W9-BTI-718

SOCIALIZATION AND SOCIETY

Social Science Research Council, Committee on Socialization and Social Structure

SOCIALIZATION AND SOCIETY

CONTRIBUTING AUTHORS

JOHN A. CLAUSEN
University of California, Berkeley

ORVILLE G. BRIM, JR.
Russell Sage Foundation

ALEX INKELES
Harvard University

RONALD LIPPITT
University of Michigan

ELEANOR E. MACCOBY
Stanford University

M. BREWSTER SMITH
University of California, Berkeley

EDITED BY JOHN A. CLAUSEN

Little, Brown and Company
Boston

LIBRARY OF CONGRESS CATALOG CARD NO. 68-15732

SECOND PRINTING

Published simultaneously in Canada
by Little, Brown & Company (Canada) Limited

PRINTED IN THE UNITED STATES OF AMERICA

To the memory of
Ben Willerman, colleague and friend

Preface

In 1960, the Social Science Research Council appointed a Committee on Socialization and Social Structure to examine theoretical formulations, existing data, and methodological issues in research on the interrelationships of social structure, socialization processes, and personality. The members of the Committee were drawn equally from the fields of psychology and sociology. During the following five years, the Committee sponsored a number of work groups, conferences, and reviews of literature and ongoing research in several subareas of the larger field of concern to the Committee. These have resulted in a number of publications and reports for participants and other specialists, though publication was not the primary objective of most of these activities.

Apart from the participation of its members in conferences and work groups, the Committee itself struggled with the analysis of relationships between features of social structure and aspects of socialization and with both substantive and theoretical issues which emerged from discussions. These discussions were sufficiently rewarding for us, the members of the Committee, that we decided to prepare the present volume. Our intent is to examine conceptual usage, approaches, and issues in the field of socialization research, especially emphasizing the effects of social structure upon the socialization process. None of the chapters of this book is intended primarily as a review of existing knowledge, though several of the chapters provide general overviews of the topics with which they deal. We have no intention of pontificating on the directions that theory and research on socialization should take, though we are interested in pointing out certain inadequacies in current theory and research and certain serious gaps in our knowledge and its utilization. We hope that these essays will have implications for subsequent theory and research and also for socialization practice.

The Committee was appointed by the Social Science Research Council at the request of a number of social scientists working in the field of socialization research. During the winter and spring of 1960, the Council brought together two groups of workers in the field of socialization to discuss the desirability and feasibility of establishing a committee to undertake a more systematic assessment of developments in the field. Following the first of these meetings, an application for support of such an effort was presented to the National Institute of Mental Health. Beginning in September 1960, the work of the Committee was supported by grant MH-4160 from the National Institute of Mental Health, Public Health Service. The grant defrayed travel and other expenses for two or three meetings of the Committee per year, enabled us to provide a part-time research assistant for each of the work groups, covered travel and living expenses for conferences, and permitted the payment of modest stipends to those commissioned by the Committee to prepare major reviews. Thus quite minor funding made possible a rather extensive program, thanks to the flexibility of the granting agency and the willingness of many behavioral scientists to give freely of their time and efforts to an activity sponsored by the Social Science Research Council.

In its initial meetings the Committee evolved several objectives which have guided the program subsequently undertaken. Perhaps most important was the decision to focus upon the linkages between social structure and socialization practice. Many studies, for example, had shown differences between class and cultural groups in socialization practices, but few had attempted to trace the ways in which such differences came into being and manifested themselves in personality development. Do working-class parents express different attitudes toward the socialization of their children and use different techniques because they themselves were socialized differently than middle-class parents were, or do particular educational and occupational experiences directly influence child-rearing orientations? To what extent do the larger social contexts and structures within which socialization takes place influence the goals and means used by socialization agents or the personality outcomes of children?

A very different kind of objective was our desire to promote interstimulation among the various disciplines working in the field of socialization research, breaking down disciplinary barriers where these had seemed to result in an undue narrowing of research perspective. Thus, in the first of our conferences, on observational techniques, we included not only anthropologists, psychologists, and sociologists but also psychiatrists and even a zoologist who had observed primates in their natural habitats. Discussion of the different objectives and methods employed proved to be extremely fruitful for many of the participants. In our discussions we became aware of barriers that existed not so much between disciplines but as a result of narrow substantive concerns — the barrier, for example, between those who had worked primarily in the area of childhood socialization and those concerned with aspects of adult socialization. Although we had originally decided to focus on the age span from birth to adolescence, we came to recognize that research on childhood socialization could benefit from consideration not only of the demands of adulthood but also of the modes of socialization and resocialization which are operative during the adult years.

We also decided that limited stocktaking through sharp focus on subareas in the field seemed more beneficial than attempting to assess the total range of research and issues in socialization. We tried to focus on areas in which there had been much ferment or, conversely, those which had been almost totally neglected. We also sought to increase our own awareness and that of other American behavioral scientists of the socialization research going on in other countries; and to this end we commissioned bibliographies and reviews of relevant literature in France, Great Britain, and Germany.

The subject matter we focused on is indicated by the titles of the conferences and work groups sponsored and the papers commissioned by the Committee. Titles alone are listed here; the details of conference and work-group location and organization, rosters of participants, and the list of publications resulting from these several enterprises are given in Appendices A and B.

Conference Topics

Observational Methods in Research on Socialization Processes
Socialization Theory: Relations between Social Structure and Psychological Structure
Socialization through the Life Cycle
Moral Development
Socialization for Competence

Work Groups

Linkages between Social Class and Personality
Sex Differences
Family Size and Birth Order as Influences upon Socialization and Personality
Social Structure and Socialization in the Elementary School Classroom
Peer Relations and Personality Development

Commissioned Reviews

American Longitudinal Research on Psychological Development
Socialization in Selected Situational Contexts
Socialization Research in Germany
Problèmes de la Socialisation: Position des Auteurs de Langue Française
The School as an Agent of Socialization (a review of British research)

As will be apparent from examination of the Appendices, each of the activities sponsored by the Committee has resulted in some publications. For the most part, papers presented at conferences were published separately, since the editing of book-length conference reports was in general not deemed feasible. In one instance where a book had been envisioned, several of the major papers were subsequently expanded to such a degree that separate publication seemed desirable to the authors.

The present volume reflects only a few of the contributions of our many coparticipants in the various enterprises in which we have engaged. The outlines of this book took shape in Committee discussions during 1964 and 1965. In June-July 1965, the members of the Committee spent four weeks together at the Center for Advanced Study in the Behavioral Sciences, elaborating outlines, writing initial drafts, and subjecting each other's products to vigorous critical discussion. All of us are grateful to Ralph Tyler, then Director of the Center for Advanced Study, and to Preston Cutler, Jane Kielsmeier, and other members of the Center's staff for making possible our month of retreat.

The inevitable chores experienced in moving from a set of diversely authored manuscripts to a book have been greatly eased by the thoughtful suggestions and editorial efforts of Eileen Mason of Little, Brown and Company. We have not striven for stylistic unity but have tried to achieve clarity and a measure of consistency in our references to the literature. Thanks are due to Arlene Vadum for help in the preparation of the index.

Finally, we wish to acknowledge our debt to the staff of the Social Science Research Council, not only for sponsorship and encouragement, but also for taking care of many of the details of grant management and "housekeeping" that are entailed in a program such as ours. In particular, we are indebted to Paul Webbink, Vice-President of the Council, and to our staff associates, who were successively, Francis Palmer, the late Ben Willerman, and Jerome Singer.

When the prospects of the present book were first under consideration, it was our hope that Ben Willerman could be a contributor to it. His death in June 1965 precluded that possibility; we dedicate this book to his memory in pleasant recollection of our association.

John A. Clausen
Orville G. Brim, Jr.
Alex Inkeles
Ronald Lippitt
Eleanor E. Maccoby
M. Brewster Smith

Contents

SOCIALIZATION AND SOCIETY

JOHN A. CLAUSEN

ONE Introduction

CONTENTS

SOCIALIZATION AS A CONCEPT AND AS A FIELD OF STUDY

Human society is dependent on a measure of consensus among its members — consensus about goals to be sought and the means of seeking to attain them. Consensus emerges through communication; it rests upon shared symbols and norms which are acquired as part of the process of socialization. But consensus is never complete, nor are the requirements of social life the same at all ages or in all parts of the social organization. New goals are constantly being evolved. From the standpoint of social demands, a man is never too old to learn. Especially in modern society, the kind of learning that we call socialization goes on throughout the life cycle.

The term *socialization* has a history of varied use. In the next chapter, we shall examine the history of the concept and of the field of study that now centers on the concept. Before going further, however, a brief discussion of the nature of socialization is called for. Most simply, the study of socialization focuses upon the development of the individual as a social being and participant in society. If one takes a developmental perspective, socialization may be regarded as the core of social psychology. As a process, socialization entails a continuing interaction between the individual and those who seek to influence him, an interaction that undergoes many phases and changes. For Elkin (1960, p. 4), it is "the process by which someone learns the ways of a given society or social group well enough so that he can function within it." For Child (1954, p. 655), socialization is "the whole process by which an individual born with behavioral potentialities of enormously wide range, is led to develop actual behavior which is confined within a much narrower range — the range of what is customary and acceptable for him according to the standards of his group." Both Elkin and Child put the stress on learning by the individual. Aberle (1961, p. 387), however, puts the stress on the social apparatus which influences the individual's learning and defines for him the range of what is acceptable: "Socialization consists of those patterns of action or aspects of action which inculcate in individuals the skills (including knowledge), motives and attitudes necessary for the performance of present or anticipated roles."

Whether or not inculcation or coercion is suggested in the definition, socialization does imply that the individual is induced in some measure to conform willingly to the ways of his society or of the particular groups to which he belongs. Indeed the first usage of the term appears to have derived from the concern of early sociologists with the problem of how society is possible; that is, how it happens that individuals with diverse goals cooperate and work together, achieving a stable unity.[1] Clearly they do so by fitting their behavior to the expectations of others, thereby acknowledging and to a degree conforming to social norms. Yet at the same time diversity and a measure of deviance from social norms are to be found in all societies. Such diversity is a condition for social change and a reflection of the fact that man is to a degree his own agent: he evaluates, chooses among alternatives, creates his own goals, and remakes his world.

Socialization may be viewed from the perspective of the individual or from that of a collectivity (be it the larger society or a constituent group having a distinct subculture). Further, individual development may be viewed generically within a given society or it may be viewed in terms of the experiences and influences that lead to significant differences among persons (both social types and unique personalities). Viewed generically, the process of socialization includes the patternings of social learning transmitted through child care and training, the acquisition of language and of selfhood, the learning of social roles and of moral norms. To a large degree, childhood socialization is the social orientation of the child and his enculturation, first within the small social world of family and neighborhood and then in relation to the larger society and culture.

Even in "simple" societies the process of enculturation is not completely standardized. No two children occupy identical positions in the social structure or experience exactly the same socialization influences. Personalities reflect differences in genetic potentialities; in the content, sequence, and contexts of socialization experience; and in the interactions of these realms. In the present volume we shall not be concerned with the uniqueness of personality but rather with patternings in personality or social participation brought about by common socialization experiences, especially as these derive from the occupancy of similar positions in the social structure.

[1] See, for example, Simmel's "How Is Society Possible?" (1895) and Gidding's *Theory of Socialization* (1897). We shall briefly review the history of the concept in the next chapter.

From the societal perspective, socialization is the means by which social and cultural continuity are attained. Fromm (1949) has suggested that socialization induces members of society to do what they must do if the society is to function properly. It engenders a social character that is appropriate to participation in the kind of institutions and organizations that are to be staffed in a given society. In the last analysis, adult performance is the criterion by which the adequacy of the socialization apparatus is to be assessed.

If socialization is to encompass all those influences that prepare the individual to fill normal adult roles in his society, the concept is manifestly broad and general. It must embrace such diverse influences as parental guidance and control aimed at teaching the child to modulate his natural impulses, the interactions through which language is learned and selfhood achieved, the effects of an older sibling as a role model, the mutual give and take of courtship and marriage as preparation for parenthood, the induction of the individual into his occupational role, and a host of other kinds of preparation and social participation.

By definition, socialization entails learning; the concept is in this sense to be contrasted with *maturation*, the unfolding of the potentialities of the organism which occurs more or less automatically except in the face of marked deprivation. But is all learning to be considered socialization, or only learning that bears specifically on future role performance? If the latter, how can one know until a life has been completely lived whether particular influences have constituted strategic preparation for future roles or whether certain lessons learned have actually provided the person with excess baggage for his life journey? A related dilemma confronts us when we consider the issue of purposiveness on the part of the agents of socialization. Shall one restrict the concept to situations in which an agent consciously seeks to modify or mold the individual's behavior toward more or less clearly envisioned outcomes? Or is the kind of incidental learning or "experiencing" that goes on, often unwittingly, when one lives among others, also to be considered socialization?

Our Use of the Concept

We shall not attempt to define or sharply delimit the concept in the present volume, but we shall focus our attention on social learning that has clear implications for future performances. Current usage in the literature varies; most often socialization designates a general area of interest, not a sharply definable process. Sharper delimitation is possible when one speaks of a subarea such as political socialization or socialization to a particular group or role relationship, but even here clear delineation of boundaries is difficult. Often other words or phrases which refer to important aspects or segments of socialization will do as well as "socialization" to designate a focus of interest — child rearing, social orientation of the child, education, enculturation, role learning, occupational preparation, preparation for marriage and parenthood, adaptation or adjustment to changing individual powers or changing social demands, changing reference groups or reference sets. As a subfield of behavioral science inquiry, socialization comprises all of these. It encompasses the learning of motives and feelings as well as skills and cognitive sets. The concept of socialization embraces equally the efforts of society's formally designated socialization agents (parents, teachers, elders, preachers) to transmit and secure adherence to existing norms and the mutual efforts of participants in all sorts of relationships (peer group, courtship, marriage, work group) to establish stable expectations.

Socialization and social control go hand in hand; they are complementary bases for social order and continuity, but they are by no means identical. In addition to the norms that constitute moral imperatives, all societies have a variety of arrangements which tend to insure the support of the moral order. Behaviors which exemplify the norms tend to be rewarded; those violating the norms tend to bring a measure of punishment. But social norms are not, for the most part, monolithic, coercive imperatives. They differ according to time, place, and the characteristics of the person. They are enmeshed with the division of labor in society. The means of support or enforcement include not only such highly institutionalized social forms as the religious and legal orders but also the informal controls and sanctions that operate within kinship, occupation, and local community relations. The effectiveness of social control rests, in the last analysis, on the transmission of the moral norms through the socialization process, on the recruitment and socialization of (witting or unwitting) control agents, and on widespread acceptance of the legitimacy of the norms and sanctions. As an underlying basis for social control, socialization efforts are designed to lead the new member to adhere to the norms of the larger society or of the particular group into which he is being incorporated and to commit him to its future. The group's values are, hopefully, to become the individual's values or at least to be recognized by him as having legitimacy. The modes of social control, especially when exercised in reaction to deviance or violation of moral imperatives, help to emphasize the importance of the norms and to strengthen the commitments of individuals to those norms.

But the transmission and enforcement of established norms is only a part of socialization. Except in the most static societies, norms are constantly being redefined and reshaped, even at the societal level. In modern, industrial societies a substantial degree of innovative behavior is, indeed, expected of those in positions of leadership. At the level of family and other intimate group relationships, the evolution of normative expectations is perhaps as important as the transmission of existing norms. Newly evolved norms become a basis for erecting control measures — more fragile and subtle than those at the societal level but nonetheless real — which help to maintain these social patterns.

In a sense, every enduring relationship may be said to entail socialization, for every enduring relationship entails a building up of mutual expectations which become to a degree normative for the participants. One sees this most clearly in marriage and in parenthood, where cultural and subcultural definitions of appropriate role behavior provide only partial guidance in the intimate give-and-take of family life. The child, we say, is socialized by his parents. This process, for any child, has its typical and its unique aspects. After they have had one or two children, parents are said to be experienced. The difference in the extent of new orientation and learning on the part of infant and parents is tremendous, but clearly the parents as well as the infant are becoming socialized to a particular relationship as well as to a social role. In any enduring close relationship or primary group, each participant is heavily involved in the orientations of his coparticipants; such involvement is the stuff of which socialization agents are made. The net effect for socialization to the norms of the larger society will, of course, depend on the consonance of the group's norms with those of the larger collectivity.

Social Learning, Social Influence, and Socialization

In the chapters that follow, we shall be primarily concerned with those kinds of social learning that lead the individual to acquire the personal and group loyalties, the knowledge, skills, feelings, and desires that are regarded as appropriate to a person of his age, sex, and particular social status, especially as these have relevance for adult role performance. Social learning usually occurs as a consequence of the attempts of others to influence the individual, but all attempts to exert social influence are not equally germane to our interests. We shall not, for example, be concerned with the efforts of others to exert influence in order to achieve personal goals in the immediate situation, as in the use of feminine charm or flattery to secure a favor. We shall be concerned with the efforts of others to change normative orientations or aspects of personality, as in marriage or in the parent-child relationship. This is not to say that actors pursuing their individual goals may not serve as role models for the socializee and thereby contribute to his social orientation and to the crystallization of his own goals and values. Attempts to exert influence may, however, be less potent forces for change than unintended consequences of the behavior of others. We have, in general, too much neglected the unwitting influences exerted by the behavior and commentaries of parents, teachers, and others (whether directed to the child or to other adults) that carry interpretations of the nature of their social world. Attempts at social influence and social control do contribute to an individual's patterns of response to others and his self-definitions, but the study of modes of influence and control *per se* falls somewhat outside the central area of socialization.

Socialization implies that norms are to become "internalized" standards, though we shall see (Chapter Six) the concept of "internalization" creates as many problems as it solves. What is important is that the individual accepts and acts upon the premise that the corpus of prevailing norms has validity for him. It does not, of course, require that he never question the appropriateness of some of the existing standards.

Further, we shall exclude from consideration the internal dynamics of the learning of skills and technical knowledge required for particular performances. Such learning is, of course, a necessary part of the socialization process. A measure of instruction must be given and opportunity must be available for the practice of skills by children and by adults if such skills are to play an important part in particular performances. A valid theory of learning is essential for an adequate theory of socialization and for the design of socialization research. The study of the learning process as such, however, is properly a separate field of specialization within psychology. Theories of learning will be touched upon in several of the following chapters (especially Chapter Six) but will not be fully treated, since our focus of attention will be on relationships between society and socialization.

Socialization efforts beyond the early period of child training increasingly are directed towards preparing the individual for change or inducing change in his outlook, ways of handling himself, activities, and value orientations. Such efforts may or may not be successful. If applied with sufficient fervor, they will almost certainly induce some kind of change in the individual's outlook, though not always in the direction intended. There is, however, an aspect of socialization which often does not directly include the efforts of others — anticipatory socialization.

Anticipatory Socialization

By virtue of man's ability for reflective thought through the manipulation of symbols, social situations and social roles can be acted out in the imagination. Small children "playing house" do not merely imitate their parents; they rehearse in advance roles they will play in the future. Their interactions are based on their perceptions of the routines and the problematics of family life; often they receive feedback from their playmates as to how *they* perceive social reality. Again, the medical student envisions himself as a doctor confronted with difficult clinical decisions;

he imagines what demands will be placed on him, what expectations he will be asked to fulfill.

Anticipatory socialization is thus a fancy name for a variety of mental activities which include daydreaming, forecasting future situations, role rehearsing, and much more. We may assume that identity is in general clarified by the individual's ability to see himself in many different situations and to predict his actions in them. In a sense, then, anticipatory socialization may seem to entail self-socialization.[2] But both the person being socialized and socialization agents participate in the process of socialization; and it would seem fruitful to examine the relative contributions of self and others in a variety of socialization circumstances. The individual can only rehearse roles or social situations that have been made known to him. Further, he is likely to rehearse those roles which have been made to seem most desirable (whether or not this was the intent of socialization agents). Some persons "work upon" their experiences, seeking thereby to shape their own destinies. Others appear to be more passive recipients or at least to do less in the way of reviewing, formulating, and reintegrating their experiences. Anticipatory socialization is, then, not a distinct process but an aspect of the broader socialization experience.

If man often creates his own opportunities and imposes his own definitions on situations, he must also, at times, adapt to changes in his ability to control his own destiny. Permanent disability, the infirmity of old age, failure in a salient role — all pose problems for the individual's identity. He must come to terms with the fact that he is not something that he was, something to which he was committed. Societies vary in the extent to which they help individuals make such adaptations. Assisting in a transition to an acceptable redefinition or in an identity transformation would clearly qualify as socialization. The individual's own effort to achieve redefinition may, in one sense, be considered a kind of self-socialization, but in another sense it is evidence that the definitions and responses of others — who serve as socialization agents — have motivated the individual to work for change.

The Concept "Unsocialized"

If socialization is a process, its end product may perhaps be called "socialized man." From the perspective of the larger society, the individual can be said to be socialized when he has learned to think and feel in the ways that someone of his age, sex, and placement is supposed to think

[2] In a sense, any socialization experience that is relevant to a given role and is provided long before the role is to be occupied may be thought of as anticipatory socialization, but most common usage confines the term to experiences and activities that are not specifically designed as role preparation.

and feel, given the necessary skills to perform accordingly. Persons who are insensitive to, or unaccepting of, the norms of their society are sometimes spoken of as "unsocialized." Deviance is explained as the consequence of poor socialization. To a degree, such usage is warranted, but it is fraught with danger. No man is ever fully aware of more than a small segment of the total culture of his society. It is doubtful that any man is at home in all of the adult male groupings of his society unless that society consists of a single, small community. Deviance may be a consequence of deviant socialization experiences — that is, of socialization to deviant norms — or of incomplete or inadequate communication of norms, or of the individual's emotional or rational rejection of norms. Nothing is explained by saying that an individual is "unsocialized" unless the nature of the deficiencies in his socialization can be specified. Conversely, conformity in itself is not evidence of successful socialization. Neither the rigidly conforming neurotic nor the person who conforms without being committed to group goals can be regarded as an ideal product of socialization.

This is not to say that a measure such as the "socialization scale" of the California Psychological Inventory (Gough, 1960) does not have a useful function in distinguishing, at least within modern societies, between relatively conforming individuals, who subscribe to those attitudes that most adult socialization agents seek to engender, and less conforming persons. Clearly it has proven useful in several Western societies. But such a scale measures attitudinal conformity to a particular constellation of norms and not socialized competence in general. True, the items represent important expressions of major themes in morality, especially the morality of the dominant middle class. Espousal of such norms does not, however, tell much about the individual's ability to relate successfully to his peers in his own subculture or about the other skills and attitudes that are required in a given milieu. On the other hand, his failure to learn or to accede to the dominant norms and expectations of the larger community does indicate that from the perspective of that community the individual lacks knowledge, motives, or commitments that are deemed essential for full acceptance as a member.

In almost every society an individual's membership in some groups results in his holding values or pursuing goals antithetical to those of the larger society. The individual may have incorporated the values of several groups and may be able to think, feel, and perform appropriately in each of these, depending on the setting and the circumstances. To suggest that the fully socialized individual will eschew all groups that hold views not wholly consonant with the established moral order of the larger society would be to deprive him of the possibility of choice and of growth. Seemingly incompatible orientations can be handled in a variety of ways. Just as no child holds all the views his parents do, so no person incorporates a consistent set of orientations and behaviors that exactly mirrors the formulation of moral norms to which most members of his society would subscribe. Even if a formulation of modal patterns at any given time were feasible, it would constantly be in a state of flux. Moreover, the degree of variation from the mode which is tolerated will depend on the characteristics and status of the actor and on the circumstances of the social situation. Individuals adequately prepared for one set of contingencies may be inadequately prepared for another, but they do not by this fact suddenly become "unsocialized." At most we can say that their socialization experience was inadequate in a particular respect. The revolutionary, who helps overthrow an existing order, may have accepted its underlying moral premises but rejected its institutional forms.

Unless there were evidence that socialization proceeded by a common set of stages in all parts of a given society, and that the accomplishment of these stages could be assessed using a relatively simple set of dimensions, it would seem unwarranted to equate any given behavior or behavioral deficit with degree of socialization. Use of the term "unsocialized" is perhaps most justified when one is speaking of a child who has not been exposed to normal interaction with others or to the inevitable imposition of social controls and definition of norms that accompanies normal interaction. Some of the feral children described in the past or children confined in isolation may be regarded as truly unsocialized (see, for example, Davis, 1947). We may, indeed, follow Cooley's lead and observe that infants and young children who are not nurtured in a primary-group relationship seem not merely to be unsocialized but to lack the basic qualities we expect in human nature. The essence of that nature is to be responsive to the behaviors and sentiments of others. A person who has not acquired the ability to respond to others differs markedly from one whose behavioral deficits result from lack of opportunity to learn the norms of a particular society or subculture, though competent in his own milieu. It would seem most appropriate to refer to the difficulties experienced in the latter instance as evidence of lack of acculturation to the new milieu.

In everyday speech, of course, people will continue to account for inept, boorish, or asocial behavior in terms of "inadequate socialization," faulty upbringing, etc. If we are to be maximally clear in our analytic attempts to understand and explain behavior, however, it will be well to avoid such usage unless specific linkages between socialization experience and behavioral outcomes can be delineated. We are certainly interested in assessing what makes for failure or success of socialization efforts. If the goals desired by the agents of socialization are not achieved, to what shall the failure be attributed? Were the techniques of socialization faulty or self-defeating, as in the use of physical punishment to curb aggressive tendencies? Were there counter forces and neutralizing influences exerted by other agents of socialization, such as delinquent peers? Or were the goals themselves inappropriate, unrealistic, outmoded? These are questions we shall be considering repeatedly in the chapters to follow.

A PREVIEW OF THE VOLUME

The essays prepared for this volume are closely related to the work groups and conferences sponsored by the Committee on Socialization and Social Structure, but they are in no sense summaries of such activities nor are they reviews of the current state of knowledge. Rather they are statements of important themes and issues in socialization research and theory as viewed by the Committee, individually and collectively. The essays are individual products, but they have been influenced by the give-and-take of discussions over the past six years.

Chapter Two, "A Historical and Comparative View of Socialization Research," sketches the development of scientific inquiry relating to socialization and notes the various topics of interest to workers in the different disciplines over the past few decades. The usage of the term "socialization" is lightly traced during the seventy years since Giddings first employed it with connotations similar to those it holds for us now. Although the term socialization is not widely used outside the United States, an understanding of the relationship of the individual to the collectivity is sought almost everywhere that one finds behavioral science. Chapter Two affords only a limited scope for a comparative review, but it does briefly note some of the major themes in socialization research and theory in Europe and, to a very limited extent, touches upon the status of cross-cultural research on child rearing.

In Chapter Three, Alex Inkeles examines society, social structure, and child socialization. He suggests that "the requisites of continuing social life come down to what is largely a set of requirements for individual socialization." Starting at this most general level, with a review of the requirements for socialization in any society, he turns next to consider a number of different profiles of demand posed by particular societies. Cross-cultural materials provide perspectives otherwise very difficult to achieve. Given the demands that societies pose for their members and the qualities that are called for, how are these inculcated? Inkeles delineates some of the social arrangements that insure that most children growing up in a given society will indeed meet the demands placed on them and will incorporate the ideals, the skills, and the defenses that are called for. But as he is well aware, this is not merely a matter of transmitting the habitual ways. What was once called for may no longer suffice. Change makes its own insistent demands. Yet both social and personal integration demand a measure of stability. Such stability is in part afforded by personal identity, itself largely a product of socialization experience. Finally, Chapter Three focuses on some of the ways in which general features of the social and political organization and even the ecological order influence the process and outcomes of childhood socialization.

Chapter Four, "Perspectives on Childhood Socialization," takes a somewhat narrower view of the aims and tasks of early socialization; particular attention is given to problems of sequence and scheduling and to the relationship of the child with the principal agents who guide his development and exercise controls over him. Coordinate with societal demands or goals for new members who are ultimately to be inducted into full adult status are the earlier needs of the infant and the child and the joint tasks that parents and children must accomplish to insure minimal competence in the offspring. In modern, industrial society, the school and the teacher soon appear, to carry out tasks too specialized, too crucial, to be left to parents. But the orientations of home and school inevitably interact, usually reinforcing each other for the middle-class child, often attenuating or conflicting with each other for the lower-class child. Peers too become agents of socialization, sometimes adding still another source of conflicting norms. How are resolutions to be achieved?

When we originally sought to delineate the scope of our stocktaking in the area of socialization, our inclination was to concentrate on the period of childhood and adolescence. Other committees of the Social Science Research Council were concerned with the effects of college and with various facets of adult behavior. Moreover, we were reluctant to set for ourselves too broad a scope at the expense of precluding intensive examination of issues in the field of childhood socialization. Yet the rapidly increasing literature on adult socialization called for some consideration, especially in view of the large number of sociologists working in this field. Psychologists and anthropologists, interested in personality and cultural transmission, have concentrated more heavily on the study of childhood socialization; sociologists, less concerned with personality development than with the processes whereby personnel are recruited and trained to fill positions in the social organization, have concentrated on socialization for occupational roles and on the institutional apparatus for the resocialization and reformation of adults who for one reason or other fail to meet the requirements of conventional adult roles.

In Chapter Five, Orville G. Brim, Jr., considers adult socialization, a subject in which the emphases are often quite different from those of childhood socialization. As a person becomes more differentiated and autonomous, he generates his own increasingly cogent demands for future performance. To a large extent, adult socialization is characterized by the acquisition of social roles and mediation among competing influences or pressures from various sectors of the role sets to which the individual belongs. Brim notes the wide variety of situations in the family, on the job, and in the community which demand new orientations or reappraisals of self and others throughout the life cycle. Some of these are direct socialization influences; others lead the individual to set new goals for himself and to develop skills and knowledge that will make such goals more attainable.

In Chapter Six, Eleanor E. Maccoby looks closely at one of the core problems of all socialization, the development of moral values and behavior. Nothing is more important than that the new member should learn to value as good the behaviors so defined in his society and to abhor what is regarded by the elders as evil. If the problem of generating enthusiasm for, and commitment to, moral imperatives is as old as man, it has only recently been studied from a nonmoral perspective. Does the moral development of the child inevitably proceed through a series of stages of cognitive development as proposed by Piaget, or is morality learned primarily through the positive reinforcement of desired responses and the negative reinforcement of those which are unwanted? Here careful examination of the assumptions and propositions of learning theory and of competing formulations is required. As Mrs. Maccoby notes, developmental theory and learning theory incorporate different assumptions and address themselves to rather different issues in considering moral behavior. The concept of "internalization," often connoting the individual's acceptance of social norms as his own standards, to be applied regardless of external controls, is here critically examined.

Psychological theories of value transmission and the development of conscience do not, in general, treat the question of changes in values that may occur over a generation or even within a relatively brief span of years. How do such changes come about, and what are their implications for theories relating to the learning of moral values? This is a neglected area of research, but one in which a number of significant questions may be posed.

If the socialization apparatus functions effectively, most individuals will acquire the necessary motives, skills, and knowledge to perform competently the social roles expected of normal adults in their society. Competence and deviance are often treated as if they were opposite ends of a single continuum, perhaps because lack of competence is often associated with deviance, especially in markedly deprived population groups. In Chapter Seven, M. Brewster Smith analyzes the relationships between competence and socialization. He develops a conception of the competent self, characterized by an interrelated cluster of personal dispositions centering on self-respect and hope. A person thus oriented is likely to make the most of his opportunities in the world and be set in positively cumulative patterns of interaction that contrast with the vicious circle of self-defeat in which persons who lack this cluster of traits are caught. How is competence, thus conceived as capability for effective role performance for self and for society, linked by socialization processes to the biological potential of the pre-social infant before selfhood is attained? In its development, what is the interplay between the developing person's intrinsic motivation toward the achievement of environmental effects on the one hand, and his search for social approval, on the other? How do characteristics of the niche that a person occupies in the social structure affect his attainment of competence? Smith draws upon evidence from a wide range of recent research and examines a number of theoretical issues in addressing himself to these and other questions.

Many lessons are not learned the first time they are taught. Teachers differ in effectiveness and learners in readiness to benefit from their experiences. Much socialization effort is haphazard. Except for a few subareas in which problems of technique and materials have been considered in the literature — especially formal education, whether lay or religious, and the orientation of parents for child rearing — little attention has been given to the study of ways in which the socialization process can be improved. This is the topic considered by Ronald Lippitt in Chapter Eight. Socialization is, in a sense, a mode of planned change; but, as in the instance of many other kinds of social change in our society, the planning has often been extremely limited and the technology of change little developed. Lippitt identifies the many different socialization agents and agencies involved in the process, the variety of goals and values that guide their efforts, and the issues of strategy and tactics that confront them. How can available resources be most effectively utilized for the accomplishment of various kinds of socialization tasks? How much initiative should be left to the socializee? How can knowledge derived from current theory and research be brought to bear in the many situations in which the socialization process is now ineffective or entails conflict to no fruitful end? Even if a certain amount of conflict is inevitable and indeed a sign of salutary creativity and potential for change, can that potential be maximized through attempts to improve the socialization process?

We have attempted no summary or final overview of the volume. Our title encompasses a far wider range of materials and themes than can be dealt with here; rather than seeking complete coverage, however, we have tried to keep both parts of the title in mind throughout the book. Far less attention is given to personality as such than to the individual's preparation for participation in his society. Some of the chapters do, nevertheless, examine the conceptualization and development of aspects of personality, and all incorporate implicit if not explicit conceptions of the nature of the behaving person or personality. We have raised questions about certain concepts that are widely employed in the field of socialization research at the present time, but for the most part we have not tried to recast the conceptual apparatus of the field. As a number of the chapters make clear, solution of many of the conceptual problems will require an examination of interrelationships which have not yet been adequately studied.

We regret that it was not feasible in this work to devote more attention to problems of methodology. The field of socialization research has not been distinguished for its methodological rigor. Many data have consisted of what parents or children said was done by or to them. Such verbalizations are far more readily and economically gathered and summarized than are direct observations. Observational methods bring their own particular problems in addition to difficulty of access and higher research costs. What the observer sees depends in large part on his premises and his relations to, or feelings about, those observed. Longitudinal studies, using a variety of research techniques with groups of individuals studied intensively for long periods of time, might seem to be an especially appropriate source of data; but, as Kagan (1964) has noted in his review of existing longitudinal studies, only minimal data on socialization have been obtained in these studies.

The reader wishing a discussion of methodological approaches and research techniques is referred to the handbook edited by Mussen (1960). Here we merely suggest the desirability of examining socialization aims and practices from multiple perspectives. In the study of socialization, one deals with interactions among community expectations, views of socialization agents, and views of those who are being inducted into some new or changing relationship. Participants in the socialization scene differ in the power they possess, the ends they seek, and in their personal security. It would be strange if they did not differ in their views of the process in which they are involved and in their interpretations of the behaviors of the partners with whom they interact.

Some of our chapters are concerned with socialization as a universal process; others focus on facets of socialization which have not yet received more than casual attention outside of our own society. The primary emphasis is certainly on socialization in modern, industrial society, even when materials from simpler societies are drawn on for contrast or comparison. We believe that in the future, research and theory will have to deal with a more complex and extended range of phenomena than are usually encompassed today in the study of socialization, but we — individually or as a group — cannot point out the direction that *must* be followed in future research. Indeed, it will be clear that we place somewhat different priorities on the various alternative approaches to clarifying the issues. Our hope is that the reader will find in the analyses some useful point of departure for his own thinking.

References

Aberle, D. F. Culture and socialization. In F. L. K. Hsu (Ed.), *Psychological Anthropology: Approaches to Culture and Personality*. Homewood, Ill.: The Dorsey Press, 1961. Pp. 381–97.

Child, I. L. Socialization. In G. Lindzey (Ed.), *The Handbook of Social Psychology*. Cambridge, Mass.: Addison-Wesley Publishing Co., 1954. Pp. 655–92.

Davis, K. Final note on a case of extreme isolation. *American Journal of Sociology*, 1947, 52, 432–37.

Elkin, F. *The Child and Society: The Process of Socialization*. New York: Random House, 1960.

Fromm, E. Psychoanalytic characterology and its application to the understanding of culture. In S. S. Sargent and M. W. Smith (Eds.), *Culture and Personality*. New York: The Viking Found., 1949. Pp. 1–10.

Gough, H. G. Theory and measurement of socialization. *Journal of Consulting Psychology*, 1960, 24, 23–30.

Kagan, J. American longitudinal research on psychological development. *Child Development*, 1964, 35, 1–32.

Mussen, P. H. *Handbook of Research Methods in Child Development*. New York: John Wiley & Sons, 1960.

JOHN A. CLAUSEN

TWO A Historical and Comparative View of Socialization Theory and Research

CONTENTS

INTRODUCTION

Concern with the proper development of offspring — with their acquisition of needed skills, the curbing of aggressive tendencies, the directing of their feet to paths of righteousness — is as old as man. Indeed, recent primate studies reveal the effort that monkey and ape parents and adults make, not only to protect their young from harm, but also to guide their learning and control their behaviors (DeVore, 1965). Thus, interest in the socialization process is an inevitable consequence of being a parent, but the scope of such interest and concern depends upon conceptions held about the nature of man (and of the human infant), the supernatural, and the organization and values of the society.[1] Moreover, we can differentiate preoccupation with the process of child training and child rearing from interest in the more philosophical issue of the individual's relationship to society or from the scientific issue of distinguishing the contributions of nature and nurture to human development. Every culture must provide guidelines for child training and child rearing, but the elaboration of views on philosophical and scientific issues obviously occurs only in cultures which have evolved some level of philosophic or scientific discourse.

Even when we limit ourselves to literature that is still of interest today, we are left with an enormous body of thought relating to socialization. Theories of socialization are to be found in Plato's *Republic,* in Montaigne, in Rousseau, and in the writings of hundreds of scholars and thinkers from the time of the first traces of written language to the present. How then can we presume to trace the development of socialization theory? We shall try to do so only in the very limited sense of examining the extent and nature of preoccupation with the process of

The assistance of Constance Boucher in searching the early socialization literature is gratefully acknowledged. I am also indebted to Gardner Murphy, W. Lloyd Warner, and Margaret Mead for very helpful responses to my requests for information about influences upon their own early perspectives.

[1] See in this connection Sunley's (1955) description of early nineteenth-century American literature on child rearing and Steere's (1964) analysis of the literature from 1865–1929.

socialization within anthropology, psychology, and sociology as these fields have developed in the United States. It may be instructive to see how the topics and issues with which the present book is concerned have been phrased in the past (to the degree that they have been of sufficient interest to be phrased). It may also be useful to trace the vagaries of usage that have characterized the term "socialization" itself. What did the term connote for various scholars? What issues were they concerned with? What other terms were widely employed in the past to designate that which we now call "socialization" or its subsidiary processes? What convergences or divergences have taken place in usage among the several disciplines?

Later in the chapter we shall briefly comment on theory and research relating to socialization as studied in other countries as well as note developments in cross-cultural and cross-national research. Within the limits of a single chapter and the limitations of readily available knowledge, it will be feasible merely to comment briefly on some outstanding contributions and to call attention both to recent reviews of work in particular areas or traditions and current programs of research which hold high promise.

In Chapter One we noted that the term socialization embraces many aspects or kinds of child training, education, enculturation, development of social character, and role learning. Many of these aspects of socialization were of interest to psychologists and sociologists from the very beginnings of these disciplines. These varied facets of the larger social process were not, however, examined in relation to one another until recent decades. Moreover, certain facets were of primary interest to psychologists, others to sociologists, and still others to students of child development or of anthropology.

Usage of the Term Socialization

As is true of many concepts employed in the social sciences, the verb "socialize" and its cognate "socialization" were current in the language well before they were used as concepts by sociologists, psychologists, or other behavioral scientists. *The Oxford Dictionary of the English Language* dates to 1828 the use of "socialize" in the sense of "to render social, to make fit for living in society." An early example of usage is taken from Lytton's *Athens*, published in 1836: "Pisistratus refined the taste and socialized the habits of the citizens." Here we seem to have the idea of perfecting the individual for society rather than merely transforming the child into the citizen. Another example, drawn from a work published in 1899, indicates that socialization is designed to produce the moral participant in society: "He (the wrongdoer) is imperfectly socialized." There were, of course, alternative meanings: to nationalize or subject to government control or ownership; to adapt to social needs or uses; and to behave sociably, though the latter usage seems largely colloquial.

Similar usages of the French verb *socialiser* and its cognate *socialisation* dating back to 1846 are noted in Robert's *Dictionnaire Alphabétique et Analogique de la Langue Française* (1963). Thus *socialisation* was early defined as "the fact of developing social relationships, of shaping into a social group or society: the socialization of men." An alternative usage — "to put under a communal or collective regime" — is illustrated by an interesting quotation from Péguy, written toward the turn of the century: "And this idea, that the socialization of teaching, the universalization of a human culture, would suffice to reconcile all of the old classes in the humanity of the socialist city, is not displeasing to us." Here we have both the idea of rendering "socialistic" in the political sense, and the idea of a universalizing of culture, overcoming differences among men. As we shall see, at least one group of influential American sociologists employed the term socialization with this latter connotation.

THE EMERGENCE OF SOCIALIZATION AS AN AREA OF INQUIRY IN THE UNITED STATES

In the following sections we shall briefly examine conceptual usage and aspects of socialization which were of interest to each of the major disciplines that now concern themselves with the study of socialization. We shall start with sociology since it was there that the term was first used, though philosophers, pedagogues, and psychologists had produced relatively sophisticated discussions of certain of the phenomena of socialization prior to such usage.

In Sociology

EARLY CONCEPTUAL USAGE

The term socialization and its various cognates began to appear with some frequency in sociological writings in the mid-1890's. As used in an early English translation of a paper by Simmel (1895), socialization referred to the process of group formation or development of the forms of association. Giddings seized upon Simmel's term but imbued it with a somewhat different meaning: "Socialization is conceived as the development of a social nature or character — a social state of mind — in the individuals who associate" (1897, p. 2). A similar idea was expressed by Ross in his 1896 paper, "Social Control." He saw "the moulding of the individual's feelings and desires to suit the needs of the group . . . as the highest and most difficult work of society," to be accomplished partly through "social influence" and partly through "social control." He referred to this "moulding" as "the socialization of the members of the group" but did not elevate the term to a position of importance as a concept.

Giddings not only employed the term as central to his analysis of social process but pronounced "the Theory of Socialization [to be] the most important part of the Theory of Society" (1897, p. 2). He regarded socialization as a by-product — albeit a crucially important one — of association. In the *Theory of Socialization* he was primarily concerned with elaborating the importance of "consciousness of kind" as the chief socializing force. Within this global conception, formulated in language that now seems strangely archaic, one finds a number of ideas current in sociological theory today, including recognition of the importance of what we now call "identification" and even of "reference groups" in developing appetites and tastes. Nowhere in the *Theory of Socialization* or in other early writing on the topic, however, do we find explicit attempts to characterize the nature of the socialization apparatus or the major features of socialization as a continuing process.

In every decade of the current century one finds at least some reference to socialization in the sociology texts published in the United States. The term continued to be used with markedly varied meanings, though it was most often employed in discussions of the bases for harmonious social relationships and for the persistence and unity of human groups. The connotation of we-feeling and of psychic or spiritual participation of the individual in collective activities was at least as common as the idea that socialization includes the gradual incorporation by the individual of the beliefs and customs of his society or group. The former idea was manifest, for example, in the doctoral dissertation of Ernest Burgess at the University of Chicago, *The Function of Socialization in Social Evolution* (1916). He noted two aspects of socialization:

> From the standpoint of the group, we may define it as the psychic articulation of the individual into the collective activities. From the standpoint of the person, socialization is the participation of the individual in the spirit and purpose, knowledge and methods, decision and action of the group. (p. 2)

Twenty-six years later, writing on "Educative Effects of Urban Environment," Burgess (1942) recalled how he had "wrestled with the meaning of the term 'socialization' " and how a socialist friend had objected to his definition (p. 9). For socialists, socialization meant collective ownership of the means of production; and of course this other definition has, as Burgess noted, an equal claim to legitimacy.[2] While

[2] It is noteworthy that when the original *Encyclopaedia of the Social Sciences* was published in the early 1930's, the article on socialization dealt with the political-economic concept, not the social-psychological one. The forthcoming

in his later writing Burgess placed far more stress upon the groups and institutions through which socialization is accomplished, especially the family and the play group, than he did in his doctoral dissertation, he held rather closely to his earlier definition. Socialization was par excellence the basis for incorporation into group life and for the integration of groups through consensus and conformity to common ethical principles.

The most influential sociological textbook of the 1920's, Park and Burgess' *Introduction to the Science of Sociology*, employed the term socialization only in a quotation from Simmel and in the following passage:

> Socialization, when that word is used as a term of appreciation rather than of description, sets up as the goal of social effort a world in which conflict, competition and the externality of individuals, if they do not disappear altogether, will be so diminished that all men may live together as members of one family. (p. 496)

It appears that the term socialization was for the most part employed rather casually through most of the 1920's but appeared more regularly toward the end of the decade. Predominantly it was used to refer to the "shaping" of the person and to the mechanisms whereby individuals were transformed into persons. It is not clear to what extent the more uniform usage of the concept in its currently accepted sense derived from the impact of behaviorism (which focused on the specific possibilities of conditioning to bring about behavioral modification), from developments in the field of pedagogy (especially the influence of Dewey), from the emergence of empirical research in sociology, or from influences derived from anthropology. By the 1930's, influences from all these quarters may be noted.

Nevertheless, socialization was not generally the rubric under which the social development of the person and of the personality was discussed. The development of interest in "culture and personality" was widespread, and during the late 1920's or early 1930's this phrasing became widely used to embrace much of what we currently connote by socialization. By the mid-1930's we find so many evidences of interdisciplinary influences that it is no longer feasible to trace lines of influence within a single discipline.

It was not until 1939 that the term socialization came to be at all widely used in its present sense. Even then a vestige of earlier usages remained. The July 1939 issue of the *American Journal of Sociology* contained two articles whose titles featured the term socialization:

International Encyclopaedia of the Social Sciences, on the other hand, will deal with the socialization of the person, not the means of production.

Robert Park's "Symbiosis and Socialization: A Frame of Reference for the Study of Society" and John Dollard's "Culture, Society Impulse and Socialization." Park continued the usage that he and Burgess had earlier elected. He wrote of "the progressive socialization of the world, that is, the incorporation of all the peoples of the earth in a world-wide economy, which had laid the foundation for the rising world-wide political and moral order" (Park, 1939, p. 23). Dollard, on the other hand, advanced socialization as one of the basic concepts of the field of social psychology. He argued for "a unification of scientific approaches . . . to study socialization," which he defined as "the process of training a human animal from birth on for social participation in his group" (Dollard, 1939, p. 60). Dollard stressed the conflicts emanating from frustration of the child's impulses and also the need to center attention "on the individual child in the family and . . . his day-to-day acquisition of social skills." Of interest for our historical perspective is his observation in a footnote:

> The "child development" movement is closely allied to the study of socialization. The trouble with this conception is that it implies that development is more or less automatic, granted certain conditions, while the socialization concept pictures development as occurring only under pressure and sometimes heavy pressure.

In 1937 and 1940, two of the most popular American textbooks of sociology appeared — those by Sutherland and Woodward and by Ogburn and Nimkoff. Here socialization came into its own as an organizing principle; each text devoted a series of chapters to the topic. Although Ogburn and Nimkoff used the heading "Human Nature" for this section of their book, they made clear on the first page of that section that they were concerned with "the process whereby the individual is converted into the person," namely, "socialization."

Although the term socialization was seldom employed in the earlier decades of the century, sociology had not neglected the phenomena of socialization. Cooley, Thomas, Park, and others had been vitally concerned with the process whereby man becomes fully human. They simply used a different vocabulary. Without attempting to do justice to sociological writing in this area prior to 1930, we shall at least note certain of the major concerns which related to aspects of socialization.

SOCIOLOGICAL CONCERNS WITH ASPECTS OF SOCIALIZATION

Throughout his writings, Charles Horton Cooley was concerned with the ways in which human nature was shaped by participation in the social order. Influenced by the writings of William James and James

Mark Baldwin on the social self and the origins of selfhood, Cooley drew on his own acute observations of social life (including the development of his children) to formulate the relationship of the individual to society. "A separate individual," he noted (1902, 1922), "is an abstraction unknown to experience." Man draws his life from heredity and from communication, and "what he gets from communication — language, education and the like — comes directly from society." He was interested in the early sociability of children and in the origin of personal ideas in the communication process. Though he did not speak of role taking, he clearly had the idea in mind when he discussed how one estimates the character of another. We do so "by imagining what we would do in various situations," drawing upon our experience with others, "trying them in various situations."

Cooley was primarily interested in the development of the subjective aspects of social life — the rise of the self and of personal meanings — through the process of social interaction. He was far ahead of his time in his description of another kind of interaction: that between hereditary potentials and social experience. Further, more than any other early writer in the fields of sociology and social psychology, he recognized the crucial importance of the primary-group relationship for the development of personality and for a conception of human nature.

The life-span of William I. Thomas was sufficiently long so that his first publication, "The Scope and Method of Folk-Psychology," appeared the year before Gidding's *Theory of Socialization*, while his last writings related to the newly emerged field of "culture and personality." Throughout his career Thomas was interested in the social processes by which the personality achieves its orientations and organization. Like Cooley, he recognized that the biological organism was to be reckoned with, and at the same time he was concerned with subjective meanings. He saw the emergence of the person as a product of both social demand and individual decision. In the Introduction to Volume III of *The Polish Peasant in Europe and America*, which he wrote with Znaniecki, we read:

> In order to become a social personality in any domain the individual must therefore not only realize the existence of the social meanings which objects possess in this domain, but also learn how to adapt himself to the demands which society puts upon him from the standpoint of these meanings and how to control these meanings for his personal purposes. (1920, p. 1850)

Thomas viewed behavior and personality in developmental perspective, something rare in sociological writing. Behavior and its meanings arise in situations. Much behavior is an emergent from definitions that are made in the process of seeking to adapt or adjust to the requirements of the situation. In a 1917 article on the influence of primary-group norms in our educational system he noted:

> The defining of the situation is begun by the parents in the form of ordering and forbidding, and information is continued by the community by means of gossip, with its praise and blame, and is formally represented by the school, the law, the church. (p. 168)

Attitudes and personalities are developed through typical lines of genesis; these derive from constellations of experiences and relationships and in turn influence the likelihood of various subsequent outcomes. "Problems of the synthesis of human personalities are not problems of personal *status* but problems of personal *becoming*" (*Polish Peasant*, p. 1843).

In his later years Thomas focused more and more on the child, drawing largely on life-history materials to study problems of adjustment and personal organization. It is significant that Volkart (1951), in his comments on the writings of Thomas, frequently employed the term socialization to refer to the topic of Thomas' interest, while Thomas himself did not use the term. Almost certainly Thomas would have objected to the connotation of moulding and conforming which the concept bore for most of those who used it prior to 1930.

We have noted that Park and Burgess used the term socialization to connote a state of universal consensus on social goals. At the same time, however, they were vitally concerned with aspects of the process of socialization as we now conceive it, even if they used a very different vocabulary. Human nature was of central interest to them — human nature as manifest in social interaction. The "reorganization of human nature takes place in response to the folkways and the mores, the traditions and conventions of the group" (Park and Burgess, 1921, p. 69). In *Introduction to the Science of Sociology*, the development of personality and of the social self was discussed under three headings: "The Organism as Personality," "Personality as a Complex," and "Personality as the Role of the Individual in the Group."

The *Introduction to the Science of Sociology* contained many excerpts from classics in the fields of sociology, enthnography, psychology, psychiatry, and even physiology, along with the theoretical scheme elaborated by Park and Burgess. Park's earlier statement "Man Not Born Human" was reproduced along with excerpts from Shinn's *Biography of a Baby*, extracts on sex and racial differences in behavior, and a remarkably catholic selection of writings on personality from Ribot, Morton Prince, Binet, William James, and others. One is impressed with the breadth of perspective which permitted Park and

Burgess to draw upon contemporary developments in psychology, genetics, and physiology while at the same time maintaining the sociological orientation. They saw the nature of the process of socialization clearly but did not elaborate on the various facets or instrumentalities through which the process takes place.

It is not possible to discuss the development of sociological perspectives on the socialization of the individual without reference to two philosophers, both concerned with the field of social psychology. The influence of John Dewey was pervasive in all of the disciplines here under consideration, but perhaps that influence was greatest on sociological social psychology. In *Human Nature and Conduct*, first published in 1922, Dewey defined "the problem of social psychology . . . [as] how different customs, established interacting arrangements, form and nurture different minds" (p. 63). Or again,

> . . . we need to know about the social conditions which have educated original activities into definite and significant dispositions before we can discuss the psychological element in society. This is the true meaning of social psychology. (p. 91)

Dewey's focus of concern was with morality, broadly conceived, and his perspective is summed up in the title of the final chapter of *Human Nature and Conduct* — "Morality Is Social." Moral conduct is to be understood as the product of social interaction:

> Connections with our fellows furnish both the opportunities for action and the instrumentalities by which we take advantage of opportunity. . . . If the standard of morals is low, it is because the education given by the interaction of the individual with his social environment is defective. . . . If a child gets on by peevishness and intrigue, then others are his accomplices who assist in the habits which are built up. (pp. 317–19)

As we shall see, Dewey influenced not only sociologists and social psychologists but also anthropologists and students of child development.

George Herbert Mead was at the University of Chicago contemporaneously with John Dewey (prior to Dewey's departure for Columbia) and with Thomas, Park, and Burgess. If Mead's influence on the thought of educators and social scientists was less pervasive than that of Dewey, it was more sharply directed to basic aspects of socialization — to the rise of meaning and of selfhood in the process of social interaction. Mead was not a prolific writer; his major formulation of social psychology, *Mind, Self and Society*, was published posthumously from lecture notes. Mead analyzed in detail the establishment of communication and the process through which meanings arise in social interaction. He gave special attention to the development of the "self" through the child's ability to take "the role of the other" — to put himself in the place of a caretaker, for example, and become an "object" to himself.

More than any other scholar, Mead established the basic premises of what has been called the symbolic-interactionist approach in sociological social psychology. One of the most frequently voiced reservations about Mead's formulations is that they have not led to direct research. Some would say that they do not *lend* themselves to direct research; and it is true that the covert aspects of the development of meaning and of the self are difficult to study, since the infant or small child cannot report on the process. But recent research in language learning and cognitive development suggests that many of Mead's formulations can be subjected to systematic study. The fact is that relatively few sociologists regarded small children as a proper topic for study. Cooley and Thomas were observers of children; Mead was not, nor were most of the social scientists who were directly influenced by his work. When sociological research began to supplement sociological theorizing, those who focused on the child tended to derive their approaches from other sources. It should be noted, however, that the symbolic-interactionist approach did lead to a substantial body of research on patterns of deviant behavior and the effects of social "labeling" on the stabilization of deviance.[3]

The beginnings of sociological research relating to socialization may also be noted in the late 1920's. The study of the social antecedents of delinquency in the subculture of the urban slum was advanced tremendously with the publication of *Delinquency Areas* (Shaw, McKay, Cottrell, and Zorbaugh, 1929), and a series of life histories of delinquents and criminals beginning with Shaw's *The Jack-Roller* in 1930. The delinquent career was seen as a consequence of "social conditioning" in a milieu that oriented the individual toward illegitimate activities and provided him with skill training in such activities rather than conventional pursuits. These works were preeminently influenced by Ernest W. Burgess, who contributed interpretive chapters on personality formation, documenting how the attitudes, standards, and philosophy of life of the criminal are built up in the milieu of the delinquency area.

The Lyndses' study of *Middletown* (1929), while not primarily concerned with socialization, devoted a chapter to child rearing and another four chapters to the schools, their programs and teachers, and "the things children learn." Data were secured on habits stressed by parents in the training of children and afforded impressive evidence of different value orientations in the middle and working classes. The Preface of *Middletown* acknowledges invaluable counsel, not only from fellow

[3] See, for example, H. S. Becker's *Outsiders* (1963). For a more general treatment of symbolic interaction see A. M. Rose, *Human Behavior and Social Processes* (1962).

sociologists, but from anthropologist Clark Wissler, psychologist Gardner Murphy, and — a name that recurs again and again in the prefaces of pioneering works on the individual and society — Lawrence K. Frank, who was then executive director of the Laura Spellman Rockefeller Memorial.

John Dollard's contributions to the study of socialization antedated by a number of years the 1939 article in which he advanced socialization as one of the basic concepts of social psychology. Particularly relevant to current concerns in the study of socialization was his *Criteria for the Life History*, which appeared in 1935. The work derived from an exploratory review of the life-history literature which was undertaken at the request of members of the Committee on Culture and Personality of the Social Science Research Council. This was at a time when life-history materials seemed to afford one of the most promising sources of data on the development of the person.[4] In canvassing the life-history literature, Dollard was struck with the uneven treatment of various facets of development. He sought to specify the kinds of information which ought to be provided in any life history to give it maximal value for making "theoretical sense" of the growth of a person in a cultural milieu; hence, his "criteria."

It is significant that six of the seven criteria are statements of requirements for the adequate study of the socialization process, while the seventh relates to the need for organization and conceptualization of materials. The criteria retain high relevance today, despite serious questions as to the feasibility of applying them and inevitable differences of opinion as to the adequacy of particular works when judged by these criteria (see Allport, 1942). Dollard's criteria were:

> I. The subject must be viewed as a specimen in a cultural series.
> II. The organic motors of action ascribed must be socially relevant.
> III. The peculiar role of the family group in transmitting the culture must be recognized.
> IV. The specific method of elaboration of organic materials into social behavior must be shown.
> V. The continuous related character of experience from childhood through adulthood must be stressed.
> VI. The "social situation" must be carefully and continuously specified as a factor.
> VII. The life-history material itself must be organized and conceptualized.
> (Dollard, 1935, p. 8)

[4] Other relevant works commissioned by committees of the SSRC in line with this interest were Herbert Blumer's *An Appraisal of Thomas and Znaniecki's The Polish Peasant in Europe and America* (1939); Gordon Allport's *The Use of Personal Documents in Psychological Science* (1942); and a volume by Louis Gottschalk, Clyde Kluckhohn, and Robert C. Angell, *The Use of Personal Documents in History, Anthropology and Sociology* (1942).

In *Criteria,* Dollard makes clear the very great influence of Edward Sapir (especially through the 1932–33 seminar, "The Impact of Culture on Personality," which Sapir and Dollard gave collaboratively), as well as his indebtedness to a number of other anthropologists (among them W. Lloyd Warner and Margaret Mead), psychoanalysts (including Harry Stack Sullivan, Hans Sachs, Erich Fromm, and Abram Kardiner), psychologists, and sociologists. Like Dollard himself, most of these highly creative contributors to theory and research on the development of the individual within his culture were not concerned with disciplinary boundaries. Beyond the mid-1930's, we deal then with a marked convergence of disciplines in research and theory on the socialization of the individual.

In Psychology

Within the broad scope of psychology as it has developed in the twentieth century, socialization was not a major focus of attention until the 1930's, though the concept was employed by a number of writers, especially in the areas of developmental and social psychology. Socialization incorporates learning, and the development of sophisticated theories of learning gave impetus to socialization research, but most learning theorists have not had a major interest in the larger process by which an individual is prepared for full participation in adult life. Socialization also entails the achievement of personality orientations and organization, and the formulation of theories of personality has likewise given impetus to socialization theory and research, though again the linkages have not for the most part been direct. We shall begin with a review of major developments in the subfields of social and child (developmental) psychology and then turn briefly to the influences of learning and personality theories.

The 1929 edition of Gardner Murphy's *An Historical Introduction to Modern Psychology* indexed neither the term socialization nor an equivalent. What we would now regard as aspects of socialization are touched upon briefly in the discussions of McDougall and of the contributions of "a group of social theorists who placed the center of gravity for social psychology not in the instinctive life but in the consciousness of *self* and of relations with other selves" (p. 295). Here were mentioned William James, Giddings, J. M. Baldwin, Cooley, and John Dewey. Murphy noted, as a rapidly growing trend, the emphasis on

> giving closer attention to the influence of those early environmental factors, especially social, which give the individual his ideas, his attitudes and his governing "habits"; on this point the views of Dewey and Cooley seem to be winning almost universal acceptance. . . . Together with this widespread movement has come a renewed interest in the mechanisms of personality itself, and (again reflecting the influence of Baldwin, Dewey,

> and Cooley), a desire to work out the principles by which the socialized "self" develops. (Murphy, 1929, p. 298)

In Murphy's 1929 chapter on child psychology, on the other hand, there is little to suggest that workers in that subspecialty were concerned with the process or instrumentalities of socialization except for Watson's studies of conditioning in small children. Surprisingly, the work of Baldwin does not receive mention here, suggesting that his impact had been greater in social psychology than in child psychology, his primary field of study. But because of Baldwin's influence on developmental thinking both in the United States and in Europe, it may be appropriate to examine the rise of interest in aspects of socialization within the field of child psychology before turning to social psychology.

CHILD PSYCHOLOGY

The establishment of child or developmental psychology as a field of scholarship in the United States can be attributed in large part to G. Stanley Hall, who also contributed so much to the introduction of psychoanalytic psychology to America.[5] Hall's interests were far ranging. After receiving his Ph.D. at Harvard under James, he had been a student of Wundt. Like Wundt, Hall viewed anthropology as an indispensable supplement to psychology, though his evolutionary perspective was biologically rather than culturally oriented. However, it was another psychologist, influenced by Wundt, who phrased the problem of developmental psychology in terms of "the social growth of personality." James Mark Baldwin, like Hall, was a Darwinian, but he was intrigued also by the analysis of the self as manifest in Hegelian philosophy and in the writings of James and the American pragmatists. Baldwin's theory of the development of the child was based in part on evolutionary recapitulation theory — the idea that the individual must go through the same stages of biological and psychic development that *homo sapiens* had gone through in the course of evolution — but it was also based upon the observation of infants and children.

Baldwin was impressed with the emergence of discrimination and adaptations by the infant in his interactions with caretakers. In the give-and-take between the infant and his caretakers, Baldwin saw the "dialectic of personal growth." Through this dialectic, the social heritage is transmitted to the child:

> . . . "culture," a body of beliefs, usages and sanctions [is] transmitted entirely by social means, and administered to growing individuals by example, precept and discipline. . . . It constitutes the *milieu*, a body of

[5] In addition to Murphy (1929), I have relied on Anderson (1931), Müller-Freienfels (1935), and Karpf (1932) for a historical overview. Ben-David and Collins (1966) was also helpful in tracing major lines of influence.

> influences which are necessary for the development of the individual mind. Such functions as language, spoken and written, play and art; such inventions as fire, building, and weaving, are not only conveniences of life; they are necessary means of growth. (Baldwin, J. M., 1913a, pp. 129–30)

Baldwin refers to play and imitation as the "tools of 'socialization according to nature.' " The meanings of life situations are learned in play and imitation; the child "tries on the varied ways of doing things and so learns his own capacities and limitations" (Baldwin, 1911, p. 20). Baldwin's formulations markedly influenced both psychologically and sociologically trained social psychologists as well as students of child development. Baldwin's influence did not, however, result in a strong focus on problems of socialization in American developmental psychology. It would appear that the introduction of psychological testing and especially of Binet's method of assessing intelligence, along with the experimental approaches of Thorndike and Watson, led to a concentration on conditioning experiments and on the measurement of attributes of the child rather than to the study of the development of the self and the transmission of the culture. This tendency is evident in the Murchison *Handbook of Child Psychology* (1931), from which the perspective of socialization was largely absent, except for the chapters by the Europeans — Kurt Lewin, Piaget, and Charlotte Bühler — and that by Margaret Mead. It is significant that the only references to the writings of Baldwin contained in the *Handbook* are in the chapter by Piaget, who to some degree built upon Baldwin's formulations.

Dorothy McLean (1954), tracing a generation of research in child development, notes that one of the early activities of the Division of Anthropology and Psychology, founded in 1919 within the National Research Council, was the establishment of a Committee on Child Welfare, subsequently renamed Child Development, to advance research and, to this end, the training of workers in the field of child development. The support of the Laura Spellman Rockefeller Memorial was secured for the work of the committee and, in 1933, the Society for Research in Child Development was organized. During this same period a number of child welfare centers or institutes at major universities were established, primarily through the sponsorship and funding of the Laura Spellman Rockefeller Memorial, represented by Lawrence K. Frank. Although Frank was a major stimulus to the exploration of relationships between culture and personality, both in his own writings and in the support of cross-disciplinary activities through the foundation he represented, workers in the field of child development tended to be preoccupied with physical development and with the development of intelligence and to remain oblivious of culture and of social interaction as crucial influences upon development.

Until the late 1920's, research on child development almost completely neglected the study of the child in the home. As Anderson (1936) noted in *The Young Child in the Home* — his report of the research carried out in connection with the 1930 White House Conference on Child Health and Protection — the home had been taken for granted:

> Unfortunately, we know relatively little about the details of home life and their relation to child development. While there are hundreds of investigations describing and measuring what the school does, there are only a few which are concerned either directly or indirectly with practices within the home. Because of this there was little to guide us in the formulation of this inquiry. (Anderson, 1936, p. 4)

Surprisingly, no reference to *Middletown* or to the anthropological literature appears in this report of the first large-scale study of child rearing in the United States. *The Young Child in the Home* showed in much greater detail than had *Middletown* the pervasive influence of socioeconomic status on aspects of child development and child rearing. Strictly the report of an empirical investigation by child psychologists, this work, impressive as it was, suggests that a large gap existed in the mid-1930's between child psychologists and leading social scientists in other disciplines who were concerned with relationships between the individual and his society.

SOCIAL PSYCHOLOGY

Social psychology emerged as a field of interest almost simultaneously in psychology and sociology. The first two English language textbooks in this new field were published in 1908 by the sociologist Ross and the psychologist McDougall. As noted above, Ross had employed the term socialization in his earlier discussion of social control. In his *Social Psychology* he again stressed the idea that most of one's mental content comes from others, but he was not centrally concerned with aspects or processes of socialization.

McDougall's *An Introduction to Social Psychology* had greater impact on the field, with its statement of the doctrine of instincts and its stress on the development of sentiments. McDougall was far more explicit in his discussion of socialization than was Ross, even though McDougall did not employ the term. He noted:

> If we would understand the life of societies, we must first learn to understand the way in which individuals become moulded by the society into which they are born and in which they grow up, how by this moulding they become fitted to play their part in it as social beings and how, in short, they become capable of moral conduct. (p. 174)

Volition or control of conduct, he noted, proceeds from the idea of self and from the sentiment organized about that idea. Building upon Baldwin, he gave a detailed examination to the growth of self-consciousness. Others who espoused instinct theory were less concerned than McDougall with studying the social shaping of the individual.

Of the social psychology texts of the 1920's, that by Floyd Allport (1924) would appear to have been particularly influential. Allport introduced experimental methods into social psychology. He also insisted on the individual as the only reality in social groups. If the realm of human culture had little meaning for Allport, he was nevertheless concerned with the requirements placed upon individuals by group life, and employed the term socialization somewhat as we do today:

> In order to be adapted to civilized society a man must not only be sensitive to the social objects about him; he must also develop permanent habits of response which are in accord with the necessities of group life. Such development may be called the socialization of the individual. It consists of a modification of the original and purely prepotent reflexes through instruction received in the social environment. (Allport, 1924, p. 123)

In 1931, Gardner and Lois Murphy reviewed the state of the field in their *Experimental Social Psychology*. A very brief historical section in the Introduction comments that "the decade 1920–30 has presented an astonishing array of investigations upon the instinctive and emotional make-up of children, the ways in which they learn and the processes by which they become socialized" (p. 2). The only indexed reference to socialization, however, was to a section of the chapter entitled "Development of Social Behavior in Early Childhood" — specifically to the discussion of the early development of smiling and crying and of responses to visual and auditory stimuli from persons.

When the second edition of *Experimental Social Psychology* appeared in 1937, it bore the subtitle *An Interpretation of Research on the Socialization of the Individual*. The influences of recent developments in anthropology are clearly manifest in an initial discussion of "the individual in relation to his culture" (pp. 18–24).

In response to a query regarding the subtitle of the revised work, Gardner Murphy (1966) comments that in the Morningside Heights world (Columbia University) of the thirties,

> the concept [socialization] was just *everywhere* around us — Dewey, Boas, Benedict, Mead, the Lynds, L. K. Frank — and the word, I think, appeared to be a rather good introduction to the "culture-and-personality" world to which all these people drew our attention.

Among others who are mentioned by Gardner Murphy as influences on his own thinking and on the thinking of Lois Murphy about positive aspects of social development are Susan Isaacs, Charlotte Bühler, the writings of Healy and Bronner, Dorothy and W. I. Thomas, Clifford R. Shaw, Kurt Lewin, Eugene Lerner, and Jacob Moreno. In that same response, however, he gives a more specific reason for using the term socialization in the subtitle of the 1937 edition of *Experimental Social Psychology:*

> Social psychology was moving rapidly along *both* of two diverging paths; it was splitting. On the one hand it was becoming a study of groups, especially of small groups: Sherif, Lewin, Moreno. On the other hand it dealt with the individual's development into a place in a (small or large) group, and learning acceptable behavior in group life; i.e. with socialization. It was the dynamics of the latter process that chiefly concerned Lois and me in the early 'Thirties . . . ; we wanted to be sure that nobody expected from our book a survey of experimental studies of groups.

The first textbook in social psychology to give extensive treatment to the development of the individual in society appears to have been that by Kimball Young, published in 1930. Young was far more familiar with the psychological literature than were most of his sociological colleagues. He devoted six chapters to the topic of personality and group participation. There is a decidedly modern note to his treatment, which considers both developmental phases — language learning, child training in the family — and social-structural influences in the play group, in the school, and in other social institutions and organizations in which the child participates. In a chapter on personality and occupational attitudes, he discussed both the antecedents and the consequences of occupational choice. No other social psychology text of the time so well foreshadowed the development of the field and so clearly stated the theme of socialization as the core of that field. The influences of Dewey, Cooley, Thomas, and Mead were strongly evident, as were those of McDougall, Floyd Allport, and Freud. With the works of the Murphys and of Young, the convergence of sociological and psychological approaches was well under way.

PERSONALITY PSYCHOLOGY [6]

The development of personality theory during the thirties largely reflected the twin influences of learning theory and psychoanalytic theory. Some workers drew their thinking from one of these alone, but there was

[6] I am indebted to Eleanor E. Maccoby for providing the basic material for this section and to M. Brewster Smith for helpful suggestions.

an active group consciously attempting to bring the two theories together and to derive concepts that proved highly influential in the psychological work on socialization which emerged later.

One of the major centers of development was at Yale, where Clark Hull and John Dollard in 1935 conducted a seminar on psychoanalytic theory. They attempted in this seminar to analyze the nature of the theory and to reformulate some of its concepts in learning-theory terms. At the same time, Robert Sears was presenting a learning-theory analysis of projection, repression, and amnesia (Sears, 1936). In the fall of 1936 a seminar on aggression was begun. It brought together not only Hull, Dollard, and Sears but also the psychologists Neal Miller, Carl Hovland, O. H. Mowrer, and Leonard Doob. They were joined by a psychoanalyst, Earl Zinn, and the anthropologists George Murdock, Clelland Ford, and, a bit later, John Whiting. One product of the seminar was the book *Frustration and Aggression*, which contained a chapter entitled "Socialization in America." The emphasis of the chapter was, in the authors' words, "to stress and perhaps overstress the frustrations attendant to the acquisition of social habits" (Dollard *et al.*, 1939). In its discussions, the seminar group had been influenced by G. V. Hamilton's application of learning theory and frustration theory to the human personality (1925)[7] as well as by the writings of John D. Watson, George Bagby, and J. F. Dashiel. But the primary point of departure for the Yale group was Hull's sophisticated learning theory, fusing the Pavlov-Watson concept of conditioning with Thorndike's emphasis on the importance of reward. Hull's formulation provided a theoretical foundation for statements concerning both successive habits acquired at different stages of childhood and regression to earlier learned behavior under frustration. The stress upon reinforcement as reward has been a major influence on subsequent psychological research on child rearing.

The primary focus of the Yale group's interest was on adult personality; the formulations of antecedent conditions associated with the development of adult personality characteristics did, however, lead to assumptions and hypotheses concerning early childhood experiences that should be significant. In the late thirties, Miller and Dollard turned to active research with children, in an effort to explicate the processes whereby children acquired the behavior patterns of the adult culture. The book *Social Learning and Imitation* (1941) was the outcome of this work.

The work of the Yale group foreshadowed several themes which were to be important in the psychological work on socialization during the forties and fifties. One of these was the use of laboratory experimental

[7] Sears characterizes this 1925 work of Hamilton as "the first sophisticated non-psychoanalytic theory of personality development" (Sears, 1959, p. 43).

methods to study such processes. When a socialization input, such as the amount or kind of punishment employed by parents, was thought to be important in the personality development of the child, it was assumed that it could be studied through "experimental analogues" produced in the laboratory. In some instances, when experimental work with children was not feasible, the experiments were done with animals. Much of the animal work on the experimental production of anxiety and the studies of the extinction of anxiety were thought to be relevant to the human socialization process, since anxiety, produced by punishment from socialization agents, was thought to play an important role in the child's learning to avoid forbidden activities and to acquire socially demanded behavior. Another influential theme emerging from this early work was the emphasis on acquired social drives or motives (for example, dependency) thought to affect the subsequent acquisition of socially demanded behavior.

Another active center of work on personality development during the thirties was at Harvard, under the leadership of Henry Murray. Murray's theoretical perspective was "guided partly by the analysts (Freud, Jung, Adler), partly by McDougall and by Lewin and partly by [his] subjects" (Murray, 1938, p. 38). Personality was seen as a dynamic process, to be understood in terms of the reconstructed biography of the individual: "Abstract biography *is* the personality, as far as it can be formulated" (p. 283). Moreover,

> since, at every moment, an organism is within an environment which largely determines its behavior, and since the environment changes — sometimes with radical abruptness — the conduct of an individual cannot be formulated without a characterization of each confronting situation, physical and social. (p. 39)

Murray noted that socialization, defined as "the inculcation of culture patterns," played a role in personality development, but he was more concerned with the relationship between environmental features and the underlying needs of the individual (pp. 99–100). Nevertheless, his conceptualization of needs-press schema and his effort to delineate the ways in which "childhood events" influence personality development (Chapter 5) foreshadowed later research on the effects of a variety of social demands and social settings in forming and changing personality. His subsequent volume with Clyde Kluckhohn (Kluckhohn and Murray, 1948) followed a 1941–42 seminar in which Murray, Kluckhohn, and O. H. Mowrer had collaboratively sought to formulate relationships between personality, society, and culture. The nature of Murray's contribution to personality theory and research is manifest in the title and contents of the volume of essays presented to him on the occasion of his seventieth birthday — *The Study of Lives* (White, 1964).

A third theoretical focus in the personality work of the thirties was that of Kurt Lewin and his students. Although not concerned with the process of socialization as such or with the past history of the individual, Lewin was concerned with conceptualizing the development of personality structure and the ways in which the life space of the individual is influenced by social-structural and situational features. Much less emphasis was placed upon early childhood events in the family, much more upon the structure and press of the immediate situation. Equally important, Lewin was not only an experimentalist but one who encouraged his students to carry out experimental studies with children. Such classic studies as the research on democratic and authoritarian group atmospheres (Lewin, Lippitt, and White, 1939) and that on regression in the face of frustration (Barker, Dembo, and Lewin, 1941) entailed continuing observation of children's activities and free play in much more naturalistic settings than those achieved in most experimental studies. The influences of Lewin's perspective are also manifest in the Parent Behavior Rating Scales of Champney (1941) and their application by Baldwin, Kalhorn, and Breese (1949), in the development of psychological ecology by Barker and his associates (Barker and Wright, 1955), and in many other direct contributions to socialization research and theory made by Lewin's former students.

In Anthropology

Developments within anthropology contributed more to the rise of interest in socialization in recent decades than did any other single influence. Yet the anthropologists' stress on viewing cultures as wholes would seem, at first consideration, a most unlikely basis for concern with the process whereby an individual is incorporated into his society, even when we recognize that becoming socialized is also becoming "culturized." Prior to the emergence of the field of "culture and personality" toward the close of the 1920's, few anthropologists seem to have been concerned with child rearing or the study of the particular arrangements, beliefs, and behaviors by which culture was transmitted from one generation to the next. Margaret Mead commented in the 1931 *Handbook of Child Psychology* that at that date there existed only three studies in the anthropological literature which dealt with childhood in primitive cultures — her own *Growing Up in New Guinea,* an account by Grinnell in his monograph on the Cheyenne, and Kidd's *Savage Childhood: A Study of Kafir Children.*

Singer (1961), in tracing the development of the field of culture and personality theory and research, notes that the most important stimulus to the rise of this field (in the late 1920's) was psychoanalytic psychology. In England, as early as 1924, Seligman called for investigation of dreams and the unconscious among primitives in his Presidential Address to the Royal Anthropological Institute. His suggestions for collecting data bearing on psychoanalytic theory were acted upon by Malinowski (1927) who examined the Oedipus complex among the Trobriand Islanders in *Sex and Repression in Savage Society*. Subsequently, through the influences of Sapir, Mead, Kluckhohn, Whiting, and other anthropologists, along with a number of psychoanalysts such as Roheim, Kardiner, and Fromm, psychoanalytic formulations offered the primary guidelines for many investigations of personality development in primitive cultures. Perhaps the dominant focus of attention was provided by the theory of psychosexual development, which stressed the importance of nursing, weaning, toilet training, and infant sexuality. Infancy inevitably became the critical phase of socialization in psychoanalytically oriented studies.

A second important source of influence, this time focusing on socialization beyond the early childhood years, was afforded by the writings of John Dewey, such as *Human Nature and Conduct* (1922). It was Dewey rather than Freud whom Malinowski quoted at the opening of *Sex and Repression in Savage Society*, and Dewey's perspective on the importance of the educational process was manifest in the following statement by Malinowski:

> Apart from the tender cares dictated by nature and endorsed by custom and tradition, there enters the element of cultural education. Not only is there a need of training instinct into full development, as in the animal instruction in food-gathering and specific movements, there is also the necessity of developing a number of cultural habits as indispensable to man as instincts are to animals. Man has to teach his children manual skill and knowledge in arts and crafts; language and the traditions of moral culture; the manners and customs which make up social organization. (Malinowski, 1927, pp. 191–92)

Although *Sex and Repression* is devoted to an analysis of the Oedipus complex in Trobriand society, it goes beyond the simple testing of Freud's hypothesis to a consideration of the process of education within the family. Malinowski was not merely concerned with cultural constellations but with sequences of interaction and changing relationships required in the education of the child.

Margaret Mead, in her earliest works, was also concerned with the process of cultural education. To a much greater extent than other early workers, she examined the ways in which children are reared and prepared for the activities they would engage in and the roles they would occupy within their society. In *Coming of Age in Samoa* (1928) Mead devoted a chapter to the education of the Samoan child, describing maternal care, the heavy reliance on older siblings for looking after younger ones, the learning of avoidances and skills, and the succession of demands, responsibilities, and privileges that go with age grades. In this and in her other early works, *education* is the key concept. She uses the term in the broadest sense to cover "the whole process by which a newborn infant becomes a member of society, a member of his particular society and an individual in his own right" (Mead, personal communication). Mead notes that it was not until the mid-thirties that she heard the term *socialization* used as a technical concept. Before then the word was simply "intelligible English" and indeed occasionally appeared in her own writing.

Both Margaret Mead and Ruth Benedict took their doctorates under Franz Boas (who had been a student of Wundt) at Columbia. Boas' students were set the task of mapping out culture areas and studying culture "as 'culture' in all its complexities of historical origins and within the physical environment" (Mead, 1959, p. 11). Mead comments further: "There was then, however, no emphasis on society or upon the study of a culture in which individuals or groups, rather than items of behavior, were the appropriate items" (p. 15). Boas did pose for his students questions about the individual in relation to his culture. For methodological tools and concepts which would prepare them for research on this topic, however, they had to turn elsewhere.

The chronology of influential works on the development of the child in his culture and on the correlative patternings of person and culture makes it extremely difficult to assess the direction of influences. Mead published several volumes before Benedict's *Patterns of Culture* appeared in 1934. But Benedict was Boas' assistant when Mead was starting graduate work, and the older student had great influence in shaping the thinking of the younger. Margaret Mead's (1959) book on Ruth Benedict affords an intimate glimpse of reciprocal influences between these two highly creative women and Edward Sapir. If Boas directed their attention to certain problem areas, Sapir served as a provocative source of ideas about the simultaneous study of the individual and the culture. Much of the interchange took place through letters and conversations, but Mead makes clear the great influence of Sapir on herself and Benedict. Later, of course, his influence was evident through his writings and his participation in the Social Science Research Council Committee on Culture and Personality.

The seminal influence of Sapir, like that of George Herbert Mead, is not explained by the magnitude of his writings (at least not in the field of culture and personality) but by the cogency of his insights. He was renowned as the foremost student of language well before he turned to a consideration of culture in relation to individual personality. Sapir does not appear to have given much thought to the apparatus of socialization; it was just there. In 1927, for example, he observed in

"The Unconscious Patterning of Behavior in Society" that a great deal of patterned behavior results from the assimilation of linguistic forms, gestures, value orientations, and other cultural forms without clear awareness even of the existence of patterns. For Sapir, culture was not, however, something exterior to individuals, having a separate existence: [8]

> The complete, impersonalized culture of the anthropologist can really be little more than an assembly or mass of loosely overlapping idea and action systems which, through verbal habit, can be made to assume the appearance of a closed system of behavior. . . . In spite of the often asserted impersonality of culture, the humble truth remains that vast reaches of culture, far from being in any real sense "carried" by the community or group as such, are discoverable only as the peculiar property of certain individuals, who cannot but give these cultural goods the impress of their own personality. (Sapir, 1934a, p. 412)

Sapir directed attention to the genesis of personality in the interaction between "the social psychological determinants of childhood" and innate biological factors, noting in his 1934 article on personality in the *Encyclopaedia of the Social Sciences* that "there is no facet of personality, however minute, which is not from the genetic standpoint the result of the prolonged and subtle interplay of both" (p. 86). He stimulated anthropologists and psychiatrists to collaborate in examining the relation of the individual to his society.

Although anthropological interest in the topic of socialization arose within the context of culture and personality studies, many of the most influential works in this field did not deal with socialization at all. Exciting and challenging as were the themes raised by *Patterns of Culture*, the focus of attention was on the *culture's* selection, not the individual's selection from among alternative possibilities. Emphasis on configurations in culture and their counterpart within personalities of individuals who share a common culture focuses on socialization only as one asks: How did these personality constellations come about?

Sharper emphasis on child rearing was brought about particularly through the influence of Abram Kardiner, a neo-Freudian psychoanalyst. Working initially with Cora DuBois and subsequently with Ralph Linton at Columbia, Kardiner gave a series of seminars which provided psychoanalytic interpretation of cultural constellations. It was Kardiner's thesis (1939) that these characteristic constellations were produced by the child-rearing practices and other "primary institutions" (family organization, subsistence techniques, etc.) prevalent in the culture. Specifically, he was preoccupied with the imposition of infant-training

[8] Margaret Mead (1959) quotes Ruth Benedict as commenting that Sapir wished to "prove that culture doesn't matter" (p. 201).

disciplines and with the ways in which institutions interfere with impulses, relying heavily on psychoanalytic theory for his basic hypotheses. Kardiner postulated also that the personality configurations produced by the "primary institutions" were themselves responsible for the distinctive forms of folklore, mythology, and religion of the culture, which he termed "secondary institutions." This theoretical scheme was to provide the model for the first efforts at quantitative cross-cultural research on socialization — the work of Whiting and Child.

Singer (1961) has examined the assumptions entailed in Kardiner's writings and the evidence for them; here we need merely note that whatever the validity of the extreme emphasis on child rearing, attention is directed to the mutual influences of personality constellations and cultural constellations. Field workers interested in personality and culture would in the future tend to look more carefully at mediating linkages.

Quite a different approach to the study of socialization in a primitive society was John Whiting's *Becoming a Kwoma* (1941). Whiting was not so much concerned with characterizing the personality orientations of the Kwoma as with trying to explain the development of the Kwoma in terms of learning theory and thereby present "a theory of the process of socialization." He was strongly influenced by John Dollard, who had by then become committed to Hullian learning theory but retained his interest in culture and in psychoanalytic theory. Whiting's subsequent work with Child (1953) followed the model of Kardiner's formulations; data from a number of cultures were mobilized to test his specific hypothesis as to the relationship between aspects of child rearing and "secondary institutions," that is, cultural features that might be regarded as expressions of dominant personality tendencies.

Another source of influence both in anthropology and subsequently in the field of human development was the teaching of Lloyd Warner. Warner notes that he was influenced by suggestions of Robert Lowie, by a brief period of work with Malinowski, and by his readings of Piaget and G. H. Mead. During the mid-1930's he gave a graduate course at the University of Chicago entitled "The Social Orientation of the Child," which was concerned very largely with socialization as such. He observes:

> It had become clear to me that one needed not only to know about social structure and the changes going on in social structure at any given time, but one needed also to know about the psychic life of the individual and the changes going on in the psychic life of the individual, and then of course the relation of the growing individual to the changing society. . . . My long time interest in kinship and the family was also directly related to my interest in the socialization of the child. Obviously the socializing process begins in the family and continues there in some societies for all the individual's life and in others for a good part of it. It is through the

> family that one can interrelate some of the body of theory and knowledge of the psychologists and social psychologists to that of the structural anthropologists. (Warner, 1967)

This brief treatment of the origins of interest in socialization within the field of anthropology prior to 1940 would be grossly incomplete without mention of Clyde Kluckhohn. Although his major influence on the field came somewhat later, he was early concerned with the interrelationships of culture and personality and devoted attention to both methodological and theoretical issues of the field in his own research. Despite all of the developments prior to World War II, Kluckhohn noted in 1939:

> With a very few notable (and mainly recent) exceptions, anthropologists have failed to give systematic attention to the problem of how specific bits of culture are transmitted from individual to individual within particular societies. Such factual material as is available in the published literature is almost wholly anecdotal in character. . . . A total conceptual scheme for attacking the question may be said to be nonexistent. . . .
>
> I feel that it is fair to say that at the moment both the substantive and theoretical aspects of socialization and culturalization (if I may coin an admittedly horrid word) acutely need investigation. (p. 98)

Among Kluckhohn's many contributions that reached beyond an audience of anthropologists were his examination of the use of personal documents in anthropological science (1945), his studies of the Navaho, and the volume with Murray previously mentioned (Kluckhohn and Murray, 1948). Kluckhohn's interests were as much focused upon the study of culture change as upon the development of the individual. Nevertheless, in his own work and through the students he trained, he contributed markedly to systematizing and more adequately conceptualizing the process of socialization.

Other Influences

Our examination of developing interest in the topic of socialization has been oriented to academic disciplines, but the disciplines are themselves subject to currents of thought in the larger society. Academicians are also parents and thereby partake in popular concerns about child rearing. Movements in adult education, public welfare, social philosophy, and clinical psychiatry have had an impact on social institutions and popular attitudes; these movements have at the same time incorporated existing knowledge derived from academic fields and modified academic perspectives.

In *Education for Child Rearing*, Brim (1959) has described the assumptions and objectives of parent-education programs in the United

States and assessed their procedures and results. In sketching the history of the broad social movement for improved education of parents, he notes both the fundamental causes for concern with child rearing and the development of organizations in response to social pressures and expressions of need. The National Congress of Parents and Teachers, founded before 1900, was one such organization. The Children's Bureau, organized within the federal government in 1912 following the first White House Conference on child welfare, was another. From 1914 to the present the Children's Bureau's publication, *Infant Care*, has been available for the guidance of parents. Here the emphasis was long derived primarily from the views of pediatric experts. If they have been increasingly influenced by psychiatric theory and socialization research, they have also tended to focus the attention of the researcher on the problems that parents confront.

Concern with social planning and with increasing the effectiveness of the individual has also inevitably focused attention upon problems of socialization even though not phrased in such terms. First immigration from abroad, then massive internal immigration during depressions and in time of war have posed problems of accommodation and acculturation for the migrant. Such problems have served to emphasize the lifelong process of socialization. Money for study that might produce practical results was available long before funding was generally available for basic social science research.

The development of clinical psychiatry outside of the mental hospital has been another important influence. When psychiatry turned to the community, it had to deal with the social matrix of personality development; consequently, it contributed much to the understanding of pathological aspects of socialization experience. Among the significant psychiatric contributions of the era in which socialization was emerging as a field of study was Plant's *Personality and the Cultural Pattern* (1937). Other psychiatrists and psychoanalysts whose writing was largely oriented to a socialization perspective were Karen Horney, Erich Fromm, and Harry Stack Sullivan.

MAIN THEMES IN THE STUDY OF SOCIALIZATION IN THE UNITED STATES

The foregoing excursion into the literature of the period prior to World War II has been primarily an attempt to trace the more obvious lines of influence in writings about socialization within each of the disciplines. It does not constitute a thorough historical review but deals with major trends prior to 1940. The volume of research and writing since 1940 has been so great as to preclude any attempt to review this literature in the present chapter. Fortunately, there exist relatively recent reviews written from the perspectives of each of the disciplines here dealt with, so that there is less need for an overview of work since 1940. Reference will be made below to a number of these reviews as well as to a few of the most influential works of the past two decades, works that have helped to establish current trends in the field.

Cottrell and Gallagher (1941) in their review of developments in social psychology during the decade 1930–1940 comment on the great increase in cross-disciplinary research which occurred in the late 1920's and the thirties. By 1939, at least some leading representatives of each of the disciplines under consideration were committed to the study of socialization processes, were using a common set of concepts, and were guided by overlapping, if not identical, theoretical interests. At a number of universities — Chicago, Columbia, Harvard, and Yale, in particular — interdisciplinary activities included seminars, research collaboration, and even degree-granting programs. Moreover, the social sciences were beginning to attract public interest and support. Recruitment and training were advancing at a much faster pace than ever before.

The formation of the Social Science Research Council was an important force in the convergence of the perspectives of the several disciplines concerned with socialization. Established in 1923 and commencing effective operations in 1927, the Council was devoted to the improvement of research facilities, organization and methods, and to the development of research personnel in all of the social sciences. Operating through advisory committees in selected areas of concentration, the Council provided a medium for effective interdisciplinary discussion. For example, the Advisory Committee on Personality and Culture, established in 1930, brought together during its early years the anthropologists Sapir and Warner, sociologists Burgess and Thomas, and psychologists E. A. Bott, C. H. Judd, and R. S. Woodworth, among others. Sponsorship of the Sapir-Dollard seminar at Yale in 1931 has already been mentioned. If parochialism did not disappear from the ranks of the several disciplines, there was at least an increasing number of workers who recognized that they could not be competent social scientists without taking into account knowledge from outside the ranks of their own disciplines.

The convergence of theoretical interests of anthropology, psychology, and sociology in the study of socialization has not by any means resulted in the obliteration of disciplinary differences. By and large, both research approaches and research objectives have retained distinctive features. Without attempting to be exhaustive, we list here the dominant aims and methods of each of the disciplines and note a few outstanding examples for each.

In Anthropology

Anthropologists have relied most heavily on direct observation of child-rearing practices and socialization arrangements in relatively small communities and have thereby been able more often to achieve a fuller picture of the total socialization process than have members of other disciplines. Among the aims pursued in anthropological studies have been:

(1) The study of the effect of particular cultural emphases and institutional constellations on the process of socialization and personality development (as in Malinowski, 1927, or Mead, 1928, and in works on national character).

(2) The documentation of the wide range of alternative emphases in modes of socialization or, more often, in valued aspects of personality, at times with the further aim of showing the plasticity of human nature (as in Benedict's *Patterns of Culture*).

(3) The study of the interrelationships between cultural change or cultural fissure and significant features of personality (as suggested by Kluckhohn, 1939, and attempted in the research of Beaglehole and Ritchie, 1958, and in the research of Spindler, 1955).

(4) Study of the statistical association between particular socialization arrangements or emphases and particular attributes of personality or of the culture, such as magic, art, or religion (as in Whiting and Child, 1953, and the many other studies using data from a large number of cultures). Cross-cultural studies of this type have been carried out both by anthropologists and by psychologists (see below, pp. 61–63).

In general, intensive studies of socialization by anthropologists have confined attention to a given society and culture, except for a very few comparative programs such as the monumental "six cultures" study of the Whitings (Whiting, Beatrice, 1963). The process of socialization in a given cultural context is then the process of enculturation. The agents of socialization are those who transmit the culture wittingly or unwittingly. Margaret Mead has commented on the tendency of students of behavior to "use the words *socialization* and *enculturation* uncritically and interchangeably" (Mead, 1963, p. 185). She prefers to reserve the concept socialization for "the set of species-wide requirements and exactions made on human beings by human societies" and suggests that the development of a cross-culturally viable theory of socialization requires a meticulous examination of the details of enculturation. Most anthropologists continue to use the terms socialization and enculturation interchangeably, though usage of the concept socialization outside of anthropology tends to put greater emphasis on the acquisition of knowledge of self and others in social interaction.

The 1940's and 1950's witnessed the publication of a large number of monographs reporting studies of the relationship of cultural orientations to personality orientations and a succession of formulations of "basic" and "modal" personality and of national character. By 1950 critical commentaries on the circularity of reasoning and evidence in many culture and personality studies began to appear in some strength (see, for example, Lindesmith and Strauss, 1950); by 1960 contributions to the field were on the whole more sharply focused on specific theoretical issues and were methodologically much more sophisticated. Of the most significant contributions to theory many were journal articles; these, on several occasions, have been gathered together in collections that have greatly influenced the development of the field (for example, Haring, 1949; Kluckhohn and Murray, 1948). Three books that appeared in 1961 — two edited by anthropologists (Cohen, 1961; Hsu, 1961) and one by a psychologist (Kaplan, 1961), all containing at least some original contributions — afford a good overview of the current state of knowledge. Singer's "Survey of Culture and Personality Theory and Research" in the volume edited by Kaplan is the most scholarly historical review of the culture and personality field.

In Sociology

Within the field of sociology we may note at least four historically significant themes which are germane to the study of socialization: (1) concern with modes of social control (and more recently with the sociology of deviant behavior); (2) the significance of social interaction in the attainment of human nature, with particular emphasis on the development of the social self and of the self-other patterns; (3) the influence of social structure and value orientations on child-rearing practices and emphases; and (4) the significance of social roles, role recruitment, and role training for the understanding of behavior. The first and oldest of these themes has tended to stress the differences between, and yet the complementarity of, regulative institutions (which insure that individual behavior will conform to cultural or group norms) and the "internalization" of norms (which produces controls from within). This process of internalization is, of course, very closely linked with the development of the self through social interaction, for it is through such interaction that norms are first defined for the child. To a great extent, the social order rests on each new generation's learning to behave in accordance with the moral imperatives of the society. In like manner, orderliness of the individual's relationships with others rests in part on his having achieved a self that is sensitive to the behaviors of others and incorporates the responses of significant others who are participants in a normatively regulated social order. This is not to say that the individual's task is solely one of learning a body of existing norms that have validity throughout the society. It is partly a manner of achieving an adequate understanding of the norms that are important to others, partly a matter of helping to shape new normative expectations. It is fair to say, however, that very little sociological research has dealt directly with these issues.

Sociological contributions to the development and understanding of role behaviors have produced a much larger body of research. One may be tempted to say "have been more empirically oriented," but this would not be an accurate statement of the problem. Formulations on socialization aspects of social control and on the rise of the social self are certainly based on empirical observations. They are, however, observations much more difficult to systematize and to incorporate in research designs, except as one focuses on particular problematic facets. When one seeks to examine particular kinds of breakdowns of social control, as in much current research on deviance, the systematic mobilizing of data becomes a more obvious and feasible strategy.

As Brim has noted (Brim and Wheeler, 1966), sociological contributions to socialization research have been most notable in the realm of adolescent and adult socialization. In this realm socialization *is*, to a large extent, a matter of role learning. Such studies of socialization have frequently taken place in the context of a particular institution or organization and have relied on combinations of participant observation and the use of interviews or questionnaires.

Where sociologists have studied child-rearing practices, they have tended to rely principally upon interview techniques, although observational and even experimental techniques have occasionally been used (for example, Rosen and D'Andrade, 1959). From the first — that is, from the time of *Middletown* (1927) — sociologists have been interested in the ways in which social status influences the orientations and behaviors of parents toward their children. Influential among the early studies were Davis and Dollard's *Children of Bondage* (1940) and the research of Davis and Havighurst (1946) dealing with child-training practices. Hollingshead's study of adolescents (1949) continued the examination of the effects of social class, while a decade later Coleman (1961) looked more closely at the effects of the peer culture on adolescent socialization.

The popularity of culture and personality studies and of the early research of workers who were guided by an amalgam of psychoanalytic and learning theory led for a time to a narrowing of focus — the imposition of disciplines on the young child — but in recent years the scope of sociological concern has broadened markedly to include value orientations, interactive patterns in the family, the nature of neighborhood and classroom contexts, parent education, and to some extent the problem of continuities and discontinuities in socialization experience from one period or setting to another. An adequate overview of current work cannot be provided here; the reader interested in recent developments as seen from a sociological viewpoint is referred to review articles by Sewell (1961, 1963) and by Clausen and Williams (1963).

In Psychology

Within the field of psychology, studies of socialization have tended to be more sharply focused on particular segments of socialization influence and more closely linked to specific theoretical premises. Theories of learning have been used loosely in most sociological and anthropological studies; they are, of course, much more rigorously elaborated and applied in psychology. Psychologists have tended to look less closely at the origins of socialization emphases and more closely at the immediate relationship between agent and inductee. They have been especially concerned with establishing the nature of the processes mediating between socialization practices and child behavior, such as identification, the development of conscience, stages or dynamics of cognitive structuring, and the shaping of motivational dispositions. As a consequence, they have conceptualized and studied child behavior itself to a far greater extent than have socialization researchers from other disciplines. Psychologists have been relatively less concerned, however, with study of the adult outcomes of socialization practices.

The variety of studies by psychologists interested in socialization and child development is great, and the substantive areas and theoretical issues touched upon often shade into one another, making it difficult to achieve any adequate, simple classification of such studies. Preeminent in number and influence have been studies seeking to establish the effects of parental influences on the developing child. Bronfenbrenner (1963) has suggested that formulations in this area may be grouped into three general families of hypotheses. The first, based principally on psychoanalytic theory, focuses on the general affective quality of the parent-child relationship (for example, nurturant versus rejecting) as the antecedent condition for the development of a particular form of behavior. The second group of formulations, employing conceptual models deriving from a fusion of psychoanalytic and learning theories, is concerned with the effects of parental rewards and punishments upon specific child behaviors. The third, based largely on the concept of "modeling" (as manifest, for example, in the work of Bandura and Walters, 1963), treats parental behaviors as providing role models for the child. One might include in another category studies deriving from field theory that attempt to characterize the total atmosphere within which socialization takes place or to analyze the complex of environmental forces both inside and outside the family as well as studies of the relationships between intentions, behavioral skills, and actions as manifest in interaction within the family.

Another kind of research on parental influence is to be noted in studies of infra-human species. Many developmental psychologists, psychiatrists, and anthropologists have been markedly influenced in their thinking by the work of ethologists and other zoologists focusing on species-specific behaviors (see, for example, Bowlby, 1957). Studies of maternal behavior in primates and lower orders of mammals (Rheingold, 1963), field studies of social behavior of animals (DeVore, 1965; Marler and Hamilton, 1966), and laboratory studies of the influences of particular forms of nurturance, of mothering, and of early experience with peers (Harlow and Harlow, 1965) have added a much wider perspective to that derived from the sharply delineated semi-experimental approaches used in many studies of the effects of human parents on their offspring.

Studies of language learning are often not couched in a socialization framework, but they constitute another major area of highly sophisticated research and theory in the field of socialization to which psychologists have been major contributors. The study of language increasingly shades into the study of cognitive development in general. Until fairly recently emphasis in this area was on cognitive processes and the development of cognitive structures, without much interest in the effects of the larger social environment. The rediscovery of poverty and the beginning of large-scale efforts at the national level to offset the effects of economic and "cultural" deprivation has, however, led to an examination of linkages between the structures of the psychological and social environment and the cognitive development of the child.

Within the school, psychologists have studied the effects of teaching techniques, classroom atmospheres, and general curriculum emphasis on the motivation and performance of the student. The effects of the "mix" of students in the classroom, as related to ability grading (variously called "tracking" or "streaming") and to sex and I.Q. of the student, are being studied in a number of countries. Less adequately studied has been the interaction between home and school socialization efforts, but beginnings have been made both in connection with Headstart operations and in the research of Biber, Minuchin, and their associates.

In certain respects, socialization research in psychology has moved faster and farther than in the other disciplines. The development of systematic theory, concern with problems of measurement and with replication of results, the use of experimental analogues of socialization experiences, and emphasis on sophisticated techniques of multivariate analysis have all helped to produce a large and increasingly well-integrated body of literature on socialization. Its theoretical sophistication and methodological rigor, however, have often been bought at the cost of limiting perspective to relatively small segments of socialization experience. Contextual modifiers of socialization behaviors and problems of continuity and discontinuity have been largely ignored. Yet it is to psychological research that we owe some of our most adequate data on the differential effects of situational contexts upon the behaviors of boys and girls or men and women of differing levels of ability and differing backgrounds.

Among the studies by psychologists that have most influenced the field in the past two decades were *The Authoritarian Personality* (Adorno *et al.*, 1950), with its examination of the family and socialization patterns found to be associated with authoritarian attitudes and prejudice, and *Patterns of Child Rearing*, by Sears and his associates (1957), the most comprehensive study of early childhood socialization in the United States. The contributions of psychologists to research on socialization have been well reviewed in a number of recent volumes, notably those edited by Stevenson (1963) and by Hoffman and Hoffman (1964 and 1966).

Increasingly, of course, major studies of socialization have involved members of several disciplines. If at times such involvement has been little more than a reflection of current fashion, there have been many instances of genuine interpenetration of disciplinary perspectives, resulting in more comprehensive theories and more adequate data collection.

Among the most fruitful collaborations that have crossed disciplinary lines one thinks not only of the early instances of Kardiner and Linton, Kluckhohn and Murray, and Whiting and Child, but of the more recent contributions of Miller and Swanson (1958), Inkeles and Levinson (1954), the Whitings, Lambert, Minturn, and others (see Whiting, B., 1963), Bronfenbrenner, Devereux, and their team at Cornell, and the ongoing program of research by Campbell and LeVine on origins of ethnocentrism. Even in the decade since the publication of *Interdisciplinary Team Research* (Luzski, 1958) there have been notable increases in the number of scholars who incorporate the knowledge and research skills of several disciplines and in the frequency with which research teams have achieved truly interdisciplinary collaboration.

A COMPARATIVE VIEW — SOCIALIZATION RESEARCH IN OTHER COUNTRIES

In tracing some of the major tendencies in the development of socialization theory and research in the United States, we have mentioned only briefly contributions from abroad. It is obvious that major theoretical impetus has come from the work of a number of European scholars —

from Freud and psychoanalysis, from Lewin and field theory, and from the steady-flowing stream of research reports by Piaget and his associates. It is much more feasible, however, to trace the development of a field of study in a single country than to attempt to encompass interactions and influences crossing national boundaries. Socialization is, moreover, primarily an American emergent, especially in its interdisciplinary expression.

There appears to be much less close communication among behavioral scientists of different nationalities than among physical and biological scientists. In general, except for scholars who regularly read journals in other languages, only such major formulations as achieve the status of classics outside of one's own language tend to come to attention. Moreover, the theories and findings of social science research are not sufficiently codified or even sufficiently coherent so that the significance of a given piece of research can be readily assessed without thorough study. Contextual influences give meaning to behavior and markedly affect the inferences one can draw from a particular interaction or a particular study. This is especially true in a field such as socialization, where one deals with the transmission of cultural and subcultural definitions by various modes which are themselves culturally specified.

Although we are likely to be aware of such classics as the works of Durkheim, Wallon, and Piaget in France, the ethnographic accounts of family and kinship influences in England, and the writings of a number of psychiatrists and psychoanalysts in various European countries, most American students of socialization are relatively ignorant of contemporary research and theory on socialization or child rearing even in Western Europe. In order to educate ourselves, the Committee on Socialization and Social Structure sponsored bibliographical reviews of the recent literature on socialization in Germany, France, and Great Britain. These reviews, indicating the substance of the work in process and commenting to some degree on trends and issues, have appeared or will appear as individual publications (see Appendix B).

Here we shall sketch only a few dominant impressions of the similarities and differences between work in the United States and work going on in the other countries for which we have information. Reference will be made to cross-national comparisons where such exist. Nowhere else have large samples of parents been interviewed or observed as systematically as in the United States; but families have been studied intensively in several countries, and surveys of parental attitudes and practices have appeared not only in Western Europe but in the Middle East (Prothro, 1961), India (see Narain, 1964, for reports on a surprisingly large number of specific projects), and Japan. Of course, there are ethnographic accounts of many preliterate societies. Major effort has, however, been confined to a relatively few countries.

In France

From France and French Switzerland have come two of the most powerful influences upon contemporary American theory and research on socialization: Durkheim's formulations relating to the shaping of individual thought and behavior by society and its "collective representations," and Piaget's seminal researches on the child's development of language and of the categories and processes of thought, his conceptions of the world and of morality. The works of Durkheim relating most specifically to socialization — *L'Education Morale* and *Education et Sociologie* — were not translated into English until recently, so that their influence in the United States has been less striking than that of *Suicide*, the *Division of Labor in Society*, and the *Rules of Sociological Method*.

One of Durkheim's earliest concerns was with the foundation of moral principles at a time when religious teaching within the public schools of France was abolished by governmental edict. Thus at an early stage in his career Durkheim's attention was focused on the transmission of values and moral beliefs.

The word "education" has much broader connotations in French than in English. The *Petit Larousse* defines it (author's translation) as "the action of developing physical, intellectual and moral faculties, . . . the results of this action, . . . knowledge and practice of the usages of society, . . . the totality of the services of public instruction." In *Education and Sociology* (1956) Durkheim's usage of "education" was remarkably similar to the conception of socialization held by many contemporary sociologists. He characterized education as

> the influences exercised by adult generations on those that are not yet ready for social life. Its object is to arouse and to develop in the child a certain number of physical, intellectual and moral states which are demanded of him both by the political society as a whole and the special milieu for which he is specifically destined. (p. 71)

We find in Durkheim an emphasis on the child's receptiveness to suggestion and to authority; he is like putty to be moulded by his teachers, but not through coerciveness. Morality is not merely obligatory; it is desirable and desired. Durkheim's analysis of moral norms and their transmission influenced not only French and American sociologists but also the thinking of Baldwin and, somewhat later, Piaget.

A number of Piaget's early works, such as *The Language and Thought of the Child* (1926) and *The Moral Judgment of the Child* (1932), were quickly translated into English and appear to have influenced sociologists and anthropologists in the United States as much as they influenced students of child development. Translation of his later works, more sharply focused on the structural properties of thought and on formulations in genetic epistemology, was less immediate. Since their publication, largely in the 1950's, Piaget's impact on the field of child development research and upon the study of cognition in general has been a dominant force (see Flavell, 1963; and Kessen and Kuhlman, 1962). The emphasis in these later publications has, however, been much less upon socialization influences, much more upon maturational processes and developmental stages.

Also very influential in French theory and research on the development of the child in society has been the work of Henri Wallon (1934, 1941). His interests in the development of the self in social interaction paralleled those of American symbolic interactionists such as Cooley and Mead (and like them he was influenced by Baldwin and by Dewey). But he also brought to the study of the child a background in medicine and experimental psychology. Founder in 1925 of the Laboratory of Child Psychology and in 1948 of the journal *Enfance*, which he edited for many years, Wallon was Professor in the College of France, the highest of all academic honors in his country. His efforts appear to have stimulated a great deal of the French research on the social development of the child.

Much of the recent French research relating to childhood socialization has been reviewed by P. H. Chombart de Lauwe (1966). He has noted five main trends or tendencies: (1) the study of identification and of the integration of successive roles; (2) emphasis on the conditions of the social milieu as these impinge upon the developing individual (socioeconomic conditions, patterns of local subcultures, ecological factors); (3) emphasis on "the function of representations, of images, of models and underlying them, the value systems subscribed to by the adults in the midst of whom the child lives"; (4) the delineation of "the stages of social maturation, . . . adaptability, the open-mindedness that allows the indispensable successive mutations to take place"; and (5) insistence on the reciprocal action of the individual on the group. Chombart de Lauwe indicates that for himself and for a number of French writers the word socialization has a coercive flavor, derived from Durkheim's usage, which makes them rather uncomfortable with the term. Yet the body of French research relating to socialization processes is sizable.

A good deal of the current research on socialization, perhaps the bulk of it, is being carried out by developmental and social psychologists in research institutes affiliated with universities or with the Centre National de la Recherche Scientifique. As in the United States, sociologists are more active in studies of adolescent and adult socialization. No major cross-national studies, comparing socialization practices in France with those in other countries have yet appeared in the literature, though a number of French and American writers have commented on apparent differences in orientation between French and American parents, schools, and peer groups (for example, see Wolfenstein, 1955; Pitts, 1960; Clausen, 1966).

In Great Britain

Psychology and anthropology are long established disciplines in Great Britain, while sociology has had a place in most British universities only in the period since World War II. Within anthropology, Seligman (1924) was among the very first to become interested in the investigation of psychological phenomena and, indeed, was credited by Malinowski (1927) with having stimulated his study of the Oedipal situation in matrilineal Trobriand society. It would appear that British anthropology has not been as heavily involved in the study of culture and personality as has an influential segment of American anthropologists, but studies of national character, by anthropologists and psychiatrists, were frequent during and just after World War II.

Himmelweit and Sealy (1966) observe that the major stimulus for research on socialization in Great Britain has been provided by psychoanalytic formulation of child development and

> by the problems brought into prominence through war and, above all, evacuation.
>
> In this type of research the names of Anna Freud and Dorothy Burlingham are prominent. Pre-war work by Susan Isaacs was of great importance and during and after the war, the observations and writings of Bowlby and Winnicott became influential both in terms of types of research undertaken and their theoretical orientations. A second mainstream of research included those studies involving close observation over a fairly long period of time of limited segments of the population (e.g., Bott [1957], Kerr [1958], Paneth [1944], and Young and Wilmott [1957]). The third main type of research includes the "programmatic" follow-up studies or sample studies by questionnaires and interview of the Newsons (1963), of Douglas and his co-workers, Hindley and Moore and Kellmer-Pringle. (p. 4)

It was the first of these streams of research that produced the substantial body of theory and research relating to maternal deprivation.[9] Research of the second type mentioned by Himmelweit and Sealy — largely deriving from anthropological and sociological studies of families in particular neighborhoods — has recently been summarized in Klein's two-volume synthesis, *Samples from English Cultures* (1965). The third type, "programmatic" research, includes several large-scale longitudinal studies as well as surveys of infant and child care.

Klein's work mentioned in the previous paragraph deserves further

[9] For an excellent review of the current status of knowledge on this topic see Yarrow (1964).

comment. It is substantively, rather than theoretically, oriented but is squarely focused on relationships between social structure and socialization. The first volume summarizes in developmental perspective three intensive studies of working-class families in different social settings and then examines other available material relating to adult life in different segments of English society. Volume Two draws heavily upon theory and research on socialization to examine the probable consequences of the family patterns described. In the Introduction to the second volume, Klein speaks of "a dearth of English studies on what parents think and do," which requires that one rely on the more systematic studies carried out in the United States (p. vii). She does list the British studies that provide quantitative data on socialization, and gives a bibliography that affords a good overview of the major British works in this field.

Klein's overview of socialization in the English family is nicely complemented by the paper by Himmelweit and Sealy (1966), "The School as an Agent of Socialization," which was prepared at the request of the Committee on Socialization and Social Structure. The nature of the British educational system, with its markedly different types of secondary school and its limited number of university places, makes secondary school placement — at age eleven or twelve — a major factor, if not *the* major factor, in determining the life chances of the individual. In the words of Himmelweit and Sealy:

> When, at the age of eleven, children are divided into secondary modern and grammar school, the segregation produces differences in opportunities for education, vocational choice, attitudes and social mobility that endure for life. (Himmelweit and Sealy, 1966, p. 2)

Elementary school becomes, then, not merely a place where fundamentals of education are obtained but a preparation for the crucial selection that takes place at age eleven. This selection is based primarily upon intelligence and achievement-test performances, supplemented by teacher recommendations. Only about 20 per cent of the elementary school students are chosen to attend Grammar Schools, which are the principal means of preparing for university attendance.

This system of education, while not by any means standardized, generates a great deal of data on school performance and on the selection process itself. Both the contributions of the home and of the organization and functioning of the school have been assessed in addition to performance differences deriving directly from the characteristics and abilities of the child. Studies of the interactions between home and school environments, of the differential effects of ability grouping upon students of high or of low I.Q., and of the differential effects of coeducational schools on boys and girls have produced an impressive body of data and generalizations about the schools and socialization in Great

Britain. Many of these studies are summarized and analysed by Himmelweit and Sealy, who also provide a large bibliography on the topic.

Turner (1960) has contrasted the nature of selective and preparatory operations of the schools in the United States and in England and is currently engaged in a major cross-national study. Comparisons of certain aspects of child rearing in the two countries are also afforded by the interview studies of Devereux, Bronfenbrenner, and Rodgers (1965) and the observational research of the Barkers (1963). Bronfenbrenner, Devereux, and their associates find many similarities in the reports of eleven-year-olds about parental practices in the United States and England, but there are some interesting differences. American parents are described by their children as more demanding and controlling yet also more affectionate and supportive than English parents. English parents are reported to rely more heavily on spanking and scolding (but also to be less consistent in their discipline), while American parents more often use psychological forms of punishment. Role differentiation between fathers and mothers is greater in England, with fathers less active in child rearing. Role differentiation between boys and girls also seems greater in England, with boys treated more severely. As Devereux *et al.* observe, their survey findings are, for the most part, congruent with the observational data reported by the Barkers. Other studies by this research team suggest that English children are far more oriented toward their peers in rule enforcement than are American children.

In Germany [10]

The following brief description of German socialization research is based almost entirely on the review prepared for the Committee by Baumert and Karl. Socialization has not been a major area of research interest for German social scientists. Although the term is employed with some frequency, it does not receive much attention in most of the

[10] Following the International Seminar in Family Research held in Washington in 1962, the late Dr. Gerhard Baumert undertook for the Committee on Socialization and Social Structure the supervision of a survey of German socialization research since World War II and began preparation of a report "giving an overview of the development of socialization research for those areas where the German language is spoken." The basic review of materials and a draft of a brief report had been almost completed when Dr. Baumert's fatal illness forced interruption of the work. The report and annotated bibliography were completed by Heinz Karl, who had assisted Dr. Baumert from the beginning in the collection of the material. In abridged form these materials have been deposited as Document No. 9624 of the ADI Auxiliary Publications Project, Photo Duplication Service, Library of Congress, Washington, D.C. 20540. To obtain a copy, remit a check or money order for $3.75 or photoprints or $2.00 for 35 mm. microfilm, payable to Chief, Photo Duplication Service, Library of Congress. Advance payment is required. Cite document number in ordering.

major handbooks, lexicons, or textbooks in social psychology and sociology. Baumert and Karl note that "no critical, comprehensive examination of the empirical studies in socialization in the German-speaking areas has been undertaken as yet," but that the nearest thing to such an examination — Thomae's "Entwicklung und Prägung" in the third volume of the *Handbuch der Psychologie* — lists an "overwhelming majority" of American titles in its bibliography (p. 6).

Speaking of the research interests expressed in German socialization studies, Baumert and Karl note:

> It is remarkable how seldom infants and children were the subject of a study. Regarding the object of socialization, we learn the most about pupils. A correspondingly high percentage of information on the role of the social mediator falls on the teachers; the role of the mother was investigated more minutely, that of the father, less. The influence of siblings, other relatives and peer groups was hardly touched upon. On the side of the social mediators, the general training attitude (autocratic vs. social-integrative) and the special variables of punishment, prohibitions and sexual enlightenment received special attention. Forms of reward and, as general variables, continuity or consistency of training were ignored to a great degree. On the side of the children and youths, the interest was focused mainly upon achievement behavior, independence and obedience or adaptation. (Baumert and Karl, p. 5)

Among the most impressive of the German studies of socialization cited in the German bibliography are those of educational psychologists Reinhard and Ann-Marie Tausch (1963) relating to socialization in the school. Using observational methods and questionnaires, the Tausches have examined teachers' behaviors and their effects on student participation and conformity in the classroom. Autocratic procedures were widespread in the classrooms studied, despite efforts to train teachers in alternative modes of handling classroom relationships and problems. Pupil responsiveness to control was, however, less favorable under autocratically imposed prohibitions than when the teachers used integrative techniques.

Conceptual issues in the German literature of socialization have been discussed by Wurzbacher (1963) in the volume *Man as a Social and Personal Being*, which bears the subtitle *Contributions to the Concept and Theory of Socialization*. As reported by Baumert and Karl (p. 8), Wurzbacher distinguishes between the processes of socialization ("guidance and moulding of the human being through the behavior expectations and behavioral controls of his partner in this respect"), enculturation ("acquisition and intensification of experiences, 'goods,' standards and symbols of the culture"), and personalization ("reactions of the individual upon the factors society and culture").

There have been a number of studies by non-Germans touching upon socialization practices and their outcomes in Germany. These include efforts to describe and explain German "national character" (for example, Dicks, 1950, and Levy, 1948), a descriptive analysis of German materials on child rearing (Métraux, 1955), and the recent work of Devereux, Bronfenbrenner, and Suci (1962). The major preoccupation of the national-character studies has been to analyze the nature of German authoritarianism and militarism. German scholars such as Horkheimer and Fromm had earlier analyzed the authority structure of the German family, and indeed psychoanalytic theory makes very clear the impact of such a structure on Freud's thinking. Extreme emphasis on obedience and discipline is manifest both in the child-rearing materials reviewed by Métraux and in the findings of studies of German youth groups and classrooms. Yet the research of Bronfenbrenner, Devereux, and Rodgers (1966) suggests in comparison with both American and English parents:

> German parents stand out for their high love-oriented methods of discipline (e.g., withdrawal of affection, appeals to guilt) as well as in their infrequent use of unconditional disciplinary methods as scolding or restricting privileges. In addition, it is in the German family that the father plays the most active role in child rearing.

While these findings, based on children's reports about relationships and practices in their families, are not incompatible with strong paternal authority, they are hardly predictable from studies of German national character. Clearly there is need for much more cross-national research, with direct comparisons of parental behavior as well as of the perceptions of such behaviors, coupled with intensive study of the meaning of particular patterns of child rearing and responses on the part of parents and children in each country.

In Other Countries

There have been a number of descriptive studies of socialization practices in other European countries but few major contributions to socialization theory or research other than those mentioned from England, France, and Germany. During and just after World War II, there were many national-character studies, some drawing on firsthand data relating to socialization practices and some drawing on "the study of culture at a distance" for whatever clues such study afforded as to the dominant emphases in personality. Such studies have been reviewed and discussed elsewhere (Mead and Wolfenstein, 1955; Inkeles and Levinson, 1954; Martingale, 1967).

Since World War II, the placing of Fulbright scholars and other

American scholars in foreign countries has furnished opportunities for collaborative study with researchers from these countries. Some socialization studies have resulted from such collaboration; others have come about through discussions held in research committees of international social science organizations, such as the International Seminars on Family Research. For a long time the reports of such seminars were a primary source of information about empirical work in process in other countries (see, for example, Anderson, 1957). The increasing number of scholarly journals in the behavioral sciences which are international in appeal, especially those like *Human Development* and the *International Social Science Journal* which are truly interdisciplinary, should help to diffuse information about important research, provided that some "centering" of reports of socialization research in a relatively small number of journals takes place. It is difficult enough in one's own country to cover the range of periodicals in which relevant materials are being published. Unless one knows the prevailing publication practices for any given country among those with a variety of scholarly journals in the fields of social and psychological studies, the task of keeping abreast is simply overwhelming.

CROSS-CULTURAL AND CROSS-NATIONAL STUDIES

Insofar as one seeks to achieve a delineation of universal elements in socialization and personality development or even an adequate understanding of the ways in which various social arrangements influence the effects of socialization experience, cross-cultural and cross-national comparisons would seem to be essential. The use of the Human Relations Area Files or of the original monographic literature for cross-cultural studies of relationships between features of the economy or ecological arrangements, child-rearing values and practices, and socialization outcomes — as by Whiting and Child (1953), Whiting (1961), Aberle (1961), Barry, Bacon, and Child (1957), Cohen (1961), and others — has produced a number of very impressive correlations which have been brought to bear on theoretical formulations drawn from psychoanalytic, learning, and role-developmental theory. It appears, for example, that the number of adult caretakers in the household will tend to influence child control and parental punitiveness in highly predictable ways. Such a finding can, of course, be checked in any given culture. When it is, as in Minturn and Lambert's *Mothers of Six Cultures*, the findings are likely to be less clear-cut. A check in our own culture might be even more difficult to interpret, for differences in the number of adult caretakers are likely to be associated with ethnic and socioeconomic differentials, with family "pathologies," and the like. But this is precisely one of the chief values of cross-cultural comparisons. One wishes to know what are the consequences of one type of modal pattern or arrangement as against another. The difficulty is that one is dealing with correlations of ecological or grouped data and may be in danger of drawing unfounded inferences (Robinson, 1950). Features other than those under immediate study may be of crucial importance.

An equally, if not more, serious difficulty comes from wrenching relatively isolated fragments of data on child-rearing practices out of their cultural context, as has been necessary if one wished to use existing data from a large number of cultures. This same kind of problem exists when a standardized interview schedule devised for one society or culture is imported into another. It may secure interesting findings and even give evidence of highly significant internal correlations or differences between cultures, but this does not mean that the most salient features of socialization practices in the second society have been established. Much depends, of course, on the magnitude and nature of the differences between the societies studied. Much depends also on the generality or specificity of inquiry about socialization tasks which must be accomplished one way or another in any society. To the extent that questions can be posed flexibly, that phrasings uniquely appropriate to their culture of origin can be avoided, a relatively standardized approach combining interview and observation should be feasible and should permit the answering of many more questions than one can address through the Human Relations Area Files.

One would hope that the collection of systematic comparative data would be coupled with intensive study of value orientations and social organization within the cultures or countries under study. The most ambitious of cross-cultural studies yet attempted — that by the Whitings and their associates — has entailed ethnographic study of the process of child rearing within the larger cultural context as well as interviews and systematic observations of samples of child behavior (see Whiting, B., 1963, and Minturn and Lambert, 1964). An adequate study of socialization (or even of child rearing) in any given society is a major undertaking; one that secures adequate data relating to beliefs, behaviors, and interpersonal perceptions of parents or other socialization agents and of children in several cultures must overcome serious problems of logistics and entails the collection of a staggering amount of data. The analysis and reporting of such data are likely to take many years or even decades. This is not to suggest that every cross-cultural study should attempt to cover the range of socialization influences or outcomes. Rather it is to note the magnitude of the undertaking when one does seek to characterize socialization processes in their cultural contexts in several societies. The gains may be enormous if the task can be accomplished. In this respect the cross-cultural study parallels the longitudinal approach in socialization research (see Chapter Four).

Somewhat less unwieldy than the truly cross-cultural study is the cross-national survey. As noted above, placing primary reliance on an interview or questionnaire has dangers, but these may at least be attenuated if the schedule used is one that has been evolved by sophisticated researchers of all the countries represented. Several major programs of cross-national research which entail at least a measure of collaboration with scholars of the countries represented are being carried out by teams of investigators from the United States. Even when such collaboration is relatively slight, provocative data may be secured, as in the studies of Bronfenbrenner, Devereux, and their associates at Cornell, which deal with parent-child relations and child-rearing practices as these are reported on a questionnaire administered in the classroom.

A number of cross-national studies of political socialization have been carried out in the past decade, and more are in process. Especially notable has been the work of Almond and Verba (1963) and the research programs of Hess and his associates at Chicago and Adelson and his associates at the University of Michigan. Whatever shortcomings cross-national research programs may have because they tend to focus on a relatively limited range of behavior with inadequate attention to the larger sociocultural matrix, they do afford a basis for going beyond the anecdotal assertions that have so often characterized cross-national comparisons. They provide the basis for asking much more sophisticated questions about the consequences of particular belief systems or social arrangements in socialization.

Perhaps the ideal kind of cross-national or cross-cultural study is one carried out by a person who has lived and worked in another culture intensively enough to achieve a measure of acculturation to it. Such comparative studies by Americans have tended in the past to be confined to Western Europe, but with the increased number of social scientists in linguistic training during and since World War II, there has been a change. Thus among others who have cross-national orientations we have workers like Caudill and DeVos, who have made long-term commitments in the study of socialization and social process in Japan; Oscar Lewis in Mexico; Bronfenbrenner in the Soviet Union; and Wylie (1957) and Pitts in France.

In the past three decades, since the major convergence of conceptual usage and of broad interests in socialization among the several disciplines, there has been not only markedly increased interstimulation and collaboration across disciplinary lines but also a delineation of somewhat distinct interests and approaches. The scope of the process we call socialization is so vast that few workers are concerned with the whole of it. It is to be expected that a number of subareas will tend to become more sharply delineated and perhaps relatively autonomous, such as political socialization and the study of language learning have become, while at the same time some workers will give increased attention to the interrelationships among phases and conceptual slices of socialization and personality development. We would also predict that a substantial amount of future research will be concerned not so much with immediate consequences of a particular aspect of socialization practices or apparatus as with the long-term consequences for the functioning of the adult within his often changing society.

References

Aberle, D. F. Culture and socialization. In F. L. K. Hsu (Ed.), *Psychological Anthropology: Approaches to Culture and Personality*. Homewood, Ill.: The Dorsey Press, 1961. Pp. 381–99.

Adorno, T. W., Frenkel-Brunswik, Else, Levinson, D. J., and Sanford, R. N. *The Authoritarian Personality*. New York: Harper, 1950.

Allport, F. H. *Social Psychology*. New York: Houghton Mifflin Co., 1924.

Allport, G. W. *The Use of Personal Documents in Psychological Science*. New York: Social Science Research Council, 1942.

Almond, G., and Verba, S. *The Civic Culture*. Princeton, N.J.: Princeton University Press, 1963.

Anderson, J. E. The methods of child psychology. In C. Murchison (Ed.), *A Handbook of Child Psychology*. Worcester, Mass.: Clark University Press, 1931. Pp. 1–27.

Anderson, J. E. *The Young Child in the Home: A Survey of Three Thousand American Families*. Report of the Committee on the Infant and Preschool Child, White House Conference on Child Health and Protection. New York: Appleton-Century, 1936.

Anderson, N. (Ed.) *Recherches sur la Famille*. Gottingen: Vandenhoeck & Ruprecht, 1957.

Baldwin, A. L., Kalhorn, J., and Breese, F. H. The appraisal of parent behavior. *Psychological Monographs*, 1949, 63, No. 2 (whole No. 299).

Baldwin, J. M. *History of Psychology*. Vol. 2. New York: Putnam, 1913a.

Baldwin, J. M. *The Individual and Society*. Boston: Richard Badger, The Gorham Press, 1911.

Baldwin, J. M. *Social and Ethical Interpretations in Mental Development*. New York: The Macmillan Co., 1913b.

Bandura, A., and Walters, R. H. *Social Learning and Personality Development*. New York: Holt, Rinehart & Winston, 1963.

Barker, R. G., and Barker, Louise S. Social actions in the behavior streams of American and English children. In R. G. Barker (Ed.), *The Stream of Behavior*. New York: Appleton-Century-Crofts, 1963.

Barker, R. G., Dembo, Tamara, and Lewin, K. Frustration and regression: an experiment with young children. *University of Iowa Studies in Child Welfare*, 1941, *18*, No. 1, xv–314.

Barker, R. G., Kounin, J. S., and Wright, H. F. *Child Behavior and Development*. New York: McGraw-Hill Book Co., 1943.

Barker, R. G., and Wright, H. F. *Midwest and Its Children*. Evanston, Ill.: Row, Peterson & Co., 1955.

Barry, H. A., Bacon, Margaret K., and Child, I. L. A cross-cultural survey of some sex differences in socialization. *Journal of Abnormal and Social Psychology*, 1957, *55*, 327–32.

Baumert, G., and Karl, H. *German Research on Socialization: A Bibliography*. Prepared at the request of the Social Science Research Council Committee on Socialization and Social Structure. Marburg, Germany, 1963. (ADI Auxiliary Publications Project Document; mimeo)

Beaglehole, E., and Ritchie, J. E. Basic personality in a New Zealand Maori community. *Journal of Polynesian Society*, 1958, *67*, 132–54. Reprinted in B. Kaplan (Ed.), *Studying Personality Cross-Culturally*. Evanston, Ill.: Row, Peterson & Co., 1961.

Becker, H. S. *Outsiders: Studies in the Sociology of Deviance*. New York: The Free Press of Glencoe, 1963.

Ben-David, J., and Collins, R. Social factors in the origins of a new science: the case of psychology. *American Sociological Review*, 1966, *31*, 451–65.

Benedict, Ruth. *Patterns of Culture*. Boston: Houghton Mifflin Co., 1934.

Blumer, H. *Critiques of Research in the Social Sciences*. Vol. 1. *An Appraisal of Thomas and Znaniecki's The Polish Peasant in Europe and America*. New York: Social Science Research Council, 1939.

Bott, E. *Family and Social Network*. London: Tavistock, 1957.

Bowlby, J. An ethological approach to research in child development. *British Journal of Medical Psychology*, 1957, *30*, 230–40.

Brim, O. G., Jr. *Education for Child Rearing*. New York: Russell Sage Foundation, 1959.

Brim, O. G., Jr., and Wheeler, S. *Socialization after Childhood: Two Essays*. New York: John Wiley & Sons, 1966.

Bronfenbrenner, U. Developmental theory in transition. In H. W. Stevenson (Ed.), *Child Psychology*. The Sixty-second Yearbook of the National Society for the Study of Education. Chicago: NSSE, 1963; distributed by The University of Chicago Press. Pp. 517–42.

Bronfenbrenner, U. Socialization and social class through time and space. In Eleanor E. Maccoby, T. Newcomb, and E. Hartley (Eds.), *Readings in Social Psychology*. 3rd ed. New York: Holt, 1958. Pp. 400–25.

Bronfenbrenner, U. Soviet methods of character education: some implications for research. *American Psychologist*, 1962, *17*, No. 8, 550–64.

Bronfenbrenner, U., Devereux, E. C., and Rodgers, R. R. Cross-cultural studies of child rearing. Progress report to the National Science Foundation. (Dittoed paper, unpublished, 1966)

Brown, J. F. *Psychology and the Social Order*. New York: McGraw-Hill Book Co., 1936.

Bühler, Charlotte. *The Child and His Family*. Translated by H. Beaumont. London: Kegan Paul, 1940.

Bühler, Charlotte. The social behavior of children. In C. Murchison (Ed.), *A Handbook of Child Psychology*. Worcester, Mass.: Clark University Press, 1931. Pp. 374–416.

Burgess, E. W. Educative effects of urban environment. In E. W. Burgess, W. L. Warner, F. Alexander, and Margaret Mead, *Environment and Education*. Chicago: University of Chicago Press, 1942. Pp. 1–15.

Burgess, E. W. *The Function of Socialization in Social Evolution*. Chicago: University of Chicago Press, 1916.

Burlingham, D., and Freud, Anna. *Infants without Families*. London: Allen & Unwin, 1944.

Caudill, W. Patterns of emotion in modern Japan. In R. J. Smith and R. K. Beardsley (Eds.), *Japanese Culture: Its Development and Characteristics*. Chicago: Aldine Publishing Co., 1962. Pp. 115–31.

Caudill, W., and Scarr, H. A. Japanese value orientations and culture change. *Ethnology*, 1962, *1*, 53–91.

Champney, H. The measurement of parent behavior. *Child Development*, 1941, *12*, 131–66.

Chombart de Lauwe, P. H. The interaction of person and society. *American Sociological Review*, 1966, *31*, 237–48.

Clausen, J. A. Research on socialization and personality development in the United States and France: Remarks on the paper by Professor Chombart de Lauwe. *American Sociological Review*, 1966, *31*, 248–57.

Clausen, J. A., and Williams, Judith. Sociological correlates of child behavior. In H. W. Stevenson (Ed.), *Child Psychology*. The Sixty-second Yearbook of the National Society for the Study of Education. Chicago: NSSE, 1963; distributed by The University of Chicago Press. Pp. 62–107.

Cohen, Y. *Social Structure and Personality*. New York: Holt, Rinehart & Winston, 1961.

Coleman, J. S. *The Adolescent Society: The Social Life of the Teenager and its Impact on Education*. New York: The Free Press of Glencoe, 1961.

Cooley, C. H. *Human Nature and the Social Order*. New York: Scribner's, 1902. Rev. ed., 1922.

Cottrell, L. S., Jr., and Gallagher, Ruth. Developments in social psychology, 1930–1940. *Sociometry Monographs*, No. 1, 1941 (whole issue).

Davis, A., and Dollard, J. *Children of Bondage: The Personality Development of Negro Youth in the Urban South*. Washington, D. C.: American Council on Education, 1940.

Davis, A., and Havighurst, R. J. Social class and color differences in child rearing. *American Sociological Review*, 1946, *11*, 698–710.

Devereux, E. C., Bronfenbrenner, U., and Rodgers, R. R. Child rearing in England and the United States: a cross national comparison. (Dittoed paper, undated, 1965)

Devereux, E. C., Bronfenbrenner, U., and Suci, G. J. Patterns of parent behavior in America and West Germany: a cross-national comparison. *International Social Science Journal*, 1962, *14*, 488–506.

De Vore, I. (Ed.) *Primate Behavior*. New York: Holt, Rinehart & Winston, 1965.

De Vos, G. A. Achievement orientation, social self-identity, and Japanese economic growth. *Asian Survey*, 1965, *5*, 575–89.

Dewey, J. *Human Nature and Conduct*. New York: Holt, 1922. (Page references are to Modern Library Edition, 1930.)

Dicks, H. V. Personality traits and national socialist ideology. *Human Relations*, 1950, *3*, 111–54.

Dollard, J. *Criteria for the Life History — with Analyses of Six Notable Documents*. New Haven, Conn.: Yale University Press, 1935.

Dollard, J. Culture, society impulse, and socialization. *American Journal of Sociology*, 1939, *45*, 50–63.

Dollard, J., Miller, N. E., Doob, L. W., Mowrer, O. H., and Sears, R. R. *Frustration and Aggression*. New Haven, Conn.: Yale University Press, 1939.

Douglas, J. W. B. *The Home and the School: A Study of Ability and Attainment in the Primary School.* London: Macgibbon and Kee, 1964.
Douglas, J. W. B., and Blomfield, J. M. *Children under Five.* London: Allen & Unwin, 1958.
Durkheim, E. *Education and Sociology.* Glencoe, Ill.: The Free Press, 1956.
Durkheim, E. *L'Education Morale.* Paris: F. Alcan, 1926.
Encyclopaedia of the Social Sciences. New York: The Macmillan Co., 1930.
Erikson, E. H. *Childhood and Society.* New York: W. W. Norton & Co., 1950.
Flavell, J. H. *The Developmental Psychology of Jean Piaget.* Princeton, N.J.: D. Van Nostrand Co., 1963.
Frank, L. K. The beginnings of child development and family life education in the twentieth century. *Merrill Palmer Quarterly,* 1962, 8, 207–28.
Frank, L. K. Physiological tensions and social structure. In E. W. Burgess (Ed.), *Personality and the Social Group.* Chicago: University of Chicago Press, 1929.
Freud, Anna, and Burlingham, Dorothy G. *Infants without Family.* New York: International Universities Press, 1944.
Fromm, E. *Escape from Freedom.* New York: Farrar & Rinehart, 1941.
Giddings, F. P. *The Theory of Socialization.* New York: The Macmillan Co., 1897.
Gottschalk, L., Kluckhohn, C., and Angell, R. C. *The Use of Personal Documents in History, Anthropology and Sociology.* New York: Social Science Research Council, 1942.
Grinnell, G. B. *The Cheyenne Indians.* New Haven, Conn.: Yale University Press, 1923.
Grönseth, E. Research on socialization in Norway. *Family Process,* 1964, 3, 302–22.
Hall, G. S. The contents of children's minds. *Princeton Review,* 1883, 249–72. Reprinted in W. Dennis (Ed.), *Readings in the History of Psychology.* New York: Appleton-Century-Crofts, 1948. Pp. 255–76.
Hamilton, G. V. *An Introduction to Objective Psychopathology.* St. Louis: The C. V. Mosby Co., 1925.
Haring, D. G. *Personal Character and Cultural Milieu.* Syracuse: Syracuse University Press, 1949.
Harlow, H. F., and Harlow, Margaret. The affectational systems. In A. M. Schrier, H. F. Harlow, and F. Stollnitz (Eds.), *Behavior of Nonhuman Primates.* Vol. 2. New York: Academic Press, 1965. Pp. 287–334.
Hess, R., and Torney, Judith V. *The Development of Political Attitudes in Children.* Chicago: Aldine Publishing Co., 1967.
Himmelweit, Hilde T., and Sealy, A. P. The school as an agent of socialization. London, 1966. (Mimeo)
Hoffman, Lois W. and Hoffman, M. L. *Review of Child Development Research.* Vol. 2. New York: Russell Sage Foundation, 1966.
Hoffman, M. L. and Hoffman, Lois W. *Review of Child Development Research.* Vol. 1. New York: Russell Sage Foundation, 1964.
Hollingshead, A. B. *Elmtown's Youth: The Impact of Social Class on Adolescents.* New York: John Wiley & Sons, 1949.
Horkheimer, M. (Ed.) *Studien über Authoritat und Familie.* Paris: Felix Alcan, 1936.
Hsu, F. L. K. *Psychological Anthropology: Approaches to Culture and Personality.* Homewood, Ill.: The Dorsey Press, 1961.
Inkeles, A., and Levinson, D. J. National character: the study of modal per-

sonality and sociocultural systems. In G. Lindzey (Ed.), *Handbook of Social Psychology*. Vol. 2. Cambridge, Mass.: Addison-Wesley Publishing Co., 1954. Pp. 977–1020.

Inkeles, A., Smith, D. H., Schuman, H., and Ryan, E. *Becoming Modern*. (Forthcoming)

Isaacs, Susan. *Social Development of Young Children*. London: Routledge, 1933.

Kaplan, B. *Studying Personality Cross-culturally*. Evanston, Ill.: Row, Peterson & Co., 1961.

Kardiner, A. *The Individual and His Society*. New York: Columbia University Press, 1939.

Karpf, F. B. *American Social Psychology*. New York: McGraw-Hill Book Co., 1932.

Kellmer-Pringle, Mea L. The National Child Development Study. *Bulletin of the British Psychological Society*, 1958, *18*, 39–44.

Kerr, M. *The People of Ship Street*. London: Routledge & Kegan Paul, 1958.

Kessen, W., and Kuhlman, Clementina (Eds.). Thought in the young child: Report of a conference on intellectual development with particular attention to the work of Jean Piaget. *Monographs of the Society for Research in Child Development*, 1962, 27, No. 2 (whole No. 83).

Kidd, D. *Savage Childhood: A Study of Kafir Children*. London: The Macmillan Co., 1906.

Klein, Josephine. *Samples from English Cultures*. 2 vols. London: Routledge & Kegan Paul, 1965.

Kluckhohn, C. Theoretical bases for an empirical method of studying the acquisition of culture by individuals. *Man*, 1939, *39*, 98–103. Reprinted in C. Kluckhohn, *Culture and Behavior*. New York: The Free Press of Glencoe, 1962.

Kluckhohn, C., and Murray, H. L. *Personality in Nature, Society and Culture*. New York: Alfred A. Knopf, 1948.

Lewin, K. *A Dynamic Theory of Personality: Selected Papers*. New York: McGraw-Hill Book Co., 1935.

Lewin, K. Environmental forces. In C. Murchison (Ed.), *A Handbook of Child Psychology*. Worcester, Mass.: Clark University Press, 1931. Pp. 590–625.

Lewin, K., Lippitt, R., and White, R. K. Patterns of aggressive behavior in experimentally created social climates. *Journal of Social Psychology*, 1939, *10*, 271–99.

Lewis, O. *The Children of Sanchez: Autobiography of a Mexican Family*. New York: Random House, 1961.

Levy, D. M. Anti-Nazis: criteria of differentiation. *Psychiatry*, 1948, *11*, 125–67.

Lindesmith, A. R., and Strauss, A. L. A critique of culture-personality writings. *American Sociological Review*, 1950, *15*, 587–600.

Linton, R. *The Cultural Background of Personality*. New York: Appleton-Century, 1945.

Luzski, Margaret E. B. *Interdisciplinary Team Research: Methods and Problems*. New York: New York University Press, 1958.

Lynd, R. S., and Lynd, Helen M. *Middletown: A Study in Contemporary American Culture*. New York: Harcourt, Brace, 1929.

Malinowski, B. *Sex and Repression in Savage Society*. New York: Humanities Press, 1927. (Page references are to Meridian Books Edition, World Publishing, 1955.)

Marler, P., and Hamilton, W. J. *Mechanisms of Animal Behavior*. New York: John Wiley & Sons, 1966.

Martingale, D. (Ed.) National character in the perspective of the social sciences. *Annals of the American Academy of Political and Social Science*, 1967, *370*, 1–163.

McDougall, W. *An Introduction to Social Psychology*. Boston: Luce, 1908.

McLean, Dorothy. Child development: a generation of research. *Child Development*, 1954, *25*, 3–8.

Mead, G. H. *Mind, Self, and Society*. Chicago: University of Chicago Press, 1934.

Mead, Margaret. *An Anthropologist at Work: Writings of Ruth Benedict*. Boston: Houghton Mifflin Co., 1959.

Mead, Margaret. *Coming of Age in Samoa*. New York: William Morrow & Co., 1928.

Mead, Margaret. *Growing Up in New Guinea: A Comparative Study of Primitive Education*. New York: William Morrow & Co., 1930.

Mead, Margaret. The primitive child. In C. Murchison (Ed.), *A Handbook of Child Psychology*. Worcester, Mass.: Clark University Press, 1931. Pp. 909–26.

Mead, Margaret. Socialization and enculturation. *Current Anthropology*, 1963, *4*, 184–87.

Mead, Margaret, and Wolfenstein, Martha. *Childhood in Contemporary Cultures*. Chicago: University of Chicago Press, 1955.

Métraux, Rhoda. Parents and children: an analysis of contemporary German child-care and youth-guidance literature. In Margaret Mead and Martha Wolfenstein (Eds.), *Childhood in Contemporary Cultures*. Chicago: University of Chicago Press, 1955. Pp. 204–28.

Métraux, Rhoda, and Mead, Margaret. *Themes in French Culture*. Stanford: Stanford University Press, 1954.

Miller, D. R., and Swanson, G. E. *The Changing American Parent*. New York: John Wiley & Sons, 1958.

Miller, N. E., and Dollard, J. *Social Learning and Imitation*. New Haven, Conn.: Yale University Press, 1941.

Minturn, L., and Lambert, W. W. *Mothers of Six Cultures: Antecedents of Child Rearing*. New York: John Wiley & Sons, 1964.

Moore, T. W., Hendley, C. B., and Falkner, F. A longitudinal research in child development and some of its problems. *British Medical Journal*, 1954, *7*, 1132–37.

Müller-Freienfels, R. *The Evolution of Modern Psychology*. Translated by W. B. Wolfe. New Haven, Conn.: Yale University Press, 1935.

Murchison, C. (Ed.) *A Handbook of Child Psychology*. Worcester, Mass.: Clark University Press, 1931.

Murphy, Lois B. *Social Behavior and Child Personality*. New York: Columbia University Press, 1937.

Murphy, G. *An Historical Introduction to Modern Psychology*. New York: Harcourt, Brace, 1929.

Murphy, G. Personal communication, 1966.

Murphy, G., and Murphy, Lois B. *Experimental Social Psychology*. New York: Harper, 1931.

Murphy, G., Murphy, Lois B., and Newcomb, T. *Experimental Social Psychology: An Interpretation of Research on the Socialization of the Individual*. 2nd ed. New York: Harper, 1937.

Murray, H. L. *Explorations in Personality*. New York: Oxford University Press, 1938.

Narain, B. Growing up in India. *Family Process*, 1964, 3, 148–52.
Newson, J., and Newson, E. *Infant Care in an Urban Community*. London: Allen & Unwin, 1963.
Ogburn, W. F., and Nimkoff, M. F. *Sociology*. Boston: Houghton Mifflin Co., 1940.
Paneth, M. *Branche Street*. London: Allen & Unwin, 1944.
Park, R. E. Symbiosis and socialization: a frame of reference for the study of society. *American Journal of Sociology*, 1939, *45*, 1–25.
Park, R. E., and Burgess, E. W. *Introduction to the Science of Sociology*. Chicago: University of Chicago Press, 1921.
Piaget, J. Children's philosophies. In C. Murchison (Ed.), *A Handbook of Child Psychology*. Worcester, Mass.: Clark University Press, 1931. Pp. 534–47.
Piaget, J. *The Language and Thought of the Child*. London: Kegan Paul, Trench, Trubner, 1926.
Piaget, J. *The Moral Judgment of the Child*. London: Kegan Paul, Trench, Trubner, 1932.
Pitts, J. The family and peer groups. In N. W. Bell and E. F. Vogel (Eds.), *A Modern Introduction to the Family*. Glencoe, Ill.: The Free Press, 1960. Pp. 266–86.
Plant, J. S. *Personality and the Cultural Pattern*. New York: Commonwealth Fund, 1937.
Prothro, E. T. *Child Rearing in the Lebanon*. Harvard Middle-Eastern Monographs, VIII. Cambridge, Mass.: Harvard University Press, 1961.
Rheingold, Harriet. *Maternal Behavior in Mammals*. New York: John Wiley & Sons, 1963.
Robert, P. *Dictionnaire Alphabétique et Analogique de la Langue Française*. Paris: Presses Universitaires, 1951.
Robinson, W. S. Ecological correlations and the behavior of individuals. *American Sociological Review*, 1950, *15*, 351–57.
Rose, A. M. *Human Behavior and Social Processes: An Interactionist Approach*. Boston: Houghton Mifflin Co., 1962.
Rosen, B. C., and D'Andrade, R. The psychosocial origins of achievement motivation. *Sociometry*, 1959, 22, 185–218.
Ross, E. A. Social control. *American Journal of Sociology*, 1896, *1*, 513–35.
Ross, E. A. *Social Psychology*. New York: The Macmillan Co., 1908.
Sapir, E. The emergence of the concept of personality in a study of cultures. *Journal of Social Psychology*, 1934a, 5, 408–15.
Sapir, E. Personality. *Encyclopaedia of the Social Sciences*. Vol. 11. New York: The Macmillan Co., 1934b. Pp. 85–87.
Sapir, E. The unconscious patterning of behavior in society. In D. G. Mandelbaum (Ed.), *Edward Sapir: Selected Writings in Language, Culture, and Personality*. Berkeley: University of California Press, 1949. Pp. 544–59.
Sears, R. R. Functional abnormalities of memory with special reference to amnesia. *Psychological Bulletin*, 1936, 33, 229–74.
Sears, R. R. Personality theory: the next forty years. *Monographs of the Society for Research in Child Development*, 1959, 24, No. 5 (Serial No. 74), 37–50.
Sears, R. R., Maccoby, Eleanor E., and Levin, H. *Patterns of Child Rearing*. Evanston, Ill.: Row, Peterson & Co., 1957.
Seligman, C. G. Anthropology and psychology: a study of some points of contact. *Journal of the Royal Anthropological Institute*, 1924, 54, 13–46.

Sewell, W. H. Infant training and the personality of the child. *American Journal of Sociology*, 1952, *58*, 150–59.

Sewell, W. H. Social class and childhood personality. *Sociometry*, 1961, *24*, 340–56.

Sewell, W. H. Some recent developments in socialization theory and research. *The Annals of the American Academy of Political and Social Science*, 1963, *349*, 163–81.

Shakow, D., and Rappaport, D. *The Influence of Freud on American Psychology*. Psychological Issues, Monograph 13. New York: International Universities Press, 1964.

Shaw, C. R. *The Jack-Roller: A Delinquent Boy's Own Story*. Chicago: University of Chicago Press, 1930.

Shaw, C. R., McKay, H. D., Zorbaugh, H., and Cottrell, L. S., Jr. *Delinquency Areas*. Chicago: University of Chicago Press, 1929.

Shinn, M. W. *Biography of a Baby*. Boston: Houghton Mifflin Co., 1900.

Simmel, G. The problem of sociology. *Annals of the American Academy of Political and Social Science*, 1895, *6*, 412–23.

Singer, M. B. A survey of culture and personality theory and research. In B. Kaplan (Ed.), *Studying Personality Cross-Culturally*. New York: Harper & Row, 1961. Pp. 9–90.

Social Science Research Council. *Decennial Report, 1923–1933*. New York, 1934.

Spindler, G. D. *Sociocultural and Psychological Processes in Menomini Acculturation*. Berkeley and Los Angeles: University of California Press, 1955.

Steere, G. H. *Changing Values in Childhood Socialization: A Study of United States Child Rearing Literature, 1865–1929*. University of Pennsylvania, unpublished doctoral dissertation, 1964.

Stevenson, H. W. (Ed.) *Child Psychology*. The Sixty-second Yearbook of the National Society for the Study of Education. Chicago: NSSE, 1963; distributed by The University of Chicago Press.

Sunley, R. Early 19th century American literature on child rearing. In Margaret Mead and Martha Wolfenstein (Eds.), *Childhood in Contemporary Cultures*. Chicago: University of Chicago Press, 1955. Pp. 150–67.

Sutherland, R. L., and Woodward, J. *Introductory Sociology*. New York: J. B. Lippincott Co., 1937.

Tausch, R., and Tausch, Anne-Marie. *Erziehungspsychologie* (Educational Psychology). Göttingen: Dr. C. J. Hogrefe, 1963.

Thomae, H. Entwicklung und Prägung. In H. Thomae (Ed.), *Handbuch der Psychologie*. Vol. 3. *Entwicklungspsychologie*. Göttingen: Dr. C. J. Hogrefe, 1959. Pp. 265–311.

Thomas, W. I. The persistence of primary-group norms in present-day society and their influence in our educational system. In H. S. Jennings *et al.*, *Suggestions of Modern Science Concerning Education*. New York: The Macmillan Co., 1917. Pp. 167–87.

Thomas, W. I., and Znaniecki, F. *The Polish Peasant in Europe and America*. 4 vols. Boston: Richard C. Badger, 1918–20. (Page references are to the two-volume edition; New York: Dover Publications, 1958.)

Turner, R. H. Acceptance of irregular mobility in Britain and the United States. *Sociometry*, 1966, *29*, 334–52.

Turner, R. H. Sponsored and contrast mobility and the school system. *American Sociological Review*, 1960, *25*, 855–67.

Volkart, E. H. *Social Behavior and Personality*. New York: Social Science Research Council, 1951.
Wallon, H. *Les Origines du Caractère chez l'Enfant: Les Préludes du Sentiment de Personalité*. Paris: Presses Universitaires, 1934.
Wallon, H. *L'Evolution Psychologique de l'Enfant*. Paris: Librarie Armand Colin, 1941. 8th ed., 1964.
Warner, W. L. Personal communication, 1967.
White, R. W. *The Study of Lives: Essays on Personality in Honor of Henry A. Murray*. New York: Atherton Press, 1964.
Whiting, Beatrice B. (Ed.) *Six Cultures: Studies of Child Rearing*. New York: John Wiley & Sons, 1963.
Whiting, J. W. M. *Becoming a Kwoma: Teaching and Learning in a New Guinea Tribe*. New Haven, Conn.: Yale University Press, 1941.
Whiting, J. W. M. Socialization process and personality. In F. L. K. Hsu (Ed.), *Psychological Anthropology: Approaches to Culture and Personality*. Homewood, Ill.: The Dorsey Press, 1961. Pp. 355–80.
Whiting, J. W. M., and Child, I. R. *Child Training and Personality*. New Haven, Conn.: Yale University Press, 1953.
Winnicott, D. W. *The Child and the Family*. London: Tavistock, 1957.
Wolfenstein, Martha. French parents take their children to the park. In Margaret Mead and Martha Wolfenstein (Eds.), *Childhood in Contemporary Cultures*. Chicago: University of Chicago Press, 1955. Pp. 99–117.
Wurzbacher, G. (Ed.) *Der Mensch als Soziales und Personales Wesen: Beiträge zu Begriff und Theorie der Sozialisation*. Stuttgart: Enke, 1963.
Wylie, L. *Village in the Vaucluse*. New York: Harper & Row, 1957.
Yarrow, L. J. Separation from parents during childhood. In M. L. Hoffman and Lois W. Hoffman (Eds.), *Review of Child Development Research*. Vol. 1. New York: Russell Sage Foundation, 1964. Pp. 89–136.
Young, K. *Social Psychology*. New York: Alfred A. Knopf, 1930.
Young, M., and Wilmott, P. *Family and Kinship in East London*. London: Routledge & Kegan Paul, 1957.

ALEX INKELES

THREE *Society, Social Structure, and Child Socialization*

CONTENTS

Were we still addicted to the more romantic forms of expression we might say that the socialization process is a struggle over domination of the development of a man's personality by three main adversaries: his innate self, the people who raise him and live with him, and the society in which he will participate as an adult member. Freudian theory in part incorporates this image in its emphasis on the tension between id, ego, and superego. Like all the popular dualisms and trichotomies, this scheme is obviously a great simplification. The need of the organism for shelter and emotional support is not necessarily opposed to, but rather may be wholly dependent for its satisfaction on, the social organization. The family which raises and intimately integrates the individual is not necessarily resistant to social demands; it is itself *of* society and may be eager to act *for* it. Yet this simplification may be useful if it makes us more aware that the socialization process is not limited to the unfolding of a set of preprogrammed innate propensities which will emerge in the course of biological maturation. Neither is the concept of socialization exhausted by consideration of the personalities or the personal relations of those who raise a child from infancy. Society intrudes itself into the process in numerous ways. Indirectly its effect is felt by its shaping of the environment of the organism — influencing diet, physical comfort, the density of population, the regularity of care, the presence or absence of the father. More directly, society shapes the socialization process by establishing the standard which the socialized individual is expected to achieve in physical development, in skills and capacities, in emotional expression, in intellective and conative activity, and in the patterning of his relations with significant others. In their efforts to socialize the child, parents are guided, however fallibly, by their awareness of such social expectation and their image of what the child must become if he is to live successfully in the world as the parents envision it will be at the time the child becomes an adult. These expectations are imposed not only by the parents but also by other adults and peers with whom the child comes increasingly in contact as he develops and spends more time outside the primary family compound. In the larger and more complex societies the socialization process is progressively taken over by formal agencies of training, and the number, extensity, and intensity of such influences may well overshadow the continuing activity of the family.

When we look at the adult outcome of childhood socialization we cannot at present state with any high degree of assurance what proportionate weight is exerted by the innate propensity of the child, the character of the parents, and the pressures of social demand. So far as research is concerned, however, the influence of society and the effects of social structure on the socialization of the child has not been the major, perhaps not even *a* major, focus of attention. Clearly there is a need for new lines of research which will more extensively and intensively explore the interaction of society and the process of child socialization.

The interrelations of society and socialization are not only complex but numerous. To review, even superficially, any large number of them would require much more space than this chapter permits. Therefore, two major aspects of this relationship have been selected for detailed elaboration, in the hope that these examples may serve to suggest how the analysis might proceed with other topics. First we seek to answer the question: What does society require of the socialization process, and what are some of the ways it seeks to obtain the expected results? In the latter part of the chapter the way in which the various features of social structure — economic, political, ecological — may exert an influence on the socialization process is examined. The former may be thought of as the intended, and the latter as the unintended, consequences for socialization that arise from the basic fact of social organization. As we shall see, however, this distinction raises a host of theoretical issues.

SOCIETY'S "INTEREST" IN THE CHILD'S SOCIALIZATION

Despite a good deal of incidental variation, almost all the current definitions of child socialization describe it as the process whereby a person acquires the attitudes, values, ways of thinking, need dispositions, and other personal, yet social, attributes which will characterize him in the next stage of his development. The social scientist is not alone in his sensitivity to the implications of current childhood experience for the subsequent organization of the personality and the public behavior of a social member. In their interaction with the child, parents and other socialization agents generally have in mind some conception of what the child is "supposed to become" and of the role which any particular child-rearing practice may play in achieving or hindering the desired outcome. In other words, both the practice and the study of child socialization are inherently "forward looking." [1] It seems obvious, furthermore, that of the various later stages which socialization looks forward to, it is the personally relatively enduring and socially important adult stage which is the critical one to consider. Therefore, a central task of the study of socialization is to inquire into the effects which the experience of the child has on the shaping of the adult.

We should note that there are two elements in the common definitions of socialization. One focus is on the input side, on the *process* of acquisition, and refers to what is "done" to the child; the other element stresses the *results* of the process, or the output side, in the form of the adult person. Many students of socialization feel it necessary to add a third element, or at least to modify the second, by emphasizing the social relevance of the acquired adult characteristics. They do so in order to maintain the distinction between "socialization" and the usual developmental processes of maturation and nonsocial learning in the typical human organism. To clarify this point, some add to the definition of socialization the specification that it deals mainly with the acquisition of those characteristics which have major relevance for the particular social roles which a person must play in his status-position as a member of a given society with a specified culture. In other words, it is not merely that socialization has a social character, but that it has important, long-term social consequences. The full development of the field of socialization requires that we extend our interests, and substantially augment the now limited energies we direct toward studying the adult outcomes of the socialization process. The immediate need is to specify those adult characteristics which seem particularly important and deserving of attention by students of socialization. When we are clearer about the adult variables, we can more effectively consider their implications for studies of the socialization process. The adult outcomes we have in mind will affect especially the researcher's choice of the age of the socializee, the socialization agent and setting, and the particular socialization practices to be studied.

What then are the characteristics which we should study? In the psychological literature literally thousands of different traits are identified and defined, and hundreds may be measured by more or less standard tests. We need some principle to guide our selection. A number of different approaches immediately assert their claim. One possibility is to study those qualities of the adult which reflect, influence, or define his psychic adjustment. This leads us in the direction of clinical measures of self-esteem, modes of defense, introversion and extroversion,

[1] To say this is not to deny that very often what is done to the child is influenced by no more long-term a desire than to get Johnny to be quiet for the next five minutes or to sleep for the next six hours.

autism, and so on. These problems of adjustment are certainly important, but to study them alone would greatly narrow the scope of our interest.

Another strategy is to maximize continuity by focusing on those characteristics of the adult which are the analogues of the behavior systems studied in childhood socialization research, such as oral and anal functioning, dependency, and aggression. Although this approach has much to recommend it from the point of view of consistency, we must enter against it a number of reservations. The behavioral systems included in the standard list may unduly restrict the range of what we can study. There is, furthermore, a peculiar process of attrition over time with many of these systems. Although orality and anality may be studied in the adult, the issues of feeding and elimination are usually not significant problems in mature individuals. In general, it is less the direct analogues of the childhood behavior systems and more their consequences in other realms which are of greatest interest.

A third strategy, which will be used here, is to select adult characteristics for study on the basis of their relevance for the adult's ability to fulfill the typical — and perhaps atypical — roles to which individuals in his society and culture are usually assigned. In other words, we can ask: What does the society expect, demand, or require of the typical member of the system when he comes to play the adult social roles he either will select, or to which society will assign him by virtue of his age, sex, color, occupation, and the like?

The Needs of Society and the Process of Socialization

If our purpose here is to illustrate an approach, not to establish a definitive list of adult characteristics that should be of interest to students of socialization, then we can be quite catholic, indeed eclectic, in our choice of variables. Yet to insure against an arbitrary choice of characteristics, we shall select those characteristics for study which are the expressed concerns of students of social structure. In the treatment of societal demands on the individual, three different levels of generality should be recognized: first, the requirements which *any* social system must put on its members; second, those which are characteristic or typical in a given distinctive society or cultural tradition; third, those which are only placed on the incumbents of selected *subgroups* or strata of certain cultures or societies. For reasons of economy, however, the last two levels will be treated as one.

WHAT ANY SOCIETY WILL DEMAND OF ITS SOCIALIZATION SYSTEM

The psychologist of personality is sometimes puzzled by the sociologist's interest in certain aspects of the individual, qualities of the person which the psychologist finds of little concern. The difference in emphasis stems from the fact that the psychologist wants to know how the *individual* got to be the way he is and what holds *him* together, whereas the sociologist wants to know how a *society* came to its present form and what integrates *it* as a system of action. Since the person and the society are such very different organizations of matter, many of the questions vital to the understanding of the one are of only marginal interest to students of the other. It is only by one of those great stretches of the imagination of which an anthropologist like Geoffrey Gorer (1949) is capable that we can find a social process strictly analogous to the individual's experience of weaning or his struggle to learn control of his sphincter. But the often patent absurdity of these analogies may blind us to a striking fact: In stating what it is that any society must have in order to survive, in presenting what are called "the functional requisites of any social system," the sociologist is, in effect, specifying a series of adult characteristics which must presumably be acquired by a substantial proportion of the population during the process of socialization. Thus the requisites of any social system become the imperatives for any system of child socialization.

In 1950 David Aberle and a group of his associates at Harvard proposed a set of conditions which any society must meet if it is to continue functioning. Marion Levy (1952) later reformulated these as "the functional requisites of any society" in his book on *The Structure of Society*. Our interest in this list is not limited to noting that one of the ten indispensable requisites is described as "adequate socialization." [2] Rather, we wish to stress that with the exception of the requirement for "adequate institutionalization," which clearly cannot have reference to a person, each of the remaining requisites of social order has a fairly direct and immediate relevance for the individual. Indeed, the whole list can be conceived of as a statement of the qualities which societal members must have if society is to survive. In other words, the list of society's functional requisites is less a statement about systems of *interrelations*, usually assumed to be the special province of the sociologist, and more a statement of the properties which *individuals* must have, even if having them in common. To examine these requisites in detail, then, may help us identify aspects of socialization that have been relatively neglected.

The first requisite is "provision for an adequate physiological relationship to the setting" and for sexual recruitment of the next generation.

[2] Levy says: "An individual is adequately socialized if he has been inculcated with a sufficient portion of the structure of action of his society to permit the effective performance of his roles in the society. There is adequate socialization in a society if there is a sufficient number of adequately socialized individuals for the structural requisites of a society to operate" (p. 187).

Meeting the problems of physical survival and continuity requires techniques and organization for obtaining food and for defense against animal and human predators, and protection against the elements. For *society* to attain this objective, *individuals* must acquire relevant information and learn adequate skills or techniques. These include sufficient knowledge of (and interest in) sexual relations to procreate the next generation, and sufficient concern and skill to insure care of the infants when they arrive. This requirement is so fundamental as to be obvious; yet it has not caught the attention of most students of socialization. From almost any good biographical account from anthropological literature, we can see how critical the acquisition of this knowledge is to the process of growing up. Don, the Hopi, reports:

> The old men took us for walks, and taught us the use of plants and how to collect them. The people pointed out that water is essential to life and taught us what to do out in the desert when we became so dry and thirsty that we could neither spit nor swallow. By the time I was six, therefore, I had learned to find my way about the mesa, to avoid graves, shrines, and harmful plants, to size up people, and to watch out for witches. (Simmons, 1942)

We have almost no recent studies which deal in any detail with the ways in which the individual acquires the knowledge and skills necessary to provide for himself and his dependents, to avoid harm to himself and others. Admittedly these issues become diffuse and very complex in modern societies, but that hardly excuses their relative neglect.

The second prerequisite is role differentiation and role assignment. Neither of these is in any direct sense a property of an individual, but the implication for socialization is that the individual must develop some sense of his identity, its similarity to the identity of certain others, and its distinctness from the identity of still others. Because of our culture's characteristic concern for individuality, research has not neglected this particular dimension of socialization. We have an especially rich resource of studies on sex differences and relatively ample materials on the differences between various age groups.[3] Extending Levy's analysis, we may mention the necessity to train the individual in some capacity for sustained involvement with others and for cooperation and loyalty, as a necessary base for the establishment and maintenance of units such as

[3] For studies on sex differences see the bibliography compiled for the Committee on Socialization and Social Structure of the Social Science Research Council by Eleanor E. Maccoby (1966). For differences between age groups see the review and bibliography prepared for this Committee by Schmuck and Lohman (1965), and that by Clausen (1965) on family size and birth order as influences on socialization.

families, work groups, hunting parties, and religious and other units concerned with symbolic activities (see Erikson, 1950). Both confusion of identity and an inability to sustain cooperation have been cited to explain the difficulty of organizing the working class in certain industrial settings, the oppressed minority groups in slavery and concentration camps (Elkins, 1961), and the villagers of a backward agricultural community in Southern Italy (Banfield, 1958).

Two other functional requisites are "shared, learned, symbolic modes of communication" and "shared cognitive orientations." The psychologist will at once recognize that for these conditions of social life to be met, individuals must be socialized to the use of a common language and a system of signs and gestures, and they must acquire certain ways of ordering and interpreting the evidence of their senses according to culturally standard cognitive maps or what Wallace (1961) calls "mazeways." The next two requisites are "a shared articulated set of goals" and "regulation of the choice of means" for the attainment of goals. The first refers to the socialization in the individual of values, needs, and motives; the second includes not only these but also the conscious executive functions of the ego or "social-self." The requisite for "the regulation of affective expression" is immediately identified as the shaping, through socialization, of the individual's modes of affective functioning, of which only the aggressive mode has received extensive study in the literature on socialization.

Closely related, yet analytically independent, is the requisite for "effective control of disruptive forms of behavior." As Levy points out, other requisites, such as the regulation of means and of expression, contribute to the same end. Similarly, the individual who is adequately socialized in his ego functions and his affective modes will be less likely to act in ways the society defines as disruptive. But, as Levy insists, we must always assume some failure in the operation of these mechanisms, in which case more direct sanctions must be applied. It is necessary, therefore, to inculcate in the individual a *readiness* to respond to such sanctions as may be applied. This obviously does not hold for direct and immediate physical restraint, but where the sanctions take the form of threats to freedom or even to life, or employ shame or guilt, then the effectiveness of the sanction depends on the responsiveness of the individual to the particular intended pressure. An individual may be trained to be unresponsive to shame, to be ready to sacrifice liberty, and even to be eager to die. The problem of controlling the behavior of such persons will clearly be quite different from that of controlling the behavior of those who do not display the same characteristics.

This completes our brief discussion of the functional requisites as indicators of the socialization demands which *any* society will make. It is readily apparent that what will terminate a society will not disintegrate an individual, at least not when he is viewed mainly as a biological organism. It should be evident, however, that the ways in which society meets its imperatives for survival have implications for the individual's socialization and that in actuality the requisites of continuing social life come down to what is largely a set of requirements for individual socialization. The elements of this set of requisites, furthermore, prove to be rather standard themes with which the personality psychologist is quite familiar and which he uses regularly in his description of personality. In Table I I have listed on one side the eight requisites presented by Levy for society and on the other side the elements of a comprehensive accounting scheme for describing personality which I earlier and quite independently developed (see Inkeles, 1963, 1966).

The issues represented in Table I should perhaps be supplemented by others. For example, the mode of orienting to authority might be viewed as one of the elements of personality most relevant to social action by the individual. Yet Levy's requisites of the social order do not specifically mention an authority structure. In addition, modes of relating to peers and subordinates, both central elements of the personality and both of particular social relevance, seem to have no precise match among Levy's social requisites, although this personality mode is clearly related to several of them. Despite these residual difficulties it remains clear that the list of requisites for any social order elaborated by sociologists is highly congruent with the list of elements which psychologists consider important parts of any personality system. This congruence suggests that there is a set of standard issues or themes which the student of socialization should regularly consider in selecting the variables to be used in his research. Thus, we would broaden the scope of our research beyond the narrow range of the primary behavior systems which until recently were an almost exclusive focus, increase the comparability of work from study to study, and perhaps most important, be assured that the results of research on socialization in the individual would have direct implications for the study of the social order. In so doing, we would more adequately fulfill our mandate to treat socialization as the study of *socially relevant* learning.

Admittedly what this list gains in general significance, it loses in specificity. It is certainly important to study the goals or values which a society inculcates in individuals. But there are so many goals and values. From the myriad values which are described in the literature on personality, which warrant study? Sociology cannot answer that question in the abstract. It must reply: It depends on the particular society or culture. Some demand one quality, others another. So we must now step down to a lower level of generality, and consider the profiles of de-

TABLE 1

Parallel Themes in the Functional Requisites of Any Social System and the Socialization of Any Individual

REQUISITES FOR CONTINUED FUNCTIONING OF SOCIETY [a]	ELEMENTS OF THE PERSONAL SYSTEM DEVELOPED IN ANY ADEQUATE SOCIALIZATION [b]
1. Provision for adequate physiological relationship to physical setting	Information and motor skills (aptitudes)
2. Role differentiation and role assignment	Self-system; personal identity
3. Shared, learned, symbolic modes of communication	Language skills; cognitive content
4. Shared cognitive orientations	Attitudes, opinions, idea systems
5. Shared articulated goals	Values
6. Regulation of choice of means	Ego development; self-system
7. Regulation of affective expression	Affective modes of functioning
8. Effective control of disruptive forms of behavior	Modes of moral functioning
(9. Adequate socialization)	
(10. Adequate institutionalization)	

[a] From Levy (1952).
[b] From Inkeles (1963, 1966).

mands on the individual which have been identified as characteristic for particular societies and cultures.

DISTINCTIVE SOCIALIZATION REQUIREMENTS IN PARTICULAR SOCIETIES AND STATUSES

We have no very satisfactory method for assessing the distinctive profile of role demands characteristic of one social structure or another. For complex societies we do not even have a master list of all the recognized positions and the associated role behavior expected of status incumbents. Even for a simple society, to our knowledge, no one has compiled a thorough list of the expected behavior patterns which the typical status incumbents will exhibit.[4] Therefore, if we wish to talk about the qualities which people in one or another society are expected to have, we must rely on the impressionistic statements of anthropological field workers, participant observers, informant reports, and the

[4] The work of Goodenough, now in progress, may change this situation, but it will certainly be only a modest beginning of what is clearly an enormous task. See Goodenough (1956, 1964) for his componential analyses of language and kinship systems.

like. We are thus faced with the same difficulties and shortcomings that arise in studying the field of national character (see Inkeles and Levinson, 1954).

Despite these formidable difficulties, we shall present brief profiles of the demands made on the "typical" member of the society in several different social systems. In so doing we bypass a host of methodological and theoretical problems. But there are some which cannot be avoided entirely or even postponed. When we speak of the "demands" of the social system we may refer either to the personal and behavioral *ideal* or we may indicate the qualities in the person which are *actually* called forth in action, rewarded in practice, and adaptive in fact. Robert and Helen Lynd (1937) dramatically illustrated the contrast in *Middletown in Transition* in which they showed through a long list of demands how America faced both ways, as in holding up the ideal, "Love your neighbor," but at the same time giving more realistic stress to the advice, "Never give a sucker an even break." We shall not resolve here to what extent the demand profiles presented are merely statements of a cultural ideal and to what extent they represent the behavior actually expected of status incumbents. Neither will we attempt to resolve whether actual manifestation of the required behavior is in fact adaptive for the individual or the society. Our purpose is not to evaluate the particular social systems discussed but merely to use information about them to illustrate the kinds of social demands different societies have been described as making.

Finally use of the term "societal demand" must be explained. To speak of *society* demanding is either to personify society or to presume a uniformity of response in any population such that a participant or an observer might think that everyone in society spoke as with one voice. This condition is, of course, seldom if ever met. Therefore, to speak of what "society" demands is to speak of something very problematic. But for our present purpose it seems a useful concept, indeed to express the underlying idea in any other way is cumbersome. The reader should keep in mind, however, that this is only a heuristic device, a kind of shorthand. Much of the time it is not "society," and not even one of its institutions, but himself and other people who make role demands on an individual, although not infrequently the individual *feels* it is society itself which addresses him. And very often others make these demands, not as agents of a larger social order, but as individuals with strong personal interests to protect or advance. This fact opens up a host of interesting problems, some of which will be discussed later in this paper.

As a start we may examine a series of profiles from the psychologically oriented anthropological literature. Erik Erikson has captured a wide audience with his description of the vicissitudes of childhood in the Sioux and Yurok cultures. It is noteworthy that in his discussion of those tribes he includes for each a very specific statement of what the individuals in those cultures must learn and be if they are to meet the role demands set for members of their respective societies.

For the Yurok, for example, Erikson (1950) says: "He must pray with humility, cry with faith, and hallucinate with conviction so far as the supernatural providers are concerned." We recognize here an expectation concerning the affective modes; his religion requires him to put on an elaborate and highly emotional display — despite what he may *feel* — in order to persuade his gods to aid him. Erikson continues to say that the Yurok

> must learn to make good nets, to locate them well, and to collaborate in the fish dam which his technology requires; he must trade and haggle with stamina and persistence when engaged with his fellow men; and he must learn to master his body's entrances, exits and interior byways in such a manner that nature's fluidways and supply routes will find themselves magically coerced. (p. 157)

In addition to these demands, Erikson mentions certain qualities which are notably *not* demanded of a Yurok, such as a requirement for great regularity or for compulsive orderliness.

In his discussion of the Sioux Erikson uses the same imperative "must" and "required," but the particular qualities now designated apply to different aspects of the personality. The prime requirement of the Sioux is apparently "the phallic aggressiveness of the fearless hunter and warrior." In addition, "generosity is an outstanding virtue required in Sioux life." Linked to this is the requirement of fortitude, by which Erikson means "the inclination to do sadistic harm to the enemy and the ability to withstand hardship and pain under torture and self-torture" (p. 121).

Erikson, of course, speaks in the language of the psychoanalytic movement. But those who have read a substantial number of the verbatim accounts of the sayings and advice given young people in many nonliterate societies will feel the resonance of Erikson's summary in such direct quotations. Here, for example, is Don, the Hopi Sun Chief, speaking about the advice given him by his maternal grandfather:

> As soon as I was old enough to take advice he taught me that it was a disgrace to be called *kahopi* (not Hopi, not peaceful). He said: "My grandson, old people are important. They know a lot and don't lie. Listen to them, obey your parents, work hard, treat everyone right." (Simmons, 1942, p. 51)

This homey advice could perhaps be given to anyone anywhere, but Aberle (1951) says it gives in concise form the ideals of the Hopi — conformity, obedience, hard work, and being good to people. Nevertheless, this ever self-effacing Sun Chief is also "aggressive, prestige-conscious, a deeply distrustful man," as are many other Hopi. Thus we see a contrast between the ideal and what, in fact, may be more common even if less "demanded" or "required" by society.

A third example will be used in support of the foregoing discussion. This model specifies the qualities required of the citizen of a democracy. After reviewing the conceptions of Alexis de Tocqueville, Jacques Maritain, Sidney Hook, and Harold Lasswell about the requirements which a democratic political order placed on participants in such systems, I summed up the characteristics of an effective citizen of a democracy:

> The citizen of a democracy should be accepting of others rather than alienated and harshly rejecting; open to new experiences, to ideas and impulses rather than excessively timid, fearful, or extremely conventional with regard to new ideas and ways of acting; able to be responsible with constituted authority even though always watchful, rather than blindly submissive or hostilely rejecting of all authority; tolerant of differences and of ambiguity, rather than rigid and inflexible; able to recognize, control, and channel his emotions, rather than immaturely projecting hostility and other impulses on to others. (Inkeles, 1961, p. 198)

To state anything so general as the personality requirements of a culture or type of social system is immediately to invite the complaint that the fact of universal role differentiation — even if only of sex, age, and prestige — makes it unlikely that the general model can have much validity. The general requirements of any system are likely to be transformed as they are translated to fit the different positions which any even moderately differentiated social structure must recognize. The Sioux may want men with an inclination to do sadistic harm, but that is unlikely to be the quality the Sioux warrior wants in the woman he comes home to. Our models of the system requirements must, therefore, always take account of the different demands society and culture may make on the incumbents of positions differentiated by age, sex, status, and the like. Aberle and Naegele's (1952) discussion of the socialization of middle-class boys in the United States permits us at once to see what some of the demand differences are in occupational, sex, and class terms. According to them:

> The ideal-typical successful adult male in the middle-class occupational role should be responsible, show initiative, be competent, be aggressive, be capable of meeting competition. He should be emotionally stable and capable of self-restraint.

Aberle and Naegele contrast the consequent concerns of the father in the socialization of his son as compared to his daughter. She is expected to be less aggressive and more emotional. She may not be bossy, and should be much more compliant. This is in accord with the expectation that her role will chiefly be that of mate, whereas the prime concern with the boy is that he be properly equipped for effective competition in the occupational world.

We could easily introduce many more examples of the demands which various authors have seen as characteristic for certain societies and for specific status positions in them, but those already given manifest sufficient pattern from which we can make some general observations. We may note the following points:

(1) There is a widespread readiness among social scientists to assert the existence of definite demands made by society and culture for certain personality traits in status incumbents. They seem quite prepared to say that individuals "should" or "must" be one way or another to fit the requirements of a sociocultural system or of a particular position in it. They are also quite ready to state what is *not* commonly required and what is firmly rejected and defined as undesirable. To the extent that there are identifiable socially required characteristics, the case is strengthened for those who argue that the variables in socialization research should be selected on the basis of their social relevance.

(2) The terms in which the requirements are stated are idiosyncratic and highly variable, exhibit very different levels of generality, and are used with widely varying degrees of precision. Thus, when Erikson says the Yurok must learn to make good nets and to place them well, we can hardly tell whether Yurok society demands a very high level of manual dexterity, or attention to detail and craftsmanship, or something quite ordinary. And we may wonder whether what is called "haggling with stamina and persistence" in the Yurok is meant to bear on the trait of compulsiveness they also are asserted to manifest, or are these two different dimensions? Similarly, we may wonder whether or not "being good to people" in the Hopi is related to the demand in democratic systems for men who are "accepting of others." Clearly, there is great need for a compulsive campaign, pursued with stamina and persistence, to evolve a more uniform conceptual scheme with common definitions and standardized measures of the basic dimensions of personality which are interesting from a social system perspective.

(3) Despite divergence in conceptual schemes and in the specific terminology favored by one or another analyst, we can discern certain recurrent themes in the socialization demands for different societies and positions. Many of them we have already encountered in Table I. Every individual must learn to be reasonably responsive to the pattern of social order and to the personal needs and requirements of the other individuals with whom he is in immediate contact. In other words, he must be basically socially conforming. He must have the ability to orient himself in space and time and have sufficient command of the rudi-

mentary physical requirements of his setting so as not to destroy himself or be an undue burden on others. The requirements of society and of its specific statuses seem usually to involve certain motor and mental skills and techniques, and some kind of specialized knowledge and information; certain ways of thinking about the world, organized in a set of opinions and attitudes and constituting a distinctive idea system; a set of goals or values to guide action, and beliefs about the appropriate and acceptable paths to the goals; a conception of oneself which gives an identity and forms the basis for a system of social relations which include distinctive ways of relating to immediate authority, to intimates and peers, and to the larger community; some pattern for the organization of psychic functioning which favors and facilitates certain distinctive modes of defense or moral functioning; and a particular cognitive, conative, and affective style.

Some of these themes, such as the modes of affective functioning, have long been central in socialization research, at least as represented by the study of aggression. Others, such as the theme of cognitive styles, have recently begun to win substantial attention in socialization research, especially as it is approached in studies of class differences (see Bernstein, 1958; John, 1963). But many of the themes are not now the object of systematic study in the current research on socialization. We have made only small beginnings in the study of language acquisition, at least as it has relevance for social adjustment.[5] The whole realm of the self as a system is little explored,[6] despite the promising beginnings which emerge from our study of competence. The modes of relating to others, especially to formal authority and society itself, have been almost completely neglected by the students of socialization,[7] no doubt because the problem does not arise in significant degree before the age of six. There is surely no need to belabor the point. A consideration of the demand, or social requirement, side of the socialization formula makes us aware of serious neglect but also points to major intellectual opportunities.

SOME UNRESOLVED ISSUES

We have argued that societies and cultures make readily identified and fairly explicit demands on the socialization process. In some sense,

[5] But see the work of Bernstein (1960), John and Goldstein (1964), and Bieri and Lobeck (1961).

[6] But see Reckless, Dinitz, and Murray (1956, 1957) and Scarpitti *et al.* (1960), and see Wylie (1961) for a review of research on the self-concept.

[7] Significant exceptions will be found in Strauss (1962), Hoffman (1963a, 1963b), Greenstein (1960, 1961), Easton and Dennis (1965), Easton and Hess (1962), and Tuma (1960).

society "expects" socialization to yield individuals with certain characteristics they share with all others in their society and yet other characteristics much more tied to specific statuses and roles. Many of the themes which societies emphasize have not been the objects of attention by students of socialization, and we urge that they be made the focus of research in the future. But there remain many unresolved issues, at least some of which must be dealt with before we can meaningfully undertake new lines of research.

To speak of *the* demands made by a social system is possible only if we assume *a* model of the sociocultural system. We can perhaps assume such simple arrangements in less complex preliterate societies, although even there we should do so with great caution, keeping in mind the long history of controversy over the nature of the required Hopi character (see Aberle, 1951). In any event, in larger and more complex societies the differentiation and diversification of activities make it difficult to insist on any general set of requirements other than reasonable conformity to social order and some ability to take care of oneself physically. We dealt with this issue, of course, by acknowledging fully the demands specific to certain statuses. But even with these more differentiated models of the socially "required," we must distinguish between the ideal which is held up by society; the qualities it actually inculcates; those which it favors or rewards; those which are in fact truly adaptive; and those which are the statistical norm quite apart from any ideal, or requirement, or even utility. Functionalists may try to resolve the problem by insisting that reference to society's "demands" is only a manner of speaking about what is needed to maintain the social system. Even then we may have some difficulty in determining exactly who it is who may define the system's requirements. Even assuming we can resolve that problem, there remains the necessity of meeting the requirements of individuals whose personal adjustment is not always congruent with the fulfillment of social requisites.

These issues are perhaps more important for the student of social structure than for the student of socialization. For the researcher on socialization the problem will be formulated more or less as follows: Assuming we can identify a "social demand," a set of "requirements" which society sets for its members, how are these qualities in fact socialized, that is, inculcated in the appropriate individuals, and if not, why not? It is immediately evident that this question suggests a series of interesting issues. To begin, the parent or other socializing agent, precisely because he is now conceived of mainly as *agent*, must have a fairly precise and detailed picture of what his action as agent is supposed to produce. Aberle and Naegele's (1952) report on middle-class fathers in the United States suggests that those fathers had a very clear picture of what society required of their sons or at least of what their sons required for "success." Reports from many other sources, however, leave one in serious doubt as to how well-formulated, specific, and articulated an image parents and other agents of at least *early* socialization have of what the end product is supposed to be. Their confusion may be expected to increase the more they realize they are supposed to raise children to satisfy something so abstract as the requirements of a social system or some significant segment of it. This suggests an important and much neglected area for research. It would be most interesting to review anthropological and other field work materials to discover with what precision societies formulate, and how thoroughly they disseminate, a clear picture of the demands they place on the socialized adult. And in future research it would be possible, both in advanced and simpler societies, to study just how clear these demands are to the individual socializing agents, how much they are in agreement with other agents, how they acquired their images of the socially necessary, and how they resolve discrepancies between the often conflicting demands which the same society may set out in its formal "requirements."

Whatever level of accuracy the socialization agent may attain in his effort to discover what is socially required — and we must assume he will succeed only imperfectly — he still faces a very great problem. He must now select those *means*, that set of socialization practices, which will attain the required end. This is no mean feat, as any frustrated socialization researcher will tell you. Of course, most people are not left so completely to their own devices. Society not only provides them with a definition of the goal, but it generally specifies the means, either by tradition or, as in modern nations, through expert advice (see Bronfenbrenner, 1958). Yet many people may not be reached by this advice, others may have trouble comprehending it, and still others difficulties in acting on it. Some of our socialization research (as in Sears, Maccoby, and Levin) has given substantial emphasis to discussions with the parents (usually the mother) about the problems and difficulties they have in implementing whatever are their *personal* objectives in socialization. There is very little research which attempts to understand better the problems which the parent or other socializing agent encounters in selecting the correct socialization procedures to attain the *socially* preferred end (see Brim, 1965). The problem is likely to be particularly acute where tradition no longer blindly dictates the approved techniques, where there has been no substitution of experts, or where the experts are in great disagreement (see Benedict, 1938; Erikson, 1950). A mother may be perfectly sure that what is wanted these days is a boy full of initiative. But how is she to know what makes a boy that way? Is she to leave him alone to discover things for himself, or is it better to push him to take responsibility? And anyhow, what does responsibility have to do with initiative? And so on.

Even if the society can recommend standard techniques to go with its standard requirements, the problems are not all resolved. Every socializing agent working with the young child must still balance at least three sets of pressures. First, there is the social imperative, and perhaps even the standard techniques recommended by society to produce the desired end. Second, the parent also has ideals and needs of his own, and in his life faces concrete and distinctive personal pressures. These may or may not facilitate or conduce to his acting merely as "instructed" agent in carrying out the social command in socialization. Third, every child will have distinctive qualities, being more passive or active, even-tempered or choleric, slow or quick, sick or healthy. These characteristics of the child must inevitably impose themselves on the socialization process, and will influence the style and the degree to which the socialization agent carries out the social imperative.

If we take account of all these forces which may be, and generally are, acting to reduce the chances that individuals will simply be "turned out" in an automatic way to fit the requirements of their society, then to be realistic we must admit that the amount of slippage will be enormous. Indeed, the number of variables involved and the nature of the contingencies make it fairly obvious that this process could not possibly produce a reasonably standard or uniform product. If we assume, however, that there are some patterned and regular manifestations of distinctive personality traits in different populations, as there certainly are of distinctive values and ways of acting, then how are we to explain the persistence of these differences in the face of the great variability of the socialization process?

The answer seems to be that we must look beyond the period of early socialization to socialization in youth, adolescence, early adulthood, and later. The experiences of early childhood may indeed lay the groundwork for later developments, but they clearly cannot in themselves give the personality the social content which it later must contain. One may, as Erikson suggests, get some image of generosity from the ready availability of the breast, but being generous also involves an elaborate set of rules and concrete behaviors in interpersonal relations which can only be acquired through a fairly long process of learning, not only in the home, and in the peer group, but often out in the larger community. Thus, generosity may mean offering your wife for the night, exchanging fresh horses for those exhausted on the trail, sharing your last bowl of rice, or nothing more than sending some freshly baked cookies across the street. And the object is never proffered without restrictions concerning time, place, form, the status of giver and receiver, and so on through the endless rules of etiquette in different cultures. It is these detailed social rules which shape and give form to the underlying dispositions, referred to as the "social content," necessary to make socialization complete.

Those who believe in the prime importance of infant and child experience will argue that unless the disposition to act a certain way, and some simple model or analogue of later behavior, are acquired during early childhood, the later development of appropriate social behavior will be impaired. They may or may not be right in all cases. Granting that the *disposition* and the basic model for the control of aggression, for obedience, and for the channeling of sexual energy may be laid down in infancy and early childhood, the acquisition of such dispositions and basic models is not in itself sufficient to qualify a person as properly or fully socialized. Society will judge him so only when he is able to *act* in the detailed ways specified by habit and custom for a person of his sex, age, and status.

Many students of socialization treat the acquisition of these secondary characteristics as if they were entirely unproblematic. They seem often to assume that if the proper ground work is laid in early life, the rest of the necessary learning will take place more or less automatically. But the acquisition of the precise knowledge, skills, and behavioral details which go with significant social roles is anything but unproblematic. However successful the infant and child learning, an individual's socialization may fail to meet society's standards because of inadequacies in social learning at later stages. Equally important, inadequacies in early socialization may be compensated for by effective social learning at later stages in the life cycle.

For both those socialized well and poorly in the early years, we must assume that it is largely through these later stages of socialization — when, in a sense, the whole social structure serves as socializing agent — that the process of socialization begun in the family is completed and that society inculcates in the individual many of its "required" characteristics. There is, then, a "second wave" in the socialization process, which we have relatively neglected in our preoccupation with the period of infancy and early childhood. In this second wave, the individual not only learns the detailed role contents socially necessary to acting in accord with earlier acquired basic dispositions, but he also acquires new dispositions and social skills which he could not appropriately learn in infancy and early childhood. Many aspects of heterosexual relations, much of the orientation and behavior appropriate to work and to political allegiance and action exemplify those realms in which, perforce, socialization must come mainly after the early years.

Even this second wave cannot always suffice, especially when a process of rapid social change constantly transforms the qualities and skills which are needed in social life and introduces new demands and requirements. Then the society must turn to a program of resocialization, a process which may be applied not only to the young but even to the adult and to the aged. And this model is still incomplete until we acknowledge that many will inevitably be socialized in ways which meet neither the individual's needs nor those of the society. Finally some may be resistant to all efforts at resocialization. The result is deviant behavior, individual maladjustment, social tension, disruption, and perhaps creative change.

How Society Influences the Socialization Process

We turn now to how society inculcates its required characteristics in the individual. In approaching this problem, we start with the assumption that our inquiry cannot be safely limited to the parent-child relationship. A complex of forces operates to produce the total socialization experience of each individual. Only by recognizing and distinguishing the several and somewhat independent elements entering into socialization can we develop new directions in research and a more adequate explanation of the total process by which animal child becomes social man.

Three approaches to the explication of the society's demands on socialization are available. One is to review the life history of the individual and to indicate at each stage the peculiar demands society makes, how it communicates them, through which agency it operates, and how each stage relates to the next point in individual development. Although all followers of the Freudian theory turn spontaneously in this direction, their interest is more in the needs of the organism than in the needs of society, and their theory is not well equipped to handle socialization beyond the early stages (see Inkeles, 1959). Erik Erikson (1950), perhaps more than anyone else in this tradition, has been keenly aware of the importance of carrying stage analysis further into adolescence and beyond. And the new view of socialization sponsored by the Social Science Research Council's Committee on Socialization and Social Structure has elevated to equal standing with child training the process of socialization throughout the life cycle. The results of the Committee's sponsored conference on adult socialization, and especially the theoretical summary by Orville G. Brim, Jr.,[8] support this view.[9]

We have seriously neglected that important source for understanding the continuity of social-communal pressures on socialization through the

[8] See Brim and Wheeler (1966); also Brim in Chapter Five of this volume.

[9] See also in this volume discussions by Clausen in Chapter Four and Lippitt in Chapter Eight on the socialization tasks of family, school, and peer group, and the social demands exerted by these important agents of society.

life cycle — the rich biographical and autobiographical accounts once so assiduously recorded by field anthropologists. If we look, for example, at the autobiography of Don, the Hopi Sun Chief, whom we have already encountered, we are struck with a recurring pattern: how, at every critical point in his life — when deciding whether to return to the white man's school, to undergo initiation, to marry, to follow Hopi custom in earning his living, or to strive for high office in the secret society — relatives, friends, and community leaders intervened to stress what was expected of him, urged him to undertake his new roles and fulfill old obligations, offered reasons for action and various forms of support, and, as he would put it, thus "showed him the way" (Simmons, 1942).

A second method for studying the implementation of social objectives in the socialization process is to select a set of key outcomes and to trace back the sources of influence which produced them. If, for example, we argue that successful adaptation in American society requires high aspirations and mobility strivings, or that women must show relatively high nurturance and compliance, then our task is to locate the various ways in which the social order defines these objectives and seeks to inculcate them in the appropriate sets of individuals. Analysis of this type is undertaken in several contributions to this symposium, in particular in the discussions of competence and moral development by M. Brewster Smith and Eleanor E. Maccoby, respectively.

The third mode of analysis will be discussed in this chapter. In this approach we focus not on the socializing agents or institutions, nor on the socially desired outcome, but rather on the means, or the social arrangements, through which the social order makes its impact felt. There is no generally accepted standard list of channels of influence in socialization, so those given below must be considered illustrative rather than exhaustive. We think they represent a large segment of the most important dimensions.

THE EXPOSITION OF THE EXPECTED

Society makes its most concentrated effort to influence socialization through direct instruction. These didactic efforts begin very early. Often before the child can understand them, parents begin to speak to their children in ways which more or less explicitly specify how "we" are, want to be, or should be. Little of this speech is recorded, but it should be. As the child begins to understand, the messages become more pointed and specific. Little girls don't lift their dresses and big boys don't cry. We've got to play fair and work hard. The guiding statements become increasingly formal and explicit as the child moves from the home to secondary socialization settings, of which the school is the outstanding instance in our cultural tradition. The sayings become maxims which the enterprising teacher mounts on large cards above the blackboards: "A fool and his money are soon parted"; "My only regret is that I have but one life to give for my country." The tales of folklore had been influential earlier, and they continue to be so as the individual shifts from oral tradition to written. George Washington cannot tell a lie — at least to his father — and little pigs who play and gambol rather than bake bricks get eaten up by wolves. The folk sayings, of course, present a model of behavior not only to the socializee but to the socializer, advising him that as the twig is bent so grows the tree, and that sparing the rod spoils the child. Where the spontaneous processes of culture fail, other sources of didactic influence insinuate themselves. Folklore is written to order, and the media of mass communication create new images of the desirable, like the little train model of American efficacy which struggles up the mountain puffing, "I think I can," and down it knowing that it could.

As the child matures, the standards and models he encounters are increasingly organized as formal and even written systems of expectation. Whether he is going through a primitive initiation or only joining the Boy Scouts, there are available an explicit model of behavior, a set of formal rules of conduct, and a rationale to support it and sanctions to preserve it, which are publicly and often ceremoniously set forth. The assumption of each new role — one's first animal to care for or a small plot to work, one's marriage, the arrival of one's children, the assumption of one's various ritual and communal roles — has associated with it ceremonies small and large which reiterate the obligations and responsibilities constituting society's expectation of the new status incumbent. It is a process which, more or less formally, goes on throughout a man's life and indeed often follows him to his burial, at which he may be instructed how properly to conduct himself as a spirit.

All this is certainly very obvious, but again it is striking how much it is neglected. The themes stressed here have not much to do with the primary drive systems, and research focused on their mastery would pass by most of these social commands. It can be argued that people act mainly in response to their deep-seated disposition and needs and not in accord with their espoused behavioral ideals. But this argument makes the very questionable assumption that the *behavioral* ideal must somehow always be at variance with the individual *need-disposition.* Of course it may be, but the chances are very much greater that it will not. Otherwise we would have a difficult time indeed explaining the persistence of any social structure. It further seems questionable to assume that where formal norm and individual disposition are not in accord, action will always, or even usually, follow individual need rather than social norm. If that were true, fewer men would be leading that "life of quiet desperation" which so many middle-class and non-existentialist American males are said to lead. Here again researchers on socialization stand convicted of neglected opportunities. Our research fails systematically to uncover and collate the formal and explicitly didactic models of behavior which societies present to their members, and neglects the places, means, and forms wherein and whereby these ideals are taught.

Again, to exemplify the point, we may turn to Don, the Sun Chief, who recalls his grandfather saying:

> Children who ignore these teachings do not live long. . . . He advised me to keep bad thoughts out of my mind, to face the east, look to the bright side of life, and learn to show a shining face, even when unhappy. . . . We grew up doing things. All the old people said that it was a disgrace to be idle and that a lazy boy should be whipped. . . . The importance of food was a lesson I learned early. My mother taught me never to waste it or to play with it carelessly. . . . I also learned that water is as precious as food. . . . [And his uncles said] Work hard, keep the ceremonies, live peaceably, and unite your heart with ours so that our messages will reach the Cloud People. Then maybe they will pity us and drop the rains on our own fields. (Simmons, 1942)

The difficulties and uncertainties of research on didactic socialization themes should not be minimized, but perhaps these difficulties add to rather than subtract from the interest of the venture. Whatever the clarity of the message society may be sending out, its reception must of necessity be impeded by many uncontrolled and even systematic sources of interference, so that many a little girl must be going around thinking: "Good Mrs. Murphy will follow me all the days of my life." Getting society's mandate expressed in a systematic and consistent way, so that the different spokesmen all speak with one voice and in the proper sequence, is a great challenge to any social system. But the problem may seem more formidable to us in the United States precisely because of the size and complexity of our system, and, perhaps most important, because as an open society we often shy away from specifying too public, official, and explicit a doctrine of individual behavior. It is less difficult for most simpler, nonliterate societies to agree on a mode of conduct; and even in modern national states the extent to which there is an agreed and formal model of conduct and character varies greatly. In countries with centralized school systems, as in France, at least that one institution disseminates precisely the same model of behavior in every classroom of the nation. In mobilized nations — those dominated by a single party with a strong ideology, as in Russia and China, and more weakly but still significantly in Ghana and Egypt — there is a very formal, explicit, and official role model which every parent, adult, teacher, government official, and even ordinary citizen is expected to know and to help inculcate in the young. In modern societies in which everyone agrees on standards and the necessity of enforcing them, the same unified effect can be obtained more spontaneously without the aid of the state. Look, sometime, for a *child* sitting in a public conveyance in Holland while an *adult*, of whatever age, is standing!

Of course these societal models are often tangential to, perhaps even in conflict with, more traditional conceptions supported by the older culture, perhaps with familial, regional, tribal, ethnic, or other points of reference. Very often the models conflict as well with individual need and desire. Such conflict cannot eliminate the effect of the official model although it may mute it, but it is in the competition and clash of alternative models of behavior and feeling that some of the most interesting problems in the study of socialization lie. There was a time when students of socialization had an interest in the marginal man, his development, and his problems (Stonequist, 1937); but today much socialization research is written as if it were already 1984 and we were all brought up in test tubes in which the environment had been carefully manufactured to screen out all conflicting pressures and disturbing elements.

EXPLICIT TRAINING

Exposition and exhortation must be implemented by demonstration and explicit training. This is a simple yet fundamental matter, one which many founders of utopias have, to their great sorrow, neglected. Many models of behavior can readily be acted on without further formal instruction. It is not likely that we can do much to instruct someone how to be cheerful or guide him in the details of being pessimistic. But many other ideals, like generosity, have meaning only in so far as very explicit and often elaborate actions are produced in the right time, place, volume, and sequence. The paucity of ritual in our own society has perhaps made us aware of the elaborate instruction required to train properly young and old to perform well in cultures which preserve complex and elaborate codes of etiquette. Although we may still send even boys to dancing school, the elaborate program of training which once was supposed to make the "gentleman" is now practiced in very few families. Other institutions have taken over. The good boys' prep school, at least until very recently, was more concerned with instructing the young man in dancing, good manners, proper dress, and other external signs of his future class standing than with the preparation of his mind. This is still true of most girls' finishing schools. Increasingly the mass media, offering instruction in good taste and gracious entertaining — and now to a much wider audience — take over the responsibility. Indeed, many lower-class women listen to and watch the daytime serial, not exclusively for the romance with which it vicariously touches their lives, but also because it teaches them how to anticipate and behave in important social situations which they otherwise feel inadequately trained to meet (Herzog, 1944).

Our insistence on the importance of explicit instruction will meet no great resistance so long as we restrict ourselves to such behavior as learning how to tie shoelaces or to write the letter *q*, although even here we have neglected to study family and cultural differences in their approach to such formal instruction. The Japanese, for example, apparently teach the young by directly guiding finger, hand, and arm in the prescribed motions, whereas we, by allowing the child to discover by accident or example, carefully avoid the direct control form of guidance.

Even more notable an example of our neglect of formal instruction as an object of research is that realm where parent and school teach complex patterns of interrelated behaviors — how to eat "properly," or how to accompany a lady like a gentleman and perhaps take punishment like a man. Students are urged, and for good academic performance are required, to develop proper study habits. We know that students vary enormously in this skill, as they do in intelligence and the motivation to achieve. Psychologists have given ample time to studies of intelligence and the achievement motive, but the acquisition of study habits has been the subject of very little research.[10] We may well ask, what are the specific behaviors of the student who "knows how to study" and how were they learned by him? By what exact parental actions is the child instructed in learning these habits, and what role do peers and the school play in teaching the specific techniques of studying?

One of the great problems of an open society, such as that of the United States, is that responsibility for giving instruction in the socially relevant and more or less public roles may become terribly diffuse and yield serious failures of socialization. In part this condition stems from our country's values, which so stress initiative and express distrust of "indoctrination." We are somewhat horrified by the example of the bureaucracy, perhaps epitomized by the army, in which one is not only told what it is like to be a soldier but in the minutest detail is instructed how to be one. A soldier is taught how to make his bed, brush his teeth, keep his back straight and chin in; he must be well versed in military etiquette and, finally, in the details of handling his weapon and relating himself to friend and enemy in combat — all done, as they say in the army, "by the numbers."

In some areas we have responded creatively to the necessity for a more

[10] There is available, of course, a good deal of advice to teachers and clinical reports by teachers on their experience in helping students with study problems (see, for example, Herber, 1965; Kranyik and Shankman, 1963). But the volume of research, especially research which is psychologically interesting and methodologically sound, is very meager (see Strang, 1955).

straightforward approach to the problems of instruction. We now rely rather heavily on programs of formal instruction in auto driving given in high school; apparently, the results have been most beneficial. But we are still not able to face the difficulties inherent in giving instruction about sex; as a result, the unmarried girls who become pregnant are much more likely to be those with less adequate information about sex (see Butman and Kamm, 1965).

The need for instruction becomes especially acute in those realms in which individuals either cannot spontaneously learn from models or lack the resources for self-instruction. One of the critical, and for many people disabling, requirements of our kind of society is the ability to fill out complex forms. Numerous bureaucratic organizations dispense these in large numbers, and for the individual much depends on how they are filled out. Formal training is not given in this essential skill, even though the later stages of schooling, through the students' taking standard tests, do provide at least some practice for later form-filling activities. Here again we may see that the mass media, especially the newspapers at income tax time, have in part taken over this function for society.

As in the setting of standards, the mass media have also become important in the process of explicit instruction. Probably the outstanding example is the instructional film, so extensively used as a socialization device by a wide variety of organizations ranging from schools to armies. Thus, during World War II every American soldier came to know about venereal disease and its prophylaxis through what he wryly called the "Mickey Mouse movie." We must see that the mass media, even as they pursue their own ends, present a great deal of instruction with regard to dressing, furnishing, manners, lovemaking, and even burglary. The results are sometimes grim, as in the case of the youngsters who followed the James Bond technique of hanging from the bottom of an elevator at the cost of their lives. But we must recognize that in many ways the media have willy-nilly taken over much of the responsibility for instructing people in a variety of behaviors and skills which are variously socially required, useful, or customary, and that by this means they contribute greatly to the integration and effective functioning of our society.

Again in the case of explicit instruction we conclude there is a regrettable dearth of systematic study. It would be of great interest to review the forms, the content, the agents, and the outcomes of *formal instruction* with regard to sexual behavior, the school pupil and college student roles, occupational roles, and parental and citizenship obligations.[11]

[11] Important exceptions are to be noted. For significant studies of the socialization of political attitudes, for example, see Greenstein (1960, 1961), Easton and Dennis (1965), Easton and Hess (1962), and Hess and Easton (1960). However, these studies focus more on the outcome of socialization than directly

The socialization literature does contain extensive studies of sex differences, but these are mainly devoted to disentangling the differences in need, value, and behavior between boys and girls (see Maccoby, 1966). They seem seriously to neglect the ideology which guides the training of boys and girls and the differences in the instruction which they receive, and there are few studies which followed the promising lead developed by Aberle and Naegele in their research with middle-class fathers. Orville G. Brim, Jr. (1959) has presented a definitive picture of our efforts to educate parents for better child rearing. These are important beginnings, but a great deal remains to be done in systematically studying the processes by which social organizations, through formal instruction, seek to socialize individuals to act correctly in fulfilling the role demands of the statuses they must assume.

SANCTIONS AS A DIRECT MEANS OF SOCIALIZATION

For instruction to be effective, it must be supported by a system of rewards and punishments. Sanctions are an essential underpinning of society's efforts at formal instruction. The mere allocation of sanctions among different acts constitutes a declaration of society's intent and sets a standard which will affect the individual regardless of whether or not he, himself, receives either the punishments or the rewards specified by the system. The more the sanction system is presented in a context of unanimity and is given special meaning through the use of ceremonial gestures of various kinds, the greater the effect. All ceremonies for meting out justice, in even the most primitive societies, are surrounded by some of the most elaborate rituals the given cultures can muster. The special nature of our courthouses, with their ubiquitous Greek columns and statues of blindfolded justice, no less than the grim demeanor of our jails and penitentiaries, are meant to convey a special message which affects many if not most people.

When we consider the multitude of commandments and the welter of instruction which confront the individual in more complex social systems, we must acknowledge that the task of completely fulfilling the society's requirements is impossible.[12] Individuals resolve the problem by choosing their course of action so as to maximize reward and minimize punishment according to the way the system is *actually* administered. If the teacher rewards memorizing more than originality, she will get more

---

on the formal instructional process. They leave us in doubt as to how the observed attitudes came to exist. An exceptional review of information about health, which reports not only what people know but examines the efforts to teach them what they know — and don't know — will be found in Veenker (1963). An experiment in teaching adolescents about sex is reported in Edelston (1956).

[12] For a revealing and rare description and analysis of this situation in the case of the Soviet factory manager, see Joseph Berliner (1957).

of the former and less of the latter, and if the factory manager is judged more by the volume of production than by quality or cost, he will increase volume at the expense of the other two even if the rules formally define both as "equally" important.

Our interest here is less in the details of how behavior is shaped by sanctions in any one of innumerable concrete situations and more in the general lessons which are taught by, or which individuals may deduce from, the application of the system of sanctions. The consistency and equality with which the rules are applied constitute a powerful lesson for the individual in how to conceive justice and judge the appropriateness of conformity to law. Inconsistency in the application of sanctions *over time* likely produces weak internal restraints on the performance of any forbidden behavior. We may also expect such inconsistency to yield a propensity to bargain and haggle so as to win the least severe punishment possible or to increase the reward offered for any given action. Inconsistency in the application of sanctions, *as between one delinquent and another,* is likely to weaken faith in the justness of the system of sanctions and thus lead to weak internalization and evasions of the system. The issues are, admittedly, complex, and any formulation so brief is open to challenge. For example, the statement about inconsistency may be challenged by those who, following the theory of partial reinforcement, expect certain kinds of inconsistency by the parent to yield firmer, more rigid internalization of parental standards. It depends, of course, on the degree of overall inconsistency, the general setting of the family, the realms in which inconsistency is manifested, and the general quality of the parent-child relation.

We begin to touch here on problems of the development of conscience and moral behavior. Since these issues are dealt with extensively in Dr. Maccoby's chapter, we limit ourselves here to one observation. In the socialization literature treating moral development, the central interest seems to have been to discover how actions, such as physical punishment or guilt induction, performed by important socializing *agents,* particularly the parents, affect the moral training of the child.[13] We have not done much to learn the extent to which the parents and others are aware of, and are conscientiously trying to convey to the child an awareness of, a *system of sanctions* which is outside the parent-child relationship and expresses the wishes and interests of *society.* Apparently not much more attention has been given to the impact of this public system of sanctions on the youngster as he moves out of the home into the street or playground, the school, the youth group, the job, and the larger community.[14]

[13] See the reviews by Kohlberg (1963) and M. Hoffman (1963a).

[14] See Matza (1964) and Weeks (1958) for studies on attitudes towards law and authority among delinquents.

RETRAINING

Not only the individual but society also gets a chance to start over again, in the sense that socialization is never complete and almost never terminal. "Development" may be over by late adolescence, but learning can and does continue until old age. Although society will sometimes admit defeat, as with the psychopath or incorrigible criminal, the prospects for retraining and for resocialization of the individual generally are sufficient to encourage substantial efforts at the second and later try. Indeed, any society must face this problem to some degree, since there are inevitably important discontinuities in the demands placed on individuals at different stages in the life cycle. The retraining becomes acute in societies undergoing rapid change, whether induced from without or within.

Every system of punishment is itself an effort at resocialization; and in part our penal system, ineffective as it may be in achieving its purpose, rests on this assumption. Religious organizations regularly strive to resocialize people according to the dictates of their belief through the use of the confessional, revival meetings, and retreats. Business organizations increasingly resort to retraining programs, sometimes going so far as to submit their staffs to the kind of group therapy practiced by the National Training Laboratories at Bethel, Maine. Educational systems currently face massive problems in retraining teachers so that they will use new methods of instruction and will teach more effectively in accord with changed conceptions of the educational process. Automation, itself only a manifestation of a more general problem of technical change which affects the entire job structure, including the professions and even the occupation of housewife, demands new programs of job training and new skills in the handling of "free" or leisure time (see Wilensky, 1961). Since Ronald Lippitt contributes a chapter to this book that treats such resocialization efforts in detail, we emphasize here only that these resocialization attempts are all fairly self-conscious. In these efforts society, through its institutional embodiments such as school, business, church, and the like, tries a second time to bring people up to a standard which is set by society. The retraining is consciously meant to advance social purposes, and in the concept of social purpose we include helping individuals to adjust effectively and to obtain *personal* happiness.

Unfortunately, we know all too little about the special character and distinctive effects of these efforts at resocialization. Prisons capture our conscience enough so that we, informed by serious concern for their effectiveness in resocializing the criminal, are beginning to turn to their study (see Wheeler, 1961, and Brim and Wheeler, 1966). The dramatic and fear-inspiring efforts of the Chinese to remake men not only ideologically but characterologically through brainwashing have spurred some serious and systematic efforts to study that phenomenon (see Lifton, 1961; Schein, 1961). Research on the effectiveness of many of the present training programs in connection with the campaigns to reduce delinquency and eliminate poverty will surely produce some interesting findings. But on the whole we have not sufficiently studied society's efforts at resocialization. We do not have as yet either a well-formulated conceptual scheme or descriptive language for handling the phenomenon of resocialization, and we are far from having a general theory to account for the outcome of these efforts.[15]

SOCIAL-STRUCTURAL FACTORS AS INFLUENCES ON SOCIALIZATION

All "views" and "perspectives" are inherently one-sided. In attempting to highlight the imbalance in socialization research which results from neglect of the more formal and explicit societal requirements, we have been working with a model which is itself quite unbalanced. Society may in the end effect its purposes, but not all of society's effects are purposeful. Socialization is influenced by social structure in many ways. Not all of the pressure is exerted in response to some clearly defined societal purpose. Indeed, the outcome may run counter to the desires and intentions of society. We must acknowledge the difficulty of determining exactly who or what is the embodiment of society and may speak for it. Society may speak with several voices. Even when there is a single source of authority in socialization matters, this source may still demand plural, and not necessarily consistent, outcomes. Still further complications are added by the fact that society cannot act for itself but must effect its purposes through organizations and individuals who are its "agents" in the socialization process. The nature of these organizations and the character, quality, and interests of the socialization agents introduce new elements of variability, which may yield outcomes at odds with society's original intent. Finally, the facts of role differentiation require that society's necessarily more general objectives in socialization be translated and interpreted by the agents of socialization. They must adapt the requirement to fit specific statuses and roles, and in this process still more substantial opportunities for uncontrolled variation are introduced.

Complex as it is, this model of the socialization process is relatively static. It assumes a high degree of continuity of the social order, so that socialization objectives and the means for attaining them will be well known and congruent. In conditions of rapid social change, however, the

[15] For this reason the Committee on Socialization has given particular emphasis to these problems. See the chapter by Brim, and the chapter by Lippitt in this volume.

objectives and methods of socialization must also change or people must be resocialized, else the qualities they bring to their social roles will be inappropriate and maladaptive both for them and society. Objectives previously valued may no longer be honored, and methods for raising children once highly appropriate may become meaningless to the parent or a severe handicap to the person who falls under their influence. Erik Erikson (1950) has given us a sensitive and revealing account of such crises in change through his account of the Sioux warriors' loss of a meaningful social role.

We can no longer use a simple, unbalanced model of the socialization process. Our discussion of the social-demand aspect of socialization will remain quite unreal unless the factors of social structure and social change mentioned above are considered. Perhaps this can be effectively done by examining in detail one dimension of socialization of the individual as he moves through the several stages of his life cycle. We cannot systematically introduce here all the different ways in which the social structure more indirectly affects the socialization process, but we will stress the role of economic and political structures, stratification systems, ecological factors, and the range and importance of the role models available. The one outcome of socialization we shall examine is the self-system, in particular the individual's self-conception. We should recall that in the discussion of the functional requisites of any social system Levy specified a system of role differentiation and role assignment. We noted that this required the socialization process to give the individual some sense of his identity, its similarity to the identity of others, and its distinctness from the identity of still others. Any society must, as a minimum, socialize the individual so that he will recognize himself as a member of his primary group, however the given culture may define that unit. It must also give him a clear image of his sex and of the different roles he will play as he ages. Some degree of occupational differentiation exists almost everywhere; and, either associated with or independent of it, there will be a hierarchy of power and authority in which every person has a defined position. In more complex modern societies the individual's positions in these structures are, of course, all distinctive and fully elaborated aspects of his identity.

It might be wise to state explicitly what is perhaps obvious to most; that is, why we believe the individual must have a definite sense of who he is. This requirement involves an interesting articulation of the needs of the social structure and of the individual as systems. From the perspective of society a division of labor is essential, but the occupational differentiation of persons is not indispensable so long as tasks are simple and routine enough. Even in the simplest societies, however, many of the tasks to be performed are fairly complex and require specialization. Some principle of economy and order seems to move all human groups, even the most primitive, toward some degree of specialization. Much impetus is presumably given to the process by the biological fact which requires that infants have easy and regular access to their mothers for nursing (see Zelditch, 1955). Once tasks are organized in systems, with definite sets of rights and obligations tying one individual to another, the further articulation of the effort of individuals depends on their *knowing* their respective positions in the system. In other words, the coordination and articulation of human interaction require that individuals know their positions in the game and be responsive to the requirements of the system in accord with their part in it. This is the primary element in identity from the social perspective, and from this primary beginning, of course, it becomes much more complex.

From the side of the individual, knowing his identity seems to be a psychological requirement for personal integration. We do not understand this need very well, but it certainly seems to exist apart from any need of society. We may suggest that the underlying need of the human organism is for orientation and cognitive order, which would be impossible to attain if all the stimuli flowing into a person during ordinary social interaction were all equally and diffusely applicable to him. It is only by knowing "who he is" — that is, by knowing his status and role — that he discriminates between the massive flow of stimuli from others and selects only those signals to which he must pay attention and perhaps respond, according to his position in the system of interaction.

In the socialization process a person not only learns who or what he is, but he also acquires a set of attitudes and feelings about himself, especially with reference to that aspect of the self which is part of his social identity.[16] Some part of this feeling will be quite private, and may be felt independently of the attitude his environment takes toward him. Some part will be social, but can be understood mainly in terms of the distinctive life history of the individual. His family constellation or his special relation to his mother may have left him uniquely vain about his looks, or uncommonly pleased with his wit, even though this judgment of him is not widely shared in the community. But to a high degree the individual will be obliged to take as his reference point what the community thinks of him, and to a marked degree the community will judge an individual according to the particular position that he holds in the network of statuses making up the social system. This affective, as against the cognitive, component of the individual's self-conception is a critical and little-studied problem in socialization. We return to it in the section on stratification, below.

[16] See Miller (1963) and the unpublished paper prepared by Miller and French (1964) for the Tucson conference of this Committee.

SOCIAL ORGANIZATION: ECONOMIC AND POLITICAL STRUCTURES

David Aberle (1961) has dealt in some detail with what many others have recognized as the "chicken and egg" aspect of the relationship of socialization to social structure. Is it that people who are raised a certain way arrange to order society accordingly, or does the nature of social organization dictate how people will be raised? He suggests that we can break out of this circle by making a comparative analysis of the relation of socialization practices to certain variable economic facts. The way in which people organize their life must in some degree be adapted to the basic natural resources available and the level of technological competence they have attained. If quite distinctive variations in the system of child rearing can be shown to be associated with variations in economic organization, Aberle suggests, then the case for the primacy of the mode of production as the determinant of child-rearing practices would be strengthened. Another important test of primacy could be made by studying cultures which had experienced important changes in their mode of production to ascertain if child-rearing practices varied accordingly.

While for some the issue remains problematic, for others there is little doubt that not only the economy but other aspects of social organization play an important, indeed prime, role in shaping the socialization practices which prevail in any society. Aberle has stated their case succinctly and forcefully:

> Thus factors not themselves the results of socialization can be seen to affect socialization practices and through them (as well as directly) the personalities of constituent members of the society. The task ahead is that of tracing the impact not only of ecological and technological factors, but of economic and political factors on units in which the bulk of child socialization occurs — the family in almost all societies, age groups where they are present, and schools in literate societies. Through their impact on social relationships in the socializing units, and on the aims of the socializers, these factors can probably be shown to account for a very large amount of the variance in socialization patterns from one society, or segment of society, to another. (Aberle, 1961, p. 383)

Since about 1950 a small but exceptionally productive group of researchers has been working within the broad limits of the framework sketched above by Aberle. Within this frame several different lines of work may be distinguished (compare Whiting, 1961). One approach is concerned mainly with discovering how some aspect of social organization — or as Whiting, following Kardiner, calls it, "the maintenance system" — influences the modal pattern of child rearing. Thus John Whiting (1961) shows that indulgence of the infant varies greatly with the type of household, being almost invariably high in the extended and polygynous cultures and generally low in those cultures in which the household includes only one mother and her children. More frequently, however, the objective of this research has been to explain some feature of the projective or cultural system as a reflection of personality characteristics which are in turn generated by the prior impact of the maintenance system of socialization. As a rule the aspect of social structure chosen as the dependent variable has been some belief or action pattern concerning religion, illness, the spirits, art, and the like; and these have been collectively termed the culture's "projective systems," again following Kardiner (1939). For example, religions may be classified according to the assumptions they are based on: gods may be controlled mainly by propitiation, or gods are more influenced by how one behaves and also by compulsive religious ritual. It develops that those societies in which infants are indulged do not propitiate the gods but rather try to control them by other means, such as wailing, begging, entreating, performing elaborate rituals, etc. (Spiro and D'Andrade, 1958).

Most relevant to our interest in self-conception are the researches of Barry, Bacon, and Child (1957), in which they considered the differences in socialization affecting boys and girls. After studying a large number of cultures, they concluded that boys are in general trained to attain quite different objectives than girls are. Boys are more firmly taught to strive for achievement and to be self-reliant and independent. The girls, in turn, are trained more for obedience, responsibility, and nurturance. From this data alone one might conclude that socialization is not so much responsive to differences in social structure as to differences in the innate characteristics of the two sexes, a difference whose effect is apparently felt across cultural lines independently of variation in maintenance systems. But the data presented by Barry, Bacon, and Child (1957) indicate more than this. The authors note that the differences between boys and girls are not the same in all cultures but rather are very much greater in those societies in which big game are hunted, large animals are kept in herds, or some form of grain agriculture is practiced. The underlying idea, of course, is that these activities, especially the hunting and herding, require men to be self-reliant and independent and perhaps achievement oriented. Working further along the same lines, these authors (1959) have shown that where production is organized in such a way as to yield a substantial surplus of food through more complex forms of coordinated or cooperative work effort, the training of the young is associated with greater pressures towards compliance. Thus, we see that socialization may vary according to economic conditions, even if that variation can be felt only within the biological limits set by sex.

If we translate these results into the terms of the self-system, it will be apparent that we are dealing here with two contrasting models of a culturally defined ego ideal, whose broad outlines are familiar and easily assimilated. In the one case we have the model of the man who is assertive, independent, fearless, perhaps aggressive, competitive, and strongly individuated. At this extreme we find the Sioux or other Plains warrior, whose individuality is shown in a multitude of ways — in his individual record in such things as war and sexual conquest, his particular dress, even in the necessity that he have a distinctive and indeed unique vision which gives him a lifelong and very personal magic. At the other end of the scale we have the Hopi to whom the very idea of competition, aggressiveness, and assertiveness represents the negation of what he is and most wants to be. Such qualities mean being Kahopi, or non-Hopi, and are to be avoided at all costs. They are not only intrinsically undesirable, but they lead to isolation from the community and eventually may produce either that unconscious harm to others which the "two-hearted" generate or an accusation by others that one is engaging in witchcraft.

In each case the relevance of this ego ideal for the adaptation of the individual to the economic and social pattern of his culture is obvious. The Hopi lived in tightly knit, highly interdependent agricultural communities which were severely restricted to their site and heavily dependent on cooperative activity for wresting a livelihood through water control in an arid land. Individuals and families were forced to live in very close proximity for economic and defense purposes. In this setting the assertive, aggressive, individuated male of the Plains, well adapted to the conditions of his life as a warrior-hunter, would have been decidedly a liability to himself, a source of difficulties for others, and a poor support for the community as a whole.

Unfortunately relatively little research is available on large-scale societies to match the impressive efforts of the comparative anthropologists. Admittedly, a strictly comparative approach is more limited when one is dealing with large-scale societies, because the range of variation in social, economic, and political structures is less than among nonliterate societies. Still an effort in proportion to the available range of variation would be most welcome, especially since in large-scale systems the degree of variation within the system is often very great. Such data as we have certainly do indicate some important variation in the values parents emphasize in different modern societies. For example, reported in "Industrial Man" (Inkeles, 1960) were the results obtained in response to an international public opinion poll in which the adults in eleven nations were asked which value it is most important to teach children. The choice was not entirely free but rather was limited to a standard list of five qualities. It is surprising that with so many countries represented the rank order of important qualities was so much alike.

Decency and honesty everywhere represented the qualities; obedience to parents and trust in God, althou competed for second place; ambition was generally quite joyment received very few votes indeed. Whether this sa would apply with a wider range of cultures is not known. purposes it is important to note that the two countries not ly part of the West-European tradition presented the most distin ive responses: Japan named ambition as the most important quality, and Brazil gave trust in God first standing. If we see these values as representing ego ideals, the data indicate that we might find occasional striking differences in the emphasis parents in different modern societies place on the qualities they most want to see in their children. And if we could study how they go about implementing these ideals in their socialization practices, the differences might well be much more striking.

When we deal with contemporary national states, the similarities in their *economic* institutions, especially in the case of the more industrialized countries, are likely to be so great as to leave little room for differences which might affect socialization practices and outcomes. But even in modern societies the degree of variation in *political* structure is sizable, and we can see fairly clear influences of that structure on socialization practices. Interest in this dimension is heightened by the fact that in nonliterate societies differentiation in political systems looms less large and has been little studied by anthropologists. Even here, however, the comparative anthropologists have been ahead of us. Aberle (1961) has suggested that in weak chiefdoms with a low level of political integration there will be less effort to discourage expression of aggression within the group, whereas in the more highly interdependent systems with fuller development of central authority inhibition of aggression within the group will more likely be stressed.

Probably the most dramatic evidence of the impact of the political system on socialization practices is contained in the report of the personal observations Urie Bronfenbrenner (1962) made in his visits to Soviet schools and nurseries. He presents a noteworthy picture of the use of these settings to socialize children in the habits of cooperative work. Even more noteworthy are the efforts of the school to teach children to accept collective responsibility and the attendant practice of everyone's serving as his brother's keeper.

The economic and political differences among cultures and nations should quite reasonably manifest themselves, even if in muted form, in the important economic and political subsystems within the same national state. Here the studies of Miller and Swanson (1958, 1960) are particularly relevant, especially *The Changing American Parent*. In that research Miller and Swanson sought to establish a relationship between the social organization of the fathers' work setting and the socialization practices followed in his home. They distinguished two main types of organization: the "bureaucratic," typified by the large-scale organization whether of production or distribution, and the "entrepreneurial," referring more to the smaller-scale, older type of family business. Their expectation, which they believe to be supported by the data they collected, was that the homes of men in the bureaucratic settings would be permissive, would particularly encourage skills at interpersonal relations and getting along with others, and would show a preoccupation with personal adjustment. The more entrepreneurial work settings were expected to yield homes and parents that were less indulgent and were concerned less about adjustment and more with individual achievement and striving.

Serious questions may be raised as to the extent to which Miller and Swanson were indeed comparing two groups which met their own criteria for defining the nature of the work organization.[17] But a number of other studies leave no doubt that there is an intimate connection between the work experience of the father and the socialization practices he adopts towards his son. The connection has been most precisely measured by McKinley (1964), although with small samples, in research in which he has divided fathers into two categories, according to how much autonomy they have on the job. He found that fathers with little autonomy on the job express more hostility towards their sons, that their wives consider those fathers too rough with their boys, and that the sons themselves more often consider their fathers as "severe." These differences seem to apply at both the middle- and working-class level.

In attempting to show that patterns of economic and political organization have implications for the socialization process, we have perhaps been lax in keeping to the forefront of attention the individual's self-conception and self-esteem. It should, however, be fairly clear that the qualities which the social organization is striving to inculcate are likely to be experienced by the individual as an ego ideal. As such they will serve as a standard he seeks to attain, which will in turn affect the degree of self-esteem he can enjoy. In order to establish the connection more clearly, we have emphasized a kind of "ideal-typical" relationship, in which the social organization seems, in its omniscience, to produce exactly the kind of man it needs and in so doing serves not only its own purposes but simultaneously contributes to the maximum adjustment of the individual. The real situation is very often quite otherwise. Especially under conditions of extreme or rapid social change, the economic and political system may no longer be able to make effective use of the qualities favored by an earlier system and adaptive in it. Erikson (1950)

[17] These doubts are intensified by the fact that a comparable distinction made by Sears, Maccoby, and Levin (1957) did not yield evidence to corroborate the claims of Miller and Swanson.

has described this situation with sympathy and sensitivity in his discussion of the physical, and in a sense psychological, unemployment and unemployability of the Sioux warrior, no longer able to find an acceptable and meaningful social expression for the aggressive fearlessness and sadistic cruelty which were so appropriate to and encouraged by the earlier economic patterns of Sioux life. Much the same pattern, even if less dramatic, is manifested today in many segments of American society experiencing the impact of technological unemployment. A comparable situation may arise in the political realm. The more obedient, compliant, unassertive, subordinate citizen may well suit the purposes of a more traditional political order; but he may not contribute much to a society seeking to develop a more self-reliant, self-directing, participant political and social order.

Even where neither change nor other considerations make the individual unsuited to his social order, it does not follow that the socialization practices which the economic and political system encourage are very adaptive for the individual as a psychic being.[18] Thus, the inhibition of aggression which is necessary to the effective functioning of the economic and political order of a society such as the Hopi, seems, with a high degree of probability, to induce all the nightmares of an intense belief in witchcraft and sorcery. It is questionable that this belief contributes much to the integration of the society.[19] Certainly it is a source of anxiety and torment to the people who live in the community. It is a consequence of social organization apparently neither willed nor actively induced, an incidental even if powerful consequence of a prior commitment to the suppression of aggression, which, given the nature of the human psyche rather than the nature of social structure, seems to have the consequence of producing people prone to believe in witches and sorcerers.

STRATIFICATION: DIFFERENTIAL ALLOCATION OF RESOURCES

In contrasting socialization practices in societies with broadly different systems of economy or polity, we lose sight of the important fact of subsystem differentiation. In particular, large-scale and complex nation-states often include subgroups whose life experience is sharply differentiated from others in a variety of ways. Sex and age may, of course, be the basis for discrimination. Generally, however, the most important differentia-

[18] For examples of research on the socialization of aggression see Berkowitz (1962), Bandura and Walters (1959), and Bandura, Ross, and Ross (1961).

[19] But Beatrice Whiting (1950) does argue that in societies with weak systems of formal control the belief in sorcery and witchcraft may serve as a substitute method of controlling behavior.

tion is expressed in the systems of stratification, usually economic and sometimes based on status and power, and is manifest in concrete form in the differential allocation of resources to families and individuals. Such differential allocation may have profound effects on the individual's self-conception, effects which are evident very early and may be reinforced and emphasized throughout the life cycle.

Most everyone can provide from his own experience illustrations of the differences in self-conception and self-evaluation which are linked to differences in social status; but it is prudent, nevertheless, to present some evidence arising from social research. Three examples, from realms very different but all based on systematic studies with large samples, may serve.

Perhaps the most striking and best documented illustration is the esteem which the community bestows on the occupations which require little education or skill and which involve contact with wastes or otherwise seem to require "lowering" the self. Even in the democratic United States, occupations like garbage collector, street sweeper, and shoe shiner are almost universally regarded as having low standing in the community. They are classified by more than 80 per cent of the population as "poor" or "below average" and achieve scores in the low 30's on a scale ranging from 20 to 100 on which numerous professional occupations make scores of 85 and above. Perhaps most important, we should recognize that there is little defense against this judgment. All groups in the population, *including those who themselves are the incumbents of the low occupations*, agree about the ratings of these and other occupations. Inkeles and Rossi (1956) have shown that much the same ranking of occupations and much the same pattern of agreement with the majority on the part of the incumbents of low-status occupations are found in other countries — indeed, we may say in all countries in the world (Hodge, Treiman, and Rossi, 1966).

The standing of an occupation is an objective fact, but recognizing it need not necessarily be accompanied by a subjective sense of inadequacy. Almond and Verba (1963) studied the subjective sense of what they call "civic competence," the individual's feeling that he understands and can influence the political process in his local community. In all five countries which they studied they found that this sense of subjective competence rose with increasing education. In Mexico, for example, only 25 per cent of those who had no schooling had a sense of civic competence, and the proportion rose steadily to 63 per cent among those with some university training (p. 237).

To offer but one more example, we note in their study of how Americans view their mental health that Gurin (1960) and his collaborators found that the tendency to see oneself as different from others increased with education. Other evidence, incidentally, indicated that to see oneself as different reflected a positive image of oneself. The increase in the frequency with which this positive image was manifested with rising education was most striking among the young. For example, for men between twenty-one and thirty-four the proportion seeing themselves as different rose from 54 for those with grade school education to 84 per cent for those at the college level.

Examples of this sort can be multiplied in great number. The evidence seems overwhelming that almost any measure of self-esteem will show marked differences when subjects are grouped by education, which reflects past differential resource allocation, or by occupation, which reflects current command over social resources and current differences in life experience.

One may certainly attempt to explain the marked differences in self-conception and self-evaluation in the several ranks of the class and ethnic hierarchy without reference to early experience. The man who works at menial tasks is apparently well aware that his job is considered poor and is given no standing in the community. Indeed, he knows that his work is demeaning and that he is avoided and perhaps considered repulsive for doing it. It does not require a caste system to yield a reasonable equivalent of untouchability even in an open society. We have an important dramatic example in O'Neill's *The Hairy Ape*. For those in somewhat more favored positions these reactions may be muted, but they are nevertheless there. The weaker sense of civic competence which characterizes those lower in education and occupational standing may readily be explained by the experiences people in those positions have — experiences which quite reasonably convince them that in fact they do not well understand the complexities of political life and that they are not as effective as others, with more power or other resources, in affecting the course of even local public affairs. The more positive self-image of the well-educated young man in the United States is a reasonable deduction from his pervasive experience of being treated with more respect and more as a distinctive human being.

We should recognize that the explanation of differential self-conceptions offered in the preceding paragraph is still an explanation in terms of socialization, albeit adult socialization. But it is of some interest to inquire whether the differences in self-conception we have noted in fact emerge only after people achieve their adult positions in society or are laid down much earlier in the life cycle. To the extent that a positive self-image is laid down earlier, might it not be a helpful factor in determining the status level which the individual eventually attains?

There is a great deal of research evidence which supports the common observation of everyday life that the children in low-status homes reflect, while still quite young, the less positive image of themselves which society is directly and indirectly expressing toward them in the resources and facilities allocated to them.

The poor and the disadvantaged minorities have less money spent on them for most of the vital services such as schooling, housing, and health.[20] Those who provide these services to the poor often are the less well equipped who have no chance to compete for more favored positions, and they may project their resentment and frustration by directing angry and demeaning behavior towards their lower-status charges.[21]

Handicapped by the deprivations which stem from under-investment, those from disadvantaged backgrounds enter the world under conditions which make it more probable that their early experiences will be experiences of failure. These failures serve to justify further denigration and discrimination, and presumably to reinforce the negative image which both environment and experience have been communicating. Thus, in time, a vicious circle is established from which escape is exceedingly difficult and which can be accommodated mainly by resignation and passivity, which in turn guarantee to maintain the disadvantaged in that position permanently.

Although at the age of six or seven children do not have an accurate picture of the relative prestige of occupations, they do by the time they are fifteen or sixteen. With this information they can begin to assess what their own father's position is and through their connection with him get some sense of how they, themselves, may be valued. Of course, children can rely on many cues other than the parent's occupational standing to judge both other children and themselves in terms of whatever the culture designates as desirable and prestigious.[22] Thus, Bernice Neugarten (1946) reports that in a typical mid-western town the children in grades five and six had a well-developed set of negative images of the children of lower-class background and classified them as poorly dressed, not good looking, unpopular, aggressive, dirty, bad mannered, unfair in play, and as never having a good time. Unhappily, the evidence does not support the notion that "sticks and stones will break my bones, but names will never harm me." The lower-class children themselves agreed in describing other lower-class children in these same terms. We grant that to so classify others of one's kind is not necessarily to so classify oneself, but it comes very close to it. And there is evidence that the poor youngsters do indeed have less positive images not only of those of their class but of themselves individually.

[20] Many details, especially concerning schooling, are given in Sexton (1961).

[21] Evidence with regard to these differences in treatment is not systematic, but there seems good ground for accepting the statement. See Clark (1965).

[22] On these issues see Stendler (1949) and Gold (1958).

The most systematic study we have of self-esteem among youths of high school age is that undertaken by Morris Rosenberg (1965) in the New York high schools.[23] On his measure of self-esteem a high score was obtained by 36 per cent of the lower-class boys, 47 of the middle, and 55 of those he classified as upper class.[24] Although not overpowering, the difference is substantial; and it seems likely that if a wider range of class background had been represented in the sample, the differences would have been greater. It is important to note that Rosenberg's scale did not test an individual's judgment of some objective rating of him by the community but rather sought to tap the presumed end product of such experiences from without, as they might result in an inner feeling about oneself. He therefore included items such as: "At times I think I am no good at all," and "I wish I could have more respect for myself." We could easily get involved in a complex argument about how to measure self-esteem. The legitimacy of such items as Rosenberg used is not in question, but it must be pointed out that they are linked to psychological dispositions of self-examination and guilt which are more inculcated in the middle-class boy. A different sort of item that measured, for example, the sense of mastery, such as "I feel I can manage most situations I must meet in life," or "I think I can go just about anywhere and be accepted and liked," would have shown sharper class differences.

These items suggest a link between the self-conception which the young man acquires according to his family's position in society and his own fate in the occupational world. Upward mobility depends on a number of characteristics, perhaps most important being a high I.Q. But there can be little doubt that it also depends on a set of psychological traits which include high energy, optimism, a sense of mastery, good personal organization, and autonomy. Douvan and Adelson (1958) tested a national sample of American boys and found that those who had upward aspirations differed in many characteristics from those who expressed interest in attaining only those jobs which would keep them on the same level as their fathers or would even place them lower in the status hierarchy. So far as orientation toward the self is concerned, they found the upward-aspiring boys showed a high degree of self-acceptance and confidence in social situations, whereas those who seemed headed for downward mobility were more unsure of themselves and more conflictive in social interaction. Since, as we have seen, these qualities of

[23] Highly relevant questions were asked by Brim *et al.* (1965) in their as yet unpublished study of the effect of testing with almost 10,000 senior high school students.

[24] Rosenberg's (1965) study and others reveal the range of self-esteem estimates to be narrower in the case of girls. The qualities which confer self-respect on a girl can be more easily attained in spite of disadvantages in education or income.

self-acceptance and self-confidence are more common in boys from middle- and upper-class families, these boys can be expected, on the average, to add this psychological advantage to the others they bring to the mobility race.

In presenting evidence concerning differences in the self-concept and self-esteem which characterize individuals of different statuses, we have hardly tried to stack the cards in favor of our point. To do that would have been easy, however, merely by selecting some exploited and oppressed minority group, the most obvious being the lower-class Negro from the southern rural community or northern urban slum. The fact that such large differences as we have observed may be found in the more benign atmosphere of an average mid-western town or in relatively properous New York State makes all the more reasonable the general proposition that the socialization process early impresses on young people an image of themselves in accord with their position in the status hierarchy and that that image is regularly reinforced at each step in the life cycle.

There are, of course, compensations. A boy who excels at sports may rise to the top in popularity and on the strength of this develop a much more positive image of himself. But the effects are not likely to be lasting if he cannot convert this advantage into a more permanent prestige income by using it as a basis for getting more education and a better job. How far much of the bravado of lower-class slum boys — their wild acting out, sexual escapades, and destruction of property — may be compensation for their feeling that they are no good, disvalued, powerless, in short "punks," is an interesting question which cannot be firmly answered on the basis of current research reports. But it seems a reasonable conclusion and deserves further study.

There are also defenses against the negative image of oneself which the stratification system induces. The poor are often cut off from media of communication and contact to a degree which may help to insulate them from too regularly facing concrete manifestations of the low esteem in which they are held. The rules of polite society contribute to help maintain this conspiracy, unless the cook overhears in the kitchen or the handyman in the yard what is being said in the living room about them and "their kind." Defense against a bad image can also be secured through the time-honored device of feeling one is doing the best one can given one's station in life, especially if one feels that one's betters cannot always make the same claim. Finally, there are the possibilities of substitute gratification in drinking, sex, or violence and the related escape into the symptomatology of mental illness. Whether any of this really helps, it is not the same thing as being given, or having restored to one, a clear sense of a valued identity, some confidence in one's capacity, and enough self-esteem to sustain oneself for the present and to prepare for the future.[25] One of our main concerns in our plans for improving the socialization process and for resocialization [26] might well be to find a means whereby we could prevent or at least mute the insidious consequences of our system of stratification so that all young people could start out with a positive self-image.

ECOLOGICAL FACTORS IN SOCIALIZATION

By ecology we mean the density of population in the home and surrounding areas, the form and arrangement of houses in the community, and the amount and type of space available to the individual and his family. This is an aspect of socialization which has not been much studied, although French research on socialization reflects some interest in the problem (Chombart de Lauwe, 1959), and Whiting has considered some of the correlates of the shape of house in his comparative studies of nonliterate societies.

The household and the neighborhood probably form the very first distinctively social point of identification, coming as soon as and perhaps before sex identity. It is in relation to his house or family that the child will first be identified and recognized by outsiders; referred to in generic terms; and treated, accepted, or shooed away, depending on the relation of surrounding households and families to his own. Therefore, we must assume that at this point the first sense of group membership as an aspect of the self is established. How this sense of membership grows, is extended, transferred to other settings, and developed or transformed has not been studied, although the subject is beginning to capture the imagination of architects and city planners. It seems likely, however, that later orientations to group membership should be much influenced by this early example. One's sense of being a member of a large and open community or, conversely, the tendency to define oneself in very narrow terms without the ability to conceive of a broader membership unit encompassing large numbers should depend in part on socialization experiences in childhood. We might ask whether the child is free to be only in his mother's or parents' room, or may freely wander through all the rooms of a house or compound, especially if different families are in the other rooms; whether the family area is enclosed by a wall; whether the immediate compound is also so enclosed, and so on. Despite the danger inherent in such analogies one cannot help but wonder about the socialization antecedents of the physical openness of the communities of the American West as compared to those of the East,

[25] These themes are considered further in M. Brewster Smith's Chapter Seven on competence.

[26] See Chapter Eight by Ronald Lippitt in this volume.

the latter being the home of the saying: "Good fences make good neighbors." One is tempted, similarly, to think of differences at the national level — of the walled compounds of Spain, the hedges of England and France, and the emphasis on maintaining the open, unfenced quality of many suburban American towns.

Ecological patterns may also affect the nature of one's identification as a member of a larger community. Individuals who grow up in highly segregated communities, especially if the relationship between subcommunities is competitive or exploitative, are likely to develop a stronger sense of ingroup membership and to base their definition of themselves on the differences rather than the similarities between themselves and other groups. On the other hand, where minorities are not discriminated against we are likely to see an erosion of distinctive identities and the transfer of the individual's sense of group membership to some larger group or entity. Later in the life cycle, the ability of adults to take on new, broader memberships or to cooperate effectively in larger community ventures may be enhanced or hampered by the degree of sharpness and the rigidity of the sense of distinctive membership laid down in childhood. The cross-national studies of the conceptions of self in children found marked national differences in the ability of children to think of those from other nations as similar to themselves: the Brazilian, Japanese, and Bantu saw little or no similarity, whereas the children of Israel, France, Canada, and the United States easily saw similarity between themselves and children from other countries. The explanation of these findings is no doubt complex. Lambert and Klineberg (1966) suggest that the second group of nations, having been reception centers for large-scale immigration, provide settings in which children may more easily learn about basic human similarities among peoples who otherwise differ in ethnic background.

In addition to the diversity of the population, of course, a good deal depends on the pattern of relations among the groups and the ideology which governs intergroup relations. It is not likely that the southern, white youngster's familiarity with Negro children in the deep South of the United States has increased his awareness of the Negro's basic human similarity. The pattern of relations between groups may also affect the degree of self-esteem the individual will develop. Rosenberg's (1965) study of high school students in New York led him to conclude that adolescents who were raised in a "dissonant" religious context — meaning essentially minority status when a religious difference exists in relation to the majority — generally had lower self-esteem. The more dissonant the context, the lower the esteem (p. 78). The differences in self-esteem were, however, not great, suggesting that minority status also does something to draw the individuals in any group together, thus acting to strengthen self-esteem.

The effects of ecology on the development of an individual's self-conception are likely to depend greatly on interaction with other influences. Living in a fairly dense apartment unit is likely to be quite different in its impact on individuation if the families inhabiting it are professional, middle-class or an ethnic and racial minority of working-class families. The same may be said of families raised in relative isolation, such as individual homestead farm families. In a comparison of French urban and farm families Lanneau and Malrieu (1957) especially note the slow social awakening of the rural children, their fear and suspicion of strangers, and their lack of experience with diverse perspectives. This much may perhaps be attributed to isolation. But their sensory motor functions are highly developed, whereas their imagination, language, and intellectual functions are underdeveloped. This should be attributed not solely to isolation but also to the occupation of their parents as farmers. Presumably, the children of a professional in the same isolation would show the reverse balance of skills. Finally, Lanneau and Malrieu note that in the farm families children grow up in an atmosphere of warm affectivity and with a strong sense of security, which again may be cultural or may be related to an ecological factor — since in French farm families the grandparents live in the home and apparently have a tendency to overindulge their grandchildren.

The density of population should have some effect on the ability of the individual to develop a sharply differentiated impression of himself — of his uniqueness or distinctiveness. In part this is a reasonable assumption simply because the development and maintenance of a distinctive identity depends on often being treated as distinct from others, a circumstance which becomes increasingly difficult as family size and general density increases. Whiting (1961) reports a very strong association between the severity of aggression training and household type, with 92 per cent of the extended family cultures severe as against only 25 per cent severe in nuclear households. Density and extension are also likely correlated. It seems reasonable to assume that density also bears a fairly direct relation to the need to control aggression. Its probable effect on the self-concept is not obvious, but possibly the sense of personal distinctiveness would be muted in those socialized to keep their aggression under extremely tight control even within the family.

Elder and Bowerman (1963) note that in the United States authoritarian and bureaucratic family practices increase with increased family size regardless of social class. This may be related to other pressures to "know your place"; that is, to avoid asserting oneself, hence to avoid marked manifestations of individuality. Developing a distinctive impression of oneself also depends on having a place and objects which are uniquely one's own, a circumstance which becomes progressively more difficult as density increases, all other factors being equal. The statement "I am nothing" or "I am nobody," so often heard in traditional rural settings, especially in Asia, may have some of its roots in this condition. One often notes the contrast between the self-confidence and aggressive individuality of the man living on the thinly populated frontier and his own countrymen in the more settled and densely populated interior. Density will also have an effect on modeling. If there is great density of population, peers rather than adults are more likely to be the most important models available a good deal of the time. Rather than the same parent or set of parents the child will daily confront a variety of relatives and other adults acting *in loco parentis*. Again this would lead us to expect a more diffuse, less individuated or distinctive self-conception. Some of these ideas can be tested by comparing families of different size in our society (see Clausen, 1966), but a more systematic test would require work in cross-cultural settings which is yet to be done. In making such studies, it would be important to explore more precisely distinctions which the above discussion necessarily tends to blur. For example, we should not be so culture-bound as to assume that the rural family always lives in relative isolation on the family farm. In many parts of Asia the population density in farming villages approaches or exceeds that commonly met in urban conglomerations. The presence or absence of age grading will also clearly influence the degree to which adults or peers serve as role models because in an age-graded society one spends the largest part of one's time, and is expected to have greatest solidarity, with one's age-mates.[27] The same degree of density may, therefore, mean more contact with either adults or peers, depending on other aspects of the social structure.

Ecological factors may also play a role in the time, vigor, and content of sex differentiation. A great deal of emphasis has recently been given to the alleged effect on identity which follows from youth's growing up in "father-absent" or "female-centered" homes. Both evidence from nonliterate societies (Burton and Whiting, 1961) and from large-scale, modern societies is used to suggest that the boy who grows up in such a household lacks a clear male figure with which to identify, later becomes panicked by fear of being overwhelmed by his female identification, and therefore acts in an excessively aggressive, assertive, and often antisocial manner to prove his maleness to himself and others.[28] Without undertaking so elaborate a psychoanalytic analysis, we can easily acknowledge that the sense of one's sex identity may be influenced by physical arrangements such as the segregation of young boys and girls; the existence of special houses for women during menstruation and after childbirth; and the degree of specialization by sex in domestic, economic, religious, political, leisure, and communal activities. In our own time

[27] See Eisenstadt (1956).

[28] For a general review of parent absence see Yarrow (1964).

and place the pervasive tendency toward erosion of the differentiation of role by sex and the almost complete absence of any strict segregation of the sexes along these lines of activity may possibly be an important factor in producing the lack of a sharp sense of sexual identity, especially among males, which is often thought to be widespread in the United States.

THE EFFECT OF ROLE MODELS

One of the indirect effects of the social system on the socialization process is achieved through the models it makes available. The punishment-and-reward theories of socialization, which dominated research in the field for over two decades, have been gradually challenged by research evidence that the older and more homely ideas of identification and imitation, now dressed up with the modern label "modeling," play a great role in the socialization process. It is clear that to an important degree we become what we see (Bandura and Walters, 1963); consequently, the challenge to society is very great indeed, since modeling implies that children will be influenced not only by being told what they should be like but by observing what important people in their environment are actually like.

The problem of modeling recalls some issues we have already encountered in considering ecological influences. We may ask: What will be the consequences of having one or a few simple and clear-cut models available as against having a wide range of such models at hand? Assuming the models are at all appropriate for the sex and culture of the individual, a clearer sense of one's identity is likely to be the outcome where the models are fewer. Where they are multiple, however, the individual may internalize the kind of variety which gives more richness and flexibility to the self, even though at the same time the difficulty of integrating this more complex set of selves is increased. We might therefore expect important differences in the definiteness and the integration of the self-conception between boys raised in rural as opposed to urban areas. There might also be important social class differences, although it is not clear whether it is more the middle- or the lower-class environment which provides the greater range of role models.

Of course, models do not have an effect simply by being there. To have an impact on the shaping of the young, the role model must have substantial and intimate contact with the socializee. Data on juvenile delinquents indicate that the absence of the parent, especially the father, is much more common in their background. Even when the father is not away, he more often has less contact with the family because of drunkenness or drug addiction, difficulties with the law, an itinerant search for work, and the like (Glueck, 1950). Quite apart from these more dramatic manifestations, a host of evidence indicates that lower-class fathers, by leaving their wives to the affairs of the home while they go off to other amusements, tend to have less involvement with their families than middle-class fathers.[29] The consequence of this should be that boys from this background must find their models largely outside the home. In public places in lower-class neighborhoods the boys are more likely to find criminal and delinquent models, and even those who are not of this character but serve as models are pushed by the lower-class culture to assert their toughness and manliness in much more exaggerated fashion than they would in their own homes. This may play an important role in influencing lower-class youths to act out in exaggeratedly violent ways against society's rules. Perhaps these cultural models are more influential in producing youthful aggression than is the alleged panic over possible identification with the female role.

We have touched here on the problem of consistency in models. Whether the diversity of models in the middle class is greater or not, it seems clear that they are more nearly *consistent*, and in a number of ways. Middle-class parents are more likely to be consistent in their individual handling of the child over time; they are more likely to be consistent one with the other in the standards they present to and uphold to the child, and probably in their public behavior as well; and they are more likely to represent and uphold principles and modes of acting which are also stressed by the school and other community agents. This consistency should not only make the impact of the models greater but should also enable the young person to integrate the models into one internal standard without excessive conflict caused by too dissonant an internal dialogue. He may not know whether he is going to be doctor, lawyer, soldier, or statesman, nor whether he will live in New York, Chicago, New Orleans, or Los Angeles; but whichever and wherever he may be, the middle-class boy has a very clear standard of the kind of person he will, in general, be.

The clarity of the self-image of the middle-class child will probably be accompanied by a higher level of self-esteem, that is, of satisfaction in what he is or may become. The Gluecks (1950) report marked differences in the proportion of delinquent and non-delinquent boys who feel that their father is an object worthy of emulation. McKinley (Table 42) reports striking differences of the same sort across the status hierarchy, with 100 per cent of upper-class boys admiring the father more than the mother, and only 44 per cent making this choice in the lowest class.[30] Many factors undoubtedly enter into this judgment of fathers by sons. Surely not the least is the differential rating which society as-

[29] See McKinley (1964) and Komarovsky (1964).
[30] Corroborating evidence will be found in Bandura (1960, 1961) and Gold (1961).

signs the low-status occupations, a rating scheme which is apparently quite well known to children at the age of fifteen. Should the child not know the rating, he can still draw his own conclusions from the evidence of his daily life. We need only imagine the difference in the impression a working-class as against a middle-class boy will get of what it means to be his father, especially if the father is a professional, when he visits him at his work or goes on the rounds with him in pursuit of some public benefit or the doing of some personal chore. He will observe great differences in how much his father is recognized by others, in the signs of deference and respect he is shown, the power he seems to be able to bring to bear, the mastery with which he handles situations. The desire to be like the father should be very different in the two cases; and quite apart from desire, the high-status model, getting more attention, may be copied more.

But desire or no, the theory of identification and a good deal of evidence suggest that a boy will end up more like his father than anyone else. And if he is internalizing a disvalued object, it must have powerful effects on the relative integration of his personal system as well as strong effects on his estimation of his own qualities and worth.

CONCLUSION

In the period between 1940 and 1960 the study of child socialization was given a firm foundation in empirical research. Developmental problems were in the forefront of attention, a state of affairs which led to relative concentration on the purely intrafamilial and interpersonal aspects of the parent-child relation. Increasingly social class and occupational differences were introduced as control variables, but the focus of research attention was still on the individual parent as socialization agent. Many of the developmental issues widely studied, such as the control of aggression and the emergence of morality, certainly seemed to have major implications for adult personality. But there was little systematic testing of the common assumption that the outcomes of childhood socialization accurately foreshadowed the personality of the adult.

We have proposed that there is a need to supplement the research experience of the decades from 1940 into the 1960's by systematically considering a whole family of variables which have not received sufficient attention in our studies of child socialization. First, we have urged that our study of the interaction of parent and child be broadened to give full weight to the interest of society in, and the influence it exerts on, the socialization process. Second, we have argued that our research should focus not only on how the child or adolescent develops his personality but also on how he learns the content of the significant social roles he will be called on to play as an adult. These suggestions are not meant to lead to replacement of a productive research tradition but rather to its supplementation and augmentation.

REFERENCES

Aberle, D. F. Culture and socialization. In F. L. K. Hsu (Ed.), *Psychological Anthropology: Approaches to Culture and Personality*. Homewood, Ill.: The Dorsey Press, 1961. Pp. 381–99.

Aberle, D. F. *The Psychosocial Analysis of a Hopi Life-History*. Berkeley: University of California Press, 1951.

Aberle, D. F. Shared values in complex societies. *American Sociological Review*, 1950, *15*, No. 4, 495–502.

Aberle, D. F., and Naegele, K. D. Middle class fathers' occupational role and attitudes toward children. *American Journal of Orthopsychiatry*, 1952, 22, 366–78.

Aberle, D. F., *et al.* The functional prerequisites of a society. *Ethics*, 1950, 60, No. 2, 100–111.

Almond, G., and Verba, S. *The Civic Culture: Political Attitudes and Democracy in Five Nations*. Princeton, N.J.: Princeton University Press, 1963.

Bandura, A., Ross, Dorothea, and Ross, Sheila A. Transmission of agression through imitation of aggressive models. *Journal of Abnormal and Social Psychology*, 1961, *63*, 575–82.

Bandura, A., and Walters, R. H. *Adolescent Agression*. New York: The Ronald Press Co., 1959.

Bandura, A., and Walters, R. H. *Social Learning and Personality Development*. New York: Holt, Rinehart & Winston, 1963.

Banfield, E. C., with Banfield, Laura F. *The Moral Basis of a Backward Society*. Research Center in Economic Development and Cultural Change, The University of Chicago. Glencoe, Ill.: The Free Press, 1958.

Barry, H., III, Bacon, Margaret K., and Child, I. L. A cross-cultural survey of some sex differences in socialization. *Journal of Abnormal and Social Psychology*, 1957, *55*, 327–32.

Barry, H., III, Child, I. L., and Bacon, Margaret K. Relation of child training to subsistence economy. *American Anthropologist*, 1959, *61*, 51–63.

Benedict, Ruth. Continuities and discontinuities in cultural conditioning. *Psychiatry*, 1938, *1*, 161–67.

Berkowitz, L. *Aggression: A Social Psychological Analysis*. New York: McGraw-Hill Book Co., 1962.

Berliner, J. S. *Factory and Manager in the USSR*. Cambridge, Mass.: Harvard University Press, 1957.

Bernstein, B. Language and social class (Research Note). *British Journal of Sociology*, September 1960, *11*, No. 3, 271–76.

Bernstein, B. Some sociological determinants of perception: an enquiry into subcultural differences. *British Journal of Sociology*, June 1958, 9, No. 2, 159–74.

Bieri, J., and Lobeck, Robin. Self-concept differences in relation to identification, religion, and social class. *Journal of Abnormal and Social Psychology*, 1961, 62, No. 1, 94–98.

Brim, O. G., Jr. *Education for Child Rearing*. New York: Russell Sage Foundation, 1959. First Free Press Paperback Edition, 1965.

Brim, O. G., Jr., and Wheeler, S. *Socialization after Childhood: Two Essays*. New York: John Wiley & Sons, 1966.

Bronfenbrenner, U. Socialization and social class through time and space. In Eleanor E. Maccoby, T. M. Newcomb, and E. L. Hartley (Eds.), *Readings in Social Psychology*. 3rd ed. New York: Holt, 1958. Pp. 400–425.

Bronfenbrenner, U. Soviet methods of character education: some implications for research. *American Psychologist*, 1962, *17*, No. 8, 550–64.

Burchinal, L. G. Sources and adequacy of sex knowledge among Iowa high school girls. *Marriage and Family Living*, August 1960, 22, No. 3, 268–69.

Burton, R. V., and Whiting, J. W. M. The absent father and cross-sex identity. *Merrill-Palmer Quarterly*, 1961, 7, No. 20, 85–95.

Butman, J. W., and Kamm, J. A. The social, psychological, and behavioral world of the teen-age girl. Institute for Social Research, University of Michigan, 1965. (Unpublished)

Child, I. L. Socialization. In G. Lindzey (Ed.), *Handbook of Social Psychology*. Cambridge, Mass.: Addison-Wesley Publishing Co., 1954. Pp. 655–92.

Chombart de Lauwe, P. H. *Psychopathologie sociale de l'enfant inadapte*. Paris: Centre National de la Recherche Scientifique, 1959.

Clark, K. B. *Dark Ghetto: Dilemmas of Social Power*. New York: Harper & Row, 1965. Especially Chap. 6.

Clausen, J. A. Family structure, socialization, and personality. In Lois W. Hoffman and M. L. Hoffman (Eds.), *Review of Child Development Research*. Vol. 2. New York: Russell Sage Foundation, 1966. Pp. 1–53.

Cohen, Y. A. *The Transition from Childhood to Adolescence: Cross-cultural Studies of Initiation Ceremonies, Legal Systems, and Incest Taboos*. Chicago: Aldine Publishing Co., 1964.

Douvan, Elizabeth, and Adelson, J. The psychodynamics of social mobility in adolescent boys. *Journal of Abnormal and Social Psychology*, 1958, 56, 31–44.

Easton, D., and Dennis, J. The child's image of government. *Annals of the American Academy of Political and Social Science*, September 1965, 40–57.

Easton, D., and Hess, R. D. The child's political world. *Midwestern Journal of Political Science*, August 1962, 6, No. 2, 229–46.

Edelston, H. *Problems of Adolescents*. New York: Philosophical Library, 1956.

Eisenstadt, S. N. *From Generation to Generation; Age Groups and Social Structure*. Glencoe, Ill.: The Free Press, 1956.

Elder, G. H., Jr., and Bowerman, C. E. Family structure and child-rearing patterns: the effect of family size and sex composition. *American Sociological Review*, 1963, 28, 891–905.

Elkins, S. M. Slavery and personality. In B. Kaplan (Ed.), *Studying Personality Cross-culturally*. Evanston, Ill.: Row, Peterson & Co., 1961. Pp. 243–67.

Elkins, S. M. *Slavery, a Problem in American Institutional and Intellectual Life*. New York: Universal Library, 1963.

Erikson, E. H. *Childhood and Society*. New York: W. W. Norton & Co., 1950.

Festinger, L., and Allen, V. *Conflict, Decision, and Dissonance*. Stanford: Stanford University Press, 1964.

Glueck, S., and Glueck, E. *Unraveling Juvenile Delinquency*. New York: Commonwealth Fund, 1950.

Gold, M. Power in the classroom. *Sociometry*, 1958, *21*, No. 1, 50–60.

Gold, M. Social class, family structure and identity process related to juvenile delinquency. Symposium on Personal-Social World of Lower Class Children,

American Psychological Association Meeting, New York, September 1961. (Unpublished)

Goodenough, W. H. Componential analysis and the study of meaning. *Language*, January–March 1956, 32, No. 1, 195–216.

Goodenough, W. H. Componential analysis of Könkämä Lapp kinship terminology. In W. H. Goodenough (Ed.), *Explorations in Cultural Anthropology*. New York: McGraw-Hill Book Co., 1964. Pp. 221–38.

Gorer, G., and Rickman, J. *The People of Great Russia — a Psychological Study*. London: Cresset Press, 1949.

Greenstein, F. I. The benevolent leader: children's images of political authority. *American Political Science Review*, 1960, *54*, 934–43.

Greenstein, F. I. More on children's images of the president. *Public Opinion Quarterly*, Winter 1961, *25*, No. 4, 648–54.

Gurin, G.,. Veroff, J., and Feld, Sheila. *Americans View Their Mental Health: A Nationwide Interview Survey*. New York: Basic Books, 1960.

Herber, H. L. Developing study skills in secondary schools. *Perspectives in Reading*, No. 4. Newark, Del.: International Reading Association, 1965.

Herzog, Herta. What do we really know about daytime serial listeners? In P. Lazarsfeld and F. N. Stanton, *Radio Research, 1942–1943*. New York: Duell, Sloan & Pearce, 1944. Pp. 3–33.

Hess, R. D., and Easton, D. The child's changing image of the president. *Public Opinion Quarterly*, 1960, *24*, 632–44.

Hodge, R. W., Siegel, P. M., and Rossi, P. H. Occupational prestige in the United States: 1925–1963. In R. Bendix and S. M. Lipset (Eds.), *Class, Status, and Power: Social Stratification in Comparative Perspective*. 2nd ed. New York: The Free Press, 1966. London: Collier-Macmillan Ltd., 1966. Pp. 322–34.

Hodge, R. W., Treiman, D. J., and Rossi, P. H. A comparative study of occupational prestige. In R. Bendix and S. M. Lipset (Eds.), *Class, Status, and Power: Social Stratification in Comparative Perspective*. New York: The Free Press, 1966. London: Collier-Macmillan Ltd., 1966. Pp. 309–21.

Hoffman, M. Child-rearing practices and moral development: generalizations from empirical research. *Child Development*, June 1963a, *34*, No. 2, 295–318.

Hoffman, M. Parent discipline and the child's consideration for others. *Child Development*, September 1963b, *34*, No. 3, 573–88.

Inkeles, A. Industrial man: the relation of status to experience, perception, and value. *American Journal of Sociology*, July 1960, *66*, No. 1, 1–31.

Inkeles, A. National character and modern political systems. In F. L. K. Hsu (Ed.), *Psychological Anthropology: Approaches to Culture and Personality*. Homewood, Ill.: The Dorsey Press, 1961. Pp. 172–208.

Inkeles, A. Psychoanalysis and sociology. In S. Hook (Ed.), *Psychoanalysis, Scientific Method and Philosophy*. New York: New York University Press, 1959. Pp. 117–29.

Inkeles, A. Social structure and the socialization of competence. *Harvard Educational Review*, Summer 1966, *36*, No. 3, 265–83.

Inkeles, A. Sociology and psychology. In S. Koch (Ed.), *Psychology: A Study of a Science*. New York: McGraw-Hill Book Co., 1963. Pp. 317–87.

Inkeles, A., Hanfman, Eugenia, and Beier, Helen. Modal personality and adjustment to the Soviet socio-political system. *Human Relations*, 1958, *11*, No. 1, 3–22.

Inkeles, A., and Levinson, D. National character: the study of modal personality and sociocultural systems. In G. Lindzey (Ed.), *Handbook of Social Psychology*. Vol. 2. Cambridge, Mass.: Addison-Wesley Publishing Co., 1954. Pp. 977–1020.

Inkeles, A., and Levinson, D. The personal system and the socio-cultural system in large-scale organizations. *Sociometry*, June 1963, *26*, No. 2, 217–29.

Inkeles, A., and Rossi, P. H. Multidimensional ratings of occupations. *Sociometry*, September 1957, *20*, No. 3, 234–51.

Inkeles, A., and Rossi, P. H. National comparisons of occupational prestige. *American Journal of Sociology*, January 1956, *61*, No. 4, 329–39.

John, V. P. The intellectual development of slum children: some preliminary findings. *American Journal of Orthopsychiatry*, October 1963, *33*, No. 5, 813–22.

John, V. P., and Goldstein, L. The social context of language acquisition. *Merrill-Palmer Quarterly*, July 1964, *10*, No. 3, 265–75.

Kardiner, A. *The Individual and His Society: The Psychodynamics of Primitive Social Organization*. New York: Columbia University Press, 1939.

Kohlberg, L. Development of moral character and moral ideology. In M. L. Hoffman and Lois W. Hoffman (Eds.), *Review of Child Development Research*. Vol. 1. New York: Russell Sage Foundation, 1964. Pp. 383–431.

Kohlberg, L. Moral development and identification. In H. W. Stevenson (Ed.), *Child Psychology*. The Sixty-second Yearbook of the National Society for the Study of Education, Part I. Chicago: NSSE, 1963; distributed by The University of Chicago Press. Pp. 277–332.

Komarovsky, Mirra, with Philips, Jane H. *Blue-Collar Marriage*. New York: Random House, 1964.

Kranyik, R., and Shankman, Florence V. *How to Teach Study Skills*. Englewood Cliffs, N.J.: Teachers Practical Press, 1963.

Lambert, W. E., and Klineberg, O. *Children's Views of Foreign Peoples; A Cross-national Study*. New York: Appleton-Century-Crofts, 1966.

Lanneau, G., and Malrieu, P. Enquête sur l'éducation en milieu rural et en milieu urbain. *Enfance*, September–October 1957, *4*, 465–85.

Larrue, J., and Malrieu, P. Types d'éducation a la ville. *In* Enquête sur l'éducation à la ville et à la campagne. *Enfance*, January–February 1958, *1*, 31–62.

Levy, M. J. *The Structure of Society*. Princeton, N.J.: Princeton University Press, 1952.

Lifton, R. J. *Thought Reform and the Psychology of Totalism: A Study of Brainwashing in China*. New York: W. W. Norton & Co., 1961.

Lippitt, R., and Gold, M. Classroom social structure as a mental health problem. *Social Issues*, 1959, *15*, No. 1, 40–49.

Lynch, K. *The Image of the City*. Cambridge, Mass.: Technology Press, 1960.

Lynd, R. S., and Lynd, Helen M. *Middletown in Transition; A Study in Cultural Conflicts*. New York: Harcourt, Brace & Co., 1937.

Maccoby, Eleanor E. The choice of variables in the study of socialization. *Sociometry*, 1961, 357–71.

Maccoby, Eleanor E. (Ed.) *The Development of Sex Differences*. Stanford: Stanford University Press, 1966.

Matza, D. *Delinquency and Drift*. New York: John Wiley & Sons, 1964.

McClelland, D. C. *The Achieving Society*. Princeton, N.J.: D. Van Nostrand Co., 1961.

McClelland, D. C., Atkinson, J. W., Clark, R. A., and Lowell, E. L. *The Achievement Motive*. New York: Appleton-Century-Crofts, 1953.

McKinley, D. G. *Social Class and Family Life*. New York: Free Press of Glencoe, 1964.

Miller, D. R. The study of social relationship: situation, identity, and social interaction. In S. Koch (Ed.), *Psychology: A Study of a Science*. Vol. 5. New York: McGraw-Hill Book Co., 1963. Pp. 639–737.

Miller, D. R., and Swanson, G. E. *The Changing American Parent; A Study in the Detroit Area*. New York: John Wiley & Sons, 1958.

Miller, D. R., and Swanson, G. E. *Inner Conflict and Defense*. New York: Holt, Rinehart & Co., 1960.

Neugarten, Bernice. Social class and friendship among school children. *American Journal of Sociology*, 1946, *51*, No. 4, 305–13.

Oetzel, Roberta M. *Selected Bibliography on Sex Differences*. Sponsored by Social Science Research Council Committee on Socialization and Social Structure, August 1962. Reprinted in Eleanor E. Maccoby (Ed.), *The Development of Sex Differences*. Stanford: Stanford University Press, 1966. Pp. 221–321.

Reckless, W. C., Dinitz, S., and Murray, Ellen. The "good" boy in a high delinquency area. *Journal of Criminal Law, Criminology and Police Science*, August 1957, *48*, 18–26.

Reckless, W. C., Dinitz, S., and Murray, Ellen. Self concept as an insulator against delinquency. *American Sociological Review*, December 1956, *21*, 744–46.

Rosenberg, M. *Society and the Adolescent Self-image*. Princeton, N.J.: Princeton University Press, 1965.

Scarpitti, F., Murray, Ellen, Dinitz, S., and Reckless, W. C. The "good" boy in a high delinquency area: four years later. *American Sociological Review*, August 1960, *25*, 555–58.

Schein, E. H., with Schñeier, Inge, and Basker, C. H. *Coercive Persuasion: A Socio-psychological Analysis of the "Brainwashing" of American Civilian Prisoners by the Chinese Communists*. New York: W. W. Norton & Co., 1961.

Sears, R. R., Maccoby, Eleanor E., and Levin, H. *Patterns of Child Rearing*. Evanston, Ill.: Row, Peterson & Co., 1957.

Sexton, P. C. *Education and Income: Inequalities in Our Public Schools*. New York: The Viking Press, 1961.

Siller, J. Socioeconomic status and conceptual thinking. *Journal of Abnormal and Social Psychology*, November 1957, *55*, No. 3, 365–72.

Simmons, L. W. (Ed.) *Sun Chief: The Autobiography of a Hopi Indian*. New Haven, Conn.: Yale University Press, 1942.

Spiro, M., and D'Andrade, R. G. A cross-cultural study of some supernatural beliefs. *American Anthropologist*, 1958, *60*, 456–66.

Stendler, Celia B. *Children of Brasstown*. University of Illinois Bulletin, 1949, *46*, No. 59. Bureau of Research and Service, College of Education, University of Illinois, Urbana, Ill.

Stonequist, E. V. *The Marginal Man: A Study in Personality and Culture Conflict*. New York: Charles Scribner's Sons, 1937.

Strang, Ruth M. *Guided Study and Homework*. What Research Says to the Teacher, No. 8. Department of Classroom Teachers, American Educational Research Association of the National Education Association, July 1955.

Strauss, M. A. Work roles and financial responsibility in the socialization of farm, fringe, and town boys. *Rural Sociology*, 1962, *27*, No. 3, 257–74.

Tuma, E., and Livson, N. Family socioeconomic status and adolescent attitudes to authority. *Child Development*, 1960, *31*, 387–99.

Veenker, H. (Ed.) *Synthesis of Research in Selected Areas of Health Instruction.* The School Health Education Study sponsored by the Samuel Bronfman Foundation, New York, 1963.

Wallace, A. F. *Culture and Personality.* New York: Random House, 1961.

Weeks, H. A. *Youthful Offenders at Highfields: An Evaluation of the Effects of the Short-Term Treatment of Delinquent Boys.* Ann Arbor: The University of Michigan Press, 1958.

Wheeler, S. Socialization in correctional communities. *American Sociological Review*, October 1961, *26*, No. 5, 697–719.

Whiting, Beatrice B. A cross-cultural study of sorcery and social control. In *Paiute Sorcery.* Publications in Anthropology, No. 15. New York: Viking Fund, 1950.

Whiting, J. W. M. Socialization process and personality. In F. L. K. Hsu (Ed.), *Psychological Anthropology: Approaches to Culture and Personality.* Homewood, Ill.: The Dorsey Press, 1961. Pp. 355–80.

Wilensky, H. L. The uneven distribution of leisure: the impact of economic growth on "free time." *Social Problems*, Summer 1961, *9*, No. 1, 32–56.

Wylie, R. C. *The Self Concept: A Critical Survey of Pertinent Research Literature.* Lincoln: University of Nebraska Press, 1961.

Yarrow, L. J. Separation from parents during early childhood. In M. L. Hoffman and Lois W. Hoffman (Eds.), *Review of Child Development Research.* Vol. 1. New York: Russell Sage Foundation, 1964. Pp. 89–136.

Zelditch, M. Role differentiation in the nuclear family: a comparative study. In T. Parsons and R. F. Bales (Eds.), *Family, Socialization and Interaction Processes.* Glencoe, Ill.: The Free Press, 1955. Pp. 307–51.

JOHN A. CLAUSEN

FOUR Perspectives on Childhood Socialization

CONTENTS

The previous chapter has emphasized the demands that societies place upon the developing child in seeking to produce the characteristics desired in adults. Beyond this, it has discussed types of direct socialization efforts by which desired outcomes are secured and the indirect ways in which features of social organization influence the socialization process. The present chapter focuses on the more intimate details of childhood socialization within the smaller social circles in which that socialization is carried out. Our purpose will be both to examine from the varied viewpoints of participants and observers the manifold influences that impinge upon the child and to note the ways in which the child acts upon his social environment in the family, the school, and the peer group. We shall stress the cumulative, processual nature of socialization, emphasizing aspects that have been relatively neglected and offering a few sensitizing concepts and propositions.

What has been termed the "widening world of childhood" spirals out from the parental home. Initially, it is the parent whose performance in behalf of the child must meet the standards set by the society; few demands can be made of the helpless infant. Gradually responsibilities are shifted and shared, and the process of childhood socialization may be viewed as the accomplishment of a series of tasks to be carried out jointly by socialization agents and children.

At no later period of life does growth occur as rapidly as it does in infancy, and this seems equally true of learning. The spectacular leaps in mastery of physical and vocal skills define the end of infancy. The helpless human infant has inborn potentials that constitute part of human nature, but another part must be supplied by society. Beyond the dependence of his very survival upon protective and nurturing behavior from other humans, the infant must be incorporated into group life in order to realize his potential for speech and selfhood. One need not postulate a specific social instinct in support of the proposition that man

In addition to my debt to fellow committee members, I wish to acknowledge here the helpful comments and suggestions of Norma Haan, Bernice Neugarten, and Ralph H. Turner.

is inherently social. His biological nature is itself a basis for an enduring tie with his mother, or a mother substitute, as the work of Bowlby (1958) and others has clearly shown.

THE STUDY OF SOCIALIZATION AS A CUMULATIVE PROCESS

Until the last decade or so, most research on childhood socialization within the family focused upon aspects of infant and child training. Recently there has been a marked broadening in the range of socialization influences which have been studied. More detailed attention has been given both to characteristic patterns of maternal behavior and to socialization influences of the father. The general allocation of authority and affection and the division of labor within the family, as well as the influence of parental values and modes of sanctioning upon the child's identifications, school performance, and morality, have been studied.[1] Nevertheless, our conceptual tools for the study of childhood socialization, and especially for encompassing the multitude of socialization influences upon children in particular social positions or for linking those influences to the larger social organization, remain crude. Indeed, the assessment of the cumulative and interactive influence of what is transmitted and what is learned in the continuing series of socialization settings through which the child passes has been little discussed in the literature, except with reference to deviant behaviors and to the problems the lower-class child faces in middle-class oriented schools.

As Inkeles has noted, socialization is accomplished both through the explicit efforts of socialization agents and through social-structural or contextual factors that influence the individual's life experiences. By definition, socialization entails incorporation into groups or relationships. It includes the transmission of cultural norms and contents and also the evolving of particularistic relationships within the broad guidelines of normative prescriptions. The ordering of the manifold phases of socialization and their outcomes will depend on the particular culture and the segment of society or the matrix of persons in which the individual is located. It will also depend, of course, on the individual's attributes, on his intellectual and physical capacities, his temperament and appearance, especially as these have been nurtured and responded to by others in early childhood.

In attempting to determine the effectiveness of any particular socialization technique employed at a given time, we face the problem of

[1] For an overview of the current status of knowledge, see the two-volume *Review of Child Development Research* by Hoffman and Hoffman (1964 and 1966).

disentangling the contribution of the technique from the effects of individual differences in potential, variations in earlier socialization experience, lack of comparability in the cultural content transmitted, and variations in the relationships between socialization agents and the individual being socialized. The enormous complexity of this task helps to explain why so much socialization research and theory has tended simply to ignore the problem of interactions among these influences. Studies which seek to establish the effects upon child behavior of socialization techniques or parental attitudes may manage to characterize the parental relationship (for example, "warm" or "cold"), but neither the cultural content, nor the social context, nor the child's capacities are likely to receive any attention. Or if the effects of cultural content and social context are examined, minimal consideration is given to techniques and relationships on the one hand or outcomes on the other. The effects of cultural content and social context, interacting with certain attributes of the child, have been studied almost exclusively in connection with educational performance. In this realm, it is feasible to study large numbers of individuals because of the availability of school records. Ecological or structural effects (of living arrangements, types of economy, etc.) have also been studied through the use of cross-cultural data and occasionally have yielded impressive correlations between structural features and socialization emphases. Here again, the nature of the data available precludes the direct study of outcomes, though some inferences may be drawn.

Adequate analysis of the interactions among the realms of variables designated above would require large samples drawn from a heterogeneous population and studied over time. Ideally one would attempt early assessment of individual characteristics and would seek data on parental practices, as well as on school and peer-group experiences at several carefully designated times. One would secure personality and social performance measures for each time sample, so as to be able to study interactions between what the person *is* and how others respond to him. Throughout, one would pay particular attention to social-structural or contextual influences within and upon the groups in which socialization takes place and would monitor the relationships of the children studied with the socialization agents involved.

This may seem an unreasonable and even infeasible requirement. Certainly, it poses enormous problems of design, conceptualization, access, data collection, and data processing. Many significant questions can be answered with the more limited and precise research designs that are so typical of socialization research at the present time. Yet with such limited research we shall not be able to go beyond the explanation of a small portion of behavioral variance in a tiny segment of the behavioral repertoire of the individual. It is true that we may obtain *correlations* between parental attitudes and behaviors on the one hand and larger segments of the child's behavior and personality on the other, but it would be perilous to impute causal significance to the parental attitudes and behaviors. The child may shape his parents' attitudes as much as he is shaped by them, especially in the years beyond early childhood.

Our primary concern in this presentation is not, however, with methodology or research strategy but with the cumulative nature of childhood socialization. The child undergoing socialization may not be aware of the significance of influences that impinge on him or even of the beginnings of shifts in his interests and identifications, yet he has an unmatched view of his own life history. He knows how tired he gets of hearing the same old admonitions from parents or teachers; he can recall how breathtakingly fresh a particular discovery was for him years ago. He has a sense of who he is and what he wants, and both come into play over the course of socialization. Parents, too, can view their children's development over the long run. They live with hopes and fears for each child. At times they see their relationships with a child grow suddenly tense and anger-laden; they know the bewilderment of having their own values and goals challenged and occasionally discarded. As a prelude to more detailed consideration of the perspectives of the child and his socialization agents, we shall begin with a brief overview of the problems posed when one considers socialization as a cumulative process, beginning at birth and taking place in a variety of settings.

From the beginning, each child presents a more or less unique constellation of constitutional attributes. His size, physical attractiveness, intellectual capacity, and temperament are to a considerable degree influenced by the genes he inherits. Any of these attributes can, however, be modified by intrauterine developments or birth injury as well as by diet, disease, and the nature of the psycho-social environment in which he grows.

His original social matrix — family, social class, ethnic background — not only provides him with initial orientations and trained abilities but carries also an implicit social stereotype of attributed characteristics. Within this matrix, the child develops characteristic ways of interpreting and responding to others. He becomes more or less dependent on others; that is, he may tend to act in his own behalf in many situations or he may look to others to meet his needs. Tendencies to assertiveness, openness to new experience, acceptance of authority — or to opposite responses — gradually become established.

Thus the child brings to each new situation or social role certain behavioral tendencies that are typical for him, some of which were built up in previous social roles, while others are manifestations of his original dispositions. Socialization agents will respond both to the social stereotype derived from appearance and background and to the child's characteristic patterns of behavior.

Within the various milieus and settings in which his socialization takes place, the child is exposed to very different "assumptive worlds." From the time he begins to master language, he is presented with interpretations of himself and of the people around him: his own attractiveness, worthiness, and what he should believe about the nature of his world and the sources of power in it; their motives, their trustworthiness, and their expectations. An adult who comprehends the nature of cultural diversity may be able to operate comfortably in several assumptive worlds; a child whose ability to symbolize is only rudimentary can hardly be expected to do so. Words themselves have different connotations in different social milieus, whether they be the more abstract references to thoughts and feelings used in one group or, in another, the simple direct references to action spiced with words forbidden in conventional middle-class speech. One's language, like his body build and facial features, serves to identify and categorize him. It will inevitably reflect, during the early years, the usage prevalent in one's original social matrix. Only very recently has it been recognized that the Negro child who speaks the dialect derived from the subculture of field slaves must, in effect, master two languages in order to learn to read. For example, linguists working in the Center for Applied Linguistics note that in learning to read the sentence, "John will be there," the southern Negro child living on a farm or in an urban slum must not only make the translation from print to sound but must learn to equate this sentence with the comparable one in his native tongue, "John go be dere."

Quite apart from the specific aims of socialization agents, the child confronts different constellations of values, beliefs, people, and opportunities depending on where his family is located socially, geographically, and temporally. Some of the most salient features of these constellations are beginning to become clear, though the problems of conceptualization are far from solved.[2] Style of life, including patterns of eating, sleeping, living together, dealing with life problems; preferred modes of association and activities; evaluations made and those received from others; long-range goals; degree of identification with one's neighbors and associates; values for one's children; personality attributes making for success in one's occupation; perception of potential opportunities for

[2] An exploration of the features and consequences of social-class differences was undertaken in the report "Linking Social Class and Socialization: Toward a Framework for Analysis and Research" prepared by Harold Proshansky (Ed.), on the basis of a literature review and work-group discussions at the University of Michigan (see Appendix B, Multilithed or Mimeographed Reports).

the attainment of prized adult statuses — these are but a few of the aspects of life experience that differ sharply according to position in the social structure. They affect the child's perception of school and peer-group socialization settings as well as the nature of family life and parental socialization efforts, and they influence the probability of achieving an integrated identity and an effective role repertoire.

The child must manage to incorporate and to some extent integrate experience from situation to situation and from setting to setting. He must become skilled at discerning not only what is wanted of him by any given socialization agent but the degree of leeway that is available to him, the congruity of any given demand with others made upon him, and the costs of noncompliance with any particular influence attempt. He must learn to restrain or give play to his dispositions differentially; that is, to learn when to act aggressively and when to act submissively, when he can effectively challenge authority and when to accede to it. He must manage his relationships across settings in such a way as to meet quite different sets of expectations.

It is obvious that there are limits to the degree to which the child can bridge conflicting demands or incompatible expectations. Within these limitations he can compartmentalize his roles and the performances they demand. He can be carefree, daring, and somewhat aggressive in the peer group and yet serious, compliant, and reserved in his role as student. He cannot, however, avoid situations where the two sets of demands conflict. At times he must choose where his primary commitment or involvement lies, declaring greater allegiance to the aims of, and his personal ties with, one group as against another. Here we encounter a very difficult problem of conceptualization. To be fully incorporated into a group, an individual must know and understand the role of group member, must be capable of performing that role, and must be motivated to do so.[3] Adequate socialization experience is a necessary, but not a sufficient, prelude to full membership status; the individual must elect to maintain a degree of commitment to the group and its purposes, but such commitment is not an automatic resultant of socialization.

With this general overview, let us turn to a more detailed examination of the aims and tasks of childhood socialization as viewed by various agents and by the child and as influenced by characteristics of the settings within which socialization takes place. We shall draw largely upon research findings that relate to a single setting at a single point in time. To round out the examination we shall rely heavily upon common experiences and problems in socialization. The problems that confront parents, teachers, and children appear in a different guise than do those

[3] For a fuller discussion, see Brim (1960).

posed by the social scientist who wishes his research to bear on theoretical issues. If our task is to extend theory so that it can cope with the phenomena that make the socialization process problematic for participants, we shall have to try to take the perspectives of those participants into account. Some of what we have to say will inevitably seem obvious. Moreover, it is difficult to combine the perspective of researcher with that of a participant in socialization; primary attention will go to the latter. Along the way, we shall try to point out issues and questions begging for research and at the end will offer more general observations about needed research.

THE TASKS OF CHILDHOOD SOCIALIZATION

Most parents are certainly not aware, when their first infant arrives, of the socialization tasks they must carry out or even of the nature of the expectations they will develop for the child within a matter of weeks. Rather surprisingly, there has been little research on the general orientations that adults who are not yet parents have toward children and how these orientations influence their parental behaviors on the one hand and are modified by the parental experience on the other. Most married couples desire children and, indeed, a good many say they would like at least three or four children (Westoff, Potter, and Sagi, 1963). Moreover, the expressed desire for several children is not, in general, markedly diminished by having experience with one, despite the protests of many new parents concerning the stress and turmoil of caring for an infant. We know from Sears, Maccoby, and Levin (1957) that pregnancies subsequent to the first are somewhat less likely to bring "delight" to the prospective mother, yet in the entire child-rearing literature there is but one study (Lasko, 1954) that examines the affectional relationship between mother and child and patterns of child care during the first few years for *two children from the same family*. There are, of course, many retrospective reports by mothers of the ways in which they improved their maternal performance with experience; to report otherwise might seem an admission of limited capacity to learn.

Few parents appear to be casual about their offspring, but some seem quite preoccupied with envisioning the future and bending their energies to control it, while others seem to live much more in the immediate present. All parents are to a degree future oriented until their children are well along toward adulthood, but in the first two years many of the tasks that face them and the child have an immediacy that makes long-term future orientations less directly significant than are current task definitions.

There are certain generic tasks to be accomplished in childhood socialization, whatever the culture. Most of these are carried out through the interaction of parents and child, each having his part to play and each only partly aware of what is taking place. The notion of developmental tasks is not new, and the present formulation overlaps considerably with that propounded nearly twenty years ago by Robert J. Havighurst (1948) and further developed in a subsequent work (1953). For Havighurst a developmental task is one typically arising at a certain period of life and requiring mastery by the individual if he is to be a successful and happy human being (Havighurst, 1953, pp. 2–4). Such tasks may be posed by physical maturation, by cultural pressures, or by the individual's own striving. Whereas Havighurst delineated a series of specific tasks, such as learning to walk and learning to take solid food, we have tried in the following pages to indicate the generic tasks to be accomplished, especially as these engage the energies of both parent and child. Whether or not they are accomplished in the family, however, we would state categorically that these tasks must be achieved if the individual is to be successfully socialized *in any society*. Obviously one could elaborate a much finer set of task categories or conceivably could reduce the number here presented. Each type or group of tasks might indeed be regarded as a set of age-graded expectations of increasing complexity, appropriate to the child's abilities and to the requirements of his particular milieu, to be worked on by the child and his socialization agents over the long course of childhood.

To a considerable degree, the tasks facing children and socialization agents necessarily parallel the functional requisites which Inkeles has noted in Chapter Three. The tasks of childhood socialization within the family constitute the first steps toward achieving the performance requirements that are posed for the participant in a given society. But from the perspectives of parent and child they will be seen somewhat differently than from the perspective of societal functioning. Many of the activities or tasks are more properly to be regarded as a series of stages or sequences beginning with initial parental demands and the child's first partial responses and building up to the demand for and achievement of fully acceptable performances at later ages.

Parental Aims and Activities

We may note the following major responsibilities which parents must to some degree fulfill if the child is to survive and to achieve sufficient competence to be acceptable to his parents and to others:

(1) Provision of sustenance and nurturance for the infant.

(2) Training and channeling of physiological needs — for food, elimination, sleep, etc. — to suit the convenience of parents and (ultimately) to meet cultural standards.

(3) Teaching, skill training, and providing opportunities for practice of motor skills, language, cognitive skills, social skills, and technical skills in order to facilitate care, insure safety, and develop potentials for autonomous behavior.

(4) Orienting the child to his immediate world of kin, community, and society in a variety of social situations and settings.

(5) Transmitting cultural goals and values; motivating the child toward parental and societal goals.

(6) Promoting interpersonal skills, concern for and responsiveness to the feelings of others.

(7) Controlling the scope of the child's behaviors, limiting "transgressions," correcting errors, providing guidance and interpretations (and here we crosscut several of the above tasks).

Most of these responsibilities or tasks are further defined in any society by norms that specify how and when parents are to carry them out; that is, a mother is expected to be nurturant in a particular way, "good parents" invest time and effort and follow accepted techniques to make sure that their children learn particular skills, avoid particular kinds of transgressions by certain ages. In all societies there appear to exist ideals of "good child" and "good parent," even though there may be a great deal of latitude in many realms of parent-child interaction.[4]

For each of these statements of parental aims and activities, we can offer a corollary task or achievement for the child. These are summarized in Table 1. The parents' provision of nurturance, affection, and warmth should permit the child to develop a sense of trust and at very least to adapt his bodily movements to those of his caretaker. Failure to adapt, either because of biological deficits in the child or anxiety and tension in the caretaker, will cause a great deal of frustration for both infant and caretaker. Descriptions by psychiatric clinicians suggest that failure to achieve mutual gratification in the nurturing relationship is likely to be associated with a long train of emotional difficulties for the child (see, for example, Sullivan, 1953).

Parental training aimed at the channeling of the child's physiological needs has as its counterpart the demand that the child control his biological impulses, expressing them only in acceptable modes and giving up unacceptable ones. As every parent knows, there can be a great deal

[4] We take these norms and ideals largely for granted; they seem a part of human nature, and to a degree they probably are. But there are cultural variations both in the ideals themselves and in the ways in which they are exemplified and transmitted. The study of such "collective representations" as they appear in literature, mythology, and other symbolic forms has been of recent origin in the United States but has been a major emphasis in France. See, for example, Chombart de Lauwe (1962).

TABLE 1

Types of Tasks of Early Childhood Socialization in the Family

PARENTAL AIM OR ACTIVITY	CHILD'S TASK OR ACHIEVEMENT
1. Provision of nurturance and physical care.	Acceptance of nurturance (development of trust).
2. Training and channeling of physiological needs in toilet training, weaning, provision of solid foods, etc.	Control of the expression of biological impulses; learning acceptable channels and times of gratification.
3. Teaching and skill-training in language, perceptual skills, physical skills, self-care skills in order to facilitate care, insure safety, etc.	Learning to recognize objects and cues; language learning; learning to walk, negotiate obstacles, dress, feed self, etc.
4. Orienting the child to his immediate world of kin, neighborhood, community, and society, and to his own feelings.	Developing a cognitive map of one's social world; learning to fit behavior to situational demands.
5. Transmitting cultural and subcultural goals and values and motivating the child to accept them for his own.	Developing a sense of right and wrong; developing goals and criteria for choices, investment of effort for the common good.
6. Promoting interpersonal skills, motives, and modes of feeling and behaving in relation to others.	Learning to take the perspective of another person; responding selectively to the expectations of others.
7. Guiding, correcting, helping the child to formulate his own goals, plan his own activities.	Achieving a measure of self-regulation and criteria for evaluating own performance.

of give-and-take and effort on the part of both parent and child before the child willingly accepts the solid foods offered him, gives up the breast or the bottle, and consistently uses the approved toilet arrangements. There *may* be much effort expended, but then again, there may not. Much depends on the vigor and skill with which parents pursue their aims and on the child's readiness. In many societies it appears that such matters do not tend to become important issues (Hart, 1955); yet in all societies children do learn the necessary measures of control and channels of gratification.

The child's learning to walk and talk are such natural phenomena that it may seem strange to view them as tasks. They are achievements, but how much difference does parental teaching and skill training really make? Maturational readiness is certainly a requisite to effective training; no amount of parental pushing can overcome this stubborn fact.[5]

[5] The early research of McGraw (1935) using twins indicated the ineffectiveness of instituting motor-skill training before maturational readiness. More recent

Given such readiness, the child will learn a language that he hears every day whether or not a special effort is made to teach him. On the other hand, such effort (or simply exposure to the rich use of language) is likely to mean increased stimulus and increased opportunity to practice rudimentary skills once they are learned. Only children and firstborn children, for example, tend to acquire the use of language somewhat earlier and somewhat more precisely than do their later-born peers (McCarthy, 1954; Koch, 1956), and one surmises that this is largely due to the greater amount of verbal stimulation from parents at the time when language acquisition is possible. Social-class differences in language learning (McCarthy, 1954) would seem to come about, in part at least, for the same reason.

Stimulation and the provision of models for the child is important, but so is opportunity to perform. The mother who always dresses and feeds her child does not maximize the child's ability to dress and feed himself. A good many tasks can probably be learned by children much earlier than we permit them to learn, partly because their early efforts are so ineffective that it seems simpler to give assistance or do the whole job oneself. For some tasks this may make little difference in the child's development; the time will come when he will insist on dressing himself, for example. But for other tasks, continued parental intervention may prevent both skill learning and development of a sense of competence and autonomy. More important than task performance per se will be the ability to exercise judgment in his own behalf, to make decisions and experience their consequences. What we call "dependency" is not a simple trait but a generalization from a variety of manifestations of the child's inability to act for himself and therefore to rely habitually upon others. Unfortunately, little of the research conducted on dependency examines developmental sequences of skill learning and task performance in the child.

One of the parent's most frequently recurrent tasks is to explain the dangers and behavioral requirements of places, activities, and social situations to the child. In part this is a matter of answering questions — who, when, why? In part it is a matter of explaining how one behaves in a wide variety of situations. From such interchanges and from direct exploration of his environment, the child builds up a picture of the nature of his world, both physical and social. Here again a question (confronted regularly by parents but largely ignored by research) arises as to optimum autonomy at any given age or skill level. Small children must be protected from environmental dangers, but in an environment

---

studies of the effects of early stimulation and environmental enrichment suggest that perceptual skills may be enhanced by such stimulation at much younger ages than previously believed. Maturation still sets limits, but they are not so sharply defined.

where dangers will be encountered they must learn to exercise judgment and handle themselves skillfully. Margaret Mead's observations on the skills of Manus children, who live over water and must early learn to balance themselves in canoes, is a case in point (Mead, 1930). The overprotective mother in such a situation may prevent early accidents but produce a child who is less well equipped to avoid later ones. Or her child may develop such timidity as to limit his performance in a variety of situations. The temperament and energy level of the child will themselves tend to modify the caretaker's role.

In general, the responses that others make to the child in any situation teach him to fit his behavior to situational demands. This is not, of course, a single task or even sequence of tasks. It is a matter of lifelong learning. And as Gregory Bateson (1947) and others have so clearly pointed out, success in this process depends on the child's learning to learn — on his becoming aware of cues and applying himself to the task of making sense of them.[6]

What parents want for their child will frequently become apparent in the concerns they express about the child's behavior at a given age. Current problems with the child may be exasperating largely because they constitute difficulties with which the parent must cope, such as the two- to three-year-old who is a dynamo of uncontrollable energy, who is into everything and seemingly quite unresponsive to parental admonition. But far more often, current problems are exasperating (and anxiety provoking) because they suggest future difficulties of inadequacies in meeting expectations. As Aberle and Naegele (1952) noted, many of the matters of concern to middle-class fathers are, from the father's point of view, "prognosticators of adult traits which will interfere with success in middle-class occupational life." One might add, success in the kind of middle-class occupational life that the father himself is most familiar with, for there are considerable differences in the kinds of traits most conducive to success in medicine, law, architecture, and business.

Coordinate with the parent's transmission of cultural goals or moral values and the parent's efforts to motivate the child in the pursuit of such goals and values is the child's development of a sense of right and wrong and standards for guiding his behavior. Again, this is hardly a task in the usual sense but rather a matter of cognitive achievements and of personal identifications. This topic receives detailed consideration in Chapter Six. Here we shall simply note that far less attention has been given to the content of what is transmitted and to opportunities for incidental learning of just what is acceptable behavior than to modes of parental sanctioning.

Finally, the parent's efforts to control the scope of the child's be-

[6] Highly relevant evidence is provided by Harlow's research on learning sets in monkeys (Harlow, 1949).

haviors, to provide a measure of autonomy while offering guidance and commentary, will be related directly to the child's achieving a measure of self-control and some criteria for the evaluation of his own performances. Parent and child must be guided by feedback in many different situations.

There are many aspects of infant care and childhood socialization that cannot, of course, be encapsulated in equivalent pairs of parental activities and child achievements. Moreover, the child's development of social skills cannot in general be directly linked to any particular parental activity, though language, social orientation, and parental guidance will all help him to learn to interpret the actions of others and to modify his own actions appropriately in different social situations. Again, the achievement of selfhood is closely linked to language learning but also to the development of moral values and to a variety of parental demands.

The Child's Perspective

Most parents probably do not explicitly formulate the various aims and activities entailed in early child rearing. Some of these are so completely taken for granted that they need not be formulated. Others become formulated in very specific terms when that which was taken for granted proves to be problematic — most often, when the child has clearly different aims from those of his parents. For the child early manifests his preferences and his will. There are many things the child wants to do, and often he is eager to learn what his parents want him to learn. On the other hand, there are skills his parents want him to learn but about which he cares little and other parental demands that are unpleasant impositions. Even a quite small child may develop strategies for avoiding certain of the learning experiences his parents attempt to arrange for him. As Jane Loevinger has succinctly pointed out: "A parent can decide to beat his child, but he cannot decide how the child will construe the beating" (Loevinger, 1959).

Parental efforts to teach cultural values and to motivate the child are likely to be seen by the child as demands to learn the things grown-ups regard as important. At times they also involve the child in awe-inspiring rituals that make him feel he is part of something powerful and wonderful. Parental control and limit-setting, on the other hand, may make him feel coerced and frustrated; when he is older he may feel that he is treated unfairly, particularly if the limits set for him are different from those imposed upon his friends. At times the child will not understand what his parents are driving at, especially if behaviors that elicit amused acceptance at one time bring forth angry castigation at another.

The small child has been characterized by Kubie as "one helpless

Lilliputian among hordes of brutal rival Lilliputians in a Brobdingnagian world of giants who are always giving too much protection or too little" (Kubie, 1957, p. 90). These Brobdingnagian giants can pick him up and cuddle him or shake him angrily, can coo at him or shout or scream at him. At times even loving parents may become furiously angry with him and may easily engender feelings of real terror in the child. But mostly, parents and other caretakers are sources of pleasure and security. The child wants their attention, wants to please them, wants to hold on to them. If family life is stable and nurturant, the child is not likely to prefer the company of others to the company of his parents until the approach of adolescence. As late as the initial year of junior high school, for example, our own unpublished data reveal that 74 per cent of the subjects of the Oakland Growth Study would choose both of their parents to be with on a desert island if they could have only three people with them.

In many ways, socialization can be seen as the imposition of restraints and frustrations on the child, especially if one concentrates attention on the demands of weaning, toilet training, and restraining aggression. For most children, however, frustration is probably less acute and less pervasively characteristic of childhood than is the zest for learning to control their bodies and to explore their world. If such exploration brings approval and if accomplishments are praised, the child gains both confidence and competence. If parental response is negative, the child may be dissuaded from certain of his explorations or he may come to treasure the times when he is not under the surveillance of his parents and hence is free to pursue forbidden sources of satisfaction.

In any event, as he is being cared for, guided, and given opportunity to learn, the child is coming to know not only his world but himself. The self is undoubtedly more than reflected appraisals, but a major contribution to self-feeling comes from the child's learning to "take the role of the other." He is able to imagine himself in the place of his parents, his siblings, or someone else who observes and comments on his behavior. In so doing, he begins to bring into his own awareness the social process and the norms that govern others. He also takes over or reflects the dominant tone of those whose commentaries and behaviors he models. We have only the most meager systematic data, largely from students of language learning, on this tremendously important stage of development. The young child frequently comments aloud on his current actions, thus providing a monologue which is directed as much to himself as to an outside audience. In time his commentaries become subvocal, but he continues to respond to his own behavior as to the behavior of others, evaluating it in much the same terms that are used by those most significant to him.

Siblings are most often part of the early socialization setting, and their role can be an important one.[7] An older sibling can provide a role model, a companion, a competitor, and an ally. A younger sibling gives his older brother or sister a new perspective, if not a role model, and an opportunity to feel protective, grown-up. The child without siblings is likely to be more adult oriented, less skilled in his later relations with peers unless he has had substantial early opportunity for play with other children.

The social interaction of the young child with his parents, siblings, playmates, and others who enter his immediate environment in the early years has been little studied. We know something of the process of successive approximations and differentiations by which the meanings of words are learned[8] but little of the ways in which the child learns to interpret the facial expressions, tones of voice, and actions of those with whom he interacts. We have little descriptive data and no evidence regarding long-term consequences of such early learning for the human, but recent research with primates suggests that interaction with adults and with peers in early childhood is crucially important to social and sexual competence in adulthood (Harlow and Harlow, 1965).

Sequence and Scheduling — Preliminary Considerations

So long as the child's activities are confined to the family, the imposition of socialization demands will be largely dependent on the convenience and convictions of his parents. Whether the child is fed on schedule or on demand, whether it has regular hours for sleeping, for being bathed, and for other routines of care, whether it is expected to be toilet trained at one year or two, and whether it is stimulated and primed for little performances as soon as it can lisp are to a considerable degree matters of parental option in a society such as our own. It is true that parents may not recognize these as matters of decision. From their own childhood experiences, from the comments of their parents or other persons experienced in the care of children, from pediatricians and family doctors, and from the mass media they may have derived convictions as to the right time for particular demands as well as the right way of imposing them.

Parents are also faced with problems in the scheduling of their own lives and with the fact that a child who has mastered locomotion with-

[7] Reviews of research evidence leave no doubt that the position of the child among his brothers and sisters significantly influences his personality development (Clausen, 1966), but we have relatively much less information about the ways in which the child's experiences are altered by his position in the family.

[8] For a description of the process, see Brown (1958). The beginnings of research on more general aspects of speech socialization and on the acquisition of linguistic competence represent a promising recent development. See, for example, Bernstein (1964) and Hymes (1962).

out having mastered certain other skills and controls can be a nuisance. The mother who wishes to hold a full-time job outside the home can hardly continue to nurse her child unless she can take the child to her place of work. Societies differ greatly in the extent to which they afford alternative institutional arrangements for infant care.

The mother of three or four young children will have reason to expect a measure of self-care and self-control from the older children while she is involved in the care of the newest infant. The available research evidence (reviewed in Clausen, 1966) suggests both that more demands for self-care are made in larger families and that firstborn children tend to have greater responsibilities.

Demands for scheduling increase very markedly when the child moves outside of the family circle. Expectations of what is appropriate for a child of a given age are, of course, not purely matters of social definition. As already noted, the child's performances depend on biological maturation. None but legendary children walk or talk at six months. There is a sufficiently broad span of maturational readiness for particular childhood performances so that expectations of the larger community are not heavily imposed on the small child but normative expectations nevertheless exist. As he moves outside the home, the walking, talking child must rather quickly come to recognize that there are limits to the liberties he can take with others and their property if he is to avoid their displeasure. In small communities at least, parents whose children are lacking in control will be the subject of comment; and, if the children present a serious annoyance, they may be excluded from some circles. Parents who are unduly restrictive will also be the subject of comment, being seen as rigid, or old-fashioned, or perhaps as not understanding children. In contemporary urban society, however, most parental behaviors will be unknown, and social pressures to influence parents whose products are not wholly acceptable will be minimal. Insofar as pressures do exist, they will come from agents and agencies asked to share in the care of the child, such as nursery schools and "baby-sitters," or from other parents or persons whose children or sensibilities have been outraged. Research on feedback to parents and its effects is almost nonexistent.

RELATIONSHIPS BETWEEN SOCIALIZATION AGENTS AND THE CHILD

As the child moves outside the family there are a number of other agents and agencies of socialization to which he will be exposed. In unsupervised play with his peers he comes to participate in autonomous groupings which have their own shared activities, codes of behavior, and controls. Through family, school, or neighborhood he may be involved in church activities, in clubs, and supervised youth groups.[9] Some of these are selected by the child or his parents as congenial or helpful. In other instances, agents or agencies may select the child for attention because of problematic behaviors. In each instance, there are particular agents pursuing particular socialization or control goals.

Any member of society may serve as a socialization agent when he influences the behavior of another, even though he may not intend such influence or may intend it merely as leading to immediate situational change. The present analysis examines the child's interactions with a limited number of the major agents of socialization. In the course of this analysis we shall examine the nature of relationships between agent and inductee as well as the aims, techniques, and timing of socialization efforts. In general, it appears that the more intimate and enduring a relationship, the less sharply are socialization aims formulated and the less directly linked to particular techniques. This is only a hypothesis, but it appears to be supported by informal observation if not by systematic data.

Socialization techniques have been studied largely as they relate to the imposition of disciplines of early childhood training, the uses of rewards and punishments, and the expressed concerns of parents of older children. To a considerable degree, the techniques of socialization in later childhood are enmeshed in the dialectic of social interaction, in personal interactive strategies, and modes of role relationship and role induction. Timing or scheduling has likewise been considered largely for the infant and toddler except in studies of age-grading in other societies. We shall not, then, be in a position to draw on systematic research but rather to ask questions about issues that seem worthy of more adequate consideration.

Let us now examine in more detail the relational patterns and loyalties involved in the major socialization settings of childhood and, subsequently, some of the implications each set of influences has for the others. These implications or consequences will depend to a very large degree on the placement of the child's family within the social structure. Social class, size of community, religion, and race or ethnic membership markedly affect what is transmitted, techniques of transmission, and the interrelationships of socialization influences. In order to be better able to examine these effects, some further conceptualization of socialization relationships may be useful.

Role Relationships in Socialization

Relationships between socialization agents and individuals being socialized tend to be subject to normative expectations for the role perform-

[9] An indication of the range of socialization settings and activities is provided in Chapter Eight.

ance of each participant as well as value orientations adhering to the relationship itself (for example, the moral injunctions relating to family ties). The normative expectations are often flexible, however, depending on the characteristics of the individuals involved, the demands of other roles, the nature of the social setting in which socialization takes place, and the nature of the goals being sought at any given time. It is therefore difficult to separate the purely normative definition of a role relationship from those aspects that are somewhat dependent on personal characteristics or situational considerations. The following appear to be the most important properties or modifiers of role relationships involving socialization agents and those being socialized.[10]

(1) Affectivity, nature of the emotional tie:
  (a) Loving-hostile (accepting-rejecting)
  (b) Emotionally involved–affectively neutral

(2) Relative power of agent and inductee, including resource control (equivalent to dependence of the inductee).

(3) Relative degree of initiative (responsibility) allocated to agent and inductee.

(4) Specificity or diffuseness of the claims of each individual upon the other.

(5) Explicitness and primacy of socialization aims (or social-influence aims) of agent as against other objectives (that is, commitment of the agent to bringing about changes in the orientations, skills, feelings, etc., of the inductee).

(6) Consonance, congruence, or resonance of the goals of agent and inductee in the relationship generally and in regard to specific socialization aims.

(7) Interpersonal skills of both parties and the clarity of communication between them.

(8) Group and contextual supports for or in opposition to agent's aims and methods (normative solidarity versus alienation, subterranean values, conflict orientation).

Each of these variables is in part specified by social-structural arrangements or by the cultural expectations and value orientations that apply to a given relationship; each is also to some degree dependent on personal characteristics or orientations of the participants, some of which may be specific to a given situation or context. In the family, where the most crucial part of primary socialization takes place, parents and children are bound to each other by the strongest moral imperatives. There is usually a strong affectional bond; relationships are diffuse (pri-

[10] This formulation draws upon several classifications of social relationships in use within general behavioral science theory as well as upon evidence from socialization research and theory.

mary, pervasive); parental power is high (complete in infancy, very high in childhood); the socialization role tends to have primacy, especially for the mother, though not in all situations; parental goals tend to be largely accepted during the early years; and parents and children speak the same language, even though they may not always communicate.

Psychological research on socialization has concerned itself most closely with affectivity and power or control in the parent-child relationship. Thus Schaefer (1959) has suggested that maternal behavior toward the child can be summarized as a function of the dimensions "love-hostility" and "control-autonomy." Becker (1964) has proposed a three-dimensional model for the classification of parental orientations toward the child and has examined the consequences of various disciplinary techniques when used by parents holding such orientations. He has labeled the dimensions "warmth-hostility," "restrictiveness-permissiveness," and "detachment-anxious emotional involvement." Becker summarizes research indicating that power-assertive techniques of discipline tend to be used by hostile parents and tend to promote aggression and resistance to authority in young children. Although it seems reasonable to assume that hostility and warmth are attributes of the parent when we are considering parental behaviors with small children, there is a point at which they are likely to become attributes of the relationship. Moreover, some parental hostility even to small infants seems to reflect the parent's feeling that the child is not as loving as the parent had expected. Such feelings have been reported, for example, in instances of severe child beating (Morris and Gould, 1963). In any case it does appear that affection, emotional involvement, and the uses of power by the parent are probably the most crucial dimensions of parent-child relationships *for the small child*. Once the child has begun to learn about the world outside the family circle, however, and especially if there are siblings who can reinforce each other's invoking of points of view that differ from the parents, other aspects of the parent-child relationship must be considered.

Unfortunately, there is not a simple relationship between these aspects of socialization roles and the effectiveness of socialization efforts. Indeed, in the case of much learning by imitation, it appears that no relationship at all is required with the model; the child merely needs to see him. Situational circumstances can be extremely important, as in cases of behavioral contagion. On the other hand, copying is more frequent when a positive relationship exists (Bandura and Walters, 1963) or when the model has high prestige (Lippitt *et al.*, 1952). In instances when an adult is trying to teach a child something important to that child's orientation or future functioning, existing research and theory support the generalization that, other things being equal, a positive, warm relationship will be more effective for almost any kind of learning except avoidance responses. Power not harshly used will be most effective when linked with positive affect but may be effective to a degree even when there is no emotional tie between the agent and the child, since power implies that the agent controls resources. On the other hand, power coupled with hostility may lead to coercion but seldom to consensus. Indeed, the use of power is likely to generate hostility; authoritarian parents generate more resentment than democratic ones, in our own society at least (Elder and Bowerman, 1963). The ends of social control may be served by such use of power, but the agents' socialization aims are less likely to be achieved. Don, the Hopi chief studied by Simmons and referred to in the previous chapter, was frightened by the powerful, masked Katchina gods who beat him, without intercession from his parents, at his initiation. Subsequently, he bitterly resented this collusive use of force and was alienated rather than emotionally incorporated into the social network by the act.

In some instances the relationship between socialization agent and inductee may be considered an end in itself; in other instances it is a means to an end. In any given situation, the substantive nature of the socialization aim or goal is, of course, an important consideration. As we have seen, socialization of the young child within the family comprises the pursuit of many goals, ranging from the transmission of cultural norms and basic orientations to the training of the child in technical and in interpersonal skills and even to the development of mutual understanding between parent and child. Few later socialization relationships entail anything like this scope, yet many will embrace multiple goals and sources of satisfaction. Whether the person being socialized welcomes the efforts of others to assist him to change or regards those efforts as coercive and to be resisted will depend both on his ideas of what he wants for himself and on the way in which the aims of others are communicated to him. How explicit is the parent or other agent in pointing out to the child the range of possibilities open to him and the various steps involved? How well does the parent enlist the child in taking responsibility for preparing himself? How adequately does the teacher involve the classroom in decisions that have to do with procedures by giving it the chance to select among various alternatives that would meet curriculum requirements? We know that communication between agent and child is often faulty and mutual perceptions distorted, but research evidence on cumulative effects is lacking. Ronald Lippitt discusses in Chapter Eight many of the possibilities that exist for improving the socialization process. Here we shall merely note that the aims and techniques which he discusses afford a crosscutting conceptualization to aspects of the relationship itself.

One may examine the scope of the activities of child and agent in a number of other respects. To what extent does the agent use his power and resources to screen out influences impinging upon the child and to limit opportunities available to it as against opening up the child to diverse experiences and opportunities? There are also matters of style or emphasis. Does the agent stress the motivations underlying the child's behaviors, or the behavioral outcomes themselves? Kohn (1963) has suggested, for example, a marked difference between the styles manifest by middle-class and working-class parents in precisely this respect, with the middle-class parent being far more concerned about underlying motivations. One may ask, also, is the emphasis on encouraging the child to try new tasks or on evaluating his skill in performing tasks especially important to his parents?

The timing of socialization efforts must also be considered. To date, timing has been examined primarily in connection with the enhancement of achievement motivation through early demands for self-reliance (McClelland, 1961) and the effects of training relative to maturational readiness (McGraw, 1935). But it is obvious that some parents anticipate certain kinds of performance requirements to a substantial degree while others do not make specific efforts to train their children for such tasks until the children appear to be late or deficient in performance by almost any standards. Some parents, for example, provide the child with instruction and opportunities to learn to swim while of preschool age, while others become aware of the fact that their children have not learned to swim only when they encounter a situation in which it is assumed that all adolescents are swimmers. Very often, of course, differences in the timing of socialization efforts reflect differences in the priorities assigned to various activities, skills, or knowledge. Should an "immature" child start the first grade at the usual age, or will he benefit from an additional year of kindergarten in which his physical, social, and intellectual skills may blossom sufficiently to permit him to experience greater competence in the classroom? Timing also rests on assumptions about appropriateness and may involve anxieties about the child getting into trouble or getting wrong ideas if a given facet of socialization experience comes too soon — or too late.

It appears that parents can have close, warm relationships with their children and yet manifest quite different styles — quite different emphases — in their socialization efforts. It is not at all evident that any given style or approach is necessarily superior to any other. Much will depend upon the nature of the environment in which socialization takes place, the attributes of the participants, and the nature of the role performance to be desired. It is equally difficult to establish, except on the basis of personal preferences, the pros and cons of conformity or good "adjustment to one's environment." There is little question but that induction of a considerable degree of conformity can have a high payoff value for the child, so far as interpersonal relationships and social mobility in contemporary American society are concerned. On the other hand, beyond a certain minimum, such conformity may not go hand in hand with either intellectual or artistic creativity. Quite possibly, also, a person may be highly conforming in certain respects yet highly innovative in others. For example, MacKinnon (1965) has noted that highly creative architects score lower on ratings of affiliation and deference and higher on aggression and autonomy than their less creative peers. Creative architects also score lower on scales of responsibility and self control, among others. In their socialization they appear to have had unusual freedom to explore their world, clear standards of conduct but at the same time "the absence of pressures to establish prematurely one's professional identity."

Rather than attempting to discuss these relationships in the abstract, let us now turn to the several major socialization settings of childhood and see how the aims, techniques, and scheduling of socialization demands and socialization opportunities interact in a complex urban society such as our own.

SOCIALIZATION IN THE SCHOOL

The family may be the ideal unit for nurturing the child and guiding his early steps toward participation in the larger social life, but insofar as technical knowledge must be imparted to any significant proportion of the population in the course of socialization, some other instrumentality or institution is required. The aims and functions of formal education vary from one society to another, and they have been variously defined from one time to another in the United States. The most general societal functions are transmitting knowledge, norms, and values, along with the orientational and motivational underpinnings that this requires, and recruiting or channeling persons into programs of preparation for social positions allocated on the basis of achievement. Obviously, educational aims are somewhat different for younger and older children, for talented or less gifted children, and for advantaged and markedly deprived children. Before turning to an analysis of certain general features of socialization within the classroom, it may be helpful to note briefly the relationship of this part of the socialization apparatus to value orientations and to the location of power and authority in the larger society.

Schools may be established and maintained by the state, by religious orders or other special interest groups, or by private groups or individuals to serve their own needs, whether educational or economic. Teachers will in general be recruited by, or in accordance with the wishes of, those who in the last analysis control the support of the school apparatus and determine its policies. But since teachers must be technically qualified, especially at the upper levels of education, there may be some disparity or tension between the orientations and aims of teachers and those of official policy makers, who are likely to be products of a different educational experience. A government or religious order that controls the training of teachers, their selection, and the curriculum to be taught is in a position largely to determine the world view of its pupil products. Schools may be used both for indoctrination and for recruitment or allocation to occupational slots.

To achieve their aims, governments established through revolution frequently attempt to offset conservative family socialization influences by setting up new educational forms for inculcating desired attitudes. Thus the Communist Revolution in Russia led quickly to edicts limiting parental power while insisting on parental responsibility to further the objectives of the revolution through the rearing of the children (Mead, 1955). Pedagogues committed to communism were given responsibility both for guiding parents and for reshaping the school system to the ideals of the revolutionary regime. Another instance of reshaping of the socialization apparatus to modify the family's role is afforded by the *kibbutzim* of Israel. The early Jewish migrants from eastern Europe brought with them values and skills unsuited to the conquest of the desert. Success in settlement and agriculture required that they throw off the folkways and mores of the traditional village life they had left behind; they established communal settlements. In so doing, they sought not merely to achieve a new form of community but to limit the transmission of outmoded ends and means by markedly limiting the functions of the family (Diamond, 1957). In each instance, the formal educational system was given some responsibilities previously lodged in the family.

But the school's role in moral as well as technical education is by no means limited to revolutionary regimes or community structures. In any democratic society where social origins are associated with grossly varying cultural orientations, the attainment of responsible citizenship by the bulk of the population is largely dependent on the educational system. The assimilation of ethnic and other minorities requires that agents from outside the family provide orientation to the larger society and its values. In rapidly developing countries, the educational system must play a major part in developing the aspirations and motivations of its students in addition to giving them the technical training needed to carry out roles of leadership in transforming political and economic systems.[11]

[11] For a discussion of these functions of education see Clark (1962) and Eisenstadt (1964).

Industrialization and urbanization require high levels of literacy and technical knowledge. Further, if alienation of large segments of the population is to be avoided, the moral commitment of citizens to the dominant values of the society is also requisite. A half-century ago, Durkheim maintained that the school must be the primary regulator of moral education for a nation, that "the school is the sole moral environment where the child can learn methodically to know and to love" his native land and all that it represents (Durkheim, 1963, p. 67). Durkheim's formulation derived from concern with a national school system in which a central authority designates who may teach and specifies a standard curriculum. Within the United States, local autonomy of school systems renders far more difficult the purveying of a standardized morality or a standardized view of the native land.

A more salient policy issue, in public education in the United States, has been the extent to which the schools should aim from the first to prepare the child for social participation as well as academic excellence. Here, of course, the most influential voice seeking to make the schools more effective socialization agents in broader spheres than the teaching of basic academic disciplines was that of John Dewey. Dewey's cogent examination of the functions of education and his case for experimentation in educational methods had as potent an influence on educational theory and practice as it had on the development of socialization theory and research noted in Chapter Two. But the questioning that has resulted complicates our task, for the aims of the schools — of school boards, school superintendents, and teachers — are not a matter of complete consensus.[12]

In the classroom we deal with socialization by cohort; that is, a group, starting together at more or less the same level of competence, is carried along as a unit. In many classrooms there may be several "tracks" or "streams," grouping children according to their presumed ability; and each group constitutes a unit for the teacher's planning. At the same time, the teacher must obviously relate to each child as an individual. In most schools any given batch of children to be inducted into the system will show a good deal of diversity. Some will have been prepared for the classroom and the role of pupil; they will be ready to pay attention and eager to learn. Others will not only be unprepared but may be immature and dependent or aggressive and difficult to control. With this general introduction, let us now turn to a closer consideration of the tasks of teachers and pupils and their relationship in the classroom.

The Teacher's Aims and Activities

In the early elementary grades, the socialization aims and activities of the teacher tend to overlap with those of the parents. To a considerable

[12] On this point, see Neal Gross, *Who Runs Our Schools?*

degree, they may be thought to reinforce and extend the parents' efforts but with a somewhat narrower focus of attention. The primary aims and activities are:

(1) Teaching and encouraging skill learning — specific cognitive skills such as reading, writing, and arithmetic, and the more general skills of maintaining attention, sitting still, participating in classroom activities.

(2) Imparting information, orienting the children to the educational system and to the intellectual heritage, seeking to commit them to its ends.

(3) Transmitting dominant cultural goals and values, making clear their meaning and relevance.

(4) Providing guidance and models for problem solving; maintaining an atmosphere conducive to learning.

(5) Overcoming gross deficits in preparation and attempting to deal with individual differences and with personal problems of the child that hinder his performance; in some instances consulting with the parents or with guidance personnel.

These are not, of course, the teacher's only aims and activities in the classroom.[13] She must exercise a measure of control over her charges. In some lower-class schools, where children are neither socially nor cognitively prepared for the disciplines of classroom learning, the maintenance of control may assume preemptive salience. Most often, the teacher will also want the children to like her, and she will bend considerable effort to this end. Moreover, there are several very general socialization issues she must deal with, relating to her use of available resources; we shall discuss these shortly. At the same time, the teacher is confronted with a mass of paper work, staff meetings, conferences, and other demands on her time and energy. While she has somewhat more predictably scheduled periods of respite from her duties than does a mother, the teacher, too, is confronted with multiple demands and periodic overloads. Many of the demands upon her have little to do with her socialization role and may, indeed, interfere with that role. As a consequence, she may invoke bureaucratic rules and modes of procedure and may confine her efforts to carrying out a quite limited definition of her socialization role.[14]

[13] The ease with which we fall into the locution "the teacher . . . she" is, of course, related to the preponderance of women teachers in the elementary grades. The implications of this sex linkage are worthy of more searching analysis than they have received. The classroom — its curriculum, activities, and trappings — tends to be markedly oriented to the interests and dispositions of the middle class, and especially those of middle-class girls.

[14] A dramatic and insightful picture of the teacher's dilemmas, as seen by an experienced teacher, is given in the fictional *Up the Down Staircase*, by Bel Kaufman.

The extent to which the teacher's aims and efforts overlap those of the parents will of course depend on many factors. Among the most important of these are the social status and ethnic background of the family, the curriculum and teaching emphases of the school, and the personal commitments and characteristics of the individual teacher. In the United States, teaching is a highly respectable, but not a highly respected, occupation. In the elementary grades in particular, teachers are expected to nurture as well as to instruct; in both public and parochial schools, the great bulk of elementary teachers are women. The pay is low, one's private life is restricted, working conditions are on the whole poor, but economic security is relatively great. At the beginning of the twentieth century, teachers were mostly drawn from rural and working-class backgrounds (Dahlke, 1958). Studies conducted since World War II suggest that while teaching is still a pathway to upward mobility, more teachers are now drawn from families whose heads are employed in middle-class occupations — the professions, business, and public service — a circumstance particularly true of female elementary school teachers (Carlson, 1961). Until very recently most teachers have, of course, been native-born whites, except for teachers in segregated schools in the South.

Some teachers are drawn to the occupation because they like children or because they feel that the contribution they can make in teaching will be a rewarding one. Others choose teaching for its economic security or its respectability or because there are relatively few other occupational opportunities available for women in their communities. Students who choose education majors are, on the average, less outstanding intellectually and socially than those who enter other professions. Moreover, insofar as college performance is predictive of ability, those who stay in teaching tend to be less able than those who give up teaching for other occupations. Nevertheless, teachers are more highly selected than parents and are certainly more explicitly trained for the duties they are to perform.

How are the aims of the teacher translated into action? She must, first of all, establish a personal relationship with the children to implement the potentialities of her formal role definition. This entails getting to know the children and what they bring in the way of attitudes, information, needs, and interests. As the structuring of friendship ties and prestige ratings begins to emerge, these become important influences on the processes of communication and control. Ultimately, accomplishment of the teacher's goals requires recruitment of interest and the achievement of involvement and commitment on the part of the students, sustained by satisfactions or rewards for their effective participation. Part of the task is to help the children to become proud of their class membership and to incorporate in that pride a sense of their being responsible for setting their own high goals. There are also, of course, aspects of the teacher's tasks that require more technical skills, such as the assessment of deficits or blocks in cognitive skills.

Teachers obviously differ in the priorities accorded to various tasks and even in the degree to which they are aware of various possibilities in implementing their curricular aims. Any given teacher has a given group of children for a relatively short time. This enhances the universalistic features of socialization in the school — one must learn to relate to a variety of different persons occupying the same position — but it has drawbacks, too. It greatly increases the difficulty both of assessing the needs of the child and of establishing a real bond with the child who has previously been traumatized in relations with adults. But let us now turn to the child and his perspective.

The Pupil's Perspective

When he enters school, the child must first learn something about the student's role with reference to activities and relationships. This may entail a measure of restraint and a bundle of new expectations quite different from anything that he has experienced. He must sit quietly for long periods, saving his boisterous expressions for the playground. He must adapt to new surroundings, large numbers of peers, and perhaps to language, foods, and expectations for personal conduct that are quite strange to him. His first task is to achieve a measure of acculturation to the school itself. Only recently have we begun to realize what a major task this may be for the child from a markedly deprived background. The expectations and preparation that the child has for the teacher and the classroom, amorphous as they may be at the beginning of school, are derived from grossly differing kinds of experience with caretakers and grossly different degrees of preparation for this role relationship.

The child's relationship to his first teacher is patterned to a considerable extent upon the relationship he enjoys with his parents. Given nurturance and trust in that relationship, the initial relationship with the teacher is likely to be easier for the child to the degree that the teacher's expectations and attitudes are similar to those of the parents. In general, however, there are more constraints and less individual involvement and personal attention. The teacher must spread her warmth over the whole class. Moreover, within the classroom there is a more consistent and compelling denial of reciprocity between teacher and child than in the family; that is, the child is not free to act toward the teacher as she acts toward him. He cannot properly make personal demands upon her or argue on equal terms with her about legitimate demands that she makes in her role as teacher. Learning these aspects of the role definition may be difficult for the child who has only experienced particularistic relationships with adults, especially if those relationships have entailed very different modes of communication and influence.

What does the prospect of school mean to the child who has not yet gone there? How is it presented to him by his parents or older siblings? How does he feel about it once he has actually begun to attend? There have been many studies of classroom sociometric structure during the primary grades but few that examine what the children think and say about their schools, their teachers, and their classmates unless the children are receiving therapy because of a school phobia or other emotional problem. Almost certainly, school has some attractions even to children who early learn from older siblings or peers that school is not fun. In one of the few studies of the impact of beginning first grade on the socialization of the child, Stendler and Young (1950) found that 93 per cent of the mothers reported the children were looking forward to starting school just prior to entrance. After two months in the first grade, 92 per cent were said to like school. Middle-class children were to a greater extent prepared by their parents for the school experience; but, according to their mothers, most children at all class levels liked school. Hess and Shipman (1967) have found sharp differences in the manner in which middle-class and lower-class mothers orient the small child to the school, with the latter presenting it in a much more threatening and unrewarding way, and with much less of the kind of information about school that will be useful to the child.

For all but a small minority of children, going to school is at least a badge of growing up, and the school becomes a social center, even if learning is not their primary aim. Moreover, most parents, whatever their origins, would like their children to do well in school and to behave in such a way as to reflect credit upon the parents.

The teacher's aims and activities are likely to be seen quite differently by children from different backgrounds. Those children who are most eager to learn particular skills and who are adequately prepared may see the teacher as a person who helps them achieve their own aims. Those for whom the teacher's aims are strange and her demands beyond their initial abilities may see the teacher as hostile and humiliating. Such differences in perspective will of course influence the course of interaction and the development of motivations and relationships among the students.

In a short time, the children in a classroom come to form friendships and relatively stable ratings of social acceptability or social influence.[15]

[15] As early as the second grade, for example, classroom social structure emerges in the early weeks of the school year and persists to a considerable degree to the end of the year and even to the following year. For a review of this literature see Glidewell *et al.* (1966).

Being acceptable to his peers, especially to peers of high prestige, becomes for the child a significant, even if not explicitly recognized, goal. This obvious occurrence has important implications for socialization. On the one hand the child learns to manage his relations with his peers, to exert and accept influence in and out of the classroom. On the other hand, preoccupation with his peers can divert attention away from the tasks that are the teacher's primary concern. The problem of multiple loyalties and of overlapping, conflicting demands is one that the child must learn to handle in school (Fox *et al.*, in press). The child who never becomes task oriented in the classroom or who becomes alienated from the teacher and her aims is likely to give his primary allegiance to others who are in the same situation. But even the child who accepts the teacher and her aims will be subject to at least occasional conflicts between the teacher's aims and the influences of peers.

To the extent that they remain residents of the same neighborhood, children will tend to go to the same school, and age-mates will tend to be in the same classroom year after year. Peer influences will then be relatively stable while the teacher will differ from year to year — or even, in some schools and classrooms, much more frequently. The personal influence of the teacher must be reestablished with each change; the institutional influences and expectations that go with the position are gradually established as the primary definers of the relationship.

A Closer Look at Aspects of the Teacher-Pupil Relationship

Let us now look more closely at socialization relationships in the school. There is here no moral injunction that teachers and children should love one another. The teacher is expected to be warmly accepting of children but not to become emotionally entangled with individual children. In the early primary grades even a modest degree of neutrality may be extremely difficult to achieve, especially since some children appear to need a great deal more emotional warmth from the teacher than others. In the later grades, expressed emotional involvement with particular students, whether resulting from annoyance or extreme affection, is likely to draw the attention of the class as a whole, to divert attention from socialization aims, and to undercut respect.

The power of the teacher is in a number of respects more circumscribed than that of parent. Inevitably, the exercise of the teacher's power is on public display. Successful exercise of influence over high-prestige pupils tends to produce "ripples" of influence over the rest of the classroom (Kounin and Gump, 1958). In the last analysis, the teacher's power rests upon the ability to exclude the child from the classroom. The meaning of such exclusion will depend on parental reactions and the possibility of legal sanctions as well as upon the child's attitude toward the school and his ties with classmates.

While the small child is likely to view the teacher as having some of the authority of a parent, the older child is very much aware of the limits on the teacher's use of force or authority. The child's own power is not negligible. Once he has become familiar with the system, he can be disruptive without being overtly guilty of violating classroom procedures. He can at times catch the teacher in statements or acts that can be used to discredit her; and, indeed, he can at times mobilize sentiment either in the classroom or outside it so as to cause the teacher serious embarrassment. Thus the child's potential power is likely to be greatest when there is a hostile relationship between teacher and the classroom group and when there are gross differences between the value orientations prevalent in the local community and those represented by the school. In this situation it is also likely that the interpersonal skills of both parties will be less effective than when dealing within their own subcultural groups. Communication is likely to be markedly hampered. The teacher will seek support in her own professional group; the child will seek to mobilize his peers or his family in opposition. This is what may, and not infrequently does, happen in the most deprived areas of a number of cities. When this does occur, the accompanying socialization experiences are not those that had been planned for, but undoubtedly social roles are learned in such situations.

It is obvious that children cannot be coerced into becoming students. When the child is not oriented toward the goals of the school, the teacher's primary task is to make those goals attractive to him. In the early years especially, this may come about through the child's identification with a teacher; in the later years it is probably most often furthered through the quality and climate of the student body. That is, as the child grows older, peer influences will become more potent; and the nature of peer influences will depend upon the characteristics of the larger student body. We know that working-class children show higher levels of achievement in schools with a predominantly middle-class student body (and attendant higher academic standards) than in schools that serve a predominantly working-class population.[16]

The school's program is closely scheduled. For the well-prepared, bright child, intellectual demands are usually not so great as to make the schedule problematic. Keeping up is easy, even in the event of absences. For the poorly prepared child, especially if he is not of superior potential, keeping up with the schedule of required achievement may present great difficulty. Inability to do so results in feelings of failure and of resent-

[16] The large-scale research on American schools by Coleman *et al.* (1966) buttresses previous research bearing on this point.

ment, even if the child is moved along with his more successful peers. An assessment of the various strategies which can be used in dealing with such problems requires simultaneous study of school and neighborhood contexts, classrooms, and children, over time, a kind of research only beginning to be carried out.

The very fact that any given teacher has a given group of pupils for only a year may provide some of the less successful students — or those who did not get along with a particular teacher — with a new chance to establish themselves within the classroom. A very positive relationship with just one teacher may be enough to arouse a child to recognize potentials within himself. Conversely, of course, an extremely negative experience can diminish motivation; but once the child has begun to recognize how he can effect his own outcome, his relationship with any particular teacher probably becomes less important.

In *Manchild in the Promised Land* Claude Brown (1965) recounts his childhood and adolescent experience in home, school, Harlem neighborhood, and various institutions. He never makes quite clear the nature of his positive experiences in school, choosing instead to write about his truanting, which began on the second day of school. Yet during his two-and-a-half year stay at Wiltwyk School for Boys, to which he was sent after a history of serious delinquency, he established a relationship with a staff member who persuaded him that he had the ability to change his life pattern and urged him to return to school. The change was several years in coming, but Brown gives a moving description of his subsequent involvement in getting an education. It would be instructive to know how often and under what circumstances such turning points occur.

If the teacher's power is less than that of the parent, it is nevertheless considerable. Real threats to the teacher's authority are rare in most schools and exceedingly rare at the lower grade levels. Teachers differ markedly in the styles they employ in the classroom, some tending toward authoritarian practices, some seeking to be "buddies" to their charges. Glidewell and his associates (1966) have noted that a large body of research attests to the impact of the teacher's use of social power and expression of emotional acceptance upon the classroom social structure. Effects upon academic achievement appear to be less significant. Both delegation of a part of the teacher's power to her pupils and a wide dispersion of emotional acceptance have been found to

> (a) stimulate more pupil-to-pupil interaction; (b) reduce interpersonal conflicts and anxieties; (c) increase mutual esteem, rapport, and self-esteem; (d) induce a wider dispersion and flexibility of peer social power as manifested by a greater tolerance for divergent opinions in the initial phases of decision-making and a greater convergence of opinion in the

> later phases of decision-making; (e) increase moral responsibility, self-initiated work, independence of opinion, and responsibility in implementing accepted assignments. (Glidewell *et al.*, 1966, p. 232)

Such influences enhance achievement of the broader socialization goals of the school even if they do not lead immediately to higher achievement-test scores. Moreover, some recent research indicates that tested achievement may be enhanced (Schmuck and Van Egmond, 1965). By enlisting the pupil in taking a greater measure of personal responsibility, group supports for the teacher's socialization aims are simultaneously built up. Both authoritarian teachers and those who yield most of their power in order to be liked by the children are unlikely to achieve solid group supports for the attainment of socialization objectives.

The examination of significant aspects of the teacher-pupil relationship and classroom atmosphere has focused also on the nature of the conceptual or belief systems employed by the teachers. O. J. Harvey and his associates (1966, 1968) have studied the relationship between the belief systems of teachers, the effects of those systems on the classroom environments created by the teachers, and the net influence upon student behavior. Teachers who espoused more abstract belief systems were more resourceful, less dictatorial, and less punitive in dealing with their students than were those teachers espousing highly concrete belief systems. Ratings of classroom behavior found pupils of teachers with abstract belief systems more cooperative, involved, active in pursuit of relevant goals, helpful, and achieving at a higher level while pupils in classrooms of teachers with concrete belief systems were somewhat more likely to seek guidance and approval. Interpersonal styles and other personality attributes are related to belief systems and undoubtedly help to explain the striking relationships found in the classrooms studied. What emerges most clearly, in fact, is the reciprocal influence of the teacher's orientation on her classroom behavior and, through that behavior, on the children's behavior and achievement.

Teachers, like parents, appear to have more difficulty — or more success — with one type of pupil than with another. The teacher's own assurance, her feeling of support or lack of support from parents and from superiors, and her understanding of the nature of the home environment of the children taught can all markedly influence ability to communicate with, and provide acceptance for, those children. We may note here a matter developed more fully by Ronald Lippitt in Chapter Eight: teachers receive relatively little feedback in response to their good ideas or regarding the adequacy of their general performance as socialization agents. The criteria on which they are evaluated are for the most part narrow, and the bases for their assessment are pitifully meager. Parents have, in general, a spouse or other relatives to offer commentaries on techniques and problems (though even parents receive relatively little feedback). Except where teaching teams or experimental programs are operative, teachers seldom have a comparable basis for non-hostile evaluation.

It is not possible to deal here with all of the many aspects of classroom social organization and pedagogical methods bearing upon socialization in the school. Recent research makes clear the complexity of assessing the effects of even so straightforward a practice as ability grouping or "tracking." On the one hand, extreme variations in ability or achievement within the classroom make difficult simultaneous communication with pupils at both extremes, suggesting the desirability of separate tracks. On the other is the finding that such grouping results in depriving the less well prepared and able students of the stimulus which their more advanced peers can provide. Moreover, even with considerable variation in the classroom, the more advanced students do not seem to lose appreciably in the absence of tracking, while the less advanced gain considerably more than if in a separate track. Yet the picture is still more complicated: apparently boys and girls respond somewhat differently to classroom grouping according to sex as opposed to coeducational classrooms.[17] Girls appear to do better in "progressive" schools, boys in more traditional schools. Boys do better in coeducational schools, girls in single-sex schools.

While peer influences in the classroom often run counter to the teacher's aims, there may be far less support for the capers of disruptive members within the classroom group than most students assume. That is, a few of the more uninhibited and dominant pupils may tend to set a classroom atmosphere antithetical to effective learning despite the fact that most of the students would prefer less disruptions. To the extent that the classroom group can be made aware of the sentiments of the majority of their peers, disruptive behavior by the few is likely to receive more unfavorable reaction. In this instance there is, of course, a greater dispersion of power or influence within the student body itself. Peers can also serve as socialization agents in the classroom; and high-prestige peers, including older boys and girls, can be employed as teacher's aides or junior instructors and tutors to the mutual advantage of both teacher and pupil.[18]

Relations between Home and School

We have already commented on the differential orientation and preparation of children when they first enter school. There is a great deal of

[17] Both of these findings are reported by Himmelweit and Sealy (1966) in their review of British studies of socialization in the school.

[18] For a description of what can be accomplished through such efforts, see Lippitt and Lohman (1966).

evidence that communication between family and school is easier and more positive in character at middle-class than at working-class family levels. Visits to the school by middle-class parents are more frequent and more often concerned with mutual exploration of ways of improving the child's performance. Participation in P.T.A. and other activities designed to give the parent a more adequate understanding of the school is likewise closely linked with social status.

Contacts between family and school need not, however, rest entirely on the initiative of parents. The school's relationship to its community can be one of aloofness or of active effort to achieve openness and interchange. Litwak and Meyer (1965) have addressed themselves to the question of alternative strategies and the optimal degree of interchange if the school is to be maximally effective in the pursuit of its educational program. They suggest that the optimum linkages established between school and community should achieve a balancing of requirements for allaying suspicions and attaining mutual understanding on the one hand and the preservation of the school's professional standards on the other. In a very real sense the school may have to accept the role of socialization agent for parents, especially in those milieus in which the school must resocialize and reorient its pupils.

Associated with the parents' involvement in school affairs is the child's perception of parental support for the school and for his own school performance. We have noted above that most parents and children appear to have a relatively favorable attitude toward the school when the child first enters. But if the child is unhappy or unsuccessful in school, parental attitudes as well as the child's feelings are likely to become more negative. Particularly in the lack of effective communication between parent and teacher, each is likely to build up a negative image of the other.

Research by Luszki and Schmuck (1963) suggests that the child's perception of parental support and interest in his school work is related to social status, is highest at the lower grades, and correlates significantly with the child's own attitude toward school and actual performance in school. Similarly, a number of British studies show that the lower-class pupil who succeeds in maintaining a high level of school achievement and remains in school has in general received a much higher level of parental support than his equally bright peers who drop out of school (Himmelweit and Sealy, 1966).

For the markedly deprived child whose parents have had very little formal education, it is likely to take prodigious effort to acquire the skills and information necessary to do well in school. Moreover, the further he progresses, the less adequate are his parents to provide assistance. Almost inevitably, the lower-class child who makes a strong commitment to being successful in school must sacrifice acceptance of many of his peers and to some degree take teachers rather than parents as his primary models.[19]

The school system not only trains but sorts out children. In the United States this sorting process tends to be gradual and goes on indefinitely — at least in theory — so that the child who drops behind and is shunted into non-academic pathways has always some potential stairway back to the highest levels of education. In England, France, and a number of other countries, sorting is more rigorous and more determinative of ultimate outcome, except for the wealthy few; and the important selection operation comes relatively early. Turner (1960) has referred to the "contest" versus "sponsored" mobility of these contrasting systems of education, for in the United States the child is at every age level engaged in a contest with his peers while in England the child who has been selected at an early age is thereafter sponsored or at least not subject to the same threat of displacement by his peers.

Under any system in which selection on the basis of performance takes place, the successful candidate is likely to be one who is aware of what he has to do and who has the ability, motivation, and support necessary to perform effectively. If parents are not in a position to appreciate fully the importance of particular academic performances or evaluations, they cannot prepare and assist their children nor can they assess the adequacy of advice given the child by teachers or counselors in the schools. Turner suggests that the "phantasy" quality of educational aspirations of many working-class children and parents derives from the contest-mobility perspective when adequate information about the nature of educational requirements is lacking. Less pervasive but equally poignant is the problem of the child of very high capacity whose potentialities for higher education are not realized because no one explained to him or to his parents the necessity of taking algebra in the ninth grade so that he could compete for a place in a first-class college. A major dilemma is posed by the fallibility of all selection mechanisms and their particularly high fallibility when operating with non-homogeneous groups and with very inadequate knowledge of the child and his socialization experiences.

Perhaps this somewhat discursive treatment of the school as an agent of socialization will suffice to give an idea of the diversity of issues that must be confronted in assessing continuities and discontinuities in socialization influence within childhood itself. It proved impossible to discuss the school without involving peers along with the teachers, for it is in school that the peer group achieves a degree of coherence. At this point, however, we shall backtrack a bit to look at earlier peer relation-

[19] Some of the discontinuities associated with the upward mobility of good students from British working-class backgrounds are described in Jackson and Marsden (1962).

ships as socialization influences and then move to an examination of changing affiliations and identifications in later childhood.

SOCIALIZATION IN PEER RELATIONSHIPS

By the time they are two or three years old, most children will have interacted with siblings, cousins, or neighborhood age-mates. The two-year-old is not, in general, ready for joint activities with age-mates. Two-year-olds may play side by side, but they have little influence on each other except as they may contest for space or objects. But three- and four-year-olds show a markedly increased ability to play cooperatively and to form relationships. Initially one can hardly talk of a peer group or play group, even though the children are together a good deal of the time. Systematic study of groupings of young children has been largely confined to the nursery school, where their play and interactions have been observed under a wide variety of circumstances.[20] For most young children, the earliest peer contacts come directly under parental surveillance or the surveillance of an older sibling or other parent surrogate. Since the caretaker is often only partially engaged in attending to the child, however, early contacts with peers no more fully socialized than themselves put a premium on learning rudimentary social skills — on being aware of the presence and wishes of others, on communicating one's own wishes to a non-protective other, on defending oneself or learning to enlist the aid of others to deal with an aggressor. The play of small children entails social learning to a marked degree.

Although preschoolers clearly learn from one another, peer pressures have little meaning at this age level. A few years later, the emergence of structures of prestige and power within the classroom and in informal groups gives to the population of peers a special significance in socialization. To be liked, to be accepted in one's own milieu, is to feel comfortable; and being liked depends upon how both physical and social attributes of the child are valued in the peer group. These evaluations are manifest in sociometric patterns revealed in many studies.

A number of the peer evaluations of elementary and junior high school students are common to both the working and middle classes.[21] The attributes of boys nominated as leaders, for example, differ little between working-class and middle-class groups — being good at sports, daring,

[20] This literature has been reviewed by Swift (1964), who notes the very considerable influence of the child's temperament and activity level on developmental readiness for participation with other children.

[21] The findings here used as illustrative are taken from Pope (1953). The changing patterns of reputational correlates with age have been studied by Tryon (1939).

enthusiastic, assured, and having a sense of humor. Popularity is somewhat related to leadership, but here being regarded as friendly and good-looking by one's peers becomes highly salient. In some respects, there are significant differences in reputational correlates that reflect different patterns of activity and of peer pressures between the classes. Thus, among twelve-year-old girls, reputations of those named as "a girl who goes out with boys" vary substantially according to social class. In the working class, they are seen as girls who "act older than they are," who have boys' interests, are assured, and are to some degree leaders but *not* popular or friendly in the eyes of their classmates. Middle-class girls so nominated, on the other hand, are highly popular and regarded as friendly, good-looking, and enthusiastic.

The implications of such findings for socialization influences within the peer group are clear, but the complexity of influence mechanisms is such that antecedent-consequent statements regarding peer-group socialization are very difficult to make. The self-assured and attractive child seems to start out with a considerable advantage in terms of peer acceptance. The timid, constricted boy is the target for jeers; to be accepted he must work to overcome his fears and to show competence in activities that are important to his peers, or he must find compensatory satisfaction in more limited relationships and activities. The overly aggressive boy may be accepted as a leader in many activities but not be chosen as a friend.

Most children are sensitive to the evaluations others make of them. They receive feedback both in the peer group and through the comments of adults relating to their difficulties or successes. Several studies have found that less popular children tend to have lower self-esteem than their more popular peers. Insofar as their lack of popularity results from attributes (or deficiencies) about which they can do something, it appears to induce desires for change.[22]

The strength of peer-group influences will, of course, depend to a marked degree on the intensiveness of peer-group involvement as against other involvements and commitments. For many children, close friendship with one or two peers may be far more important than pressures for popularity and for conformity with peer norms. For most preadolescents incorporated into stable families, friendship will bring new opportunities for developing social sensitivities, for resolving differences of opinion and making decisions without adult intervention, but will not pose a threat to parent-child relationships or parental socialization aims. Parents by and large continue to be the primary influences upon the child well into adolescence. Joint parent-child activities and association tend to diminish

[22] Research on peer acceptance as an influence on socialization has recently been reviewed and summarized by Campbell (1964) and by Schmuck and Loman (1965).

in the later years of elementary school, and participation with peers increases; but if parents are available to their children there is unlikely to be a sharp break in the relationship.[23]

On the other hand, the child either without a stable home or at odds with his parents is likely to be assimilated into a group of peers who become his primary source of reference. Moreover, since such a child will tend to be less friendly and therefore less acceptable in the dominant peer groupings of the school, he is likely to choose and be chosen by others whose status is also in some sense problematic. In neighborhoods where seriously deviant behavior is widespread and opportunities for participation in a deviant subculture are readily available, such children are more likely than their peers to become delinquent.[24] In general, children become available for recruitment to delinquency inversely with the degree to which their self-images and self-esteem are anchored in satisfactory relationships in the home and in the school.

In many societies the transition from childhood to a substantially increased participation in adult activities is marked by initiation rites or *rites de passage*. Males are symbolically and often physically removed from close attachment to their mothers; females on the other hand may be more closely associated with, and watched over by, their mothers. There is a clear demarcation of one's responsibilities and appropriate activities as an adult man or woman, even though all the privileges of the position may not be immediately available. This does not, in most cases, mean that the individual leaves his parents' home or becomes less subject to their wishes for him. Socialization certainly does not require a sharp break with one's parents in order to achieve adult status, though such a break is not infrequent in our own society. Its occurrence is, indeed, a sign of difficulty in the socialization apparatus, and indication that the family and the school are not completely adequate instruments for preparing children for adult role performance.

As Eisenstadt (1962) has noted, youth groups tend to arise in societies in which the family or kinship unit cannot insure the attainment of full social status on the part of members. In such societies the division of labor is not linked to the kinship structure; and major political, economic, and religious functions are performed by specialized groups. Where participation in the family is an inadequate basis for developing full identity or full social maturity, Eisenstadt suggests that the adolescent seeks in youth groups "some framework for the development and crystallization of his identity, for the attainment of personal autonomy

[23] The most adequate data available on changing activity patterns as the child matures are those of Bowerman and Kinch (1959).

[24] See, for example, Reckless, Dinitz, and Murray (1956), and Dinitz, Scarpitti, and Reckless (1962) on the relationship between self-concept and delinquency during the age-span of twelve to sixteen years.

and for his effective transition into the adult world" (Eisenstadt, 1962, p. 36). Yet paradoxically, the values of the youth culture tend to be quite different from those of the larger adult society. The adolescent may be questing for identity; but as a participant in the youth culture he is, in Erikson's terms, experiencing a moratorium, not a rational transition. In any event, the pressures of the youth culture and the recognition that the life of the parental family has little new to offer him do bring about a marked change in association patterns and identifications of the adolescent in such societies. By the beginning of senior high school in the United States (around age fourteen), most children are more attracted to activities with peers than family activities. This does not mean that the values of parents are thrown over and that those of the peer group are ascendant, though such *may* be the case. Most adolescents do not appear to experience a major transformation of values or of identity but rather become more open to new experiences and begin to exercise markedly increased autonomy.[25] This is precisely one of the places where longitudinal study is most needed, however, so as to identify the precursors of sharply disjunctive shifts and the circumstances under which they tend to occur.

Peer socialization pressures are perhaps nowhere stronger than in asserting that the adolescent should be emancipated from parental restrictions. Nothing is more devastating to an adolescent male than to be viewed as under the control of his parents and especially of his mother. Thus the peer group enforces conformity to its definition of age-appropriate activities and norms. The sanctions employed are, in the last analysis, largely those of acceptance or rejection. And since there is no injunction that peers must be kind to one another, peer acceptance is likely to become a goal in its own right and the mastery of peer-valued skills a means to attaining that goal.

Explicit socialization aims are generally minimal in peer relations. Insofar as we deal with personal friendships, the relationship itself is the objective. Mutual selection may derive from living next door to each other, from the discovery of similarities in interests and values, from contacts initiated by parental friendships or associations, from shared misery, or from a variety of other circumstances. Friends provide acceptance, share experiences and confidences, and by and large do not boss each other around or seek to change each other. Yet the very mutuality of the relationship and the freedom for joint exploration lead to increasing convergence of opinions and values.[26]

[25] In addition to the research of Bowerman and Kinch, previously cited, evidence on this point comes from Riley, Riley, and Moore (1961), and from Douvan and Adelson (1966).

[26] This convergence has been documented most impressively by Newcomb (1961).

Most parents, particularly in the middle class, know the friends of their preadolescent children and at least know something about the friends of their adolescent offspring. They may seek to influence the choice of friends and may indeed be successful in doing so with the young child. But by and large friendships and peer-group influences are outside the orbit of parental control once the child is in school. For many parents, especially those living in crowded slum areas where social deviance is rife, the peer group represents the threat of loss of control. The relationship of peer-group norms and standards to those of the larger society may, however, vary greatly. Bronfenbrenner (1962) has provided a dramatic description of the way in which peer relations are used to buttress rather than to undermine conventional adult standards within the Soviet Union. Starting with the early years in the classroom, groups of peers are simultaneously thrown into competition with other groups, and the members of each group are made responsible for the showing of their unit. Each unit is, of course, part of a larger organization, and its performance and adherence to standards reflects credit or discredit on others. Under this system of peer control, deviance is likely to arouse a quick response. Indeed, Bronfenbrenner reports that Soviet children respond to a hypothetical situation entailing an instance of socially disapproved behavior quite differently than do children in the United States. Not only are the Soviet children less willing than their counterparts to say that they will engage in the disapproved behavior, but they are *less* likely to say that they will engage in it if told that their classmates will see their answers. By contrast, American children say they would be *more* likely to engage in the behavior when told that their answers would be seen by their classmates (Bronfenbrenner, 1966).

Control of peer relationships in the interest of a standardized morality is hardly consonant with American valuing of individual freedom. There are, however, many instances in which the allocation of responsibility to peers is demonstrably feasible. Particularly in regard to the adolescent, as Coleman (1961) has suggested, it would appear that more effective use might be made of the influence potential of the peer group itself by allocating to it a greater measure of responsibility for setting and maintaining standards within educational and community spheres. Only systematic research based on action programs can establish whether or not such increased responsibility will tend to carry over to other areas of social participation.

Although there is widespread recognition that "the peer group" is often treated much too glibly as though it were a monolithic force, there has been relatively little research on the direct influence of individual peer relationships (and sibling relationships) in the socialization process. Groups of friends do not merely participate in a youth culture where fun and glamour are to be pursued. To a considerable extent they are likely to try to formulate and examine their own dilemmas; to influence each other's interests and commitments; and to share experiences that call into question authoritative pronouncements by parents, teachers, and other adult socialization agents. To the extent that moral issues have been oversimplified in order to impose a more coherent, compelling basis for the normative order — as they tend to be oversimplified by parents, teachers, and legal systems — the examination of such issues by peers freed from adult constrictions becomes a basis for a more realistic view of the social order. Parental values are not so much repudiated as recast, despite the fact that a direct confrontation of parent and adolescent on issues relating to values may polarize each to positions far different from those taken in another context.

One of the most striking illustrations of the grossly different perceptions of the adolescent on the part of teachers, parents, and peers is given by Goldman's research on actual and ideal images of the contemporary high school graduate (1962). Teachers, parents, and high school students agreed reasonably well on the characterization of the ideal. They varied greatly in their views of the extent to which the actual high school graduate approached the ideal, with teachers most negative and students least negative in their views of the actual adolescent. For many adults the monolithic image of the youth culture is taken as a description of youth rather than the caricature that it is.

By adolescence, the nature of the socialization process has markedly changed. The child has become far more active in defining his own goals and in seeking the kind of socialization experience that will help him achieve them. The initiative is now largely his except in situations where specified requirements must be met in order to secure some further opportunity or where behaviors deriving from deviant modes of socialization call into action resocialization or reformative efforts on the part of the community. The characteristics of such socialization activities and the involvement of the individual's identity in his later socialization experience are discussed in Chapter Five.

The transition from childhood to adolescence and adulthood is not, we have noted, marked by ceremony or by sharp change in our society. It is a transition that has to be worked out through gradual changes in role relationships and commitments.

CHANGING RELATIONSHIPS BETWEEN PARENT AND CHILD

Changes in parent-child interaction in the course of socialization reflect both the child's maturing and the nature of his role involvements outside the family. At every stage of development, the parent is confronted with decisions concerning how much control he should attempt to exercise, how much autonomy he should grant. In the early years we have noted that parental power is very high and that it may be exercised either through the use of superior strength or through direct control of the child's environment. As the child matures, less and less of this physical and social environment is under the direct surveillance or control of the parents. Power can still be used punitively by the parents, but such use is likely to alienate the child and to increase the amount of time spent away from home engaged in activities disapproved by the parents.

The parent must, then, yield initiative and responsibility to the child to the degree that seems consonant with the child's capabilities. Here parents have few guidelines other than impressionistic ones. The claims of the child upon the parent are also likely to be quite different beyond early childhood than they were when the parent was the primary source of both nurturance and orientation. In our society, these claims are less well formulated, however, by either parent or child, with the consequence that many children feel that their parents are less available to them than they would wish, at the same time that parents feel their children are rejecting them. This availability does not seem to be merely a matter of parental time, though that may be part of the problem.

There appear to be rather significant class differences in the extent to which socialization aims continue to have primacy in parent-child relationships. Studies of the working-class adolescent suggest that there may be more demand for help in the home (without significant relinquishment of controls relating to home life) but more acceptance of freedom outside the home. Lesser parental awareness of alternative developmental pathways and greater preoccupation with the adolescent's immediate situation are likely to result in lesser efforts to help the adolescent take stock of his opportunities and his current status.[27] Once the adolescent begins to earn money outside the family, he is less subject to parental control by manipulation of resources. For the middle-class child who has long-range plans entailing college attendance, parents are obviously better able to continue exercising influence through control of resources and also are more involved in joint exploration of opportunities and requirements.

The adolescent is the intellectual equal of his parents, if lacking their experience. Moreover, he is likely to be much more *au courant* with changes occurring in social patterns and moral norms. He is aware of alternatives to his parents' perspectives and is likely to reject some of the beliefs to which they are strongly committed. Where such matters can

[27] Again our evidence is limited largely to impressions from research focusing on other problems (for example, Komarovsky, 1964) except for a study by Psathas (1957).

be discussed on a more or less equal basis, they may not seriously interfere either with the affectional relationship between parent and child or with the congruence of their aims. Often, of course, these matters become a basis for bickering and polarization of other attitudes. It appears that few parents are prepared to acknowledge to an eighteen-year-old that his assessment of what is important is as valid as their own, partly because they do not believe that it is, and partly because they find it difficult to modify a role relationship in which they have been interpreting the world to the child.[28]

The child early acquires a basic identification with his parents; they are the center of his universe. If they insist on remaining the center of his universe well into adolescence, however, and pressure him to resist widely accepted peer practices, the child is likely either to make a choice in the direction opposite to that wished by the parents or to become profoundly ambivalent. The direction of socialization influence within the family must, to some degree, be reversed if there is to be successful communication; that is, beginning with the child's first excursions outside the orbit of his home and becoming increasingly significant in later childhood and adolescence, the parents must rely upon the child for orientation to his world. Since they are not privy to full participation in it, they are as dependent upon him to know the meanings of activities in that world as he was upon them for his early orientation. If the child alone is aware of the contradictions in norms that are presented to him in various settings, so that no one else knows the extent to which the tasks he is asked to do are discordant or meaningless by the standards of another setting, the whole task of resolution and synthesis remains for him to accomplish without assistance. In the last analysis, of course, only he can achieve such resolution, but this is a place where skilled socialization agents can offer guidance and enhance understanding.

What kinds of problems do children take to their parents? What kinds do they take to their peers? More important, how do their patterns of discussing what is important to them within the family and outside of it change over time? We have only the most meager data about the antecedents within the family and the external pressures that modify communicational and affectional patterns. Parents appear in our culture

[28] What data we have on this point come largely from studies of family interaction (often using the technique of revealed differences) and from reports of adolescents about the extent to which their parents listen to their views and yield responsibility for decisions. When such interaction is under observation, it is likely that most parents bend over backwards to show that they are democratic and willing to give the adolescent his say. It would be desirable to study the perceptions parents and children have of family conversation and especially of discussions that generate heat or that are broken off without resolution of tensions.

to be less free to reject their children than are children to reject their parents. Rejection by children of the standards of their parents and even of the parents themselves is not, of course, a new phenomenon despite recent concern about alienated youth. It has always been an especially acute problem in the face of major social conflict and social change. Social disorganization because of a breakdown of traditional ways among immigrant groups tends to be most serious for the second generation, which seeks to accept new patterns but is often not accepted in the new environment. A similar problem confronts militant Negroes, who face a poignant dilemma in the socialization of their children. Shall they be oriented to fight against any indication of discrimination, or shall they be prepared to compete as effectively as possible within the larger society? One cannot achieve acceptance by constantly contending with his associates, yet one may thereby achieve a reallocation of power and influence. It is likely that explicit parental socialization efforts will be less crucial here than the effects of social action and the commentaries the child hears — the exultations and the lamentations — about the plight of his people.

This kind of dilemma is not confined to the markedly deprived or to conflict groups, however. Similar, if less drastic, choices confront parents in considering the kind of education and orientation a very bright daughter should receive, or the kind of sex education to be given a child in the era of "the pill." Inevitably social change makes for discontinuity of influences between the home and some segment of the larger society in which the child participates. A parent or a teacher may feel that certain kinds of information are better kept from the child but may be completely unable to exert the control he would wish for. Under the circumstances, then, he must either ask how he can best prepare the child to handle the information when it comes, provide the information himself, or — and this may well be the modal response — he may simply abdicate his socialization role, hoping that the child will be able to manage somehow.

SUGGESTIONS FOR FUTURE RESEARCH

In reviewing childhood socialization across settings and over time, one becomes more sharply aware of the great number of influences acting upon the child and interacting with one another. At the same time, such a descriptive account may seem overly pat, making the process of socialization appear more obvious and less issue laden than it actually is. In every setting, socialization agents are confronted with problems of strategy, yet relatively few of these problems have been studied. Systems of rewards and punishments and effects of variations in restrictiveness have been examined to a considerable degree, though mostly as they bear upon the socialization of the younger child. But the effects of restrictiveness in one setting — the family, for example — upon the child's performance in the classroom under different systems of classroom control or different degrees of restrictiveness have not been examined. Again, it is widely recognized that the child from a deprived minority background, or any ethnic background that has value orientations different from those of the dominant culture, will learn both sets of values, will experience conflict, and will have to deal with that conflict one way or another. Yet the modes of conflict resolution and the action of various socialization agents in facilitating such resolution have been little studied except in immigrant groups and in analyses of the ways in which delinquent or other deviant behaviors are rendered acceptable through rationalization and through the neutralization of the norms of the larger society.[29] It seems reasonably well established that delinquents and non-delinquents alike are aware of both the conventional and the subterranean value systems that exist in the urban slum. But we know less of the way in which the non-delinquent handles value conflict in this milieu than of the orientations of the delinquent.

To take another simple example, we know from several recent studies that the preparation a child receives for school — the orientation he is given and the cognitive skills he has acquired in the family — will influence his performance in preschool programs and in the first grade. From other research with older children we know that the combinations of control and support provided for, and of autonomy granted to, the child by his parents are related to his classroom performance and his acceptance by peers. But we have almost no data on the ways in which parental attitudes and behaviors toward the child change by virtue of the child's reports of his school and peer experience. We can cite examples of a variety of possible changes, and we can readily believe that such interactions between events and influences in one setting make a difference in the other setting and in the child's integration of his experiences. What we need to know, however, is how often, under what circumstances, and with what consequences do such interactions occur? What are the most salient interactions, from the standpoint of particular constellations of settings, agents, and aims?

Do parents respond to the child's disappointment and failures in school with emotional support and encouragement toward more successful performance, do they offer the child excuses so that he will be less inclined to try for success, or do they respond punitively because he has

[29] A cogent analysis of the use of "techniques of neutralization" is given in Sykes and Matza (1957).

let them down? More generally, what is the degree of interpenetration of the influences of various agents in the major socialization settings of childhood? There is much evidence for a more consistent, cohesive network of socialization influences in the small community than in the larger city. Not only are there far fewer bases of differentiation, but controls are exercised and affirmed through an interlocking network of personal relationships across settings. Beyond the confines of the small community, cultures differ markedly in the extent to which the child's behavior is everybody's business.

The call for more attention to sequences of influence and to the overall effect of a myriad of competing and interacting sources of influence may dismay those who are dedicated to rigorous experimental studies of socialization. Such studies have added immensely to our understanding of psychological processes underlying social influence. Comparable rigor in problem analysis and methodological design in the study of sequence and of the interactions among agents and agencies is needed if we are to understand the linkages among influence systems and their effects on personal commitment and personality development.

Concepts for the analysis of relationships among socialization settings are few and crude. They need elaboration. How can the interpenetrations or the linkages between systems best be characterized and indexed? How can the explicit and implicit value orientations of different settings be assessed as they impinge upon the child at different age levels? To what extent can one identify transferable and non-transferable (or even detrimental) skills fostered in different settings or roles? How are various roles that are potentially available to the child defined by his significant socialization agents? What attributes of character or personality are most valued by each of these agents, and how does the child perceive these valuations?

Through all of our efforts to trace developmental sequences and socialization influences it is necessary to view the child as an active agent, forging his own identity, no matter how problematic that identity may be. Large segments of the world's population take a fatalistic view of their influence and power when considering their potential impact on the social order or even upon their own futures. Yet it is hardly to be doubted that the great majority of persons in most societies are aware of their ability to make choices that will affect their lives. They make such choices at many points in the course of becoming adults. An examination of the range of socialization influences over time can give some indication of the kinds of choices that are available, the circumstances under which they are made, and the ways in which the individual maximizes his ability to fill the roles available to adult members of his society.

REFERENCES

Aberle, D. F., and Naegele, K. D. Middle-class fathers' occupational role and attitudes toward children. *American Journal of Orthopsychiatry*, 1952, 22, 366–78.

Bandura, A., and Walters, R. A. *Social Learning and Personality Development*. New York: Holt, Rinehart & Winston, 1963.

Bateson, G. Social Planning and the concept of "deuterolearning." In T. M. Newcomb and E. L. Hartley, *Readings in Social Psychology*. New York: Henry Holt & Co., 1947. Pp. 121–28.

Becker, W. C. Consequences of different kinds of parental discipline. In M. L. Hoffman and Lois W. Hoffman (Eds.), *Review of Child Development Research*. Vol. 1. New York: Russell Sage Foundation, 1964. Pp. 169–208.

Bernstein, B. Elaborated and restricted codes: their social origins and some consequences. In J. J. Gumperz and D. Hymes (Eds.), *The Ethnography of Communication*. Special publication of the *American Anthropologist*, 1964, 66, No. 6, Part 2, 55–69.

Bowerman, C. E., and Kinch, J. W. Changes in family and peer orientations of children between the fourth and tenth grades. *Social Forces*, 1959, 37, 206–11.

Bowlby, J. The nature of the child's tie to his mother. *International Journal of Psycho-Analysis*, 1958, 39, 1–24.

Brim, O. G., Jr. Personality development as role learning. In I. Iscoe and H. Stevenson (Eds.), *Personality Development in Children*. Austin: University of Texas Press, 1960. Pp. 127–59.

Bronfenbrenner, U. Response to pressure from peers versus adults among Soviet and American school children. Paper delivered at the XIX International Congress of Psychology, Moscow, U.S.S.R., August 1966.

Bronfenbrenner, U. Soviet methods of character education: some implications for research. *American Psychologist*, 1962, 17, No. 8, 550–64.

Brown, C. *Manchild in the Promised Land*. New York: The Macmillan Co., 1965.

Brown, R. *Words and Things*. New York: The Free Press, 1958.

Campbell, J. D. Peer relations in childhood. In M. L. Hoffman and Lois W. Hoffman (Eds.), *Review of Child Development Research*. Vol. 1. New York: Russell Sage Foundation, 1964. Pp. 289–322.

Carlson, R. O. Variation and myth in social status of teachers. *Journal of Educational Sociology*, 1961, 35, 104–18.

Chombart de Lauwe, Marie-José. La représentation de l'enfant dans la société urbaine contemporaine. *Enfance*, 1962, No. 1, 53–67.

Clark, B. R. *Educating the Expert Society*. San Francisco: Chandler Publishing Co., 1962.

Clausen, J. A. Family structure, socialization, and personality. In M. L. Hoffman and Lois W. Hoffman (Eds.), *Review of Child Development Research*. Vol. 2. New York: Russell Sage Foundation, 1966. Pp. 1–53.

Coleman, J. S. *The Adolescent Society*. New York: The Free Press, 1961.

Coleman, J. S., *et al. Equality of Educational Opportunity*. Washington: U.S. Government Printing Office, 1966.

Dahlke, H. O. *Values in Culture and Classroom: A Study in the Sociology of the School*. New York: Harper, 1958.

Diamond, S. Kibbutz and Shtetle: the history of an idea. *Social Problems*, 1957, 5, 71–99.

Dinitz, S., Scarpitti, G. R., and Reckless, W. C. Delinquency vulnerability: a cross-group and longitudinal analysis. *American Sociological Review,* 1962, 27, 515–17.

Douvan, Elizabeth, and Adelson, J. *The Adolescent Experience.* New York: John Wiley & Sons, 1966.

Durkheim, E. *Education and Sociology.* New York: The Free Press, 1963.

Eisenstadt, S. N. Archetypal patterns of youth. *Daedalus,* Winter 1962, 28–46.

Eisenstadt, S. N. Education and political development. In D. C. Piper and T. Cole (Eds.), *Post-Primary Education and Political and Economic Development.* Durham, N.C.: Duke University Press, 1964. Pp. 27–47.

Elder, G. H., Jr., and Bowerman, C. E. Family structure and child-rearing patterns: the effect of family size and sex composition. *American Sociological Review,* 1963, 28, 891–905.

Fox, R. R., Lippitt, R., Schmuck, R., and Van Egmond, E. *Understanding Classroom Social Relations.* Chicago: Science Research Associates. (In press) Especially Chap. 17.

Glidewell, J. C., Kantor, Mildred C., Smith, L. M., and Stringer, L. A. Socialization and social structure in the classroom. In M. L. Hoffman and Lois W. Hoffman (Eds.), *Review of Child Development Research.* Vol. 2. New York: Russell Sage Foundation, 1966. Pp. 221–56.

Goldman, S. Profiles of an adolescent. *Journal of Psychology,* 1962, 54, 229–40.

Gross, N. *Who Runs Our Schools?* New York: John Wiley & Sons, 1958.

Harlow, H. F. The formation of learning sets. *Psychological Review,* 1949, 56, 51–65.

Harlow, H. F., and Harlow, Margaret. The affectational systems. In A. M. Schrier, H. F. Harlow, and F. Stollnitz (Eds.), *Behavior of Nonhuman Primates.* Vol. 2. New York: Academic Press, 1965.

Hart, C. W. M. Contrasts between prepubertal and postpubertal education. In G. D. Spindler (Ed.), *Education and Anthropology.* Stanford: Stanford University Press, 1955. Pp. 127–62.

Harvey, O. J., Prather, M., White, B. J., and Hoffmeister, J. K. Teachers' beliefs, classroom atmosphere and student behavior. *American Educational Research Journal,* March 1968, 5.

Harvey, O. J., White, B. J., Prather, M., Alter, R. D., and Hoffmeister, J. K. Teachers' belief systems and preschool atmospheres. *Journal of Educational Psychology,* 1966, 57, 373–81.

Havighurst, R. J. *Developmental Tasks and Education.* Chicago: University of Chicago Press, 1948.

Havighurst, R. J. *Human Development and Education.* New York: Longmans, Green, 1953.

Hess, R. D., and Shipman, Virginia. Maternal attitude toward the school and the role of the pupil: some social class comparisons. In A. H. Passow (Ed.), *Fifth Work Conference on Curriculum and Teaching in Depressed Areas.* New York: Columbia University, Teachers College, 1967.

Himmelweit, Hilde T., and Sealy, A. P. The school as an agent of socialization. London, 1966. (Mimeo)

Hymes, D. H. The ethnography of speaking. In T. Gladwin and W. C. Sturtevant (Eds.), *Anthropology and Human Behavior.* Washington, D.C.: Anthropological Society of Washington, 1962. Pp. 13–53.

Jackson, B., and Marsden, D. *Education and the Working Class.* London: Routledge and Kegan Paul, 1962.

Kaufman, Bel. *Up the Down Staircase.* New York: Prentice-Hall, 1964.

Kellam, S. G., and Schiff, S. K. Adaptation and mental illness in the first-grade classrooms of an urban community. American Psychiatric Association, Psychiatric Research Report No. 21: Poverty and Mental Health. (Mimeo)

Keniston, K. Social change and youth in America. *Daedalus,* Winter 1962, 145–71.

Keniston, K. *The Uncommitted: Alienated Youth in American Society.* New York: Harcourt, Brace & World, 1960.

Koch, H. L. Sibling influence on children's speech. *Journal of Speech Disorder,* 1956, *21,* 322–28.

Kohn, M. L. Social class and parent-child relationships: an interpretation. *American Journal of Sociology,* 1963, *68,* 471–80.

Komarovsky, Mirra. *Blue Collar Marriage.* New York: Random House, 1964.

Kounin, J. S., and Gump, P. V. The ripple effect in discipline. *Elementary School Journal,* 1958, *59,* 158–62.

Kubie, L. S. Social forces and the neurotic process. In A. H. Leighton, J. A. Clausen, and R. N. Wilson (Eds.), *Explorations in Social Psychiatry.* New York: Basic Books, 1957. Pp. 77–104.

Lasko, Joan K. Parent behavior toward first and second children. *Genetic Psychology Monographs,* 1954, *49,* 96–137.

Lippitt, Peggy, and Lohman, J. E. Cross-age relationships — an educational resource. *Children,* 1966, *12,* 113–17.

Lippitt, R. Processes of curriculum change. In R. E. Leeper (Ed.), *Curriculum Change: Direction and Process.* Washington: National Education Association, 1966. Pp. 43–59.

Lippitt, R., Polansky, N., Redl, F., and Rosen, S. The dynamics of power. *Human Relations,* 1952, *5,* 37–64.

Litwak, E., and Meyer, H. J. Administrative styles and community linkages of public schools. In A. J. Reiss (Ed.), *Effects of School Administrative Ogranizations on Youth and Community.* New York: The Free Press, 1965.

Loevinger, Jane. Patterns of parenthood as theories of learning. *Journal of Abnormal and Social Psychology,* 1959, *59,* 148–50.

Luszki, M. B., and Schmuck, R. Pupil perceptions of parental attitudes toward school. *Mental Hygiene,* 1963, *47,* 289–99.

Maccoby, Eleanor E. Effects of the mass media. In M. L. Hoffman and Lois W. Hoffman (Eds.), *Review of Child Development Research.* Vol. 1. New York: Russell Sage Foundation, 1964. Pp. 323–48.

MacKinnon, D. W. Personality and the realization of creative potential. *American Psychologist,* 1965, *20,* 273–81.

McCarthy, Dorothea. Language development in children. In L. Carmichael (Ed.), *Manual of Child Psychology.* New York: John Wiley & Sons, 1954. Pp. 492–630.

McClelland, D. C. *The Achieving Society.* Princeton, N.J.: D. Van Nostrand Co., 1961.

McGraw, Myrtle B. *Growth: A Study of Johnny and Jimmy.* New York: Appleton, 1935.

Mead, Margaret. *Growing Up in New Guinea: A Comparative Study of Primitive Education.* New York: William Morrow & Co., 1930.

Mead, Margaret, and Calas, Elena. Child-training ideals in a post-revolutionary context: Soviet Russia. In M. Mead and M. Wolfenstein (Eds.), *Childhood in Contemporary Cultures.* Chicago: University of Chicago Press, 1955. Pp. 179–203.

Morris, M. G., and Gould, R. W. Role reversal: a concept in dealing with the neglected/battered child syndrome. In *The Neglected Battered Child Syndrome*. New York: Child Welfare League of America, 1963. Pp. 29–49.

Newcomb, T. M. *The Acquaintance Process*. New York: Holt, Rinehart & Winston, 1961.

Parsons, T. Family structure and the socialization of the child. In T. Parsons and R. F. Bales, *Family, Socialization and Interaction Process*. Glencoe, Ill.: The Free Press, 1955. Pp. 35–131.

Parsons, T. Youth in the context of American society. *Daedalus*, Winter 1962, 97–123.

Pearlin, L. I., and Kohn, M. L. Social class, occupation, and parental values: a cross-national study. *American Sociological Review*, 1966, *31*, 466–79.

Pope, B. Socio-economic contrasts in children's peer culture prestige values. *Genetic Psychology Monographs*, 1953, *48*, 157–220.

Psathas, G. Ethnicity, social class and adolescent independence from parental control. *American Sociological Review*, 1957, 22, 415–23.

Reckless, W. C., Dinitz, S., and Murray, E. Self concept as an insulator against delinquency. *American Sociological Review*, 1956, *21*, 744–46.

Richey, R., and Fox, W. *An Analysis of Various Factors Associated with Selection of Teaching as a Vocation*. Bulletin of the School of Education, Indiana University, Division of Research and Field Services, May 1948.

Riley, M. H., Riley, J. W., Jr., and Moore, M. E. Adolescent values and the Riesman typology: an empirical analysis. In S. M. Lipset and L. Lowenthal (Eds.), *Culture and Social Character*. New York: The Free Press, 1961.

Schaefer, E. S. A circumplex model for maternal behavior. *Journal of Abnormal and Social Psychology*, 1959, *59*, 226–35.

Schmuck, R., and Loman, Anita. Peer relations and personality development. Institute for Social Research, Ann Arbor, Michigan, 1965. (Mimeo)

Schmuck, R., and Van Egmond, E. Sex differences in the relationship of interpersonal perceptions to academic performance. *Psychology in the Schools*, 1965, 2, 32–40.

Sears, R. R., Maccoby, Eleanor E., and Levin, H. *Patterns of Child Rearing*. Evanston, Ill.: Row, Peterson & Co., 1957.

Stendler, Celia B. Social class differences in parental attitude toward school at grade 1 level. *Child Development*, 1951, 22, 37–46.

Stendler, Celia B., and Young, N. The impact of beginning first grade upon socialization as reported by mothers. *Child Development*, 1950, *21*, 241–60.

Sullivan, H. S. *The Interpersonal Theory of Psychiatry*. New York: W. W. Norton & Co., 1953.

Swift, Joan W. Effects of early group experience: the nursery school and day nursery. In M. L. Hoffman and Lois W. Hoffman (Eds.), *Review of Child Development Research*. Vol. 1. New York: Russell Sage Foundation, 1964.

Sykes, G. M., and Matza, D. Techniques of neutralization. *American Sociological Review*, 1957, 22, 664–70.

Tryon, Caroline M. Evaluations of adolescent personality by adolescents. *Monographs of the Society for Research in Child Development*, 1939, *4*, No. 4 (whole No. 23).

Turner, R. H. Sponsored and contest mobility and the school system. *American Sociological Review*, 1960, *25*, 855–67.

Westoff, C., Potter, R. G., and Sagi, P. *The Third Child*. Princeton, N.J.: Princeton University Press, 1963.

Wylie, L. Youth in France and in the United States. *Daedalus*, Winter 1962, 198–215.

ORVILLE G. BRIM, JR.

FIVE *Adult Socialization*

CONTENTS

INTRODUCTION

One may be surprised at the lack of study given to adults by scholars in the area of socialization. After all, most of the world's great drama and literature is about adults, not children, and most of it describes the passage of adults from one role to another — how it happened, who demanded it, how one meets the new demands or avoids them. "One man in his time plays many parts," wrote Shakespeare; husband, father, old man, widower, soldier, employee, colleague, leader — these and many other roles are required of a person during the course of his adult years.

Socialization is continuous throughout life, for though individuals enter the adult world with some anticipatory socialization, the socialization experienced in childhood is not enough to meet the demands of the later years. This is especially true in modern industrialized societies and particularly so in the United States. In these rapidly changing societies, the lives of the new wave of twenty-one-year-olds who each year join the ranks of adults do not follow those of their predecessors. The younger adults must find new models or develop new styles of life without them; meanwhile, the older adults try to adjust to the conflicts created by the rapid rate of ideological and technological change.

Among those roles for which anticipatory socialization might take place, some require intolerable demands upon the person to practice, so to speak, the role which lies ahead. Lawyers and insurance men know how difficult it is to get most wives even to contemplate life as a widow, much less think through carefully what the role will require, and even perhaps to practice on occasion living alone and being independent while the husband is still alive. Downward mobility is a fact of many adult lives, but it is not reasonable to expect one, ahead of time, to practice life at a lower standard of living.

Adults must change and must be socialized into new roles. This essay

Prepared with the assistance of Peter J. Stein and Ruth Felsher Schreiber.

presents an informal overview of some of the things the American adult will confront in occupations, in the family, and in the community, as he lives through a fifty-year period. It is a selective survey of contexts and types of adult socialization experiences and an identification of certain research and theoretical topics of adult socialization. What will others demand of him, and what will he come to demand of himself? How will he be able to meet these demands for change, and how can he reconcile his own wishes with those of society?

The review deals with the non-deviant adult — the average person and his experience. A good portion of what little research has been done on socialization of adult life has been concerned with the deviant individual. This well-known body of work includes the sociological analyses of the attempts by society through its institutions to socialize the delinquent or criminal in order to return him to a non-criminal way of life. Another major body of studies deals with socialization of the addicted, that is, the alcoholic or the drug addict. A third group of studies is concerned with the processes and effects of various therapies for the emotionally ill. The literature on these types of deviant behavior and the attempts to alter it through adult socialization are available in good recent reviews such as those by Wolfgang, Savitz, and Johnston (1962), or Becker (1964).

The studies of life changes associated with the changing physical state of the adult constitute another important body of socialization research, even though most were not made from this viewpoint. It is fairly obvious that important changes in socialization prescriptions for the adult will accompany changes in his health or the onset of a disability. Discussion of such studies is omitted from this chapter because much of the material is familiar to the reader and is readily available. Accidents which are disabling in minor or major ways render the adult unable to carry out his ordinary roles and require him to learn new roles. The adjustment of the disabled, of the physically handicapped, and of the blind have been analyzed and reviewed in some well-known sociological studies (Barker, 1953; Scott, 1968; Sussman, 1965). Other important work includes analyses of the impact of illness on the person (Davis, 1963) and of the consequences of physical stigma (Goffman, 1963). Aging itself, of course, is associated with changed demands for behavior because of the various increased disabilities which are correlated with the aging organism. Beginning with the middle years there frequently is a decline in strength, vigor, and memory, which leads to inability to carry out satisfactorily some of the customary roles the adult performs, which in turn leads to a readjustment of expectations and of performance levels. Socialization in later years that is a direct consequence of changed physical states can be reviewed in Riley (1968), and in Williams, Tibbitts, and Donahue (1963).

Individuals and groups differ greatly in the evenness of their lives, that is, in the degree to which they are under pressure to change as they move through the stages of the adult years. Some live very simply and have undemanding lives, with little change in their environments or their personalities. Even though socialization in later life is more characteristic of modern societies, with their increased rate of change and customs, their greater rates of social mobility, and their more rapid obsolescence of information, the quiet life still is the rule for most adults. In later sections of this chapter many life episodes in the family, work, and community are noted which cause socialization. We must stress that no single person will experience all of the episodes; for instance, except in unusual cases, one is not highly mobile both upward and downward in his lifetime. For the typical adult in the United States, most days ask very little in the way of change, and most people seem to like it this way. But other persons are beset by a wide array of demands, from society or from themselves, far exceeding those that the normal person faces. The life-spans of some are broken into separate phases by the demands upon them for radical change arising from divorce, family deaths, illness, loss of job, etc. It seems certain, also, that different categories of people face different types and degrees of adult socialization — for example, men versus women, rich versus poor. In this review we note many such differences in which sex, ethnicity, or social class seems to be correlated with the kind of demands for change which adults face.

THE DEMANDS OF SELF AND OTHERS

In our view socialization is the process by which one learns to perform his various roles adequately, and our concern here is with the acquisition of social roles. This may not encompass the whole of socialization, but role acquisition is an extremely important, if not the most important, component of adult socialization. In each instance of socialization a key element is the role prescription or expectation that someone else has for the person in question, which involves a change in, or addition to, that person's beliefs, attitudes, or behavior, or motives or values, with reference to some social situation. But the prescriptions by members of society for how an adult should change — that is, the demands of others — are only part of the picture. The person himself has many self-initiated ideas and prescriptions for his own personality and behavior change, and in many cases the self-initiated socialization is a greater source of adult personality change than are the demands of other persons.

The Demands of Others

Individuals or groups have an interest in changing the behavior of an adult so that his behavior will be more in accord with the wishes of the individual or group. In a complex, pluralistic society, such as the United States, many persons and groups compete for effective influence over the behavior of an adult and seek to alter the adult's personality in large or small ways to accommodate their own desires. The differences and conflicts between the objectives of these various persons are manifest in the efforts at adult socialization. The employer, the wife, the child, the advertiser, the physician, the politician — each in his or her own way has an interest in the adult's personality and behavior and seeks to remake it to his own advantage. The fashion industry conflicts with the husband's wishes about his wife's behavior, while the liquor industry competes with the wife in attempting to change her husband's habits. Each group has its own modes of attempted influence, and each has its relative persuasive power. The control over powerful rewards and punishments in the hands of the employers and family members make them especially effective in socialization efforts, while on the periphery of influence are neighbors, political groups, advertisers, and others.

We do not consider here the relative effectiveness of different "methods" of adult socialization. Much research has been done (Mann, 1965) on the effectiveness of various methods — including the one-minute radio talk and the use of drugs and other devices to influence prisoners of war — in inducing attitude and behavior change. In the sophisticated studies, the interactions of methods with the social conditions under which the effort at change is made and with adult personality characteristics are considered. Conceptually, these must be classed as studies of adult socialization, with a special focus not on content but on the efficacy of different procedures.

The focus of this chapter, as indicated earlier, is the substance of the demands made upon the adult, classified roughly according to the work situation, the family, and the community as the setting of the demands. We can say generally that in any of these adult socialization contexts those persons making the socialization effort can, and often do, make use of a whole range of procedures to induce attitude change and behavior. These persons seeking to socialize the adult employ various mass media to influence him and also engage in direct face-to-face interaction, the manipulation of group pressures, the use of economic sanctions in some instances, and other techniques to bring about change.

The cause of changed prescriptions for an adult's role performances are the more basic changes in economic resources, population pressures, density of and proximity to other kinds of persons, physical and emotional makeup of persons with whom the adult is closely associated, and other facts of life. The changes demanded of the adult may be at a very general or societal level, entailing alterations in the law, in the formal sense, on a regional or national basis. The demand that one desegregate his store, inn, restaurant, theater, or private club requires for many white Americans, both southern and northern, a change in beliefs and attitudes that contrasts sharply with earlier and deeply learned views toward the Negro. Changes in laws in a complex society follow from the more basic changes in the economy, from the available pool of trained talent, the need for men to fight the country's war, the growth or decline in population, the obsolescence of certain occupations, and so on.

The demands from others for change occur more frequently at the immediate level of social interaction than as a result of a change in the nation's laws. A person's occupational role, for example, may alter. The owner of a private filling station may no longer be able to compete with others and may be forced to join a larger petroleum company chain; as a consequence, his relation to his suppliers and his clients will no longer be the same. A man may be told that he has risen as high as he can go in his place of work and that his present position must be accepted by him as the achievement level for his lifetime; thus it is demanded that he deal in some way with his achievement motivation — his orientation toward success — and do so without displacing frustration upon something else or making a desperate and unwise change of occupation. The wealthy person who loses his money must adjust to a new place of residence, to new social groups, and to new consumption patterns, and, the impact of downward mobility being what it is, must also handle the deeper adjustment involving his self-esteem. Or change may result in the family because the increasing strength and knowledge of the eldest son enables him to challenge effectively the authority of the mother and father and to force a realignment of customary relationships within the family. The married woman who is widowed is faced with demands to substitute autonomy in decisions and actions for the customary dependency which characterized her relationship with her husband. Some women make this transition while others reestablish the familiar relationship through remarriage or alliance with a more autonomous woman friend.

The socialization of an adult is tied to the characteristics of that person, apart from changes in the outer world which lead to altered prescriptions on the part of others. Aging, in particular, is a source of changed demands on the adult. As one ages he progresses through the age-graded positions in society, from marriage to parenthood, through increased responsibilities in the community, and through positions of authority and leadership in employment, into a period of declining responsibility. There is, of course, nothing mystical about the fact that aging is associated with such progression. The natural accumulation of experience and power through maturation enables a member of society to assume roles which he could not take on before. The successful fulfillment of these more important roles is desirable from the viewpoint of society because of the contribution made to the general welfare. Hence there is strong pressure upon an adult to take on such roles and, indeed, to be enthusiastic about his progression "upward" and the chance to discharge his adult responsibilities to society. In the area of the family one is expected to marry and have children and rear them to maturity. In the occupational world, as one progresses he is expected to accept the advancements, along with increased rewards, of course, and not to refuse promotion. Senior professors who turn down deanships are frowned upon, and it is not easy to find a college where one can be a lifetime assistant professor, much as one might wish to. Thus the demands of the outer world are fitted to the perceived abilities of the adult, and these are closely associated with age grading in most societies; maturation itself leads to changes in the demands of others and to pressures toward socialization for new responsibilities (Riley, 1968; Williams, Tibbitts, and Donahue, 1963; Williams and Wirths, 1965).

Self-initiated Socialization

Many people have characteristics of their personalities — some aspects of their behavior and life styles — which are not what they wish them to be. Of these, a large number, perhaps larger than is commonly recognized, seek to change themselves to become more acceptable in their own eyes. Most analyses of socialization, whether of children or adults, view the process as one in which social groups or persons are training the child or adult for some role. Little attention has been given to the quite obvious self-initiated attempts by a person to change and improve his performance of certain roles in his life. As far as we have been able to find out, no major investigation has ever been made of the kinds of changes adults may be seeking to make in their personalities; that is, evidently no one has systematically asked adults about this, even though adults, clearly more than children, are able to, and surely do, initiate their own socialization. For some adults one could even say that most of their personality change is the result of their own efforts rather than the result of the demands of others. And it appears that self-initiated socialization may be on the increase because of the greater affluence of the average adult and the greater leisure for experimenting in new areas of life.

Some of the drive toward change is economic in origin. One attempts to improve upon his performance in the world of work so that he can rise in the occupational world and live better. The economic source of this striving for improvement may be more important for those from lower-income levels. At the upper-income levels, other motives may underlie the desire for change. Dreams of power, of recognition and fame, of nobility of character, or the wish to create something of one's own, or to contribute in some larger way to the common pilgrimage of man may motivate a person to change.

To speak of self-initiated socialization and contrast it with demands coming from others suggests that the former is independent of the influence of other persons. This is not true, of course. Theoretically, self-initiated socialization has its roots in the expectations that significant others have had for the individual's performance. The distinction really is between whether the demands are current, immediate, and from persons real and present, or whether the "others" involved are distant and symbolic. In the drive toward change, the person is always trying to please someone, but in self-initiated socialization, it is he who is the significant judge of his performance. We all have made or heard statements such as "I am not happy about the way I did that," and "I should be able to do better than that," and even, more rarely, "I think that was about as well as I could do." How does this "I-me" component of personality, in which the individual views himself as if he were another person observing himself, develop?

The individual, when looking or acting toward himself as an object, must initially do so from the point of view of some significant other person. This viewpoint gradually becomes disassociated from any specific person so that the individual is no longer able to recall or identify the other person in the interpersonal relation. How does this happen?

> It appears that both generalization and the inability to discriminate are the sources of the "I-me" type of relationship. The "I-me" relationship is the product of a body of learning generalized from interaction with a number of reference figures now nameless because their identity has been lost in countless learning trials. In the most frequent case the information derived about one's self from interaction with others has been given by a great many people so that no specific individual remains linked to this self-other relationship. This is true about basic components of the self such as size, sex, ability, or appearance, and also one's conformity to and deviance from norms widely shared in society. . . . Secondly, there is a companion process also leading to generalization, namely, a lack of ability to discriminate on the part of the child in his early interactions with his parents. In these interactions a child's experience has been so limited that he has no basis for differentiating (discriminating) between the reactions of his parents and their demands upon him and the reactions and demands of the entire objective world. In largest part this inability to discriminate exists because communication between parent and infant is preverbal, and the infant lacks symbolic tools to facilitate discrimination between different sources of reward and punishment. What

> is learned from parents thus is viewed as inherent in the world at large, that is, in the generalized social order. It follows that elements of personality thus acquired provide a good foundation upon which the further process of generalization mentioned above may proceed. (Brim, 1966).

Thus we see that the "I" to which one refers his beliefs and behavior for approval is a product of early and still continuing learning and generalizing of the expectations of important others for his own behavior, and that as the "I" is gradually established, the demands one places upon himself become just as powerful as if the parental and other early influential figures were the source (Brim and Wheeler, 1966).

The role prescriptions which come from the self may change under the impact of new experience. Experience provides the raw material from which the self grows; it leads to the introduction of new elements in one's conception of a desirable style of life. The adult meets new people and gets ideas from books, conversations, travel, or from observation of others' lives. A person's changing health and strength may cause conflict in his existing self. New ideal states for an individual's personality evolve and can be seen just ahead; thus the individual directs himself toward these new ends.

Certain persons may have more initiative toward change than others. M. Brewster Smith in his companion chapter on socialization for competence directs attention to this. Analyses of the organization of personality and the role of the motivation for "self-actualization," such as Maslow has presented (Maslow, 1954), stress individual differences in this kind of behavior. We do not know whether there are group differences in self-initiated socialization, and in the absence of data we can do no more than raise the question for further consideration.

We emphasize here that self-initiated socialization need not involve less significant changes in personality than those which result from demands of the outside world. Large changes in personality have been demonstrated to come from within. Dramatic religious conversions, perhaps the most familiar example, have been described in recent articles (Lofland and Stark, 1965) and, of course, in the analysis by William James (1902), and also in Frank's recent book (1963).

Other changes in personality, not so abrupt or dramatic but still deep and important, result from self-initiated socialization. Behavior, motives, and beliefs can be transformed gradually through a process of "personality drift." Minor changes in expectations that an individual holds for himself may occur over a period, without there being any noticeable demarcation. There may be small but incremental shifts from time to time in what an individual asks of himself, and the resultant day-to-day alterations in his behavior, rewarded by himself, lead to a cumulative change which over the years makes him much different from what he was when younger. Thus what a person proposes to do with his life — both where he would like to arrive and how he wants to live along the way — can be substantially affected by these successive minor alterations, until one day he finds himself a person quite different from that of a decade earlier, without knowing how the change occurred.

SOME THEORETICAL ASPECTS

Role and Status Changes

Demands from others or from oneself are the same in certain respects. Both encompass two theoretical kinds of changes: an alteration of a role associated with a continuing status or social position and the assumption of a new status and the learning of a new role related to that status. In the first case, the new socialization demand may come from someone with whom the adult has had a continuing relationship, such as a spouse, employer, or friend. Here we might say that new and different demands are made upon the adult in the same old relationship. In the second case, socialization involves new and different persons and new types of social relationships; here the adult must learn to meet the new demands issuing from a new relationship, for example, from working with a new employer, being married to a new husband or wife, or having a new child.

Conflict and Congruence in Socialization Demands

As we see, many persons and groups compete to influence the adult's behavior, and the adult himself has his own ideas about the way in which he wishes to change. The inevitable result is frequent conflict between the direction in which the adult wishes to move, with respect to his career, family, or role in the community, and the direction in which others wish him to change, or not to change.

Where the same change is desired on both sides, there can be co-operative effort between the person and society. In some roles, such as the profession of medicine or the law, one's colleagues and clients as well as the professional person himself expect a continuing growth on his part, manifested in the acquisition of new techniques and knowledge. Joint development of the social skills of both the husband and wife in a marriage, as in the instance where both take social dancing lessons, and the joint effort to save a marriage itself, as when a husband and wife together decide to seek marriage counseling, are illustrations.

Where the demands of the society for change truly are counter to the wish of the individual to stay the way he is, then resistance, antagonism, evasion, and outright revolt may ensue. Rare is the person who does not have many experiences as an adult in which pressure is exerted on him to change when he would rather not. From young adulthood to older age, the conflict between the demands for socialization and the wishes of the individual leads to draft evasion, avoidance of marriage, quitting a job, staying away from home, and in extreme cases self-imposed isolation from society.

Where the reverse is true — the adult seeks to change himself but those with whom he lives or works want him to stay the same — he must find a way to move ahead against the resistance. It may be that the friend or the husband or wife fears that the other is moving out of his reach, or the employer or the community may be threatened by the innovations sought by the person. Family controls, economic sanctions, or bureaucratic controls in the work situation, or community legal and informal controls may be used to thwart the attempts of an adult to change himself when this change is not acceptable to others. Wanting an early marriage, wanting to enlist in the military service but being rejected, trying to move an organization ahead but meeting opposition, trying to alter a habitual pattern in a marital relationship or in the parental role are common experiences of this type.

Unmarried young adults have more freedom to leave home, to change jobs, or even not to work at all, because they are not yet locked in with responsibilities and they have not been fully socialized into the values of adult roles. Still, on balance, it would seem that adults more frequently than children can select the kind of socialization experiences they want, and have greater power to resist external demands, through deciding whom they will expose themselves to, what groups they will join, what teachers they will have, and what ideas they will examine. For example, the mass media research shows that adults routinely select confirming evidence from the mass media to substantiate their existing attitudes and beliefs. Moreover, adults have financial and other resources with which to fight back, even though we recognize that there are differences in power between certain groups to resist the influence of others, depending on one's wealth, social status, and political influence.

Most important is that adults have a wider set of reference figures to draw upon for counteracting sets of values and opinions. Resistance to the immediate local demands for conformity springs from reliance on non-immediate significant others in one's life, so that the person is not necessarily concerned with approval and acceptance at this time and place. The increased number of interpersonal relationships, that is, the richness of the gallery of significant others, gives the adult greater autonomy and independence from many groups. The extreme instance is the adult martyr who can pursue his distinctive purpose even though strong coercive measures may be used against him by many groups in society, because he is supported by others whose approval is of higher significance to him and so sustain him in his independent course, whether they be future generations of men, the host of dead poets, his father or his mother, or perhaps his God.

Aids to Socialization

As we will see throughout this review, a great many social institutions have developed to aid the adult in socialization. Most of these are familiar and include a wide variety of forms: the citizenship class for the immigrant, the programs of employers to retrain their employees to handle a new technology, family-life education and parent-education programs for newlyweds and first-time parents, college programs for women reentering the labor force or entering it for the first time, etc. Some of these express the demands of society that the individual be changed, as in the various correctional institutions supported by society to which persons are remanded. Others express the collective desires of individuals to change their lot, as seen in the creation of continuing education programs for physicians sponsored and paid for by the participants themselves.

Usually overlooked in adult socialization are the many informal ways, as opposed to the above-mentioned institutional aids, in which socialization is aided. An adult customarily will seek out, informally, people with similar experiences so that he may learn from them. He restructures his friendships and primary groups to fit the particular growing edge of his interests: pregnant women find each other and discuss their progress, newly elected departmental chairmen chat informally about their common problems and how they handle them in this new role, and army recruits socialize each other in a way that the formal institutions of the military service could never achieve (Brim and Wheeler, 1966). We cannot really, of course, say that most adult socialization occurs in informal primary-group relationships rather than in the formal and tutorial organizations, but certainly it must be stressed that if we look only at what goes on in the institutions, we will miss a substantial portion of the continuing day-to-day, hour-by-hour socialization of adults in informal primary-group relationships.

This leads us to recognize an important fact about the relationship between a person and his world with reference to adult socialization: in many cases other persons do not demand that the adult change, nor do they actively collaborate with him as he seeks his own change. Rather they provide conditions in which he can pursue his own development. In seeking change, the individual frequently is dependent on a group, and by his own initiative he must find and get into the groups which provide him with the socialization experiences that he needs. The alcoholic who wants to quit drinking and searches for Alcoholics Anonymous is an illustration, as is the person entering into a relationship with a psychotherapist to bring about the change in his personality that he desires. The good teacher or the good guidance counselor, adviser, friend, spouse, or parent can provide a human relationship in which his information and emotional support and expectations will encourage and stabilize the adult's own efforts to change.

We see that in these cases of adult socialization the distinction between the inside and the outside becomes blurred and the adult, in order to achieve his own socialization ends, must find a supportive social relationship. We know quite a bit, at an abstract, general level, about how and why such supportive relationships should exert their influence. The story we have not been told is how adults search and find among the variety of groups in society those which can aid them in completing the changes they want to fashion in their own personalities. Nor have we been told how many persons, in their attempts to change, are defeated by the absence of the human relationships necessary to sustain them in their efforts.

The Degree of Change

To many scholars the most important, most difficult question about adult socialization is how much change can take place in adult personality. How durable are the effects of life up to age twenty-one? How much change can a person look forward to in his personality or his style of life during adulthood? Are the changes that occur just on the surface in behavior and knowledge, or in deeper motives and values? We might ask how recognizable is a person in later years, say at age fifty, by a person who has not seen him since he was twenty years old? And if a man is unrecognizable, is the change one of breadth or of depth: have there been many changes in manners, voice, appearance, political attitudes, and the like, with the same basic personality characteristics still there; or is he the same outwardly as in early years, but with some fundamental change in feelings or values, say a change from being open and autonomous to being defensive and afraid?

Social research is not much help to us on this question. Data are thin and not decisive; it is not settled how much stability or change there is in adult personality (Brim and Wheeler, 1966; Neugarten, 1963; Frank, 1963; Olesen, 1966). What we can do is direct attention to this highly important question and note its great relevance for many of the topics discussed in this chapter. The demands upon an adult, whether his own or others, vary considerably in the amount of personality change that is required. In some instances only a simple addition to, or expansion of, one's existing skills is asked, and this extension of knowledge or behavior may generate little conflict with other previously learned characteristics of one's personality. In other instances major changes in one's orientation to life are demanded, as in prisoner-of-war camps; and there is discontinuity and conflict between what was learned earlier and what is now required. Rather than building upon existing personality structure, it is necessary to replace earlier learning with later; or the stringent demands for new attitudes and behavior may be difficult not because of conflict but because the elements necessary to permit one to learn these new motives and attitudes were not acquired in childhood.

In the material that follows we note the numerous predicaments of life — episodes confronted by many which make life difficult and demand adaptation. Perhaps we do not stress enough the durability of the person in the face of these predicaments or the continuity in his personality from one year to the next in spite of the alterations he must make to cope with the new demands coming from marriage and work and moves to new communities. Certainly most people at age fifty are recognizable from age twenty, and continuity of personality, not change, is the more common experience. Still, occasional changes of a dramatic nature do occur in adult personality, a circumstance demonstrating that adults do have potentialities for change as great as those which existed in earlier years. The conditions of change, how frequent change occurs, and the character of the change in motivational terms are still quite open questions needing much more study.

SOCIALIZATION IN OCCUPATIONS

Entry

Learning an occupation is one of the great demands after childhood. In some instances the job-specific technical skills required are nil, and the worker remains completely unskilled. Only the interpersonal relationships between employer-employee and between fellow workers are left to be developed. In other instances the job-related skills and information make immense demands upon the learning capacity of the adult.

In our modern world, with its greater freedom of occupational choice, not much of the required occupational learning can be anticipated and taught during childhood. The family cannot do it informally, for most children do not enter the same occupation as their parents (Goode, 1964). The schools cannot do it because the child's future work cannot be predicted. Only in rare instances is an occupational choice made early and anticipatory socialization undergone prior to the adult years.

In sharp contrast is the case of anticipatory socialization for military service for adult males in the United States. Some military service in peacetime is required by society from many of its adult males, the premise being that many components of the actual wartime role differ from what is expected of the male in his customary work role and require special training. Following World War II the influential argument in favor of continuing military conscription was that the country must never again be confronted with the great socialization task faced in the period 1940 through 1945, in which development of a military force was made extremely difficult by the lack of any anticipatory socialization of basic military skills for the male population.

In such an instance, where one can foresee that many males will experience military service in their lifetime, some socialization of a preliminary nature can take place. It is probable, also, that in societies with less freedom of choice, manpower needs can be anticipated and youth assigned to different occupations, such as engineering or technical work; thus, occupational socialization is begun early. In the United States the relative freedom of occupational choice makes this early anticipatory socialization unimportant.

Thus the typical adult during his first years in the labor force experiments with various jobs and passes through his trial work period. People become differentially attracted to occupations on the basis of income, accessibility, and the fit of the job to their skills and their personalities (Inkeles, 1964) so that an individual's discovery of a compatible occupation is a result of his shifting from one line of work to another until he finds work that he likes. This is not to imply that in the process of finding work, the individual makes an "occupational choice"; rather, this process is not rational or deliberate. Often the individual leaves jobs which he does not like until he stumbles upon something better. It is during this period that he acquires the knowledge and skills suitable for his more mature occupational choice (Form and Miller, 1960) and enters that phase of his occupational history in which he is likely to continue in the same general line of work for the next thirty years. But settling into an occupation and learning what is needed to carry out the job does not mean that the individual's socialization in the world of occupations is over by the age of thirty-five. Much more than this is demanded of many adults in the labor force during their work history.

Changes in or on the Job

The probability that during his working life an adult will face demands from others for substantial socialization for new kinds of jobs is related to the vulnerability of his job to the decisions made by others and to the rate of obsolescence of his particular information or skills. In regard to involuntary job changes, either through being transferred by the employer or being discharged, most members of the adult world are vulnerable to the demand that they learn a new job. The alternatives in modern nations include more than just starving: one can go on relief, take a simpler job with less pay, and so on. Still, these alternatives are less attractive in many cases than the task of learning the new job. Only a very few adults have an occupational status where they are invulnerable to this requirement; judges, in certain courts, and university professors, at certain levels, are familiar examples.

Vulnerability to forced change is related to the income or prestige ranking of an occupation. The semi-skilled and unskilled worker generally shows a career history of a disrupted nature, with multiple job changes and with a higher likelihood of military service. But there are exceptions. Vulnerability of jobs is greater in the field of advertising than of skilled labor. Informational obsolescence may be more rapid among the medical profession than in any other field. Moreover, the phenomenon of being transferred within an organization from one type of work to another, and indeed from one region of the country to another, in connection with promotion to successively higher levels, is a characteristic of the middle and upper levels of management in business, and not of the skilled or unskilled labor group. Overall, the greater vulnerability to job changes of the less skilled worker may be offset by the fact that the amount of change expected of him in shifting from one job to another is less than at the higher occupational levels.

Negroes in particular have an uneven work history, for they still are concentrated disproportionately in unskilled occupations of high vulnerability; in addition, discriminatory dismissals add to the frequent need for finding new jobs. Now there are planned and deliberate efforts by many groups to increase the opportunities for employment at higher levels for the American Negro, a circumstance requiring major socialization in the early and middle years of adult life in order that the Negro work effectively in these new and unfamiliar positions. Perhaps the extent to which the demands upon the upwardly moving Negro, in response to these new opportunities, involve changes in some fundamental beliefs and attitudes has not been widely enough recognized. Socialization programs have focused on occupational skills but have not aimed at socializing the person in the important areas of values and interpersonal behavior. In any event, there seems little question that in the next generation the adult Negro male may be facing some of the most dramatic socialization demands to be found in the occupational world and that studies of the white-collar Negro male and especially the growing number of business executives in the years ahead should be given high priority in the social sciences.

Women in the labor force deserve special mention here. The facts show that work for women is a common experience: at least nine out of ten women work outside the home at some time during their lives, and at any given time one-third of the working population consists of women. Although the 90 per cent participation rate includes women who have worked a few months at some time in their lives, for many work is a major lifelong experience (Gross, 1958; Goode, 1963).

Their youthful, initial participation in the world of work may not be very different from that for males, in that socialization into an occupation takes place early and in both instances job relevant skills and behavior are acquired. But it is the woman who enters the labor force for the first time after child-rearing years, on whom the demands of adult socialization may rest most heavily. Some thirteen and a half million women who work currently are married and living with their husbands. Some substantial percentage of this number are mothers with children either in school or who have grown up and left home. And for the large percentage of these who are entering the labor force for the first time, the demands of the work role are very different from the demands they have met in the wife and mother roles in the preceding years. The working women who are reentering the labor force after a period of absence, because of marriage and child rearing, may have an easier time. Their earlier experience may stand them in good stead, giving them a basis for more rapid learning of the skills they need to get back to work. The secretary returning to a job after a fifteen-year layoff finds much of it familiar, but the woman taking training as a secretary and working for the first time at the age of forty finds both the technical skills and the interpersonal relationships novel and demanding. This process has been analyzed in several studies (for example, Rossi, 1964), and experimental programs such as those at Radcliffe College have been created to help socialize the women for entry into the occupational world after child rearing.

Many women evidently must make the change, adding the world of work to family life, for financial reasons. Still, the relationship of family income to female employment is not entirely clear from the data we have. It seems that the highest incidence of working wives (who are currently married) have husbands whose income is in the category of eight to fifteen thousand dollars; where the husband's income is less than this amount, fewer, not more, wives are working. At least two of the many possible contributing factors come to mind. Firstly, we know that many women enter the work force voluntarily for various personal (rather than economic) reasons; thus taking a job is a response other than to economic need. Secondly, the data described above are not controlled either for age or for stage of the family life cycle, and it is plausible that the entry or reentry of women into the labor force in the post-child-rearing years occurs at about the same time that their husbands' incomes are reaching their highest levels.

We should learn much more about the reasons women work so that we can make the correct prognoses for the type and depth of their socialization in the marital and parental relationships and the subsequent influence on other family members' personalities.

As a response to the need for adult socialization, a large social institution has grown from its nineteenth-century origins. Although adult education encompasses other aspects of socialization to be referred to later, its largest area of activity is in job-related skills. Ziegler (1964) writes:

> In the nineteenth century, if adults wanted further education they had to get it by attending evening high schools for youths (and these only in the larger cities) or by enrolling in Farmers' Institutes or courses presented by the Chautauqua circuit or in institutions like the Cooper Union in New York or the Junto in Philadelphia. Churches, fraternal societies and labor organizations offered occasional lectures, and the high schools in eastern seacoast cities provided English lessons and "Americanization" for the foreign born.
>
> Consider what the term adult education now includes: the credit and non-credit or "informal" courses at all institutions of high education open to adults; programs of the public schools, evening high schools and junior colleges; the secretarial and vocational work offered at commercial schools; the technical and management courses given by technical institutes and professional graduate schools as well as by business and industry themselves; the recreational and educational programs of social, civic, religious, fraternal, professional and public affairs organizations, associations and clubs; the religious education, public affairs forums and creative arts courses to be found in many churches and synagogues; the lectures, films discussion groups, art fairs and music festivals offered by public libraries, museums and other civic institutions; the home demonstration and technical-agricultural work provided by the Cooperative (Agricultural) Extension Service; the courses offered by government agencies and the armed forces to government employees (and others); the field of community development; education by television; the commercial correspondence schools and home-study departments of many universities; and finally, the enormous and increasing amount of independent self-study or self-education.

One may not be fully aware of the extent of adult education. In a 1961–1962 survey the National Opinion Research Council (Johnstone, 1963) found almost twenty-nine million persons engaged in some kind of adult education course or activity. The distribution of interests showed nine million studying job-related subjects or skills, five million in hobbies and recreation, three and a half million in home and family life, and nearly two million in personal development. We will have occasion to refer to these figures again later.

Participation in adult education is unequally distributed among different groups in the American population. It is mostly the younger group of adults (under forty) rather than the older adults (over forty) who are engaged in adult education. There are about equal numbers of men and women, and it is important to note no significant differences in religious background or in race. The clearest distinguishing characteristic of those participating in adult education is that they are already among the best educated. In the data reported only 4 per cent with no schooling sought adult education, while 47 per cent of those with more than sixteen years of schooling sought more. These figures suggest that a given amount of education may be a threshold over which one must cross, both to awaken interest in self-growth and self-improvement leading to self-initiated adult socialization, and also to reach occupational levels where the job demands are for continuing updating of one's occupational skills.

NEW WORK SKILLS

The work histories of most adults show changes from one job to another which require learning technical or professional skills and knowledge associated with the new occupation. One may be promoted to a new kind of work; one may be reassigned to a different job; and, of course, one may be discharged. Society itself may "reassign" the male worker in the case where military service is demanded; this is theoretically the same as a job change.

The worker resists the disruption of his occupational world. Often he feels that the demands of a promotion are greater than the rewards gained at the higher level. There are familiar instances of men who accept promotions but then want to go back to their earlier, easier, already learned jobs; they say that the promotion did not work out. The "draft" certainly is viewed by most males as a disruption of their life, and their attitudes toward military obligation being the rule are negative (Janowitz and Little, 1965). As for the right to job tenure, that is, the right not to be moved or dismissed, both individual and organized-labor efforts to this end are manifest in contracts with employers restricting the right of the employers to disrupt the stability of a man's work career.

Of course, these have their parallels in the demands which the individual places upon himself. If promotion does not occur, he may leave the organization for a higher-level job in another place. So, too, he may move sideways from job to job, searching for something better suited to his wishes. Whether from the outside or from the individual's own demands, job histories are interrupted with demands for new learning.

A change of occupation at the unskilled level may involve interpersonal, but little technical, learning. Where the task is on an assembly line — for example, making sure certain bolts are tightened down — then a job change or a reassignment might be to another comparatively simple task, and the retraining might be fairly easy. Where higher skills are involved, then more must be demanded. The Wall Street lawyer who takes a job as a company or house counsel, the medical man who becomes the chief of the hospital, the assembly-line worker who is promoted to foreman, and the engineer who ends up in charge of the controller's office — all face changes substantially greater than those demanded of the factory worker who shifts from one machine operation to another.

In general, we can say that as society advances in complexity and technical knowledge, the percentage of unskilled labor decreases and the general level of information and technical skill necessary to participate in the occupational world rises. Thus we can speculate that with increased specialization, the differences between jobs increase, and the new learning associated with change from one kind of work to another must be greater.

Even if the individual remains at the same job, he may have to retrain himself periodically in the newer knowledge and skills associated with his particular task. In the decade ahead increasing numbers of men and women in the United States will find their knowledge obsolete as they enter the forty- to sixty-year-old period. The increased growth rate of knowledge and technical inventions makes, for a man at age forty, a world very different from the one for which he was prepared when he was twenty; and instead of being more competent than younger men, because of the years of experience, he actually is less competent because he does not control the new and more powerful knowledge produced since his formal educational. As a consequence of the more rapid growth of knowledge, there has been an expansion of attempts to keep up with new information and to avoid the obsolescence of knowledge and skills.

We should note that not all of these efforts at adult socialization are self-initiated. The demands for keeping up-to-date on one's job come frequently from one's employer or organization. Business executives may be required by the management to take month-long "brush-up" courses and to participate in staff seminars at "training schools." Airline pilots are required to take refresher courses to keep up with new equipment and new procedures. Many engineers are required by their companies to take time off and return to specialized schools to upgrade their professional skills. Although in medicine and law the individual practitioner has been the one to initiate such efforts, we should note that in Russia the physician is required, like the airline pilot, to upgrade his qualifications continually and to pass recurrent examinations.

NEW INTERPERSONAL RELATIONSHIPS

Important new interpersonal relationships must be learned in almost every new work situation. Promotion brings one into contact with new people, as does reassignment to a new job at the same level. Especially demotion requires some difficult interpersonal learning. Where job changes are self-initiated and where the adult seeks a change of occupation, clearly the same things occur; moving to new occupational settings brings him into a circle where his existing interests, motives, beliefs, habits, style of relating to others — each or all — may need to be altered to fit what is expected of him by his new colleagues, employees, and employer. Even if he continues in precisely the same work, he will find himself at times with a new supervisor, new work colleagues, or new subordinates, any one of whom may react to him differently. In some cases the personnel turnover leads to complaints that things are not like they used to be in the old days; and the individual quits and seeks a "new," but more comfortable, social environment. That he may or may not like the people whom he works for or works with, that he cannot adjust to the demands they make on him, or that he wants to change his own behavior in a certain way but they will not let him — these are clear and basic realities of the occupational world.

Most of the descriptions of adult socialization in the family and in the community deal with interpersonal situations and accommodations of one person to another. It is surprising, then, to find that for the occupational world there is no comparable body of information on the process of socialization which undoubtedly takes place between colleagues or between an employee and his boss. Clearly the changes in the person demanded by the varied interpersonal relationships of his work situation over time are more significant than the informational learning associated with the performance aspects of a new job. In spite of this, studies here are rare, although the richness of this area of research is evident in a recent report (Hodgson, Levinson, and Zaleznik, 1965). In future studies, the relationships between the interpersonal demands of the job changes in family relationships should be analyzed, and the two-way process of influence between the world of work and the world of the family in their varying demands upon the adult should be charted.

NEW LEVELS OF ASPIRATION

There is a third area of socialization related to work to be noted at this point, even though the changes in personality that are involved may seem general rather than related to occupations alone. We refer to the fact that many American males must adjust their career aspirations of earlier years to the probable realities of the levels of achievement to be reached in their lifetimes. For example, Chinoy (1955) reports that automobile workers, comparing their career dreams with what they have actually accomplished, solve the problem of discrepancies by considering their work to be temporary and by maintaining their hopes of becoming an entrepreneur or farmer. Eventually, though, "the worker faces a day of reckoning when he is called upon to admit that he is 'trapped,' that his American dream of being his own boss is not to be fulfilled." If one can no longer postpone to the future hopes for achievement, as time begins to run out during the middle-years period, then one may change one's goals. It is indeed puzzling that there are so few sociological studies (there are, of course, many plays and novels) of male efforts to adjust aspirations with achievements in their careers.

One report (Gross, 1958) shows that many students at the secondary school level have unrealistic expectations about their achievement in later life and that these earlier expectations are not fulfilled in later careers. Comparisons of the actual jobs which high school graduates obtain six years after graduation and their aspirations when in school show that substantially fewer than wished to be were engaged in the professions (over half the seniors had aspired to professional status and less than one-seventh reached it) and substantially more were in clerical jobs (one-fifth were in clerical jobs although only one-twentieth had planned to be). One handles these discrepancies for a long period of time by successively displacing fulfillment of aspirations into the future, but the day of reckoning does come. The socialization which must take place is in the self-image, where changes in self-esteem, and probably in one's basic achievement values, must occur.

It is in this context that we understand better the so-called "repotting," whereby a man makes substantial changes in his career (this probably occurs more frequently in the professions and high management groups). Repotting occurs for some men about the age of fifty. As time runs out on a man's achievement aspirations, it is easy for him to say that he is in the wrong kind of work. He thereby avoids the demands for change in his self-image and substitutes in its place the need to learn a new kind of work. Lawyers go into business, professors turn to novel writing, physicians give up private practice and seek research jobs, and business executives talk about finding a job as a teacher but usually end up in some form of public service.

Not all, or even most, middle-years job changes spring from attempts to resolve the aspiration-achievement discrepancy. Military officers, their years of service completed, turn to civilian occupations (Biderman, 1964). For others the shift of occupation at this age reflects leisure and wealth; now one can afford the luxury of recasting one's career to better fit one's interests. Still, many career shifts constitute a search for a different occupation where one's early aspirations might yet be realized.

SOCIALIZATION IN FAMILIES

Many of the changes in behavior and attitudes which the adult must make are tied to the new interpersonal relationships which he establishes in the family. These demands for change start with marriage and continue through the normal sequence of evolving and increasingly complex familial relationships as children are born, members of the family die, relatives of one or the other spouse's family join the married couple, and as divorce and remarriage may take place. Families, like persons, have developmental stages with which socialization is correlated, and these stages are tied to the ages of the members. One must first adjust to his or her spouse; then to children, in infancy, adolescence, and later as young adults; one must reestablish a relationship with the spouse after the children have left home; and finally learn to live alone as a widow or widower.

Some descriptive statistics from the *Monthly Labor Review* (1963) tell us how deeply engaged in such changes people are. More than 90 per cent of the population marries. For women, the median age at marriage is twenty years. Most families have one or two children; the typical pattern of spacing shows the first child appearing two years after the marriage, with subsequent children (two) following at intervals of two years. The mother typically completes child bearing at age twenty-six and sees her last child enter school at age thirty-two. The period of time during which spouses live together after children have left the home is lengthening; almost a fourth of married life now is lived together in this post-parental phase.

Many of these families will be broken by death, or by separation or divorce. Statistics show that of women age fourteen and over, eight and one-half million are widowed, and of males, over two million are widowers. Of new marriages contracted, it is estimated that one in four will end in court; this breakup usually occurs within one or two years of marriage. This figure does not take account of unregistered permanent separations or of desertions which add substantially to the rate of breakup. In the United States well over 90 per cent of those who lose a spouse through death or divorce will eventually remarry, if this loss occurred between the ages of twenty and thirty-five, that is, prior to the middle years. Generally, four-fifths of divorced men and three-fourths of divorced women can expect to marry again, whatever the age. Note, though, that two out of five of these remarriages will again end in divorce or separation. Often these family breakups occur while young children are still in the home, so that many families have a single parent. (Parents Without Partners has grown into an international organization providing a place where millions of single parents, rearing some seven million children, may ask for information and aid.)

The family, then, even though it may be the most stable social institution that we have, in many cases loses and gains members. Spouses are replaced by others, and the size of the family expands and contracts. Meanwhile, even where the personnel may remain the same, maturation has its effect, and the expectations of each member for the others shift over time.

Marriage

The relationship between a husband and wife is probably the most influential relationship of adult life and the major source of demands for socialization upon the young adult. Novels, drama, and social science have described the seemingly endless variety of adaptations, large and minute, deep and superficial, of husband and wife in attitudes and beliefs, in highest values, and fundamental motives. Whether it be learning to manage a joint checking account, catching the nuances of meaning in gesture or voice or expression of a person from a different cultural background or social-class origin, learning manners or style of dress or to enjoy new foods, the marital relationship is rich in day-to-day and year-to-year socialization experiences.

It does seem that the degree of similarity in the cultural background of the two spouses affects the need for socialization. Homogamy in background should make it easier to develop new roles and meet each other's expectations because more general cultural values are shared. We gain some insight into the socialization process which must go on in marriage from information on demographic characteristics of the marital relationship and correlated family events.

Data on divorce rates, for instance, show more frequent divorce among persons marrying from unmatched class and cultural backgrounds. This would seem to confirm the hypothesis about homogamy if one makes the inference that a divorce is an indicator of the inability of the partners to meet the demands for socialization in the marital roles (Mogey, 1964). It should be noted that rates of social events such as divorce are frequently used as indicators of strains and failures in the adult socialization process. Also rates of suicide, illness, alcoholism, and so on, by age, race, region, and social background, have been taken as indicators of man's relationship to his society at least since the time of Durkheim.

Probably most marriages still are intra-social-class marriages and occur between people who live within a mile or so of each other. Data on marriages (Goode, 1964) suggest, however, that there is an increase in interclass marriages. Still, on examination, these marriages often turn out to be between young people of currently similar life styles and areas of residence, in spite of their different class origins. Usually one of the spouses comes from a family which has been socially mobile and has taken on the way of life of the class of the potential spouse (Goode, 1964). There remains, nevertheless, a very large number of marriages between persons from quite different cultural backgrounds. Since most of the important beliefs and attitudes which will serve to regulate behavior in the marriage have been derived from experience in the individual's own family, the research showing large social background differences in marriage behavior leads to the conclusion that need for new learning on the part of one or both marital partners must occur where their origins are different (Cain, 1964). For example, patterns of sexual behavior differ in notable ways by social class, and adjustments must be sought. Modes of disciplining children differ, and there is a strain to reconcile these. At the upper social-class levels there are more feelings of companionship and marital love reported, while at the working-class level there is less communication between husband and wife, with the spouses spending their free time with those of the same sex in their own individual and different ways; their interpersonal contact primarily is an exchange of services, rather than of expressions of affection or companionship. In the working-class groups the wife has more power in the marital relationship, compared to wives of other backgrounds; the middle-class spouses tend to be equal in decision making and authority; and the husband has the primary decision power in the upper classes.

Marriages between spouses of different backgrounds would affect the male and female differently. Among whites in the United States, the female often marries "up," and the male marries "down." Women more frequently exchange their beauty for a man's social rank or power, or his potential achievement, rather than the other way around (Goode, 1964). This means that more lower-lower-class men do not marry and more upper-upper-class women do not marry, because women marry upward and leave the lower-class males behind, and the upper-class female cannot marry down so there is a shortage of eligible males for her. In interracial marriages, where Negro and white are involved, we find the Negro male marrying down even more than in all-white marriages, because he exchanges his rank and power in the Negro stratification system for its lower equivalent in the white hierarchy.

Intermarriage between spouses from differing religious groups is increasing, and may become a more frequent source of socialization demands than are interclass marriages. Jews are most likely to marry endogamously, Catholics next, and Protestants least likely. There is considerable variability by region in the actual rates, but it appears that 80 per cent of Jews marry endogamously, while the variation for Catholics ranges from 80 to 90 per cent in New Haven to 50 per cent in cities in the South. Intermarriage of Jews to non-Jews still meets the greatest opposition among Jews and probably demands more from the marital partners than Catholic and Protestant intermarriages. However, the effects of interfaith marriages usually are moderated by similarities in the social class and ethnic backgrounds of the spouses; one does not often find a marriage where the spouses come from differing ethnic, social class, and religious lines.

In marriages between persons from different cultural backgrounds, one might expect that there is convergence in learning on some central ground, for example, the upper-class male takes on certain lower-middle-class patterns of behavior while his wife is learning upper-class manners. However, it may not be convergence at all, and socialization demands may rest much more heavily on one member than another. It is likely that in interclass marriages the pressure is for the lower-class member to move up. Thus, the woman would seem to have more to learn as she adapts to the higher-status position of the male, but this may be offset by the fact that women seem to undergo more anticipatory socialization for marriage than do males. In interfaith marriages and interracial marriages, it is probably the actual reference group of the couple who enter marriage that would explain whether, and to what extent, one partner would bear a heavier socialization demand.

At a different level of socialization there are demands on each marital partner to adapt his or her personality to that of the spouse, regardless of similarity or difference in cultural background. Studies of mate selection and of psychological similarities and differences between spouses suggest that personality characteristics such as dependency, nurturance, and aggression are linked in complicated ways in the marital relationship. For example, some data (Winch, 1958) indicate that spouses tend to have complementary needs, suggesting that if this is the normal pattern of marriage in current society then instances where complementarity does not exist require socialization of the desires of one or the other spouse. For example, if two marital partners are high on a need for dependency, one may have to learn to control or eliminate this need. The complexity of the interrelations of unconscious personality characteristics in marriage is documented in numerous case histories (e.g., Stein, 1956) and again indicates the complexity and depth of the demands for change in personality which can exist in the relationship between spouses. However, scientific studies of such mutual adaptation in personality are rare. We can cite the work of Vincent (1964), which shows that the personalities of a group of young married people change to a much greater degree than the personalities of a control group of unmarried persons and, moreover, that those persons marrying earliest showed the largest personality change following the marriage. For the most part, the adjustment of spouses over time has been documented only informally, and investigators of this process have large potential rewards in new knowledge before them. The degrees and character of personality changes could be studied in relationship to the sociological nature of the marriage, that is, whether or not it is interclass, or interethnic; it is a first or second marriage, for one or both partners; there are large or small age differences. The degree and character of these important changes in adult life also can be studied in relationship to the initial personality inputs, that is, the kinds of personalities the marital partners take into the marriage. Much interesting and valuable research awaits the social scientist here.

We noted that more than a quarter of the adult population engaged in a second marriage, and for some there is a third and a fourth and more. This is more frequently true for those in lower occupational groups than for those in the higher, and for the less educated than the better educated (Glick and Carter, 1958). In the United States population, more than one in four of the adults with an elementary school education, but only one in ten of those graduated from college, have been married two or more times. Moreover, these rates do not reflect the actual number of broken marriages in the less educated population. Here the cost of divorce is so high that unregistered separation and desertion are common, a circumstance made very clear by the fact that increased free legal aid to the poor has been utilized primarily (in one state over 80 per cent of all cases of requests for aid) to obtain divorces.

We might use the remarriage rate to conclude that socialization into the marital relationship is more difficult or strenuous for the lower-income groups than for the higher, for, in some instances, the second marriage certainly must continue the socialization process which was underway in the first. Still, for others, the breakup of a marriage and the subsequent remarriage may be a flight from a situation where much was demanded that was new and difficult to learn, to a simpler marital relationship in which an earlier learned mode of interaction with the opposite sex can be drawn upon, that is, in which the marital partner is less demanding of change. Similarly the lower rates of marital breakup in the middle- and upper-class groups may not reflect a smooth course of socialization but instead may reflect social values against divorce and thus may mask strenuous efforts of the spouses to try to adapt to each other's desires in order to "save the marriage."

Parenthood

The role of parent is the second fundamental role to be learned in the new family. Persons meeting parenthood differ in the repertoire of attitudes and behaviors which they bring to this new situation, and the amount of personality change which is necessary varies accordingly. The background of experience in a large family of one's own, with the pattern of sharing possessions and space with siblings and of learning to care for younger siblings in a quasi-parental relationship, may have prepared some rather well; while others, growing up as only children or, for other reasons, with little contact with small children, have less informal training for the parental role.

The prescriptions for parental role behavior come from society's representatives or surrogates, and from other family members, that is, the other spouse, grandparents, relatives, and the like. In addition, the infant himself makes direct demands of an emotional kind upon the parents, and even though he has little power of his own, these demands are backed by agents of society. Students of the family (Le Masters, 1957; Dyer, 1963) have suggested that new parents are unprepared for the realities of actually living with a baby and have romanticized the role of parenthood, so that there is an observable impact of the firstborn child upon the adult personality as the child's highly immediate and imperative needs demand the attention of the parent. What is to be learned is not aspects of culture different from the adult's, as might be the case in marital adjustment, but attitudes and motives pertaining to the satisfaction of another person's actions and wishes, which on the whole require of the adult unselfishness, control of aggression, mature handling of numerous mild frustrations, and adaptation to an interrupted work schedule and interrupted leisure.

The parent-child relationship, like the marital relationship, has a deeper level where unconscious feelings exist. The parent's feelings are in part a residue of attitudes and motives remaining from the relationship with his or her own parents. Clinical appraisals give many illustrations; for example, the man (Billig and Adams, 1965) who had an authoritative father whom he unconsciously hated and who became emotionally disturbed during the pregnancy of his wife because of his increasing apprehension that the child would be a son and would feel the same way toward him. At this level of personality, normal feelings toward a child would be difficult to develop since repressed personality characteristics acquired early in life and not subject to change by socialization in the usual sense have already been developed. Parenthood, then, with first and later children presents the adult with new interpersonal relationships for which both overt attitudes and behavior elements must be learned and often deeper motivational characteristics altered.

The great concern for learning and improvement in role performance manifested by American parents apparently is unique in history (Brim, 1959). Millions of parents actively participate in programs designed to improve their competence in the parental role, and hardly a literate young mother in the United States is not reached by one or another mass media attempt to influence her maternal behavior, whether or not she has sought it. Most parents who are concerned with their role performance and ways to improve it seek counsel from the medical professions, customarily the pediatrician; and the concerns dealt with are not primarily medical, but are the reactions of the parent to the growth and development of his or her child. In addition, participation in parent group discussions concerned with parental role performance and its change numbers in the hundreds of thousands.

With this vast group of parents being educated or educating themselves about child rearing, there are systematic differences among the social classes. The evidence (Brim, 1959) drawn from major studies dating from 1920 to the present clearly demonstrates that the percentage of participating parents varies directly with the person's socioeconomic status. Participation here comprises membership in study groups, individual counseling under public health or pediatric auspices, and the various mass media experiences, including books, pamphlets, and magazines read, radio talks listened to, and articles on child care read in newspapers or magazines. As one would expect, these studies also show that it is more frequently the mother than the father who engages in educational activities for the parental role. These sex differences are much less at the lower-class than at the middle-class levels, an indication that the greater participation in parent education of the higher socioeconomic class members comes primarily from a greater participation of the women in that group.

Changes within Family Roles

Marriage and parenthood involve changes of status and the assumption of new roles. Within the family, once established, there are many gradual and subtle changes in the hopes and expectations of family members for each other; and much of the individual's socialization in the family in later years is a consequence of adaptation to changes in what others in a family expect of the individual.

HUSBAND AND WIFE

Changes in husband and wife, as a result of other forces, lead to continuing mutual socialization into new and continuously shifting and evolving relationships between the spouses. There have been few studies of the marital relationship over time; again, we must draw on the informal observations of marriages in biography and fiction as well as on common experience.

Some of the change is the result of events in the world outside the family. The male's occupation may change, which in turn can gradually change him in ways that spill over into his relationship with his wife and alter it. As we have seen in many instances, the wife herself may enter the labor force, again precipitating a change in the customary expectations regulating the marital roles (Nye and Hoffman, 1963). For example, Neugarten and her colleagues report (Neugarten, 1965) on the basis of Thematic Apperception Test responses that the male over time becomes more dependent, passive, and conforming in the occupational world, while at the same time the woman's authority increases around the home. These dual changes result in a shift in the balance of power in the marital relationship.

Families usually move to new communities or to new neighborhoods as they rise or fall in the social hierarchy, and the novel acquaintances and activities which follow influence both spouses and become translated into new role prescriptions for each other. The impact of mobility upon the husband and wife is not always an even matter, and the influence may be felt more by one marital partner, usually the wife, as a result of the heightened aspirations held for her following her husband's promotion and change of residence. Frequently the wife has a hard time keeping up with the increasingly sophisticated husband and his new colleagues and acquaintances, who generate new ideas and new prescriptions for her behavior at what from her point of view must seem an unreasonable rate.

And, of course, though we are not considering the impact of physiological aging, or of illness or accident, in this overview, changes in sexual interest and vigor on the part of one or both spouses as they grow older affect the marital relationship. Since such changes seem only infrequently to coincide in marital partners, new attitudes and expectations guiding the sexual relationship in marriage must be developed and accepted, willingly or not.

Other sources of change between the husband and wife are simply tied to the stage of the marriage and are the result of alterations in the number, age, and sex composition of the family. Studies (Blood and Wolfe, 1960; Terman, 1938; Bowerman, 1957; Pineo, 1961) report marital happiness to be highest in the first year and then to decrease gradually for the next fifteen years, after which it rises and then levels off at a higher plateau at the time of launching the last child into his own occupational and marital settings. It thus appears that the post-parental period in a marriage is one of greater satisfaction than before. For most, this is not a crisis period but rather a "golden period" in which there is an increase in shared activities with the spouse, a decrease in mutual concerns about money, and less individual community participation (Deutscher, 1959). These changes seem to create a period requiring resocialization into the marital roles of husband and wife as they reemerge as separate roles after the long confusion they have had with parental roles. There is possibly a "discovery" of the personality of the marital partner as it has evolved during the twenty-five to thirty-year period of child rearing.

An unmeasured, unknown, but possibly very great amount of change in the husband-wife relationship is the result of self-initiated efforts by one or both spouses. Husbands and wives exhibit a variety of attempts to improve their role performances; working more around the home, saving more money, being smarter in their purchases, creating a better scheduling of activities in the household, solving disagreements about sex, finding a long-range answer to a working relationship with their parents-in-law — these and other concerns like them are on the agenda of self-improvement for many American husbands and wives. In response to these self-generated efforts to change have come large commercial and public enterprises that provide instruction pertaining to these family concerns; for example, books and articles on marriage for consumption by husbands and wives as they strive to improve their role performances. Seeking the advice and aid of one's clergyman in these matters is common, and voluntary entry into marital counseling is an increasing phenomenon, while the profession of marital counselor continues to grow. All of these attest to the conclusion that change is common and often constant in the marital relationship.

PARENT AND CHILD

In the parent-child relationships, meanwhile, the children continue to develop and change; and the parent must learn new styles of child rearing and develop new beliefs, attitudes, and feelings over the course of his relationship with the child. As the child matures, he learns increased skills in manipulating his parents: he gains in ability to appeal to authorities of the outside world and thus to bring pressure to bear upon the parents on behalf of society; and the increasing physical growth of the male child, and to a lesser degree the female, enables the child to confront the parents in a showdown of physical power. Thus the wishes of the growing child become a very real force in the adult parent's life and cause the parent to make a number of changes. The child may be dissatisfied with his parent's behavior, beliefs, and modes of attempted control, and may seek to influence the parental behavior to correspond more to what the child expects of the parent in his work, the home, or community life.

Probably because children are not supposed to be able to influence parents, in a normative sense, the quite evident effects of children upon parents' personalities have escaped the attention of the research social scientist. Apparently no one has even asked in a systematic way of a sample of parents whether they perceive their children to have had any influence on their own values, life plans, personal desires, work orientation, or marital relationships. It is a commonly, if informally, reported experience by most not overly defensive parents that one or more of their children influenced them in profound ways and at deep levels on occasion and that they are different persons because of their continued intense interaction with children. It is erroneous to think of the socialization process in the parent-child relationship as a one-way process. Many interesting studies suggest themselves here, among them studies of personality changes of unmarried adults, married adults without children, and married adults with children.

As children move ahead in the social hierarchy, dissatisfaction with parental practices becomes more common, and, unless the parent is able to adapt, which he usually is not, a gulf opens between the child and parent. Less frequently reported on is the relationship between the parent and the downwardly mobile child, not an infrequent case, and what, in this case, is required of the parent. In the first instance, the expectations of the child for the parent are to learn and become accustomed to new styles of life, manners, and attitudes consonant with the higher-class position that the child has attained. In the second instance, the demand upon the parent is not so much for change in class mannerisms and attitudes as it is for shifting his aspirations and hopes for what the child might become, to correspond to the realities of the child's achievement.

The final outcome of the ever-growing influence of the child on the parent is the gradual inversion of the relationship between the two, as it shifts from the initial position in which the parent has complete responsibility and authority to the reverse, at a later age period, when the child has come to assume these same responsibilities of the parental role, toward his aging and less able parents. In many states the responsibility for the care of family members legally shifts from the parents' responsibility for the children to the children's responsibility for the parents. Research on aging shows that in some families this transformation of the relationship takes place gradually and without conflict between the two generations; in other families the loss of authority and power is hard to accept by the parents, and socialization into the older age role vis-à-vis the child is colored by continuing challenge and conflict; and, of course, in some families the socialization into this older-age family role never is successful, and the relationship between the generations is broken off.

SOCIALIZATION IN THE COMMUNITY

The adult's life in his community of residence brings him into recurrent interaction with his friends, members of his social clubs, the church, school personnel, political parties and action groups, volunteer organiza-

tions, and other groups which constitute the structure of the commu[n]
As an adult participating in community life, he will be confronted wit[h]
prescriptions for his behavior that will differ from what is customary
for him, what he has learned from earlier times in his life. In the simple and primitive community the continuity of culture might be such that very little that is novel is encountered through the life-span. But this is not true of modern American communities, in which both the membership and the culture are under continual alteration. We might view the socialization in later years arising from community participation as falling into two major types: that coming from changes in the current community or residence and that associated with the adult's move to a new community.

The Existing Community

Changes in an adult's existing community occur in several ways. The community is part of the larger society and is the social and political unit in which most of the values of the society as a whole are manifest. There are frequent occasions in which the demand for change upon individuals is effectively expressed within the life of a community even though it issues from sources external to that community. We mentioned earlier the example of federal legislation for desegregation, which bears heavily on traditional beliefs and actions at the community level. Innovations in educational practice, public health practices, or in transportation, made at the supra-community level, show us how state and federal requirements entail demands for changes in the way of life of members of given communities. Fluoridation, desegregation, regional high schools, and the like — all may confront the adult in his later years as new ideas, and it appears that there will be no lessening of these community-mediated demands in the generation ahead.

A community itself may be vitally altered by change in the characteristics of the resident population. Changes in population density, either increases or decreases, and changes in the age composition are one matter but are not nearly as important, one would think, as the effects upon a community of the shift in composition according to cultural background. Communities customarily have certain ethnic characteristics, and these are changed by persons from different backgrounds moving in and displacing the older residents. Communities change their social-class, religious, racial, and national-origin characteristics. Thus a continuing member of a community may find himself interacting with members of diverse cultural backgrounds with different ideas about what should take place in the community and what customs should prevail. Some residents move on to find a community more in tune with their own backgrounds and personalities, but others must stay, and for these

…n which must take place as the community around them …ut the same, theoretically, as that which confronts an …o a new and strange community. Of course, in perhaps … the old-time residents feel that they need not change at …at the new residents, whatever their backgrounds, must … adapt to the standards of the old-timers.

Some socialization pertinent to community life certainly is initiated by the person himself. This may be more characteristic of those at the level of the middle classes in the community, but certainly some persons at any level in society seek to advance in the world of acquaintance and friendship, and in social class. Well ahead of any occupational advance or change in residence, one may have learned the values of the aspired membership groups and the weights they assign to different values, learned the beliefs of those particular groups to which one wants to belong and their ways of behaving.

Initiative also is shown in the drive for participation in community political life. Studies of political activities show that the American public, to be sure, has little interest in political participation. Still, we cannot overlook the move toward voter registration in the South at the present time as one of the many powerful illustrations of the fact that the individual's desire to take part in the activities of his community leads to efforts to learn and to change which cost the individual something. There is often strong urging on the part of volunteers to encourage Negroes to take part in political activity in their communities in the South, so that at first participation would seem not to be self-initiated. However, the fact of strong prohibitions on this new activity coming from various parts of the white community leads us to ask who the Negroes are, given the same outside encouragement as others, that press toward a new role as active participants in the local community, with all of the demands it puts upon them, while the others do not.

Last, probably the greatest demands for change in life and personality that the adult conceivably could meet follow from the destruction of his normal community life by the great disasters of mankind. Most likely it is because the United States has never been overrun and occupied in war, or seen famine or plague, that the great impact of these disasters on adult life has been virtually unstudied by scholars in this country. In vivid contrast, for hundreds of years the postwar literature in vanquished countries in Europe and Asia has called attention to the change in personal lives and fortunes: broken families, shifts in occupations, gain or loss of wealth, dislocation of residents, the need to live by harsher, less humane values, the need to reorient oneself to a day-by-day rather than year-by-year or decade-by-decade mode of existence, that is, to forego life planning and to learn to live with no assurance at all about the future.

The New Community

An adult's work and his family may cause him to move and take up residence in a particular new community. Both social and geographical mobility are involved, and it is difficult to separate them in discussion. Usually both reflect either the desire of the adult for improved economic position or the fact of its achievement. Sometimes people are moved by their employers, or they move for reasons of health or climate, just as sometimes people move up in the social order through inheritance or move downward through loss of a fortune rather than through occupational promotion. Still, the prime mover here is economics. We should add that since the moves seem voluntary, this socialization may seem to result not so much from the demands of others as from the individual's demands; however, although the mobility might be self-initiated, the new socialization which is consequent upon the move is the result of expectations of others, not of the individual.

Most frequently a move to a new geographical community is coordinate with an upward mobility move such as moving from one community to a more desirable neighboring community or from one area of a town to a better area. The exceptions are purely lateral moves from one region to another, in which case the new socialization may be minimal. A movement from one locale to another which involves no social mobility means that the individual can carry along the major elements of the various roles he plays in the community and be able to use them; only the people are different.

Both social and geographic mobility imply a change in the nature of the groups in which the adult takes part and to which he refers his behavior as model or judge (Litwak, 1960). Both ask for change in social activities, consumption patterns, allocation of leisure time, mode of dress, political attitudes, child-care practices, and many other aspects of his style of life.

IMMIGRATION

In the decades between the Civil War and World War I immigration to the United States totaled approximately twenty million persons and averaged nearly a million new persons a year shortly after the turn of the century. The adjustment of these immigrants to a new culture is perhaps the greatest continuing process of socialization of adults in history. This same process continues today in the United States, although at a reduced level, in the great urban centers which are points of entry for new immigrants from countries different from those of their predecessors. These millions of persons had been socialized to one set of cultural patterns, including the motivations, abilities, and knowledge necessary and appropriate for active membership in their society of birth, only to find themselves, at a later point in their lives, in another society which asks for other values and behavior for membership. From the person's point of view, as Eisenstadt (1954) points out, he is required to learn new roles and must acquire new primary-group values, new skills, a new language.

These successive waves of immigrants were for the most part peasants who were drawn to the American industrial development where they worked in mines, mills, and factories, with consequent radical changes in their way of life. The records show that the immigrant's process of adjustment to the new demands may be a long and painful one, since he has lost many of his old social relationships and the stable and rewarding situations which are inherent in them, and a new set of rewarding, coherent, and understandable social relationships has not yet evolved. It is this unstructured social situation which creates the feelings of anxiety and insecurity described by many analysts of the immigrant process, for example, Thomas and Znaniecki (1918–1920) in *The Polish Peasant in Europe and America.* Significant general reviews of immigration are those by Gordon (1964), Handlin (1951), Jones (1960), and Young (1932).

Many immigrants, of course, sought to protect themselves from the demands of new and strange ways of life by re-creating in the United States communities which were familiar to them and which were isolated from the new society as little enclaves from the old world in the great cities of the new world. The socialization which then occurred was specific to those roles in which there was contact with the larger society, namely, in the area of work. The more basic attitudes and values regulating life in the community continued much the same, and it was not until the maturation of the children of the immigrants, the second and third generations, that socialization into American society ran its course.

MOBILITY IN THE UNITED STATES

The estimates from research are that one-fifth of the American population changes its residence every year. In general, the pattern for local moving differs from the pattern for more distant moves. The rates of local moving are highest for those who have "attended high school" and slope off slightly for the less educated and better educated groups. For migration to different countries, contiguous states, or even more distant states, the highest rates of migration are for those with some college training and the lowest are for the less educated (*Current Population Reports: Population Characteristics,* 1966). In a move to a new community the individual is confronted with new styles of life which he will be expected to learn. The demands are similar in substance to those of the immigrant to the United States but surely are lighter and easier to meet because the cultural differences between old and new neighborhoods is rarely as great as those facing the immigrant.

Sometimes the upward social mobility associated with change of community may take one into a much different style of life. As Goode (1964) has said, much mobility takes place within a given ethnic system, so that each ethnic group has its own internal class structure, and one moves up or down within this hierarchy. But on occasion, the adult may rise through the top of his ethnic group and move into a larger pyramid of social strata; in this case it is both social-class mobility and a move out of a familiar ethnic group into a strange one which lie behind intensified demands for large changes in the adult's way of life. The adult may, when he moves, enter a neighborhood which differs from his former one in religion or ethnic background or, in the unusual case, his race. Williams (1964), in his book *Strangers Next Door*, analyzes the experience the adult may have when he finds himself a member of a minority group in a community and must learn to fit into this role. We hardly need add that the adult's first experience with discrimination from his fellow members in the community will have a powerful influence on his own personality and behavior.

The adult socialization required of the husband or wife in the mobile family may differ from one case to the next, but we can speculate a bit about systematic differences. Studies of adjustment of immigrants report the new learning demands to be greater for the husband than the wife and the problems of adjustment more severe for the male. It is he who is confronted by the prescriptions from the new world to which they have moved, while the wife, to a greater extent, is protected from these new ways by isolation in the home. There will be conflict between her and her children as they acquire values and behavior differing from her expectations, but it is doubtful that the conflict is as harsh as that for the male who not only has the same intergenerational adjustment as the wife but must face the current day-to-day world of work. Still the wife may pay a price for the relatively less conflict and pressure: she may be left behind in the socialization process. Probably this occurs also in currently mobile American families, although we do not have enough information about the effect upon the wife of the husband's occupational mobility. What insights we do have (Cavan, 1964) indicate that the wife is not socialized into the new patterns of values and behavior as her husband progresses occupationally. She has less occasion to confront the new demands, for she is home rearing children and busy in her familiar community. It would seem, then, that when a move is made it may be the wife, rather than the husband, who is underprepared and will have more to learn, for she has not been socialized along the way, so to speak. If she is successful in staying in the home, then these demands may not impinge upon her, except perhaps through children or through the husband himself. Frequently, though, upward mobility of this kind coincides with later stages of the child-rearing period so that there is little to do at home, and the wife is confronted not only with an empty house but a challenging new community.

To sum up, the socialization demands upon the adult resulting from his upward mobility range from the small and simple to the large and complex. How far one moves — far in terms of differences in the values and attitudes of the new groups — is the key factor: we might say that the greater the move, the greater the amount the adult must learn, the greater the stress, and the greater the adult personality change.

Downward Mobility

Many adults, when they change their residence, move to a less desirable neighborhood than the one they were living in previously. Downward mobility, like upward mobility, is an event which frequently incorporates a geographical change with the change in social class. Even though the family may try to stay where they are — not give up the good house and neighborhood — a change of job and lowered income may force the move. Analyses of the frequency and consequences of downward mobility are few in number and of relatively recent date. Basic data are presented by Goode (1964), who has brought together information on a cross-national basis concerning the rates of downward mobility and who gives a summary of the compilation by Miller (1960) of social-mobility studies using data from fourteen countries. The results make it unmistakably clear that each person is potentially subject to downward as well as upward mobility. For example, Scandinavian data show that within three or four generations, there is no discernible difference between the descendants of families which earlier were respectively at the top and bottom of the social-class distribution (Goode, 1964).

The data on the United States are not as extensive as for some of the other countries, nor does the United States have as long a history. (For example, in some Scandinavian countries, the mobility data are available since the fourteenth century.) The evidence seems to show that levels of income, education, and occupation are on the rise in general, so that the potential growth of the economy and technology of the United States results in a population rising in the social order according to these indices. But, of course, our interest is in the individuals who fail to participate in this improvement of position and who stay the same or fall below the level of income, education, or occupation of their fathers.

The personality characteristics of high aspiration and achievement motivation and the genetically given high ability, associated in an open class society, such as the United States, with upward mobility, suffer in transmission from one generation to the next. Intelligence of offspring regresses toward the mean for the population, and children reared in an upper-class environment seem subject to child-rearing practices which lead directly to a lower need for achievement. Nor is it possible in most cases to transmit intact an acquired family fortune which could protect offspring from their own failings, because of taxes and because the number of children involved in most instances requires a division of the estate. This ancient problem in intergenerational mobility still must be solved by rich families in the United States. For these several reasons, then, children may not be in a position to advance beyond or even maintain their level of origin.

Downward mobility, also, is a consequence of divorce, where the economic impact is such that neither spouse, after separating, may have a status as high as that held previously. Widowhood, too, as in other instances of broken families, is often the cause of a move into a less desirable residence and an associated loss of status, for the death of the husband reduces the income below the level where the old patterns can be maintained. A widow, much more often than not, must find a new circle of friends.

Much downward mobility is associated with deviance from the normal code, such as crime, alcoholism, or emotional disorder. These deviant characteristics are correlated with unemployment and exclusion from, or rejection of, other significant positions in life; but it is still unclear whether the downward mobility itself, springing from other reasons, may lead to crime, alcoholism, and emotional disturbance, rather than be caused by them.

A downward move also takes place through no fault of the individual when the society itself is in an economic depression (in contrast to the advancing economy noted earlier in which everybody "rises"). The impact of this kind of downward mobility is much worse for the lower than the upper social classes (Cavan, 1964): during the American depression of the 1930's there were 6 per cent unemployed among the upper classes and 72 per cent unemployed among the lower classes. The upper-middle status group generally maintained its position, although in some cases the wife had to return to work. For the lower-middle and upper-lower classes there was prolonged unemployment and a lower social status; the adjustment strain apparently was the worst for those in this group who were at that time "on their way up," that is, moving ahead. For them it was a difficult time because they found themselves going back down. Among working families of the lower levels, there was extensive degradation and application for public relief.

And finally, of course, some downward mobility must be accepted as deliberate, self-initiated, a matter of choice. Many adults turn their backs on successful careers and choose others with less income and less prestige that are more satisfying to them. The artist who works without recognition but still resists commercialization or the professional who chooses to live in a smaller community with a smaller practice rather than join his father's office or firm are among familiar examples.

Yet, of all this downward mobility we know little about the probable impact on the adult in terms of how he must change to meet the situation. The downward mobile path seems to be virtually undiscussed and unanalyzed in social science literature, except for a few studies. One study by Clark (1960) analyzes how the new junior colleges serve the function of getting students to recognize their own limited abilities and the unreality of their aspirations to go to a major four-year college; Clark referred to this as the "cooling out function." Goldner's study (1965) of demotion in industry examines how the institution attempts to "make it easy" on the demoted executive. But we still do not know for how many persons downward mobility is a problem. Some may view it as a relief, as they settle into a way of life which makes lesser demands upon them. For others, the adjustment may be intense and dramatic, with a deep reevaluation of their personal worth and their relationships to their family, friends, and work colleagues.

CONCLUSION

Adult socialization has not been a familiar and common object of study in the workshops of social scientists. The main theoretical and research questions here derive from, and in due course will contribute to, our knowledge of the variable consequences of childhood socialization. They also derive from, and in time will enrich, our insight and theory concerning the relationships between personality and social structure — how the former transforms the latter, and how the latter channels and regulates the former. From the many items noted in this chapter we call attention here to a few from different facets of the adult socialization process that need study.

The depth of personality change in adulthood has never been charted in a systematic way; individual cases of fundamental alteration of personality are familiar to most of us, but the frequency of these changes and their distribution by types of persons is not known, nor do we know very much about the social episodes, whether external or internal, which produce these changes. We noted also the importance of studying the adult seeking personality change and his need for a supporting environment (that is, social, interpersonal, immediate, and real) during his attempt to change; otherwise he must fall back upon symbolic reference figures who support him with rewards and punishments in a more distant and necessarily less organic manner. But at the same time, we noted that symbolic reference figures on many occasions provide the support the individual needs to change, for they can be a counteractive force to the real, immediate reference figures. The parameters of these complicated processes, not to speak of systematic analyses, are still to be established.

In the world of occupations we called attention to the importance of studying career socialization of adults whose earlier lives left much room for adult learning, such as Negroes entering the executive world. In the same vein we noted the need for more study of post-child-rearing female participation in the labor force, with attention given to the fit of earlier socialization to the new occupational demands and with more attention than has been heretofore devoted to the reasons for this change of status. And interpersonal relationships change in one's job — familiar faces disappear, new colleagues or employees or supervisors arrive. How one learns to get along with the new personalities and the new styles of life, and the impact of this learning on work or the family or on one's more secret aspirations deserve more study. So also does the process of reconciliation of achievement to aspirations in the middle-years period. The majority of men and women face a time in their lives when what they thought they could do proves to be unachievable. The varieties of adaptations to these middle-years realities are a social process, taken as a whole, which warrants more study than it has received.

In the institution of the family, the sizable adult socialization that takes place in new relationships (as between parent and child) and in the changes in continuing human relationships (as between husband and wife) demands study; the impact of the family upon the adult is evident if one takes the time, and perhaps has the courage, to reflect. Notable among the topics here are the influence of children upon adults over the span of child-rearing years and the influence of husband and wife upon each other.

Finally, downward mobility and its demands for behavioral, attitudinal, and motivational change pose problems for many women and men in the United States and have been neglected in contrast to the elaborated concern of American social scientists with upward mobility. The social analysts and artists of England, for example, have been sensitive to, and concerned with, the causes and impact of downward mobility, but this country's social scientists and its artists and novelists still look mostly upward.

References

Barker, R. G., *et al.* Adjustment to physical handicap and illness. *Social Science Research Council Bulletin*, No. 55. Rev. ed., 1953.

Becker, H. S. (Ed.) *The Other Side; Perspectives on Deviance*. Glencoe, Ill.: The Free Press, 1964.

Biderman, A. D. Sequels to a military career: the retired military professional. In M. Janowitz (Ed.), *The New Military*. New York: Russell Sage Foundation, 1964. P. 287.

Billig, O., and Adams, R. W., Jr. Emotional conflicts of the middle-aged man. In C. D. Vedder (Ed.), *Problems of the Middle Aged*. Springfield, Ill.: Charles C Thomas, 1965. Pp. 121–33.

Blood, R. O., and Wolfe, D. M. *Husbands and Wives: The Dynamics of Married Living*. Glencoe, Ill.: The Free Press, 1960.

Bowerman, C. Adjustment in marriage: overall aid in specific areas. *Sociology and Social Research*, 1957, *41*, 257–63.

Brim, O. G., Jr. *Education for Child Rearing*. New York: Russell Sage Foundation, 1959.

Brim, O. G., Jr., and Wheeler, S. *Socialization After Childhood: Two Essays*. New York: John Wiley & Sons, 1966.

Cain, L. D., Jr. Life course and social structure. In R. E. L. Faris (Ed.), *Handbook of Modern Sociology*. Chicago: Rand McNally & Co., 1964. Pp. 272–309.

Cavan, Ruth S. Subcultural variations and mobility. In H. T. Christensen (Ed.), *Handbook of Marriage and the Family*. Chicago: Rand McNally & Co., 1964. Pp. 535–81.

Chinoy, E. *Automobile Workers and the American Dream*. New York: Doubleday & Co., 1955.

Clark, B. R. The cooling-out function in higher education. *American Journal of Sociology*, 1960, *65*, 569–76.

Davis, F. *Passage Through Crisis*. Indianapolis: The Bobbs-Merrill Co., 1963.

Deutscher, I. *Married Life in the Middle Years*. Kansas City: Community Studies, 1959.

Dyer, E. D. Parenthood as crisis: a re-study. *Marriage and Family Living*, 1963, *25*, 196–201.

Eisenstadt, S. N. *The Absorption of Immigrants*. London: Routledge & Kegan Paul, Ltd., 1954.

Form, W. H., and Miller, D. C. *Industry, Labor, and Community*. New York: Harper, 1960.

Frank, J. D. *Persuasion and Healing*. New York: Schocken Books, 1963.

Glick, P. C., and Carter, H. Marriage patterns and educational level. *American Sociological Review*, 1958, *23*, 294–300.

Goffman, E. *Stigma*. Englewood Cliffs, N.J.: Prentice-Hall, 1963.

Goldner, F. H. Demotion in industrial management. *American Sociological Review*, 1965, *30*, 715–24.

Goode, W. J. *Family and Mobility: A Report to the Institute of Life Insurance*, September 1, 1964.

Goode, W. J. *World, Family, and Revolution Patterns*. New York: The Free Press, 1963.

Gordon, M. *Assimilation in American Life*. New York: Oxford University Press, 1964.

Gross, E. *Work and Society*. New York: Thomas Y. Crowell Co., 1958.

Handlin, O. *The Uprooted: The Epic Story of the Great Migrations*. New York: Grosset & Dunlap, 1951.

Hill, R., and Rodgers, R. H. The developmental approach. In H. T. Christensen (Ed.), *The Handbook of Marriage and the Family*. Chicago: Rand McNally & Co., 1964. Pp. 171–211.

Hodgson, R. C., Levinson, D. J., and Zaleznik, A. *The Executive Role Constellation*. Cambridge, Mass.: Harvard Business School, 1965.

Inkeles, A. *What is Sociology?* Englewood Cliffs, N.J.: Prentice-Hall, 1964.

James, W. *The Varieties of Religious Experience*. Modern Library Edition. New York: Random House, 1902.

Janowitz, M., and Little, R. *Sociology and the Military Establishment*. Rev. ed. New York: Russell Sage Foundation, 1965.

Johnstone, J. W. C. *Volunteers for Learning: A Study of the Educational Pursuits of American Adults*. Chicago: University of Chicago Press, 1963.

Jones, A. M. *American Immigration*. Chicago: University of Chicago Press, 1960.

Le Masters, E. E. Parenthood as crisis. *Marriage and Family Living*, 1957, *19*, 352–55.

Litwak, E. Geographic mobility and extended family cohesion. *American Sociological Review*, 1960, *25*, 385–94.

Litwak, E. Occupational mobility and extended family cohesion. *American Sociological Review*, 1960, *25*, 9–21.

Lofland, J., and Stark, R. Becoming a world-saver: a theory of conversion to a deviant perspective. *American Sociological Review*, 1965, *30*, 862–75.

Mann, J. *Changing Human Behavior*. New York: Charles Scribner's Sons, 1965.

Marital status of working women. *Monthly Labor Review*, January 1963.

Maslow, A. H. *Motivation and Personality*. New York: Harper, 1954.

Miller, S. M. Comparative social mobility. *Current Sociology*, January 1960.

Mogey, J. Family and community in urban-industrial societies. In H. T. Christensen (Ed.), *Handbook of Marriage and the Family*. Chicago: Rand McNally & Co., 1964. Pp. 501–34.

Neugarten, Bernice L. Personality changes during the adult years. In R. G. Kuhlen (Ed.), *Psychological Background of Adult Education*. Chicago: Center for the Study of Liberal Education for Adults, 1963. Pp. 43–76.

Neugarten, Bernice L., and Garron, D. C. Attitudes of middle aged persons toward growing older. In C. D. Vedder (Ed.), *Problems of the Middle Aged*. Springfleld, Ill.: Charles C Thomas, 1965. Pp. 12–17.

Nye, F. I. and Hoffman, Lois W. *The Employed Mother in America*. Chicago: Rand McNally & Co., 1963.

Olesen, Virginia. Paper presented at the Sixth World Congress of Sociology, Evian, France, September 1966.

Pineo, P. C. Disenchantment in the late years of marriage. *Marriage and Family Living*, 1961, *23*, 3–11.

Riley, Matilda W. Socialization for the middle and later years. In D. A. Goslin and D. C. Glass (Eds.), *Handbook of Socialization Theory and Research*. New York: Rand McNally & Co., 1968.

Rossi, Alice S. Equality between the sexes: an immodest proposal. *Daedalus*, 1964, *93*, 607–52.

Scott, R. A. *Social Science and Work for the Blind*. New York: Russell Sage Foundation, 1968.

Stein, M. H. The unconscious meaning of the marital bond. In V. W. Eisenstein (Ed.), *Neurotic Interaction in Marriage*. New York: Basic Books, 1956. Pp. 65–80.

Sussman, M. B. (Ed.) *Sociology and Rehabilitation*. Washington, D.C.: American Sociological Association, 1965.

Terman, L. M., with Buttenwieser, P., Ferguson, L. W., Johnson, W. B., and

Wilson, D. P. *Psychological Factors in Marital Happiness*. New York: McGraw-Hill Book Co., 1938.
Thomas, W. I., and Znaniecki, F. *The Polish Peasant in Europe and America*. 5 vols. Boston: R. G. Badger, 1918–20.
U.S. Bureau of the Census. Mobility of the population of the United States: March 1965 to March 1966. *Current Population Reports: Population Characteristics*. U.S. Government Printing Office, Series P-20, No. 156, 1966.
Vincent, C. E. Socialization data in research on young marriers. *Acta Sociologica*, August 1964.
Williams, R. H., Tibbitts, C., and Donahue, Wilma (Eds.). *Processes of Aging: Social and Psychological Perspectives*. Vols. I and II. Behavioral Science Series. New York: Atherton Press, 1963.
Williams, R. H., and Wirths, Claudine G. *Lives Through the Years*. New York: Atherton Press, 1965.
Williams, R. M., Jr. *Strangers Next Door*. Englewood Cliffs, N.J.: Prentice-Hall, 1964.
Winch, R. F. *Mate Selection: A Study of Complementary Needs*. New York: Harper, 1958.
Wolfgang, M. E., Savitz, L., and Johnston, N. (Eds.) *The Sociology of Crime and Delinquency*. New York: John Wiley & Sons, 1962.
Young, D. *American Minority Peoples: A Study in Racial and Cultural Conflicts in the United States*. New York: Harper, 1932.
Ziegler, J. M. Continuing education in the university. *Daedalus*, 1964, 93, 1162–83.

ELEANOR E. MACCOBY

SIX *The Development of Moral Values and Behavior in Childhood*

CONTENTS

INTRODUCTION

For the purposes of the present chapter, it is assumed that moral behavior is behavior a social group defines as good or right and for which the social group administers sanctions. Moral values are beliefs, again shared in a social group, about what is good or right. Some moral imperatives are nearly universally found in all social groups, others vary from one cultural setting to another, and of course it is possible for an individual to belong to different groups whose moral precepts differ, so that moral dilemmas are posed for the individual. In the early stages of the child's development, however, conflict over morality more often comes not from the pressure of alternative value systems but because the moral demands of society are incompatible with the individual's needs and desires for immediate gratification. Conflict for the individual may be produced either when others demand that he should *not* do something he wishes to do, or when the social demands are that he *should* do something that he does not want to do. The material for this chapter will be drawn largely from the child-development literature, where more attention has been given to the problem of inhibiting the child's socially undesirable actions than to the conditions which govern the development of positive altruism and responsibility-taking. Research and theorizing about moral development in children have centered around such issues as resistance to temptation, guilt over deviation, postponement of gratification, and the learning of rules about what behavior is proscribed under what conditions. Our discussion must, therefore, emphasize these matters rather heavily, but this one-sidedness does not mean that we consider the

This chapter stems in part from papers (together with the discussions which followed them) which were presented at a conference on moral development sponsored by the Social Science Research Council's Committee on Socialization and Social Structure and organized by Martin Hoffman. Several of these papers are now in expanded form: Kohlberg (in press), Aronfreed (in press), Hoffman (in press), and Reiss (1965). We wish to acknowledge our indebtedness to the participants in the conference for clarification of the issues discussed in this chapter.

"thou shalt nots" to be more important than the "thou shalts" in the acquisition of moral social behavior.

While moral behavior in childhood often involves a conflict of interests, this conflict should lessen with increasing training. That is, while the unsocialized person may want immediate sexual gratification without restriction as to time, place, or obligations to his partner, or may want to acquire attractive objects without regard to property rules, the successfully socialized person will have come to want what society wants him to want, at least to a large degree, so that he experiences little conflict or temptation when he confines his sexual activities to socially prescribed settings, or avoids stealing.

From the standpoint of the larger society, one of the objectives of the socialization process is to produce individuals who will not only conform to the socially prescribed rules of conduct but will, as members of society, accept them as their own values. Thus the concept of "internalization" has been a central one in the study of moral development, and it will be one of the objectives of this chapter to examine this concept and consider what utility it now has in the light of recent thinking.

It is clear enough, in any case, that while some individuals who conform to social values have accepted them as their own, others have not, and conform unwillingly as a result of external pressures. Still others, despite what appears to be fairly mature knowledge and understanding concerning social rules, do not conform to them. There are some puzzling problems in the relationship between moral judgments, moral knowledge, and moral behavior. The cognitive and behavioral aspects of morality appear not to follow the same developmental paths, nor to predict one another reliably. For this reason, some students of morality have concluded that the cognitive aspects are of little importance and have confined themselves to the study of overt behavior, on the grounds that it is what people do, not what they believe about right and wrong, that will make a difference in the way society functions. We consider it a mistake to write off cognition in this way and will discuss the conditions under which the two aspects of morality ought to be interdependent, as well as the validity of studying each for its own sake.

A related issue concerns the generality of morality within either the cognitive or the behavioral sphere. When we talk about moral development, it is important to be as clear as possible about whether we are discussing a unitary process or a set of relatively independent changes. When we describe some major schools of thought, we will inquire about the degree of generality that each assumes.

We will now turn to a presentation of two major positions concerning moral development — the "developmental" position and the social-learning one — making use of the child-development literature as it bears on these two points of view. This literature has not dealt extensively with social-structural variables. Since it is a major purpose of this volume to investigate the role of social structure, we will note the occasions when aspects of social structure have been referred to in an account of moral development, and we will further consider in what respects our understanding of the processes involved might be improved by more extensive attention to these variables.

THE DEVELOPMENTAL VIEWPOINT

Piaget

The work of Jean Piaget, presented in his *The Moral Judgment of the Child* (1948), is well known and has been extensively described and reviewed elsewhere (Flavell, 1963; Kohlberg, 1964). We will not attempt to give a full exposition of it here but will present briefly some of the salient elements of his point of view as they relate to the major concern of this paper. We will then turn to a discussion of the work of Kohlberg, which grew out of that of Piaget. Piaget and Kohlberg have been concerned primarily with the cognitive aspects of moral growth: with judgments of right and wrong. Basic to their theories is the view that the development of moral judgments is part of the more general process of cognitive development. The child's understanding of moral rules must be limited by the level his thought processes have attained. Piaget described a stage of "realism" in children's thinking, during which they do not entirely distinguish between external reality and thought processes about reality. At this stage, they tend to believe, for example, that the names of things are an integral part of them, instead of being arbitrarily assigned. Realism extends to moral judgments, and during this phase of development the child will believe that rules of conduct are absolute and unchangeable, having a kind of existence of their own; at a later stage, it is possible for him to view rules as representing a social contract arrived at among individuals who are free to change them. Furthermore, the moral judgments of the young child are seen as bound by his "egocentrism." During the preschool years, the child is unable to subordinate the immediate stimulus field as it stimulates his own sense organs sufficiently to imagine how it would affect someone approaching it from a different perspective. In moral judgments, egocentrism would take the form of not being able to take the role of the other — not being able to base judgments on how others are likely to feel about, or be affected by, the child's actions.

What are the implications of Piaget's viewpoint for "internalization" of moral rules? He believes that rules may be "interiorized" to a greater or less degree and distinguishes three phases in development toward greater interiorization. Rules are first seen by the young child as entirely external to himself. Then comes a period in which the child accepts the obligation to conform to the rules, even though he does not feel he had a part in creating them. In this stage, he obeys the spirit, rather than simply the letter, of the rule. He can generalize a rule to new situations and identify the situations to which it does *not* apply in a fairly differentiated fashion, so that his application of the rule is now more thoughtful and less mechanical than it was initially. But the rule is still something emanating from external authority; moral judgment does not become truly autonomous (fully interiorized) until the phase of mutual respect and cooperation is reached. At this point, the child comes to feel that he has agreed to be bound by certain rules of conduct for the sake of others and, in return, they have agreed to regulate their behavior for *his* sake. Morality at this level is said to be fully interiorized because the individual feels that he has some control over the rules — they are maintained by his assent, not imposed by external authority. Piaget holds that this morality of reciprocity is usually not attained until about age eleven.

The reader will note that this position differs from the Freudian one, where internalization is thought to occur earlier and to involve the child's taking over parental strictures in fairly unmodified form. From the psychoanalytic point of view, the rules remain the same after "internalization" as they were before. What changes is the locus of their enforcement, which shifts from external authority to the child, himself. Internalization in the Freudian sense is similar to the state of affairs prevailing at Piaget's intermediate stage, but in Piaget's system this stage is succeeded by another in which moral concepts and the social basis for them change. For Freud, the moral values internalized from parents persist relatively unchanged through life.

Concerning the relationships between moral judgments and moral behavior, Piaget has two things to say, and they are not entirely consistent. He notes that children make more mature moral judgments when they are questioned about familiar incidents than when they are told stories which present new situations. They are likely to judge an action in real life on the basis of the intent of the actor, for example, while in a hypothetical story they will fall back on judgments based on the seriousness of the consequences of the act regardless of what the actor meant to do (a type of judgment more common among younger children). Piaget says:

> Now since thought in the child always lags behind action, it is quite natural that the solution of theoretical problems such as we made use of should be formed by means of the older and more habitual schemas rather

> than the more subtle and less robust schemas that are in the process of formation. . . . Children may perfectly well take account of intentions in appraising their own conduct, and yet confine themselves to considerations of the material consequence of actions in the case of the characters involved in our stories, who are indifferent to them. (Piaget, 1948 edition, pp. 132–33)

The child's real-life actions, then, will reflect greater maturity of moral judgment than will his answers to hypothetical questions. At the same time, Piaget notes that young children will verbalize the highest respect for the rules of the game or for their parents' commands, believing them to be obligatory and unchangeable, and yet will in fact not always abide by them. In part this occurs because the young child does not yet have the motor and intellectual skills to put the rules into practice; in part because he becomes preoccupied with (or distracted by) other aspects of the game than its social and rule-bound aspects — he may go off into experimentation with bodily movements, deriving pleasure from these, and momentarily forget the socially defined objectives of the game.

We see then that in some instances thought lags behind action and in others action lags behind thought. Piaget was well aware of the fact that thought and action may not appear to correspond. But this fact did not suggest to Piaget any lack of functional relationship between thought and action. It simply meant that cognitive development does not occur smoothly with all related properties changing at once. Thus, achievement of a new level of moral judgment may not generalize immediately to all situations to which it might be applicable; and possession of certain cognitive elements necessary for a "moral" action (for example, knowledge of a rule) does not imply possession of other cognitive elements necessary for performing the moral action (for example, being able to remember several aspects of a rule at one time). But it may be assumed that for Piaget, moral action is always based upon cognitions, including moral judgments as he defined and measured them.

A cornerstone of Piaget's position about the development of moral judgments is that a mature level of these judgments involves concepts of equality, "fairness," and the right of others that can only come from interaction with an equal-status peer group. The presence of what Piaget calls "adult constraint" in the child's relationships with his parents, while functional for the early phases of moral development, is inimical to what Piaget sees as the most advanced levels of moral thought:

> Through imitation and language, as also through the whole content of adult thought which exercises pressure on the child's mind as soon as verbal intercourse has become possible, the child begins, in a sense, to be socialized from the end of its first year. But the very nature of the relation between child and adult places the child apart, so that his thought is

> isolated, and while he believes himself to be sharing the point of view of the world at large he is really still shut up in his own point of view. The social bond itself, by which the child is held close as it may seem when viewed from outside, thus implies an unconscious intellectual egocentrism, which is further promoted by the spontaneous egocentrism peculiar to all primitive mentality. (Piaget, 1948 edition, p. 26)

In discussing the development of the concept of justice, Piaget underscores once more the limitations of adult authority:

> The conclusion which we shall finally reach is that the sense of justice, though naturally capable of being reinforced by the precepts and the practical example of the adult, is largely independent of these influences, and requires nothing more for its development than the mutual respect and solidarity which holds among children themselves. (1948 edition, p. 196)

Parent and child, as Piaget sees it, can never free themselves from the relationship of "unilateral respect" that is established in early childhood, a circumstance which makes it impossible for the parent to be the socialization agent who will teach the child a mature morality based on mutual respect and cooperation. Only other children can do this. Hence it is only between the ages of about eight and eleven, when parental control is diminishing and strong peer bonds are being formed, that the morality of mutual respect begins to develop.

Piaget did modify this view somewhat by suggesting that a good schoolmaster, or even a parent, could assist somewhat in the development of autonomous morality by putting himself on an equal plane with the child and his peer group — by agreeing to be bound by the same rules as the children and acknowledging his own difficulties and failures of compliance.

Piaget recognizes differences among children in their rate of progression through the developmental levels in moral judgment. He suggests furthermore that in certain primitive cultures where religion is transcendental and social organization authoritarian, moral judgments may be "fixed" at the level of realism, and the morality of mutual respect and cooperation may never be reached by a majority of the members of the society. Still, he was primarily interested in charting the modal course of development of moral judgments in Western society, and he did not set out in detail what variations in children's life settings or in the socialization practices of their parents ought to be associated with individual differences in the rate of development.

Others have made deductions from his theory concerning these relationships in an effort to test his views about the role of adult authority and peer groups. The assumption has been made that the more authoritarian the parent (the more strict, severe in discipline, restrictive, punitive, or undemocratic), the less mature the moral judgments of the child will be. A further deduction is that the more (or earlier) the child is integrated into a strong peer group, the more strongly (or earlier) he ought to develop a morality of reciprocity. Kohlberg (in press) has summarized and evaluated the evidence based on these assumptions. He finds: "The moral realism dimensions . . . do not appear to be related to either the parent's or the child's reports of the parents' controllingness"; and "peer group participation has not been found to be specifically associated with advance on Piaget-like measures of intentionality and reciprocity."

An interesting possibility is that the kind of parental influence which would be most effective in accelerating a child's progress through the "stages" of morality would be a changing level of controllingness. Piaget seems to mean that a child can never develop a mature morality unless he has gone through a morality of constraint at an earlier point. If he does mean this, then too much democracy during the early life of the child might interfere with the developmental sequence.[1] Perhaps only the parent who begins by being authoritarian, and thus helps the child to consolidate a morality of constraint, can have a child who is ready at an early age to progress into a more mature morality. If the parent shifts to an egalitarian mode of interacting with the child at this point, he might augment the influence of the peer group in producing a morality of reciprocity. Stage-related shifts in parental behavior have not been studied. As noted above, the single-stage studies of the only social-structural variables with which Piaget dealt — namely, the nature of the authority and peer relations the child is bound into — have not proved very useful for ordering or explaining the phenomena of moral judgment. Are there nevertheless other aspects of the developmental point of view which do stand up under empirical test and which must be taken into account in our effort to understand moral development? Here we turn to Kohlberg's (in press) reformulation of developmental theory.

Kohlberg

Kohlberg insists that there are indeed aspects of the child's general cognitive growth (other than the specifically moral ones) which provide a framework for, and impose restraints upon, the nature of the moral judgments that are possible for children of different ages. He asserts further that, with respect to the development of moral judgments themselves, the child progresses through an invariant sequence of stages which are to some degree independent of cultural or subcultural variations.

Kohlberg begins his analysis by summarizing the evidence bearing upon the nature of the developmental sequences Piaget outlined. He

[1] The author is grateful to Mr. Ralph Turner for suggesting this possibility.

shows that certain elements of the child's moral ideology, as described by Piaget, do meet the test of developmental progression, at least in that they show regular, replicable changes with age. The dimensions which show this progression include objective responsibility (an act is judged according to its outcome rather than its intent), fixity of rules (lack of adaptation of rules to specific situations), absolutism of values (belief that everyone shares a set of values), definition of wrong by punishment (an act is wrong *because* it is punished), expiative rather than restitutive justice, and immanent justice (punishment can emanate from anywhere, including the inanimate environment). The dimensions which do *not* show a regular developmental progression include duty defined as obedience to authority, obligations defined in terms of reciprocity, and conformity to peers. Even the dimensions which do change regularly with age should be formulated in a different way than Piaget has done, Kohlberg holds. He takes issue with Piaget's description of the morality of the young child in terms of respect for rules. Kohlberg agrees that young children are governed by rules in the sense that they try to discover what adults consider to be right and wrong. But he believes that they conform to these rules out of simple hedonism — they want to avoid punishment and maximize reward — instead of believing, as Piaget asserts, that the rule has an absolute power of its own. On the basis of his analysis of Piaget's findings and utilizing new data he has accumulated himself, Kohlberg formulates a somewhat different set of stages, defining three levels, subdivided into six stages, as follows:

Level 1. Pre-moral level:

1. Punishment and obedience orientation (obey rules to avoid punishment).
2. Naive instrumental hedonism (conform to obtain rewards, have favors returned).

Level 2. Morality of conventional rule-conformity:

3. Good-boy morality of maintaining good relations, approval of others (conform to avoid disapproval and dislike by others).
4. Authority-maintaining morality (conform to avoid censure by legitimate authority and the resulting guilt).

Level 3. Morality of self-accepted moral principles:

5. Morality of contract and democratically-accepted law (conform to maintain the respect of the impartial spectator judging in terms of community welfare).
6. Morality of individual principles of conscience (conform to avoid self-condemnation).

Kohlberg takes seriously the responsibility for demonstrating that these are indeed "stages." He rates the judgments which a given child makes of a wide variety of hypothetical situations according to the above stage categories and reasons that if these steps really do constitute stages, the following things should be true: (1) each should change regularly with age, the frequency of judgments of the lower-level types decreasing with age, that of the higher-level types increasing; (2) there should be some generality across situations; (3) the frequency of judgments rated in any given category should be more highly correlated with the frequencies in neighboring categories than with the frequency in categories removed by several steps; and (4) it should be easier to shift a child one step up than to produce any other shift in judgments. He presents evidence that all these conditions do indeed prevail.

Does Kohlberg's position imply that the child's progress through the stages is in some way predetermined so that it simply unfolds according to genetic laws of its own? Is there any way that culture can get at the individual and shape the course of his development? How does Kohlberg account for individual differences among children of the same age? What role does socialization play in his system?

First of all, it should be noted that Kohlberg does not claim that his stages account for all of the variance in moral judgments. He only claims that there is a "g" (general) factor in moral judgments which accounts for a substantial portion of the covariance among these judgments. Hence there is room for a variety of individual environmental factors to affect the child's moral judgments without invalidating the "stage" position. Kohlberg holds that at Level 2, the process of internalization begins, primarily through the child's identification with his parents. He conceives of identification as role taking and says that the child does not identify at an earlier age because his capacity for taking the role of another is limited in the early years.

Value acquisition through role taking implies, of course, a wide variation in the content of the values which are being taken on by the child. The content will vary from one family to another and from one culture to another. It is possible that the child will begin to internalize a strong value for being a good thief, if he is growing up in a society of thieves and can get approval from the authority figures on whom he is dependent by developing the skills and values of thievery. But this is not to say that Kohlberg's position permits pure cultural relativism. He would have to say that the young child in the thieves' culture would at first conform to thieves' values only to obtain rewards or avoid punishments. At a later point he would begin to role-play the authority figures and in this way come to accept the values as his own, even ultimately feeling the necessity to enforce the values on others. He would go through the developmental stages, in other words, regardless of the content of the values being internalized. The extreme example of the child in a thieves' society is a poor one from the standpoint of Kohlberg's theory, for he does not believe that "delinquent subcultures" within the larger society really have, or can maintain, values which are dissonant with those of the larger society (although, of course, they can have a lesser degree of commitment to the general social values). A more important issue, for him, is the rate at which an individual progresses through the stages toward complete internalization of social values. Certain positions in society provide greater stimulation for role taking and hence more rapid development. Greater peer-group participation does this, he believes, as does membership in a higher social class. The major differences between children from different social classes (or children with high or low sociometric status), then, is not that they are acquiring different values but that they progress through the stages of internalization at different rates. Stages are not skipped over by any group. As Kohlberg observed in his conference paper:

> Both middle class and working class children seem to be growing up in the same direction . . . but the middle class children are more advanced or sophisticated with regard to those attributes (Piaget dimensions). Were children growing up into distinct adult sub-cultural value systems, age trends would be in divergent rather than convergent directions.

If certain positions in the social structure provide more adequate conditions for movements up the moral-judgments ladder, does the limiting case occur in which the stimulation is so minimal that the child simply fails to progress and becomes "fixated" at an immature level? Kohlberg does not deal frontally with this issue, but he implies that it may indeed occur. He gives an example of a bright seventeen-year-old delinquent who says:

> Laws are made by cowards to protect themselves. Everybody is a crook at heart. You can take a child from birth and raise him to be any type of character. We raise people to kill rabbits, we could just as well raise them to kill people. As far as I am concerned, what is right is to go by my own instincts.

This boy has clearly not arrived at a "morality of contract" nor even a morality of conventional rule-conformity, despite being at a chronological age when moral development should be nearly complete. Presumably Kohlberg would diagnose such a case as one in which the conditions of intra-family life did not motivate the child to identify with (role-play) his parents, and hence he never moved from Level 1 to Level 2 or 3. The exact conditions which do stimulate or retard movement through the stages in Kohlberg's system are not fully spelled out. Simply pointing out that differences in social class or sociometric status are correlated with such movement leaves unanswered a host of questions about exactly how these social-status attributes produce more or less role playing and hence internalization of values. Nevertheless, social-structural variables are important in Kohlberg's system, and the parents, serving as they do as models for identification, play a more central role in socialization in this system than they do for Piaget.

Kohlberg distinguishes different degrees of internalization in the acquisition of moral values. At the pre-moral level, standards of judgment are external to the child, and the motivation for conforming to the standards is also external in the sense that the child is governed by external rewards and punishments. At Level 2, standards are still largely external, although the child can now be governed by his own knowledge and anticipation of what his parents consider right and wrong. The motivation to conform has become more internal, however. Although he feels he himself cannot judge what is right and wrong, he feels an inner compulsion to conform to what his parents have defined as right and wrong. Even if he knows he could escape detection for wrongdoing, or may not get a reward for right-doing, he still feels discomfort over deviance and pleasure over conformity. At Level 2, he also feels some obligation to enforce upon others the rules which he has accepted from identified-with authority figures. At Level 3, the standards as well as the motive to conform have become inner; they are felt as emanating from the self, and no longer depend upon the support of external authority. They are the product of multiple role taking, with many models other than the parents (Kohlberg here draws upon Mead's concept of the generalized other). At this stage, it is much more difficult to get the child to change his standard on the basis of authoritative pronouncements. Kohlberg says that "conscience" at this age means "not only a painful feeling or a warning voice associated with violating an external rule, but an inner process of thought and judgment concerning the right." It is at this later stage that moral judgment has become fully internalized and also rational. In one sense, it is only at this stage that the individual may be thought of as being truly "moral" at all. The taking on of parental values through identification is regarded as an intermediate stage, appropriate to an earlier stage of cognitive development than that typically found at Level 3.

If values are being internalized in the above ways, should it not be true that they guide behavior? Should we not require that measures of moral judgment predict actual overt conformity, as a test of the validity of the moral-judgments analysis? Kohlberg recognizes the importance of the issues involved in the mesh between moral values and moral behavior. He does insist that moral judgments are of importance in their own right — that society cares not only about what an individual does but cares also about the nature of the moral judgments an individual is able to make concerning his own behavior and that of others. He points out that the law requires that the individual shall be able to distinguish "right from wrong" before he may be punished for a deviant act and that, furthermore, the law judges behavior in terms of the intent as well as the consequences of an individual's actions. Therefore, it is important to understand the development both of concepts of right and wrong and of the ability to judge on the basis of intentionality, even if these aspects of moral development are unrelated to overt deviant or conforming behavior in specific situations. For Kohlberg, morality itself is defined more by the cognitive contents of moral judgments than by individual items of behavior.

Nevertheless, Kohlberg does concern himself with the correspondence between the two classes of phenomena. He states:

> The fact that children do not always do what they say when the chips are down does not mean that *development* of judgment and *development* of conduct go along two different tracks. Verbal judgments may not be "trustworthy" reports of conduct, but they may still reflect the same basic developmental processes.

He cites evidence to show that there are low, but positive, correlations between the maturity of moral judgments and resistance to cheating, teachers' ratings of conscience, and teachers' ratings of fairness with peers. He notes, further, that maturity of moral judgments is associated with a child's ability to resist external pressure to commit an "immoral" action. Kohlberg's interest in conceptual development stems in part from his assumption that thought and action are not really separable, and hence he is impelled to search for instances in which one can be predicted from the other and to suspect that in cases of lack of correspondence the wrong thing has been measured.

The developmental systems of Piaget and Kohlberg have in common the fact that they emphasize *change* within the individual during his growth period and *similarities* among individuals at the same developmental level. So far, individual differences have been thought of as essentially "noisy" variables by Piaget and Kohlberg, while individual differences are central for the account of moral development given by the social-learning theorists. We will now turn to a brief analysis of this position.

THE SOCIAL-LEARNING POINT OF VIEW

Reinforcement and Modeling

Social-learning theory has been the dominant point of view in socialization work for the past twenty-five years. It is the theoretical base from which Miller and Dollard, Sears, Whiting, Bandura, Walters, Aronfreed,

Cairns, and Hoffman, among others, have worked. The theory has been enunciated quite fully, with some important individual variations, by these writers. The basic concepts of the theory — reinforcement generalization, discrimination, habit strength, drive, mediation, and the stimulus-response associationist base of learning itself — are well known and need no exposition here. A discussion of the learning-theory point of view about moral development will have a number of themes in common with psychoanalytic theory, particularly with respect to the choice of issues to be studied and variables to be measured. Many of the leading figures in research on socialization were influenced by psychoanalytic theory and were centrally concerned with restating psychoanalytic concepts and hypotheses in social-learning theory terms. The discussion which follows will bring out the aspects of the social-learning position which are particularly relevant to the socialization process, noting points of contrast with the developmental position outlined above and noting differences between the several positions within social-learning theory, with the relevance of social-structural variables being stressed whenever possible.

For social-learning theorists, the acquisition of moral behavior and values is not different in any significant way from the acquisition of any other class of behavior. If one wishes to understand the acquisition of morality, one must study the processes which underlie the acquisition of any behavior, that is to say, the processes of learning. However, for the social-learning theorist, certain dilemmas arise in an attempt to understand the acquisition of moral behavior. In this theory, either the acquisition of behavior or its performance will be controlled by reinforcement (positive or negative). Moral behavior, as noted at the beginning of this chapter, quite often involves behavior which is contrary to the individual's most immediate hedonistic interests — he must do work, undergo discomfort, or forego immediate gratification for the sake of the interests of the social group. The process of socialization for moral behavior is essentially a difficult process, then, for it often involves substituting behavior which does not carry its own immediate reinforcement for behavior which does. Furthermore, a desirable outcome of the socialization process from the standpoint of the social group is that the individual will conform without constant surveillance from society's formal or informal policemen and, indeed, will be able to function as policeman and teacher of the norms to the next generation. This requires that the individual be able to administer reinforcements (both positive and negative) to himself and others. Punishing or criticizing oneself is a response which should be very difficult to acquire, and a number of learning theorists (notably, Aronfreed) have been centrally concerned with the problem of how an individual can learn to do this.

While social-learning theorists have made the assumption that the child acquires moral behavior primarily through direct reinforcement of this behavior by parents and other socialization agents, the acquisition of behavior through "identification" has long been assumed and studied. Bandura and Walters have demonstrated experimentally that behavior can be acquired through observation of models, without direct reinforcement to the observer. Observational learning is limited by the extent to which the observer attends to the appropriate eliciting conditions which control the model's responses. But under conditions where these cues are clear, situation-appropriate behavior can be acquired observationally. This process, then, in comparison with influence through direct reinforcement, may greatly extend the range of sources of influence on the course of the child's moral development. For example, the mass media may become a source for the acquisition of behavior through observational learning, and Bandura and Walters (1963) argue convincingly that they do indeed function in this way. Still, whether one emphasizes modeling or direct reinforcement or both, the parents still play a crucial role in the socialization process for any social-learning theorist, for the parents serve as the most consistently available and salient models as well as the primary dispensers of reinforcement during the early part of the child's life. Furthermore, although a child may *acquire* elements of social behavior through observation of a model with whom he is not directly interacting, the *performance* of the behavior tends to be controlled by the immediate reinforcement contingencies; hence, the people who are in a position to control these contingencies will have the greatest effect upon what the child *does*, even if they have less exclusive control over what he learns how to do. The parents, then, are the central figures in early socialization, and this makes them central for the whole of moral development, for in social-learning theory, early learned behavior tends to persist. Behavior once learned will be maintained unless the reinforcement contingencies are changed. There is no inner programming producing change as there is in the cognitive-developmental approach. Stability of behavior tends to be maintained by the tendency of the individual to seek or stay in environments which will not demand change of him. Therefore, socialization during early childhood is of great importance for the social-learning theorist, and much of the research stemming from this point of view has dealt with the preschool child and the effects upon him of variations in parental socialization practices.

The Generality of Moral Behavior

How much generality of moral behavior from one situation to another does social-learning theory assume or demand? If one focuses on reinforcement contingencies, the degree of generality of moral behavior should depend on how consistent the parents are in their treatment of the different content areas of morality. The social-learning theorist does not have to commit himself about how this ought to operate in reality. If moral behavior is shown empirically to be quite specific to situations, he will assume that this occurs because the parents use more effective socialization techniques or set higher standards with respect to some of the transgressions of their child than other transgressions. If, on the other hand, a child who conforms to moral standards in one situation does so in other situations also, the social-learning theorist can point to a presumed consistency in parental behavior across situations. He can also refer to cognitive variables in his discussion of this problem: verbal mediation, in which a variety of actions are called by the same name (for example, "honest" or "unfair"), would produce generalization of behavior across the situations so labeled. Nevertheless, the development of verbal statements about how one ought to behave can take a different course than the development of overt conformity behavior — the correspondence between the two will depend on whether they are subject to the same treatment from socialization agents.

In fact, the findings on the intercorrelations of aspects of moral behavior have often indicated a rather low level of generality. Following the classic study by Hartshorne and May (1928), who reported low correlations between various aspects of honesty as well as low correlations between "moral knowledge" and honest behavior, the theme of a lack of generality has been reiterated in a number of studies. We can mention several of these here, although the following list of researches bearing on the point is by no means exhaustive. Aronfreed (1963) has shown that the tendency to criticize oneself following a transgression is independent of the tendency to repair the damage done. In fact, he has demonstrated experimentally that these two aspects of morality have different antecedents, with self-criticism being a function of the amount of derogatory labeling of deviant behavior that socialization agents do, and reparations varying with the extent to which a child is offered the opportunity to administer his own sanctions. In a recent study by Sears and his colleagues (1965), resistance to temptation and emotional upset (guilt) over transgression tend to be uncorrelated and each related to a distinct set of parental socialization practices. Parental reports of the level of "conscience" a child displays at home have been found to be unrelated (or even slightly negatively related!) to behavior measures of resistance to temptation, and again, the correlates of the two aspects of morality with child-rearing variables are quite different (for example, Burton *et al.*, 1961). Findings of the kind listed above have led social-learning theorists to challenge the psychoanalytic theory of the acquisition of morality through a process of identification in which the young child is presumed to incorporate a wide range of parental values and behavior tendencies at the same time and to the same degree.

This lack of generality constitutes a challenge to some aspects of the social-learning theorist's own position. He should expect that new situations should be reacted to with behavior generalized from what was learned in previously encountered similar situations. As Kohlberg (1963) notes, social-learning theory depends heavily on the conditioning of anxiety as a basis for the acquisition of avoidance responses and assumes that this conditioned anxiety (the "warning voice of conscience") generalizes to a wide variety of situations (especially those given the same verbal label) unless the individual has undergone discrimination training. Furthermore, from the standpoint of the acquisition of behavior through modeling, one might expect a fair degree of generality. The nature of the factors which influence the potency of a model will be discussed below; for the present it is sufficient to note that they do not appear to act piecemeal. That is, a parent who possesses strong model characteristics should be imitated in a wide range of his behavior. Insofar as the parent himself conforms to a wide range of moral standards, his child should acquire a generalized morality through modeling himself on the parent. Generality would be weakened, of course, if the child were subject to the influence of several nurturant models who were inconsistent with one another in their moral behavior.

Actually, the empirical issue of generality is not settled. Burton (1963), in a factor analysis of the original Hartshorne and May data, found a strong "g" factor which accounted for more than 40 per cent of the variance in the table of intercorrelations among the measures of honesty. With corrections for attenuation, the "g" factor accounted for more than 60 per cent of the variance. Burton cites other studies which have found a general factor in honesty, although he does indicate that "the cognitive aspect of morality seems for the most part to be independent of the behavioral choice situation." Sears *et al.* (1965) found consistently positive correlations among several tests of resistance to temptation. Kohlberg, as noted above, found internal consistency in a set of measures of moral judgment.

It should be noted that correlational analysis may not always be the best way to discover generality if acquisition of moral behavior proceeds stepwise so that one element is a necessary, but not sufficient, condition for another. In this case, a Guttman scale analysis is a more appropriate means for discovering the relationships among different aspects of moral thought or behavior. Unfortunately, this approach has not been widely employed. In any case, we probably will not find, and should not expect, a simple answer to the question of whether moral behavior is made up of an aggregation of independent elements, each individually acquired, or a generalized "trait." The question of the generality or specificity of traits is, of course, an old one in psychology, still widely debated with respect to intelligence and many attributes of personality other than "morality," and we cannot hope to settle it here. The evidence would appear to indicate that there is at least one general factor, and possibly several, which accounts for a portion of the variance of behavior in a variety of situations. There are also many "s" factors which reflect situational specificity. We do not yet have a clear enough formulation of the nature of the general factor or factors to permit us to predict what aspects of moral behavior ought to be correlated and what ought not.

Socialization

In most instances, when the social-learning theorist has studied some aspect of moral development, he has chosen a dependent variable which he assumes has some degree of stability and generality. These variables include "conscience," "internal versus external moral orientation," "resistance to temptation," "delinquency," and "self-criticism" — to name only a few. The research strategy has been to study individual differences in these attributes (either differences produced experimentally or those found in a state of nature) in relation to the behavior of socializing agents. In most studies, the nature of the dependent variable has been such that the researcher feels he can assume a reasonable degree of homogeneity among socialization agents concerning the outcome they would like to achieve. That is, the assumption is made that most parents would like to have children who are non-delinquent, have highly developed "consciences," are able to resist temptation when adults demand that they should do so, etc. The differences among children in performance, then, are usually not studied in relation to differences in what socialization agents are demanding of them but in relation to the effectiveness of the techniques being employed to inculcate culture-wide values. When socialization is viewed in this way, the child will either have the values of the parent generation (if socialization techniques are effective) or he will be inadequately socialized — amoral or pre-moral. There is no provision in this conception for a new generation to acquire a set of values systematically *different* from those held by their parents. This point will be taken up again in the section on macro-social influences.

What then do the social-learning theorists have to say concerning the characteristics of the socialization process that are most and least effective in transmitting parental norms? The characteristics which have been studied vary from global, pervasive characteristics of parental interaction with children (for example, the "warmth" of the parent), to highly detailed, microscopic features of parental behavior (for example, whether the parent stops a child while he is reaching for a forbidden object rather than after he has picked it up). In experimental studies, these fine-grained variables have proved to be powerful in determining outcomes in child behavior (Aronfreed and Reber, 1965; Walters and Demkow, 1963; Aronson and Carlsmith, 1963). The large majority of socialization studies, however, have not involved experimental manipulation of the antecedent variables but have made use of normal variations in the practices employed by a population of parents insofar as it is possible to determine what these practices are. In this research, one faces not only the issue of what generality there is in the moral behavior of the child but also the issue of the generality of parent behavior. Are parents consistent enough from one time to another and from one situation to another so that it is justifiable to identify one parent as "permissive" and another "restrictive" on the basis of a limited sample of his behavior? Astonishingly little attention has been given to this problem in studies of socialization practices. It is very difficult indeed to find any measures of test-retest reliability of either observational or interview measures taken with parents. The most common means of assessing parent behavior, the parent interview or questionnaire, usually simply assumes some consistency in parental behavior and asks the parent about what he "usually" does or how he "usually" feels when his child behaves in a specified fashion. No doubt there is a good deal of situational variability in the behavior of the parent as well as that of the child: he may punish only when he is alone with the child, not when others are present; he may follow through on a demand when he is rested, not when he is tired, etc. Still, if one is to believe that variations in moral behavior among children are to any degree traceable to differences in their parents' behavior toward them, there must be some degree of stability within individual parents with respect to their position on the dimension which differentiates them from other parents. Socialization research stemming from social-learning theory has made this assumption.

Before we proceed to list some of the conclusions emerging from this research, we must digress briefly to consider a methodological point. When research deals with certain attributes of parental behavior, it must be concerned with the problem of whether any correlations with child behavior that are discovered are a function of the attributes which were measured or other attributes which are correlated with these. For example, it has been repeatedly found that parents from different social classes differ in their child-rearing practices, the middle-class families being more permissive and less punitive than working-class families. If one works with a cross-section sample of families, including families with a range of social-class memberships, and finds relationships between child behavior and some aspect of parental practices that is correlated with social class, the finding may, of course, be an artifact of some characteristic of social class other than the socialization practice whose effect is being studied. The problem of intercorrelations among the antecedent variables has led to three approaches: (1) deliberate selection of samples that are homogeneous with respect to the variables whose effect one does not wish to study; (2) efforts to measure the "confounding" variables so as to hold them constant statistically in the analysis of results; and (3) factor analysis of the antecedents so as to reduce large sets of intercorrelated variables to a smaller number of relatively independent variables. Aspects of social structure have usually been dealt with under the first two approaches. Most students of socialization practices have not been greatly interested in social class or other aspects of social structure per se. The findings relating class to child rearing have emerged primarily as by-products of studies with other concerns. Since social-structural variables do not relate to the theoretical constructs from which most socialization research (at least that done by psychologists) proceeds, variance associated with these variables has been treated as "error variance" — something to be cleared away so that the effects of the child-rearing techniques of the parents can be more clearly seen.

The intercorrelations among child-rearing variables themselves are another matter. Here the effort has been to identify underlying dimensions. As might be expected, the dimensions which emerge from factor analysis of any particular set of measures of socialization practices are a function of the nature of the variables which were included in the initial set of measures. The effort to find a single limited set of dimensions which will describe most of the variability in parental behavior regardless of the specific measures taken is probably foredoomed to failure. Still, in order to reduce the number of attributes of parental behavior to a manageable set for the discussion which follows, it may be useful to list some of the variables which have emerged from factor analytic studies (Baumrind and Black, in press; Lorr and Jenkins, 1953; Sears, Maccoby, and Levin, 1957; Slater, 1962; Becker *et al.*, 1962; Nichols, 1962; Cline, Richards, and Needham, 1963) as underlying attributes of parental behavior or attitudes:

Warmth (versus hostility or rejection)
Permissiveness (versus restrictiveness)
Child-rearing anxiety
Sex anxiety
Inhibitory demands and discipline
Responsible child-rearing orientation
Physical punishment
Dependence encouragement
Democratic attitudes
Authoritarian control
Punishment (versus non-punishment); punitiveness; punishment orientation

General family adjustment
Marital conflict
Firm discipline
Independence-achievement orientation
Seclusiveness

Schaefer (1959) has attempted to order a variety of child-rearing variables with respect to two basic dimensions — warmth-hostility and control-autonomy — and has shown that these dimensions fit the data from several studies of socialization practices, although some studies have identified additional dimensions orthogonal to these. Becker (1964) has subdivided the control-autonomy dimension into two — restrictiveness-permissiveness and calm detachment versus anxious emotional involvement — while maintaining the warmth-hostility dimension as separate and unitary. A number of researchers have felt that not only the basic power and affection variables but techniques of discipline such as withdrawal of love or "induction" (appeals to the child's own sense of right and wrong) are important in their own right. However, as Becker (1964) cogently points out, techniques of discipline tend to be correlated with the warmth dimension. Physical punishment tends to be used by hostile parents, while warm parents more often use praise, reasoning, and induction. Hence it is often difficult to study the effect of specific techniques apart from the effects of the more pervasive affective relationships in which they are enmeshed.

There are several recent reviews of the relationships of parental socialization practices to aspects of the moral development of children (Becker, 1964; Hoffman, 1963; Kohlberg, 1963). These reviews point to the inconsistency in the findings, stemming in part from differences in the way aspects of parent behavior have been defined and measured. It is not possible to go into the complexities of the findings of many studies here, but two of the major themes that emerge are discussed below.

WARMTH VERSUS REJECTION OR HOSTILITY

High degrees of parental warmth have been found to be related to non-delinquency, to responsibility, and in some instances to indicators of "guilt" or "conscience." In experimental situations where the amount of nurturance offered by an experimenter to a child subject is varied, it has been found that children will more often imitate a nurturant model than a non-nurturant one, a circumstance suggesting that one of the factors underlying the greater success of warm parents in inculcating moral norms is that their children are more likely to learn from them through modeling. In addition, warmth promotes the socialization process because, as Becker puts it, warmth "makes the parent important to the child and obviates the need for more severe forms of discipline to gain compliance." The child who feels strong positive attachment and little fear toward his parents will want to stay in their presence (and hence the opportunities for teaching and modeling will be increased) and will also be motivated to gain their approval and avoid their disapproval. In this connection, it is interesting to note that the use of withdrawal of love as a technique of discipline appears to be most effective in a context of high warmth.

There is some evidence that withdrawal of love has more influence on "guilt" or "conscience" (socialized responses after transgression) than it does on behavioral conformity — the ability to avoid transgressing. Aronfreed has shown that a condition which will increase self-critical responses in children is what he calls "high cognitive structuring," that is, labeling of actions by derogatory names when the socialization agent considers them undesirable. It is possible that derogatory labeling often forms part of the parental behavior which has been identified as "withdrawal of love"; in any case, both are likely to occur *after* a transgression has occurred and hence control the post-transgression responses, such as apology, confession, self-criticism, and emotional upset, rather than the behavior which occurs at the point of initial temptation.

CONTROL VERSUS AUTONOMY

The findings concerning the effects of a high degree of control exercised by parents are less consistent than those relating to warmth. Much seems to depend on the emotional context within which power is exercised by the parent. Becker's summary indicates that parents who are restrictive (highly controlling) and warm have children who are well socialized in the sense that they are conforming, obedient, neat, and polite, but that these children also tend not to be as creative, independent, or socially outgoing as the children of parents who are warm but less restrictive. The work of Baumrind (1967), on the other hand, showed the combination of parental warmth and control to be most effective in producing "ego strength" in children — competence, friendliness, and an absence of either babyish, passive immaturity, anxious withdrawal, or overimpulsive, disruptive forms of behavior. Hoffman, on his measures of moral development, found that the most mature children had parents who were moderately controlling in a context of warmth. Bronfenbrenner also found a curvilinear relationship between the extent of parental control and the child's responsibility-taking and leadership in adolescence.

Some of the differences in the findings of different studies may be traced to differences in definition. In the Hoffman work, high degrees of control are represented by what he calls "unqualified power assertion" — an insistence by the parent that the child should do what he is told simply because he has been told. For Baumrind, high control is a matter of consistent follow-through on demands: a parent is called controlling if he sees to it that a parental demand is met, even though there may have been a good deal of reasoning, explanation, and even negotiation with the child before the demand was established.

In any case, it appears that with a variety of definitions of control or its absence, ultra-permissiveness does not produce a well-socialized child. An ultra-permissive, rejecting parent is perhaps better described as neglecting, and his child tends to become antisocial. Even when the parent is warm, an absence of at least moderate parental control is likely to be associated with low impulse control in the child and low levels of achievement, although the child's hostility level will usually not be high. High degrees of restrictiveness by warm parents, on the other hand, may mean that the child is over-controlled and inflexible, remaining dependent upon external authority for the control of his actions instead of developing the ability to make his own judgments and administer his own sanctions.

It is clear from the experimental studies on the effectiveness of models that the model who is powerful (in the sense of having control over resources the child wants) will more often be imitated spontaneously by a child who observes his actions than will the powerless model. We seem to have a rather paradoxical situation here: the parent who has a high degree of power may not have to use it often. That is, the controlling parent will find it relatively easy to elicit behavior which is like his own because the child will have acquired the requisite repertoire through observation. The acquisition process need not be coercive, although the child may sometimes need pressure to *perform* the adult-like actions that he has learned through observation.

The amount of control exercised by parents, then, and the way it is exercised are important for the achievement of moral behavior in children. We have noted that it makes a difference whether power is exercised by hostile or affectionate parents. It probably is important also whether the exercise of parental power is arbitrary or reasoned — whether the parent explains his reasons for his decisions and gives the child an opportunity to participate in the decision making.

The above brief account of some of the main themes in socialization research is, of course, highly oversimplified. Only the findings relevant to two major dimensions of child rearing were referred to, and these two dimensions, important though they are, do not by any means account for all the variance in parent behavior. There is an almost infinite variety of patterns of socialization practices impinging on children in different family settings. Perhaps partly because of the radical reduction involved in selecting only two aspects of child-rearing practices for study, the findings of different studies have not been entirely consistent; but the main findings do indicate that the effects of one dimension cannot be understood except as the one dimension interacts with the other. Thus, the addition of further variables may be expected to increase the complexities of interpreting findings because of the additional interactions which may be expected to emerge as important.

Nevertheless, it would appear to be amply demonstrated that differences in moral behavior and values among children of the same age are associated with differences in the socialization practices of their parents. It might be argued, of course, that no cause-and-effect relationship has been established and that the parental practices might be responses to the child's behavior, not vice versa. This point seems to have some force in relation to the evidence cited above concerning parental warmth. Is it not reasonable that parents would respond more warmly to a well-socialized child than to one who does not conform to parental and societal demands? The findings on power and control, however, are not so easily understood in this light. The more socialized a child is, the less control a parent would need to exercise. Yet the bulk of the findings go the other way, with at least moderately high control being associated with socialized behavior in the child. It would seem unlikely that high parental control is a response to a child's good conduct.

Even more telling are the findings of the experimental studies, in which it has been possible to have experimenters reproduce at least some aspects of parental behavior and obtain changes in children's behavior which parallel some of the findings of correlational studies (for example, Aronfreed, 1963; Bandura, Ross, and Ross, 1963). Such results make us more confident that the characteristics of children are indeed to some degree the outcome of the parental practices with which they covary.

DEVELOPMENTAL AND SOCIAL-LEARNING THEORY CONTRASTED

Of course, it comes as no surprise to the social-learning theorist that the child's moral behavior and moral values will reflect the training he has received. But does this constitute a problem for the developmental theorist? As noted earlier, the developmentalist does not think of children as taking divergent paths depending upon the nature of their socialization experience. He thinks of them as taking the same path but does allow that an individual's rate of progress along this path will be a function of accelerating or retarding conditions some of which are provided by socialization agents. Of course, for the developmental theorist, the primary determinant of a child's rate of progress through the stages of moral development will be his rate of cognitive growth, so such a theorist will look for correlations between level of moral development and such variables as I.Q. But he does allow for certain interpersonal factors as well. First of all, the rate of development of I.Q. itself may be influenced by socialization practices. In addition, conditions which promote role playing will facilitate the transition into higher levels of morality—presumably into the morality of contract. While Kohlberg does not specify what the parental practices are which should facilitate role playing (other than to say that membership in "participating groups," such as higher social classes, will do so), the work of Bandura and his colleagues, on the conditions which increase an observer's imitation of a model, may provide a point of contact between Kohlberg's theory and social-learning theory. If one makes the assumption that an observer learns from a model through covert role playing, then the conditions which facilitate modeling ought to be facilitating role playing, and it would follow that the nurturance (warmth) and power of socialization agents would facilitate transition to higher levels of morality on the Kohlberg scale just as they appear to be associated with the aspects of moral behavior that the social-learning theorists have measured.

However, this is speculation. The relationships between the standard socialization variables described above and children's standing on the Kohlberg scale have not been measured. More important for our present purposes is the fact that the two theories do have different things to say concerning the nature of the changes that occur with time in a given child. The social-learning theorist would say that if a child's parents employ the appropriate child-rearing techniques, the child will directly acquire the more "mature" forms of moral behavior without having had to pass through the "less mature" stages.

Let us, as an example, contrast the work of Hoffman (1967; in press) with that of Kohlberg with respect to this issue. On the basis of seventh-grade children's responses to moral-judgments items, Hoffman distinguishes three "conscience types"—the external, the conventional-rigid, and the humanistic-flexible. When the child's moral judgments seemed to be based on concern for external punishment, they were coded as external. When they emphasized moral convention or moral authority, they were coded as conventional-rigid. When they emphasized the consequences of action for others and interpersonal values such as mutual trust, they were coded as humanistic-flexible. Kohlberg notes the parallel between this classification scheme and his own set of developmental levels, where Hoffman's "external" type would be roughly equivalent to Kohlberg's stage 1, his conventional type to stage 4, and his humanistic-flexible type to either stage 2 or 6, depending on whether the child's concern for others was concern over losing their approval (stage 2) or a concern based on taking the role of the other and thus understanding his point of view. The major difference between the positions is that Kohlberg has arranged these "types" into sequential order, offering evidence that there are regular progressions from one to the other with age. Hoffman, on the other hand, assumes that parental practices are fairly constant over the lifetime of the child (that is, that a warm or controlling parent is fairly stably so through the major part of a child's growth period) and that different parental practices cause children to diverge in moral orientations. The child is "external" because his parents have been relatively cold and have used high power assertion and physical punishment, while the humanistic-flexible child has developed his moral orientation because his parents were warm, used induction, and used moderate levels of power assertion. Hoffman's view would not provide for the possibility that children who are now humanistic-flexible were characteristically "external" types at a younger age. It would seem that only longitudinal research, tracing the development of moral judgments in individual children and contrasting this development in children growing up in different socialization settings, will settle the issue of sequentiality versus diverging types.

At present a reasonable prediction is that both formulations will turn out to be right to a degree. Kohlberg's data on age changes are convincing evidence that, taking populations of children as a whole, there is indeed a developmental progression. Of course, the social-learning theorist can claim that this progression stems from systematic changes in the nature of the socialization techniques employed with children of different ages. Perhaps young children have an "external" orientation because their parents employ physical punishment more often at this age than they will do later, when they feel that the child is old enough to respond to reasoning and other "induction" techniques. Or perhaps the fact that as the child grows older he has increasing contact with socialization agents other than his mother (for example, his father) may help to explain shifts in his moral orientation. We have very little information indeed concerning the changes in socialization practices within a family as the child grows older. There is some evidence that warmth is more stable over time than parental behavior with reference to the power dimension (Schaefer and Bayley, 1960), but there is clearly a pressing need for research which traces changes in socialization patterns in more detail so that we can determine how well the changes that do occur match the systematic change in moral behavior and moral judgments that occur with growth.

Even if it does turn out to be true that parents adapt their child-rearing practices to the developmental level of the child (and indeed they *must* do so to some degree), the developmental theorist will have scored a point, for he will have additional evidence that the developmental timetable of the child does in one sense control the course of moral development; the social-learning theorist will have to concede this point but will insist that the child's development is mediated by the changing behavior of parents as training agents and perhaps is even produced by these changes, instead of occurring as part of an internally controlled "unfolding" process.

Even if systematic changes in parental behavior with the age of the child were uncovered, there would still be room for considerable variation among families in the nature of the affective and power relationships with a child of a given age and in the techniques of discipline employed. Such variation ought to serve as a starting point for understanding individual differences among children of the same age. It is doubtful whether the developmental view that parental practices serve only to retard or accelerate progress through a fixed sequence of stages will ever provide an adequate account of individual differences. The amoral seventeen-year-old delinquent cited earlier is a case in point: he is intelligent and sophisticated, and his amorality is very different from that of a five-year-old. Surely it is not satisfactory to view him as morally "retarded" — as a person who has simply failed to develop. There seems more promise in looking for socialization factors which have produced a diverging pattern of character development, not only in such a deviant case as the one Kohlberg described, but for variations within the normal range as well.

The above discussion has centered on the problem of whether differences in the moral orientation of children tend to be sequential within a child or whether they represent fairly enduring characteristics of different groups of children that may be traced to differences in the socialization experiences they have had. As noted earlier, this issue is part of the larger question of the extent to which moral development is controlled by cognitive development. The developmental theorists hold that the relationship is a close one, and they have some evidence for their position in the positive correlations (though they are not large) between level of moral judgments and I.Q., as well as in the systematic increases in level of these judgments with age.

The evidence for a significant role of cognitive development is not nearly so strong if one considers moral *behavior* rather than moral judgments. There have been some attempts to determine whether individuals behave in a more "moral" fashion as they grow older. In his summary of the scanty evidence on this point (1964, p. 392), Kohlberg indicates that studies of cheating and stealing show that older children are as likely to show these forms of deviation as younger children in experimental situations. McFarlane *et al.* (1954) report that the frequency of lying (as reported by parents) declines with age through the age range six through eight. The frequency of overt aggression decreases with age, but we do not have good evidence concerning the more subtle and disguised forms of injury to others. Certain deviant acts, such as stealing cars, are possible only for older children and of course increase with age, at least through the teen-age period, while the frequency of children's stealing coins out of their mothers' purses would very likely decrease with age. It is evident that the cognitive growth occurring through childhood, if it plays any role in moral behavior, can serve not only to increase the pro-social forces on behavior but can also increase the motivations, opportunities, and capabilities for certain kinds of antisocial behavior. What has intellectual development to do with moral behavior, then?

Festinger (1964), in an article on the relationship between attitude change and behavior, has pointed out that we have no clearly documented instances in which change in attitudes produced by persuasive communications is associated with change in the relevant behavior. Thus it is possible to convince mothers of young infants that they ought to toilet train their children at a later age than they originally thought was proper, and this change in attitudes may be relatively lasting, but they do not actually start toilet training later than a control group (Maccoby *et al.*, 1962). Festinger discusses the nature of the environmental and behavioral supports that must exist before attitude change can be effectively translated into action. Clearly we cannot expect that progressive changes in children's knowledge and understanding about what people *ought* to do will automatically be translated into moral action. Still this does not mean that the level of knowledge and understanding of which a child is capable is irrelevant to his moral behavior. For the developmental theorist, the relevance of cognitive level is not just a matter of what attitude and values the child holds. The term cognitive development is broader than this and refers to growth in the kind of thought processes that occur. The matter is obviously highly complex, but it may be worthwhile to speculate about the nature of possible interactions between cognitive development and moral behavior, in the hope of uncovering some areas that would repay further fact-finding efforts.

As a starting point, we might note that while Hartshorne and May (1928) did not find any increases in morality with age, they did find positive correlations between moral behavior and I.Q. Brighter children did not cheat so often, either at school or on school work done at home, as did the less intelligent children. A developmental theorist might be inclined to interpret this fact in the following way: brighter children are more able to put themselves in the role of other children and to appreciate the effect their own cheating might have on lowering the grades of others; their more mature moral judgments, then, would lead them to inhibit their own cheating as part of the peer-group-based morality of contract. It should be noted, however, that the bright child cheats just as much as the dull child at party games; this fact suggests another interpretation, namely, that the bright child cheats less on examinations because he has less need to do so to achieve his academic goals. He has alternative means. In a situation where his intelligence gives him less advantage (for example, party games), he cheats as much. The growth of cognitive abilities with age, then, may contribute to moral behavior in that it equips the individual with pro-social means to achieve his goals. The older, more competent child can, for example, earn some money with which to buy what he wants. The younger child, not having this alternative, might be more tempted to steal a small amount of money if the opportunity arose.

One aspect of cognitive growth which might be related to moral behavior is increasing time span. The young child can neither plan over an extended time nor easily foresee delayed consequences of his actions. Increasing understanding of time sequences should facilitate moral behavior in that it permits more sophisticated understanding of the consequences of actions for oneself and others and permits balancing alternative outcomes in such a way that the individual can forego immediate gratifications for the sake of maximizing long-term gains and minimizing long-term losses. However, increasing time span can have its antisocial implications as well: The young child would not be capable of carrying out a well-planned crime nor a subtle and extended program of injury directed at an enemy. The young child will hit out and forget; the older child can brood, dissemble, and plan for revenge. He can delay his antisocial act until circumstances arise that shield him from being caught and punished. Thus the nature of antisocial behavior clearly changes with the time-binding aspects of cognition that are achieved with age, but it is not clear that age changes will necessarily result in a total lesser amount of such behavior. The balance should depend, at least in part, on the extent to which society provides the individual with pro-social avenues that have a high probability of achieving his goals.

Another obvious connection between level of cognitive development and the nature of moral behavior lies in the nature of the rules which a child can understand. It is possible to teach a child of three not to cross a given street. It would be much more difficult to teach him that he could cross it except after five o'clock when the rush-hour traffic begins. In the same way, it is easier to teach a child that he must never lie (although the limits of the category "lie" are not always easy to establish) than to teach him that he must not lie unless to tell the truth would do such injury to another person that the child would be justified in lying in order to spare the person that injury, despite the losses in mutual trust that might ensue from the lie. To perceive and balance different values which are not altogether compatible in a given situation ought to require more cognitive maturity than the application of a single, simple rule. And even in the case of simple rules, the ability to understand the nature of the category of acts referred to in the rule should be a necessary condition for obeying it. If the child is told, "You are not to play with matches," he can only obey if he can tell matches from toothpicks and distinguish play from necessary use. Even a very young child can do reasonably well with such simple matters of rule reference, but it takes considerably more ability at verbal abstractions to be able to distinguish instances of "justice" from "injustice." Even assuming that what Festinger calls "behavioral supports" are forthcoming, the child will not follow the rule correctly in new instances unless he has abstracted the correct category of instances to which the rule refers.

Developmental theorists refer to increases with age in the child's ability to put himself in the place of another. The social-learning theorist is less impressed with the age changes in this respect, for he is able to demonstrate observational learning in very young children, and presumably such learning is empathic to some degree.

Parenthetically it should be pointed out that it is not clear just how much or what kind of "covert role playing" is required in the process of learning from a model, and hence it is difficult to trace age changes in the relevant empathic skills. In one study of delay of gratification (Bandura and Mischel, 1965), the effects of observing a model's delay choices were determined. In one experimental condition, the children saw a model make his choices and listened to the model discuss his reasons for his choices. In another experimental variation, the child subjects were merely told what choices a model had made and were asked to read the model's statement of the rationale for his choices. The children's choice behavior was influenced in both conditions, and about equally for the two conditions (at least in the immediate post-test). Thus it would seem that the "observational learning" situation may be interpreted as one way of telling the child what behavior is appropriate to the situation, but the child need not actually see a model perform the behavior — he only needs to know verbally what the behavior is. Thus the "symbolic modeling" situation comes close to being a persuasive communication — in this case, one which successfully influenced an aspect of overt moral behavior.

The more traditional modeling situation, in which the subject sees the model perform certain actions, is one where covert "playing the role of the other" is more clearly involved, and the experimenters working with preschool children have had their models perform very simple, clearly identified actions. They have not been concerned with limitations on the nature of the actions which observers can copy nor with the cues of reward or punishment for the model which the observers are able to utilize. Given the fact that changes do occur with age in the child's ability to understand the nature of the stimulus situation impinging upon others (Flavell, 1963), it would seem likely that there are improvements with age in the quality of observational learning when models perform subtler actions and respond to less obvious cues than those which have been employed so far in studies of observational learning.

All of this argues that the level of cognitive maturity will indeed make a difference in moral behavior. A reasonable degree of cognitive maturity would appear to be a necessary, but not sufficient, condition for certain levels of overt, mature moral behavior. As noted earlier, Bandura and Walters (1963) have pointed out that subjects may *learn* a bit of behavior (by observing models or otherwise), but they may or may not *perform* the behavior they have learned. A child may learn an antisocial action but never perform it because the relevant conditions never arise or because of the fear of external sanctions. Or pro-social behavior may be learned but not performed because of the lack of relevant motivation or for some other reason. We are faced with the dilemma of the intelligent delinquent who knows and understands the social rules very well but who either does not believe that they apply to him or, not appearing to be disturbed over discrepancies between his verbalized values and his behavior, accepts them at a superficial level. We are dealing here with the problem of different degrees of "internalization," and it may be a good idea at this point to contrast the two theoretical viewpoints we have been examining with respect to their treatment of this concept.

A good deal of the work on moral development done by social-learning theorists has been motivated by an interest in internalization. In recent years, the usefulness of this concept has been challenged. Some of the issues raised are these: Is *internalizing* different from *learning* itself? When an animal learns to take a left turn in a maze, has he "internalized" the left-turning response? If so, what is the utility of the concept of internalization — why not simply say learning? If one wishes to label as internalization only a certain subset of instances of acquisition of behavior, by what criterion is the subset to be identified? One approach has been to classify behavior as internalized only when controlling functions are exercised by the individual himself rather than by an external controlling agent. The assumption is that controls were originally external (through the administration of rewards and punishments by an external agent), but that behavior becomes independent of these external sanctions, and the individual comes to administer his own rewards and punishments.

A great deal has been written on the problem of distinguishing behavior which is externally controlled from behavior which is not. A basic issue has been that the individual often avoids deviant behavior or performs onerous duties because he anticipates social rewards or punishments which, in actuality, may never be forthcoming. These anticipatory responses represent control from within the person (external actions being absent). Yet it would seem reasonable to regard the behavior as externally controlled whenever it is motivated by fear of external punishment or promise of external reward. Thus only certain self-controlling acts would be evidence of internalization — those motivated by the wish to avoid self-condemnation or merit self-approval.

Aronfreed (1963), in his studies of self-critical responses, has shown that such responses tend to be acquired when they are paired with the termination of external punishment. Hence self-criticism becomes a means of avoiding or terminating external punishment. When looked at in this way, it is difficult to say whether self-critical responses should be looked upon as an example of external or internal control.

Bandura (1963) makes two points concerning internalization: (1) Behavior is always under the control of external, discriminative stimuli. He gives the example of the lonely motorist waiting for a red light to turn to green in the middle of the night when no one is there to see whether he obeys the light or not. In waiting for the green light, he may be exhibiting internalized behavior in one sense, but he is still under the control of an external signal — the stop light. Thus behavior which is "internalized" is not entirely free of external controls; it is simply that *sanctions*, potential or actual, are internal. (2) It is very difficult to tell the difference between sanctions that are internal, in the sense of punishment or reward by the self, and actual or potential punishment from external agents; when an individual appears to be maintaining a standard of behavior in the absence of social support, or even in defiance of social standards, he may actually be attempting to please a rather specialized external person or group. Bandura and Walters say (1963),

> The size of the group by reference to which a particular person evaluates his behavior may vary considerably; when a person's immediate reference group is small and select, and does not share the values of the majority of persons of his social class, it may sometimes appear that he is making an independent self-evaluation, and displaying "inner-directed" behavior, whereas he may be, in fact, highly dependent on the actual or fantasied approval or disapproval of a few individuals whose judgments he values highly. (Bandura and Walters, 1963, pp. 163–64)

Bandura and his colleagues do not doubt that the individual comes to administer rewards and punishments to himself; indeed, they have studied the acquisition of self-rewarding and self-critical responses. They do question, however, whether these are ever truly independent of a selected set of external agents. In an experiment related to this issue, a model rewarded himself only when his performance on a task reached a particular standard of excellence. His standard was adopted by the child subjects who observed him; they tended to reward themselves, subsequently, only for performances which reached this standard. But when the status of the model was deflated (models who had been described as big-league ball players were revealed to be convicts), the subjects no longer adhered to the standards these models had displayed. Hence, the self-administered standard was shown to be dependent on a reference person and to vary with the status of this reference person. Is it then truly internalized?

The account of moral development provided by this group of learning theorists, then, would appear to end with Kohlberg's Level 2. The transition from control by external agents to self-administration of sanctions is recognized, but the standards remain externally based (though they may need only periodic external support). The final stage in Kohlberg's system, in which the standards themselves become internalized, based upon "an inner process of thought and judgment concerning the right," and in which standards are felt to emanate from the self rather than from a reference group, does not appear in the Bandura-Walters' system. It would not be incompatible with their system to assume the existence of standards for which the reference-group source has been forgotten or for which the external reinforcements have emanated from such a wide variety of sources that the standard no longer has a specific reference-group base, so that they rest for their validity on the "generalized other." If one makes the further assumption that standards which do not have a specific and identifiable reference group seem to emanate from the self, then there would be a basis for contact between Kohlberg's Level 3 and the Bandura-Walters' account. However, Bandura and Walters have not made these extensions, and would not be likely to do so, since with their behavioristic orientation they would not consider it especially important whether standards "seem to emanate from the self" or not; the important question for them would be whether the individual does or does not behave in a manner consistent with social standards, and whether he does or does not produce self-controlling responses.

A number of writers on moral development have described the emergence of altruism as one characteristic of the highest level of moral development. Piaget and, somewhat less explicitly, Kohlberg refer to a kind of morality in which the individual judges (and presumably controls) his own actions on the basis of their actual or anticipated consequences for others. This altruism may be based on self-interest in a very generalized sense. That is, the individual may recognize the values for himself of living in a society where justice, law, and order are maintained. Still, one of the characteristics of mature morality for the developmental theorists is that the individual shall recognize morality as a social contract — he must accept the obligation to promote the interests of others in return for their agreement to promote his, and he must act in accordance with others' interests even when he obtains no gratification through social approval for doing so. And for this stage to be reached, the individual must have achieved a fairly advanced level of cognitive development, one which permits him both to use abstract principles of law and justice and to take the role of the other.

Bandura and Walters (1963) do not discuss altruistic behavior as such. Presumably they would say that in instances in which the individual takes a risk or sacrifices his own interests in the service of others, even when his actions are anonymous and hence cannot be reinforced by others, his behavior represents generalization from many instances in which unselfish behavior *has* been rewarded and selfish behavior punished. Beyond this, Bandura (1965) says that the individual's behavior may be affected by vicarious participation in others' experiences in a number of ways. In the first place, the individual may learn, from observing the consequences of other people's actions, which actions are likely to be rewarded and which punished; he then governs his own actions accordingly. Walters (1964) notes that certain models are more influential than others in this regard — that the observer searches for cues as to whether imitating a given model would be likely to bring reward or incur punishment for himself. But this sensitivity to the behavior of others and the consequences for others is still motivated by self-interest and may not properly be called "altruism." Of greater relevance is the question: What happens when an action by A is followed by injury or benefit to B? What effect, if any, does this have on strengthening or weakening the response of A? Bandura (1965) analyzes this question in terms of the conditioning of matching emotional responses. If A has had enough experiences in which his fate has been joined to that of B, so that when B underwent pleasant or painful experiences A did so as well, then signs of pleasure or pain in B will arouse matching emotional states in A, and A will be motivated to behave so as to produce signs of pleasure, or terminate signs of pain, in B. Aronfreed (in press) has recently carried out a series of experiments on altruistic and sympathetic behavior in children, based on a similar theoretical analysis. He gives children an opportunity to forego something they want for the sake of either giving another child pleasure or relieving the other child's discomfort. Working with children younger than the level at which "social contract" morality ought to appear (age six through eight), he can increase the frequency of occurrence of altruistic responses by making sure that two conditions are met: first, the child's own discomfort or pleasure must be repeatedly aroused at the same time that another child undergoes similar experiences; and second, the other child must emit reliable signs of his discomfort or pleasure. These signs then become signals for the altruistic or sympathetic behavior of the observing child.

The occurrence of altruistic behavior in these experimental situations does not appear to depend on the child's having achieved a mature level of moral judgments. It would be interesting to discover whether older children would display altruistic behavior without the direct conditioning to their own affective states that Aronfreed finds necessary in younger children. Certainly in adults altruistic behavior occurs without any clear opportunities for such conditioning to occur. We would expect, for example, that the behavior of parents would be controlled by sanctions administered to their children, even if the parents themselves had not concurrently undergone the same sanctions and had not thus been conditioned to give vicarious emotional responses. When the consequences of an individual's actions impinge upon someone to whom he is emotionally attached, it is as though these consequences had befallen himself. What kind of "extensions of the self" are possible? Can the individual be controlled by consequences of his actions to his dog, his business associates, his school, his country? Developmental theory, with its emphasis on the growth of role taking, would presumably expect to find increasing flexibility of the boundaries of the self and increasing altruism on this basis. For social-learning theory, there seems no reason to believe that young children would be less capable than older children or adults of establishing altruistic behavior on the basis of the conditioned arousal which is presumed to underly such behavior.

A final point of comparison between learning theory and developmental theory concerns the role they assign to such social-structural variables as social class. For Kohlberg, as noted above, membership in a social class is a "participation inducing" factor which promotes role playing and hence moral maturity. For Bandura and Walters, social status determines access to desired goals through legitimate channels and hence helps to govern the value to the child of postponing gratification and resisting temptation. If the child has an open opportunity to obtain the education and skills which will entitle him to the things he wants, he is less likely to try to get them by antisocial means. Social status probably plays another role in the Bandura-Walters' system, although they do not say so explicitly: when a parent is treated with deference by others, his status as a powerful model in the eyes of the child probably increases and thus the likelihood that the child will adopt his standards spontaneously through modeling is increased. For both theoretical points of view, then, higher social status is a factor which should promote adult-like and pro-social moral development, but the implied mechanisms differ.

THE PROBLEM OF INTERGENERATIONAL CHANGE

As noted earlier, social-learning theorists have tended to think of the socialization process as one of moral replacement — a process in which each new generation must acquire the values and conform to the behavioral standards laid down by the preceding generation. Kohlberg similarly discusses stages in the child's acquisition of the rules — whatever these rules may be — that are laid down for him by parents and other authority figures, although Kohlberg does provide for some autonomy in rule making at Level 3. In both systems, the child either takes on the values of the parent generation or because of inauspicious conditions fails to do so, but it is not immediately obvious how the child would acquire a systematically different set of values under either of the two systems. Both systems would predict a fairly high degree of parent-child matching in values — more so under family conditions which promote modeling or role playing — with individual children tending to be more similar to their own parents in values than they would be to other children's parents.

Albert Reiss (1965), a critic of the two individual psychological approaches to moral development discussed above, points out that there is lack of evidence concerning the validity of even so elementary an assumption as that of parent-child matching in values. But beyond this, he focuses attention on the changes in modal values which occur from one generation to another — changes which seem to be related to society-wide changes in social organization, economic conditions, population movement, etc. — and asks how these changes are to be accounted for if we view moral development as a process of "internalization" of the values of preceding generations. Reiss points out that there are shifts in a single generation in the norms for behavior in a specific situation, such as the change in behavior on Halloween from an emphasis on "tricks" to an emphasis on "treats." It would appear evident that there have also been extensive shifts over the last several generations in deeper, more pervasive values systems having to do with work and thrift, with sexual behavior, with respect for elders and authority figures, etc.

How do these changes come about? Reiss, believing that the values learned early in the family setting are not internalized in the sense of becoming self-maintaining, de-emphasizes the role of the family in the transmission of values. He holds, rather, that values must be continually reinforced and maintained by inputs from the social setting in which an individual finds himself, and will change if these inputs change. Thus it is possible for the same individual, conforming successively to drastically different sets of values and behavioral demands, to function successfully under the Weimar Republic, the Nazi regime, and the post-war German democratic political system. According to Reiss, in a modern, complex society, the maintenance and transmission of values is a fairly specialized function that is concentrated in a set of social institutions (the courts of law, the police, and to some extent the schools). If there are changes in the nature of the behavior they demand and reinforce, the behavior of the population in the social system will change. And the specialized institutions are responsive to economic and political factors characterizing the society, so that they will demand patriotic self-sacrifice during wartime, thrift during periods of industrialization where accumulation of capital is necessary, etc. The family in its turn is susceptible to some degree of influence from the specialized institutions, but this influence is a one-way street. The family cannot exercise counter-influence to any significant extent. The family, then, is not a particularly significant element in mediating change, in Reiss's scheme of things.

That values and behavior do change with changing social conditions we cannot doubt. Either this means, as Reiss claims, that the family is of little importance in transmitting values that will govern an individual's behavior in his adult life (because the larger social system counteracts the parents at a later point and replaces the values the parents have taught) or else socialization agents within the family must be responsive to changes in social-system conditions and thus change, in comparison with their own parents, the nature of the values they transmit and the methods they employ to do it. If parents bring up their own children in a different way, demanding a different kind of behavior from that demanded of them by their own parents, then their own early learned values were not internalized in the sense of being both enduring and strongly enough held to motivate transmission to their children.

The question of the importance of the family in the transmission of values is an intricate one, and full discussion of the issue would require a much more extensive treatment than is possible here. Let us simply say that studies of the early history of deviants, by comparison with individuals who do not become deviant, do seem to point to the importance of early-life, intra-family conditions in producing individuals who are socialization failures from the standpoint of the requirements of the larger society. Furthermore, there is enough evidence from the clinical literature concerning the failure of individuals to change and adapt themselves to new circumstances to justify our assuming at least a moderate degree of persistence in early learned values and modes of behavior. We could reasonably assume, then, that if there is a shift from one generation to another in a set of values, this shift has occurred partly because the socialization practices employed with the new generation, or the values being taught them, have changed by comparison with the teaching received by the previous generation in its childhood. This assumption does not imply that the change from one generation to another is *entirely* mediated by changes in socialization practices, and neither the social-learning position nor the developmental one would require that this should be so. The developmental position provides for values rationally arrived at in adulthood that are different from the values the individual learned from his parents. And there is nothing in social-learning theory that says that behavior, once learned, cannot be unlearned, or that new learning cannot take its place. If an individual moves from a family setting, in which one set of values is being taught, to a different setting (such as an employment setting, or the army), in which a different set of values is being taught, and if the conditions for learning are adequate, his values and behavior can change, although there will likely be evidence of conflict. Furthermore there will be some instances in which the individual cannot make the change, as in the case of the army inductee who cannot bring himself to shoot his weapon at the enemy in combat. The differences between initial socialization in the family and later socialization, or resocialization, of the adult have been fully discussed by Brim and Wheeler (1966), who point out that a major difference may lie in the nature of the affective and power relationships between the teacher and the learner. The power differential being great and the affective relationship being intense in childhood, it may be possible to obtain genuine acceptance of values more easily at this age, while external conformity is more likely to be the outcome of training efforts in adulthood.

A number of writers have pointed out that the importance of early socialization in the family may lie not so much in the specific values that are taught but in whether the family implants the necessary social motivation that will permit later socialization inputs to be effective. That is, needs for affiliation and approval, acquired early, may later motivate conformity to whatever standards exist in the social setting the individual enters. This may seem to produce chameleon-like shifts in values, away from those which the parents themselves held, but the shifts do not necessarily mean that early-childhood socialization was ineffective.

Assuming, however, that there is some component of the *content* of adult values that reflects the content of values taught to the individual in childhood, how do we get shifts in values from one generation to the next? Of course it is likely that we do *not* get shifts that are as great as they ought to be if we considered only the requirements of changing social conditions. We have cultural lag, where the behavior of individuals continues to be to some extent adapted to conditions which prevailed in their early lives. But assuming that we do get some shifts which are mediated by changing socialization processes, how do the requirements of changing social conditions get through to parents and affect their child-rearing practices?

Very little thought has been devoted to the question of what sustains the behavior of socialization agents. It is reasonable to expect that when a child does something which is contrary to a value the parent himself holds, the parent will be made anxious, and will act to change the child's behavior in order to reduce his own anxiety. In addition, there are certain actions on the part of the child that directly reward or punish the parent. For example, aggression directed by the child to the parent causes pain to the parent, and the parent may be expected to behave in such a way as to terminate the child's aggression. Or when the child damages valuable and essential property, the parent must either do additional work to earn the money to replace it or forego buying something he wants; therefore, he obviously will attempt to control the child's behavior so as to minimize the effort he must expend or maximize the purchasing power of his money. Without considerations of this kind, it is possible that the anxiety he feels over a child's behaving in a way that is inconsistent with his own values may not be sufficiently compelling to motivate a sustained socialization effort on his part. Let us consider as an example waste versus thrift. A parent who was himself raised during depression years might have been severely punished in childhood for losing a small amount of money, for damaging clothes that had to be replaced, or for throwing away a small amount of food which might have been used as a leftover. Under such training he might have developed habits of frugality and care about material possessions which would persist with reasonable strength and consistency throughout his lifetime, even though he later would become part of a much more affluent society. Will he teach his child to be as frugal as he is? Parents undoubtedly concentrate their control efforts on the aspects of the child's behavior that seem most important, most worth the effort and the cost in affective solidarity between parent and child that is often involved in obtaining compliance. A mother may experience a twinge of discomfort if she sees her child pour a half-glass of milk into the sink. This is an action she would never perform herself, but she may say nothing if the child does it in the course of cleaning up after a meal — a helpful act she wishes to encourage. Only if the food budget is very tight and the cost of milk really matters will she make an issue of this bit of waste. In prosperous times, the controlling act is unlikely to occur. Thus the economic conditions in which the family exists can help to determine whether a value that a parent holds will be transmitted. It should be noted that certain parental values are not especially susceptible to modeling; the child cannot easily observe certain aspects of the parent's frugality, such as the instances in which the mother did not buy something she wanted, and it is primarily the occurrence of direct teaching in such value spheres that will determine what the child learns. From the child's point of view, also, there will probably be a good deal of inconsistency in the reactions of his parents: they will occasionally show strong emotional reactions to aspects of child behavior toward which little teaching effort has been directed.

John Whiting (1966) has offered the hypothesis that ecological conditions will determine certain aspects of socialization and that changes in these conditions will produce changes in socialization practices. A social group moving from open to crowded living conditions, for example, will increase its control of aggression, he suggests, because aggression is more disruptive in close quarters. Thus environmental conditions which affect how directly the child's actions impinge upon his parents will affect their responses to his actions and the degree of emphasis they give to the inculcation of such value as aggression-inhibition in the ingroup.

With the above considerations in mind, it would seem that the existence of change in values from one generation to another need not be thought of as in any sense a refutation of the psychological theories of value transmission. Nor need it necessarily be taken as evidence against the significance of the family as a mediating agency between social conditions and the acquisition of values by the child. Focusing on intergenerational change does, however, bring to light a gap in the work which has stemmed from psychological theories. The preceding comments on the conditions which might cause a parent not to transmit a value he himself holds are speculative, for students of the socialization process have not focused their attention on the reinforcement conditions which sustain the training efforts of parents nor on the ways in which larger social and economic conditions affect the parents and push them toward change. Very little evidence relevant to these issues exists. Clearly, there is a neglected research area here, and work is needed on the socialization practices of parents functioning under different social, ecological, and economic conditions.

In attempting to account for intergenerational change in values, however, it is important not to lose sight of the continuities that do exist. There has been an impressive persistence of the Judeo-Christian ethic in a very large culture area for a very long time. This persistence has undoubtedly been facilitated by the incorporation of the ethic into the specialized institutions that Reiss refers to, so that early-learned morality receives institutional support throughout the individual's lifetime. But it also depends on certain minimum childhood socialization of the large majority of individuals in the society, so that the society can function without devoting too high a proportion of its resources to controlling or attempting to resocialize adult individuals.

REFERENCES

Aronfreed, J. *Conduct and Conscience: The Socialization of Internalized Control over Behavior*. New York: Academic Press. (In press)

Aronfreed, J. The effects of experimental socialization paradigms upon two moral responses to transgression. *Journal of Abnormal and Social Psychology*, 1963, *66*, 437–48.

Aronfreed, J., and Reber, A. Internalized behavioral suppression and the timing of social punishment. *Journal of Personality and Social Psychology*, 1965, *1*, 3–16.

Aronson, E., and Carlsmith, J. M. Effects of the severity of threat on the devaluation of forbidden behavior. *Journal of Abnormal and Social Psychology*, 1963, *66*, 584–88.

Bandura, A. Externalization of the superego. Comments on *Conduct and Conscience* by J. Aronfreed. Paper presented at SSRC conference on moral development, 1963.

Bandura, A. Vicarious processes: a case of no-trial learning. In L. Berkowitz (Ed.), *Advances in Experimental Social Psychology*. Vol. II. New York: Academic Press, 1965. Pp. 3–55.

Bandura, A. and Mischel, W. Modification of self-imposed delay of reward through exposure to live and symbolic models. *Journal of Personality and Social Psychology*, 1965, 2, 698–705.

Bandura, A., Ross, Dorothea, and Ross, Sheila. A comparative test of the status envy, social power, and the secondary reinforcement theories of identificatory learning. *Journal of Abnormal and Social Psychology*, 1963, *67*, 527–34.

Bandura, A., and Walters, R. H. *Social Learning and Personality Development*. New York: Holt, Rinehart & Winston, 1963.

Baumrind, Diana. Child care practices anteceding three patterns of preschool behavior. *Genetic Psychology Monographs*, 1967, *75*, 43–88.

Baumrind, Diana. Effects of authoritative parental control on child behavior. *Child Development*, 1966, *37*, 887–907.

Baumrind, Diana, and Black, A. E. Socialization practices and parental attitudes related to dimensions of nursery school behavior for boys and girls. *Child Development*. (In press)

Becker, W. C. Consequences of different kinds of parental discipline. In M. L. Hoffman and Lois W. Hoffman (Eds.), *Review of Child Development Research*. New York: Russell Sage Foundation, 1964.

Becker, W. C., Peterson, D. R., Luria, Zella, Shoemaker, D. J., and Hellmer, L. A. Relations of factors derived from parent-interview ratings to behavior problems of five-year-olds. *Child Development*, 1962, 33, 509–35.

Brim, O. G., Jr., and Wheeler, S. *Socialization After Childhood*. New York: John Wiley & Sons, 1966.

Burton, R. V. The generality of honesty reconsidered. *Psychological Review*, 1963, *70*, 481–99.

Burton, R. V., Maccoby, Eleanor E., and Allinsmith, W. Antecedents of resistance to temptation in four-year-old children. *Child Development*, 1961, 32, 689–710.

Cline, V. B., Richards, J. M., Jr., and Needham, W. E. A factor analytic study of the father form of the parental attitude research instrument. *The Psychological Record*, 1963, *13*, 65–72.

Festinger, L., Behavioral support for opinion change. *Public Opinion Quarterly*, 1964, *28*, 404–17.

Flavell, J. H. *The Development Psychology of Jean Piaget*. Princeton, N.J.: D. Van Nostrand Co., 1963.
Hartshorne, H., and May, M. A. *Studies in Deceit*. Book I. New York: The Macmillan Co., 1928.
Hoffman, M. L. Development of internal moral standards in children. In M. Strommen (Ed.), *Review of Research in Religious Development*. Des Moines, Iowa: Meredith Publishing Co. (In press)
Hoffman, M. L. and Saltzstein, H. D. Parent discipline and the children's moral development. *Journal of Personality and Social Psychology*, 5, 1967, 45–57.
Hoffman, M. L. Parent practices and moral development: generalizations from empirical research. *Child Development*, 1963, 34, 295–318.
Kohlberg, L. *The Developmental Approach to Moralization*. (In press)
Kohlberg, L. Development of moral character and moral ideology. In M. L. Hoffman and Lois W. Hoffman (Eds.), *Review of Child Development Research*. Vol. 1. New York: Russell Sage Foundation, 1964. Pp. 383–432.
Kohlberg, L. Moral development and identification. In H. W. Stevenson (Ed.), *Child Psychology*. The Sixty-second Yearbook of the National Society for the Study of Education. Chicago: NSSE, 1963; distributed by The University of Chicago Press. Pp. 277–332.
Lorr, M., and Jenkins, R. L. Three factors in parent behavior. *Journal of Consulting Psychology*, 1953, *17*, 306–8.
Maccoby, N., Romney, A. K., Adams, J. S., and Maccoby, Eleanor E. Critical periods in seeking and accepting information. *Paris-Stanford Studies in Communication*. Stanford: Institute for Communication Research, 1962.
MacFarlane, J., Allen L., and Honzik, N. *A Developmental Study of Behavior Problems of Normal Children between 21 Months and Four Years*. Berkeley: University of California Press, 1954.
Nichols, R. C. A factor analysis of parental attitudes of fathers. *Child Development*, 1962, 33, 791–802.
Piaget, J. *The Moral Judgment of the Child*. Glencoe, Ill.: The Free Press, 1948. Translation of book originally published in 1932.
Reiss, A. J. Social organization and socialization: variations on a theme about generations. Working Paper #1, Center for Research on Social Organization, University of Michigan, Ann Arbor, Michigan, 1965. (Multilith)
Schaefer, E. S. A circumplex model for maternal behavior. *Journal of Abnormal and Social Psychology*, 1959, 59, 226–35.
Schaefer, E. S., and Bayley, Nancy. Consistency of material behavior from infancy to preadolescence. *Journal of Abnormal and Social Psychology*, 1960, *61*, 1–6.
Sears, R. R., Maccoby, Eleanor E., and Levin, H. *Patterns of Child Rearing*. Evanston, Ill.: Row, Peterson & Co., 1957.
Sears, R. R., Rau, Lucy, and Alpert, R. *Identification and child rearing*. Stanford: Stanford University Press, 1965.
Slater, Philip E. Parental behavior and the personality of the child. *Journal of Genetic Psychology*, 1962, *101*, 53–68.
Walters, R. H. Modification of social behavior through the observation of consequences to others. Paper read at the University of Illinois, June 1964.
Walters, R. H., and Demkow, L. Timing of punishment as a determinant of response inhibition. *Child Development*, 1963, 34, 207–14.
Whiting, J. W. M., Chasdi, Eleanor H., Antonovsky, Helen F., and Ayres, Barbara C. The learning of values. In E. Z. Vogt and Ethel M. Albert (Eds.), *People of Rimrock*. Cambridge, Mass.: Harvard University Press, 1966. Pp. 83–125.

M. BREWSTER SMITH

SEVEN Competence and Socialization

CONTENTS

What do we know, and what do we need to know, about the conditions under which people come to function as competent members of society? The question arises with urgency as the first generation of crash programs to instill competence in the poor and "culturally deprived" comes under skeptical review, and the path to the millenium remains to be discovered. It was in this context of contemporary social action that, near the end of its tenure, the Committee on Socialization and Social Structure considered the topic of socialization for competence.

In its preliminary discussions, the Committee identified a number of currently active lines of research that seemed to bear upon positive outcomes of socialization — outcomes viewed from a frankly evaluative perspective. Several of these diverse, but potentially convergent, strands — ranging from the effects of early experience on the neonate to the evocation of competence among the citizens of newly independent developing countries — were brought together for examination and critical discussion at a conference held in San Juan, Puerto Rico in the spring of 1965. This chapter builds on the conference discussion but departs freely from it in the attempt to see the bearing of socialization on the origins and development of competence from a more coherent perspective than the lively exchange between specialists of disparate interests and backgrounds could attain.[1] As the reader will see, a coherent framework within which questions are posed rather than a substantive synthesis is aimed at: too many pieces of the puzzle are still missing. To the extent that synthesis is attempted, it must remain conjectural.

I am indebted to Arlene Skolnick for stimulating discussion, to Dieter Bruehl for extensive bibliographical assistance, and to an informal seminar, with Neil Altman, Dieter Bruehl, Diana Solar, Ronald Weisberg, and Arlene Vadum, that helped me to explore concepts of self-evaluation.

[1] Participants in the conference are listed in Appendix A. Since an account of the conference has been published elsewhere (Smith, 1965), and some of the working papers have since been printed in revised versions (Colson, 1967; Inkeles, 1966), I have made free use of the ideas that it stimulated without feeling the obligation to treat them in the form presented at the conference.

TOWARD A CONCEPTION OF THE COMPETENT SELF

In any attempt to look evaluatively at the processes and outcomes of socialization, terminology makes a difference. The terms we use carry with them a freight of implicit assumptions, and the changing fashions in evaluative terms reflect shifts in what goes without saying, what is taken for granted. Thus before World War II sealed the fate of extreme cultural relativism in the social sciences, a favored concept to which a highly productive committee of the Social Science Research Council devoted its attention was *social adjustment* (Young, 1941), which for present-day readers bears an unwelcome connotation of uncritical obeisance to the sociocultural status quo. *Mental health* (see Jahoda, 1958), more recently fashionable and probably more durable because of the institutional recognition it has received in law and government, is currently under attack as connoting a bio-medical frame of evaluation that is out of tune with the contexts in which we want to employ it (Smith, 1961; in press). The term *competence* (*Webster's* defines *competent* as "answering to all requirements, adequate; fit; capable"), on the other hand, is presently acquiring connotations that commend it for our purposes. This chapter is intended to increase its popularity — but also to clarify some of the issues that arise in conceptualizing the nature and development of competence.

Alternative Conceptions of Competence

In adopting *competence*, we were influenced particularly by Robert W. White, who in a series of important essays (1959, 1960, 1963) urged the relevance to human development of intrinsic motivation toward competence — toward effective interaction with the environment — that, in White's view, man shares with the higher mammals. White marshalled evidence for the separate and major role of such motivation, which he designated *effectance*, in distinction from the "drives," based on tissue needs, of the motivational theory that until recently prevailed in experimental psychology, and from the quiescence-seeking instincts of orthodox psychoanalysis. For White, the important motivational ingredient missed by traditional theories is contributed by the feedback that the developing person gets about the environmental consequences of his own actions. Later, we will compare White's view with alternative possible emphases on *social* feedback from the approval or disapproval of significant others — social reinforcement — or on intrinsically motivating aspects of information processing as such. We will see that important issues are involved here that as yet are far from resolved. At this point, however, we are not ready to pursue them. Rather, what is relevant is to note that we are attracted to competence as an evaluative concept partly because of the connotations that White has given it: rootedness in a view of the organism-person as an *active* (rather than merely *re*active) participant in *inter*action with the environment, and close linkage to motivational processes.

These connotations point to a focus on biological origins and concern with the developmental vicissitudes of individual motivation and capacities. Given the Committee's task and orientation, however, a complementary focus on societally relevant outcomes was required of us. In his paper for the Puerto Rico Conference, Inkeles offered a definition of competence that stresses the societal referent: "the ability to attain and perform in three sets of statuses: those which one's society will normally assign one, those in the repertoire of one's social system that one may reasonably aspire to, and those which one might reasonably invent or elaborate for oneself" (Inkeles, 1966). At the Conference he argued vigorously — as he does in his contribution to this volume — that the study of socialization should be approached from the standpoint of societal requirements and socialization outcomes rather than from that of biological origins and the impact of practices of child rearing. His proposed definition of competence is well adapted to this strategy.

It is also congruent with the emerging public interest in finding ways in which *all* citizens may become equipped for effective participation in modern society, with the public distress that a submerged minority have been trained in *in*competence that leaves them unable to benefit from most "opportunities" that are opened to them. This concern was paramount to a group of staff members of the Community Research and Services Branch, National Institute of Mental Health (Rae-Grant, Gladwin, and Bower, 1966), who proposed a concept of social competence quite similar to Inkeles' as the focus of an alternative to the traditional mental health strategy that centered on psychotherapeutic intervention to reduce inner conflict.

In a report on a conference of mental health professionals held at the National Institute of Mental Health shortly after the Puerto Rico Conference, Gladwin (1967) develops the implications of this concept in an important statement.

> Competence . . . develops along three major axes, all closely interrelated. First is the ability to learn or to use a variety of alternative pathways or behavioral responses in order to reach a given goal. . . . Second, the competent individual comprehends and is able to use a variety of social systems within the society, moving within these systems and utilizing the resources they offer. Third, competence depends upon effective reality testing. Reality testing involves not merely the lack of psychopathological

> impairment to perception but also a positive, broad, and sophisticated understanding of the world. (p. 32)

Programs of remedial intervention appropriate to this conception were seen as operating primarily

> through the provision or adaptation of a social environment designed to maximize rewarding and effective social experience within a setting relevant to the real world in which [the] clients lived. The modality through which such an experience must be achieved can be referred to as an ecological unit encompassing within a single interacting system the individual and as much of his social environment as is relevant to the behavior under consideration. (p. 32)

The approach to social systems implied in the concept of the ecological unit is highly congenial, it will be seen, to the point of view developed in the present chapter, and the examples that Gladwin provides of current programs that seek to maximize social competence through deliberate intervention with ecological units of differing scope supplement my treatment very usefully. What I wish to emphasize here, however, is the essential congruence of Gladwin's conception of social competence with Inkeles': the three components of competence that Gladwin offers to define goals for programs of social intervention are, in effect, abilities to use social systems to achieve one's goals — to perform effectively for self and society in one's social roles. In contrast with White's conception and with the view of competence to be developed in this chapter, the motivational aspect of competence remains implicit. Reference is rather to knowledge and ability.

It is instructive to view Inkeles' conception of social competence in relation to an earlier sociological formulation on which Gladwin (1967) draws, which also contributed connotations that predispose us to be attracted to it: *interpersonal competence*, as introduced by Foote and Cottrell (1955) in their programmatic framework for family research. These authors, seeking an evaluative concept for family research from a "planning" orientation (a context similar to the present one), conceive interpersonal competence as skill or ability "in controlling the outcomes of episodes of interaction" (p. 36) and as comprising six components: health, intelligence, empathy, autonomy, judgment, and creativity. They organize their suggestions for research around hypotheses concerning the antecedents and correlates of each of these presumptive aspects.

Viewed in historical perspective, the variant versions of competence offered by Foote and Cottrell and by Inkeles correspond rather neatly to the two major strands in modern sociological role theory. For both, indeed, competence is a matter of capacities for role performance. What differentiates them is the frame within which role performance is conceived. Inkeles writes in the structural tradition of role-status theory, anchored near its origins by Ralph Linton's *The Study of Man* (1936), and more recently summarized and codified by Gross, Mason, and McEachern (1958). In this tradition, adequacy of role performance is to be measured against the role requirements of the various statuses or positions in the social structure that a person may occupy. Foote and Cottrell, on the other hand, embody the so-called symbolic-interactionist tradition stemming from George Herbert Mead (1934) and assimilating congenial influences from neo-Freudian psychiatry, especially Harry Stack Sullivan (1953). Emphasis in this tradition is on interactional *process* in role relationships that are conceived primarily in interpersonal rather than social-structural terms. Socialization is viewed more as a process through which personality and selfhood emerge in the course of role-taking in progressively more sharply attuned communicative interaction than as one in which persons become equipped with beliefs, knowledge, skills, motives, and values that fit them to occupy a sequence of niches in the social structure. While Foote and Cottrell do not exclude a constitutional-genetic component from their criteria of interpersonal competence, their conception amounts to a view of successful socialization — successful within the framework set by Mead and Sullivan, just as Inkeles' definition states a conception of successful socialization within the structuralist framework.

Clearly there is no necessary clash here between competing versions of the Truth. Just as modern versions of role theory have sought to weave together the strands deriving from Linton and from Mead (an early attempt was made by Sarbin, 1954), so a role-relevant conception of social competence as successful socialization might well incorporate ingredients from both the Foote-Cottrell and the Inkeles versions. A comprehensive view of social competence should also keep in simultaneous view the two perspectives that are differentially emphasized by Inkeles and by Foote and Cottrell: that of society and its "manpower" needs, and that of the person himself as the locus of humanistic values. To repeat, competence involves effective role performance for self and for society.

Competence as Differentiating Vicious and Benign Circles of Development

As we contemplate these two sociological conceptions of competence in relation to White's bio-psychological one, bridging the gap between them with explicit conceptual and empirical links becomes in effect the major agenda of the study of socialization, when it is phrased evaluatively. It is the problem of how to get from beginnings in the infant organism to the person participating competently in communicative interaction within the framework of a social system. Intuitively, it looks as though the gap from White to Foote and Cottrell is narrower than that from White to

Inkeles: Inkeles' concern with outcomes for the larger social system introduces a variety of specific requirements beyond the more generalized capacities in which Foote and Cottrell are interested. Be that as it may, the view of competence that emerges in the foregoing discussion creates severe problems for the writer of this chapter. For if the topic of competence is to be identified with the outcome of socialization taken evaluatively, the task of this chapter is hardly distinct from that of the entire volume. What would be its distinctive content? Indeed, the chapter by Inkeles works out the implications of his conception of competence for the study of socialization in such rich detail that there would be no gain from reviewing the same considerations here.

Faced with this predicament, I have adopted a strategy of selection based on empirical assumptions that go beyond the bounds of knowledge that can currently be regarded as firmly established. I will assume, in implicit agreement with a good many contemporary theorists, that there is a core of interrelated personal attributes — short of the entire complement of cognitive, motivational, and behavioral variables implied by Inkeles' conception, and even of the more limited list proposed by Foote and Cottrell — which in some way plays a crucial role in the person's effectiveness in interaction with the environment. The cluster of attributes that I am looking for is one that would make a decisive difference in the cumulative direction of the outcome of a person's interactions.

Underlying my search for such a key cluster is a view of causation in personal and social development as inherently circular or spiral, rather than linear in terms of neatly isolable causes and effects. As the very concept of *inter*action implies, developmental progress or deficit is typically a matter of benign circles or of vicious ones, not of persistent effects of clear-cut single causes (see Myrdal, 1944). In social life, there is much bitter truth to the biblical maxim, "To him who hath shall be given; from him who hath not shall be taken away even that which he hath." Launched on the right trajectory, the person is likely to accumulate successes that strengthen the effectiveness of his orientation toward the world while at the same time he acquires the knowledge and skills that make his further success more probable. His environmental involvements generally lead to gratification and to increased competence and favorable development. Off to a bad start, on the other hand, he soon encounters failures that make him hesitant to try. What to others are challenges appear to him as threats; he becomes preoccupied with defense of his small claims on life at the expense of energies to invest in constructive coping. And he falls increasingly behind his fellows in acquiring the knowledge and skills that are needed for success on those occasions when he does try.

The picture is familiar. In instance after instance of contemporary attempts at planned social intervention to remedy human ineffectiveness, whether under the aegis of the schools, of poverty programs, of corrections, or of "mental health," the practical problem is becoming conceptualized as one of how to break into well-entrenched vicious circles of social causation so as to convert them into benign ones, in which Hippocrates' "curative power of Nature" can then be relied upon. The *practical* problem is typically immense because of the way in which a multitude of causal factors interlock, so that remedial efforts applied to any single factor are ineffectual: the inertial properties of the rest of the system suffice to drag the person down again in spite of initial gains. The *conceptual* problem is that of distinguishing the components of the interdependent system and, especially, of identifying those that are central and strategic in regard to causal linkage with other variables in the system and also in regard to accessibility as leverage-points through which the state of the system as a whole can be altered from a "vicious" to a "benign" condition.

Related Concepts and Themes in Recent Research

Provisionally, then, I want to focus in this chapter on attributes of the person that are likely candidates for such a strategic role. For the developed person who has attained selfhood, the place to look for them is in attitudes and motives related to the *self*, as the entity around which a person's enduring orientations to the environing world are organized. The recent literature contains a number of terms and concepts that seem to belong in the domain with which we are concerned. Some of these are common English terms that have acquired enriched meaning from the sensitive commentary of Erik Erikson (1959): trust and confidence, initiative and industry, autonomy, and, especially, hope. On the other side of the coin, there are self-doubt, passivity, dependence, fatalism, and despair. No one will question which of these lists goes with the Haves, which with the Have Nots! Nor is the idea novel that these are important human qualities: humanistic wisdom has always known it. What is new is their recognition within the specialized and deliberately cumulative enterprise of social and behavioral science.

This recognition has also engendered a technical and not very rewarding literature concerning the dimension of self-evaluation usually called self-esteem (Wylie, 1961; Rosenberg, 1965; Coopersmith, 1967). While the technical difficulties of measurement, given people's motivation to put on as good a face as they can manage for themselves and others (Goffman, 1959), still elude satisfactory solution, the persistent research that is being invested in the study of self-esteem as an independent or a dependent variable reflects the common acknowledgment of its key status.

Perhaps, indeed, part of the difficulty that has hampered empirical research on self-esteem has followed from the assumption that it *can* be treated as an unidimensional variable; we might profitably return to McDougall's conception of the *self-regarding sentiment* (McDougall, 1921) as suggesting a complex, multidimensional structure more in keeping with the part that we expect it to play in human experience and behavior.

Developments in the post-Freudian psychoanalytic tradition of ego psychology make further terms available to us for dealing with these decisive properties of the self. Erikson, of course, writes from within this tradition, as does White, whose contributions to the conceptualization of competence might be seen as an attempt to follow through on the otherwise unrealized invitation extended by Heinz Hartmann (1958) for an integration of psychoanalytic ego psychology with the findings of "academic" psychological research. Lois Murphy's (1962) conception of the child's emerging *coping strategies* for mastering the environment — as distinguished from the defenses against anxiety stressed by earlier psychoanalytic writers — initiated a productive shift of emphasis; the distinction has been further developed by Haan (1963). The notion of *ego strength* (Barron, 1963) as resiliency in handling stress may be too globally evaluative to be satisfactory in the long run, but it too can be seen as a foray into the present area of concern. Recently, Jane Loevinger (1966) has cast a variety of current ideas about ego functioning into a coherent and sophisticated developmental perspective. Her proposed progression of ego development, from impulse ridden through opportunistic and conformist to conscientious, autonomous, and integrated stages, offers a framework, with diagnostic "milestones," for treating the emergence of qualitative features of the personality system that make for personal integrity and for relative independence from the vicissitudes of biological impulse or environmental contingency.

Essentially out of contact with the foregoing developments, a succession of loosely-linked experimental approaches to the study of goal-setting behavior is just now coming into coherent focus as highly relevant to our concern. These began with the studies of *level of aspiration* by Kurt Lewin and his students (Lewin, Dembo, Festinger, and Sears, 1944), who investigated the effects of success and failure on a person's hopes and expectations for performance on experimental tasks. These studies gave rise to a number of interesting experimental findings and conceptual distinctions, but the line of research that they stimulated seemed until recently to have been played out without major impact on personality or developmental theory. From the standpoint of his social-learning theory of personality, Rotter and his students (Rotter, 1954) carried out a relatively independent program of research on goal setting, in which the value of the goal and the subject's expectancy of success were central variables. This line of work, too, seemed to have found its place, without major impact, in the not very coherent literature of personality research.

Meanwhile, Atkinson and his students (Atkinson, 1964; Atkinson and Feather, 1966) began a series of studies of goal setting in relation to McClelland's conception of achievement motivation (McClelland, Atkinson, Clark, and Lowell, 1953) — a topic to which we return later in the chapter. Sharing with Rotter a value-expectancy approach to conceptualizing goal setting, the Atkinson group found different patterns of goal setting to distinguish persons whose orientations toward achievement stemmed from hope for success from persons whose orientations stemmed from fear of failure, the latter characteristically setting their levels of aspiration unrealistically high or very low. Level of aspiration now became relevant to the study of the person's fundamental orientations that affect his engagement with challenge and opportunity.

New research developments, again under the leadership of Rotter, bring us to the present, when research on this interrelated cluster of issues is very active indeed. Rotter's group had observed that success on an experimental task has very different consequences for a person's subsequent goal setting, depending on whether the person believes that the outcome — the "reinforcement" received — results from chance or from his own skill. In a number of studies this belief was manipulated experimentally. Recently Rotter has developed and validated a measure of "generalized expectancies for internal versus external control of reinforcement," and has shown that people differ consistently from one another in their general tendency to attribute the outcomes of their endeavors to external factors, such as chance or fate, or to internal ones, such as their own skill and effort (Rotter, 1966; Lefcourt, 1966). As Rotter summarizes the substantive findings that bear upon the construct validity and hence the theoretical interest of his I-E scale, there is

> strong support for the hypotheses that the individual who has a strong belief that he can control his own destiny is likely to (a) be more alert to those aspects of the environment which provide useful information for his future behavior; (b) take steps to improve his environmental position; (c) place greater value on skill or achievement reinforcements and be generally more concerned with his ability, particularly his failures; and (d) be resistive to subtle attempts to influence him. (1966, p. 25)

Rotter notes the relationship of perceived internal versus external control to research on achievement motivation (high need for achievement implying some belief in one's capacity to determine the outcome of his efforts), to White's conception of competence motivation, and to the sense of *powerlessness* as an aspect of the sociological concept of alienation (Seeman, 1959). He also notes apparent, but less direct, convergences with Riesman's (1950) well-known distinction between inner-directed and other-directed character types, and with the distinction between "field-dependent" versus "body-oriented" tendencies that the Witkin group derived from the study of individual differences in perceptual responses (Witkin, Lewis, Hertzman, Machover, Meissner, and Wapner, 1954).

Still an additional line of investigation that warrants notice in this partial roll call is Mischel's work (1966) on children's preference for small, immediate rewards or larger, deferred ones. Capacity for delayed gratification as an aspect of impulse control has figured prominently in discussions of ego strength. Whether such a capacity for forbearance is at issue or rather an attitude of trust that promised gratifications will actually be delivered, Mischel has provided methods that permit the systematic study of one component of an effective orientation toward the environment. The relevance of voluntary inhibitory control is further indicated in a study by Maccoby and her collaborators (Maccoby, Dowley, Hagen, and Degerman, 1965), who found among nursery school children, both boys and girls, that although an index of general activity level in free play was unrelated to measures of intellectual functioning, the children's ability to inhibit movement voluntarily showed moderately strong correlations with these measures.

This hasty overview of concepts and research themes from the recent past serves to define a terrain of relevance: from a variety of intellectual heritages and research traditions, students of personality have been converging on a cluster of interrelated, overlapping ideas that seem to bear upon the extent to which a person is oriented to make the most of his opportunities in the world, upon the likelihood that the interactive circles of causation in which he involves himself will be benign, not vicious. Having spread a sampling of these ideas and themes before us, let us see if we can find in them some provisional order.

A Provisional View of the Competent Self

In a first approximation to a formulation of the competent self, then, we would look for distinctive features in the person's attitudes toward self and world. The self is perceived as causally important, as effective in the world — which is to a major extent a world of other people — as likely to be able to bring about desired effects, and as accepting responsibility when effects do not correspond to desire. In near equivalent, the person has self-respect. With self-respect go at least moderately favorable levels of general self-evaluation — self-esteem or self-acceptance — but favorable self-evaluation in the general terms according to which it has predominantly been studied would seem less important than the sense of efficacy or potency. (In terms of Osgood's semantic differential [Osgood, Suci, and Tannenbaum, 1957], research on the self has overstressed the preemptive evaluative dimension, to the neglect of the coordinate dimensions of activity and potency.)

Distinctive attitudes toward the world are linked with these attitudes toward the self as the opposite side of the same coin. Coordinate with the feeling of efficacy is an attitude of hope — the world is the sort of place in which, given appropriate efforts, I can expect good outcomes. Hope provides the ground against which planning, forbearance, and effort are rational. Corresponding to generalized favorable self-evaluation is an attitude of optimistic trust. While as Erikson has asserted, some degree of basic trust is essential to personal adequacy, I would think that given that essential minimum, hope is the more critical attitude. In the lack of hope, attitudes of fatalism and passivity that make a bad world tolerable at the cost of giving up the possibility of constructive action are natural adaptations that have been rediscovered perennially by individuals and cultures the world over.

With these positive attitudes toward self and world goes a characteristic behavioral orientation that throws the person into the kinds of interaction that close the benign circle. Here we find alternative phrasings that amount to much the same thing. The person is attracted to moderate challenges that have an intermediate probability of success. By setting his goals realistically at a level somewhat higher than that of his previous performance, he reaps the maximum cumulative gain in sensed efficacy from his successes. This is, in effect, an active, coping orientation high in initiative, not a passive or defensive one characterized by very low goals (which can yield little sense of efficacy when attained) or unrealistically high ones (the main virtue of which is the readiness with which non-attainment can be explained away and "failure" neutralized).

These attitudes and behavioral orientations, I propose, constitute the generalized core of the competent self. As I will shortly suggest, they seem to be relevant across societies and cultures. Accompanying these dispositions of the self are the array of knowledge, habits, skills, and abilities that are required to translate hopeful expectations and active orientations into effective behavior. This equipment for competence is clearly part of the interlocking system, since its possession gives a person warrant for feelings of efficacy and for hopeful expectations, and his constructive engagement with the environment in turn establishes habits of industry and provides the experiential background from which he can acquire knowledge and skill and make the most of his potential abilities. But these attributes are bound to be more specific to the person's particular roles and station in society than are the ones I have proposed for the generalized core.

Some of these cognitive and behavioral qualifications nevertheless have rather broad applicability, such as Foote and Cottrell's (1955) proposed components of interpersonal competence — intelligence and empathy. Also high in generalized relevance are skills in inquiry and in the use of informational resources — particularly valuable in a fluid world in which pat solutions and right answers do not stay valid. But these suggestions already seem to arise with special relevance to contemporary middle-class society; one can think of other cultural situations where their payoff would be small. From another perspective, however, modern technical society is itself increasingly universal (with the middle class embodying its major values). As Inkeles points out, within this modern framework one can go a long way toward specifying the repertory of cognitive and characterological equipment that is necessary for effective participation in terms of modern society's common role requirements: orientation to the clock and attendant habits of temporal regularity and dependability, verbal and numerical facility, accommodation to work relationships of authority and collaboration in complex organizations, and many others.

In keeping with the strategy that I proposed at the outset, I will focus henceforth on the proposed core of the competent self, without intending to minimize the importance of these additional personal dispositions that engage with particular societal role requirements. Before turning to issues pertinent to the relation of this competence syndrome to socialization and social structure, I need first to strengthen somewhat the case for its relevance as a syndrome and to examine more closely the case for its transcultural generality.

Illustrative Evidence for the Competent Self

My own conviction about the relevance and coherence of the syndrome arose in the course of my study of Peace Corps teachers (Smith, 1966), whom a colleague and I interviewed near the end of their first and second years of service in Ghana.[2] From close study of selected tape-recorded interview transcripts in the light of field experience, we developed a set of descriptive items to characterize the personalities of the volunteers as they appeared through the job-focused interviews. These items were then used by judges other than ourselves to characterize each volunteer as his interviews portrayed him, by "Q-sorting" the cards according to a prescribed distribution in nine categories, ranging from items seen as saliently characteristic of the volunteer to ones seen as saliently *un*characteristic of him. We intercorrelated the resulting personal profiles of item ratings and factored the matrix of correlations (by the principal components method) to get at patterns of personality as displayed overseas in the challenging situation of Peace Corps service.

[2] This account is adapted with only minor change from Smith (in press).

As might be expected, the first principal component turned out to be a highly evaluative factor. Table 1 lists the items that were especially characteristic of volunteers who received high loadings on it, in order of declining factor scores; the items that defined what is *un*characteristic of these volunteers are given in Table 2, in order of increasing factor scores. Items referring to basic self-attitudes of self-confidence and self-esteem head each list, and the positive list contains the further item, "feels . . . that it matters what he does with his life," reflecting self-respect and

TABLE 1

Personality Items with High Factor Scores on First Principal Component

ITEM	FACTOR SCORE
Generally self-confident.	73
A genuinely dependable and responsible person.	69
The values and principles which he holds directly affect what he does.	65
Feels his own life is important, that it matters what he does with his life.	65
Open to experience, ready to learn.	62
Tolerant and understanding.	61
Characteristically maintains a highly articulate intellectual formulation of his situation and problems.	60

TABLE 2

Personality Items with Low Factor Scores on First Principal Component

ITEM	FACTOR SCORE
Feels a lack of worth; has low self-esteem.	24
Basically a dependent person; characteristically leans upon others for support.	33
Has had a characteristically high level of anxiety during the time in Ghana.	33
Tends to expect little of life, pessimistic.	33
Seems generally to lack energy, to operate at a markedly low key.	35
Tends to be suspicious of others.	35
Tends to give up easily when faced with setbacks.	36
Would be unable to accept help from others when in need.	37
When things go badly, would tend to let them drift.	37
Tends to be preoccupied with matters of physical health.	38
Irritable and over-responsive to petty annoyances.	38
Engages in "posturing" to self and others; concerned with maintaining "face."	39
Tends unrealistically to minimize or deny the difficulties that he faces.	40

efficacy. The negative list contains opposites of autonomy (dependence), hope (pessimism), active orientation (low energy, gives up easily, lets things drift), and trust (suspiciousness). Both lists contain items pertaining to realistic openness to experience. All of these traits are highly congruent with our tentative picture of the competent self.

The lists contain some other items whose presence is instructive. On the list of positively distinguishing characteristics, the qualities of principled responsibility and tolerance are clearly dictated by the requirements of the Peace Corps role. Perhaps they are intrinsically related to general competence, but we cannot be sure. The remaining items on the negatively distinguishing list are accounted for by those psychological states and processes which especially interfere with competent coping: anxiety and the psychological defenses through which anxiety is contained.

The Peace Corps study contains further evidence for the present formulation of the competent self in its sole modest predictive success. My colleague Raphael Ezekiel (1968) had devised a procedure in which the volunteers-in-training wrote three mock autobiographical essays: one on their immediate alternative plans should they not be accepted by the Peace Corps, one covering the three years after their return from Peace Corps service, and a third covering their fortieth year. The essays were rated for *differentiation*, the extent to which the essays showed complex and detailed mapping of the future; *agency*, the extent to which they showed the self as the prime agent in determining the course of the respondent's future life; and *demand*, the extent to which they described a life viewed by the respondent as demanding long-term, continuing effort. The sum of these ratings correlated moderately (.41) with the overall administrative evaluation as of the second year.

Table 3 shows the Q-sort items, again based on the overseas interviews, that were characteristic of the high-scoring volunteers. Apart from items that primarily show personal consistency from the time of essay writing until that of the interviews one and two years later, the picture of inventiveness, initiative, job-elaboration, and self-testing or responsiveness to challenge indicates that the procedure indeed tapped qualities that contribute to a more than routine performance. Ezekiel's interpretation of his measure is highly relevant to the picture of the competent self with which we are concerned here. The volunteer's readiness to engage himself with demanding tasks and to take the initiative in bringing about well-cognized futures that he desires, as crudely indexed by the ratings developed from the essays, provides a basis for his response to the Peace Corps assignment with commitment, initiative, and effort.

Volunteers for the Peace Corps are undoubtedly a self-selected elite in regard to these qualities, and my study of them, though intensive, was small in scale. More convincing evidence of the cogency of one central

TABLE 3

Items That Are Characteristic of Volunteers with High Sum Scores on Mock Autobiographies

ITEM	P*
Personality Q-Sort	
Envisions a challenging and demanding personal future.	.05
Characteristically maintains a highly articulate intellectual formulation of his situation and problems.	.05
Shows inventiveness, ingenuity.	.05
Has developed a well-balanced, varied, and stable program for self of work, relaxation, relief or escape.	.05
Devotes much of his energy to a deliberate program of self-improvement (creative activity, study, etc.).	.10
High in initiative; active rather than reactive.	.10
Performance Q-Sort	
Elaborates his performance of teaching duties in non-routine, imaginative ways; invests self creatively in teaching job in and out of class.	.01
Values his Peace Corps assignment as relevant to his career plans.	.05
Actively employs self in useful, school-related activities outside of class.	.10
Concerned with using his Peace Corps experience to test himself.	.10

* By t-test comparing extreme thirds of the distribution.

component of the proposed competence syndrome comes from the massive study, under the auspices of the United States Office of Education, of factors affecting the educational achievement of children of various ethnic groups (Coleman *et al.*, 1966). Data were gathered in the fall of 1965 from 645,000 pupils in grades 3, 6, 9, and 12 in 4000 American public schools. To quote the summary of this unprecedented study (p. 23):

> A pupil attitude factor, which appears to have a stronger relationship to achievement than do all the "school" factors together, is the extent to which an individual feels that he has some control over his own destiny. . . . The responses of pupils to questions in the survey show that minority pupils, except for Orientals, have far less conviction than whites that they can affect their own environments and futures. When they do, however, their achievement is higher than that of whites who lack that conviction.
>
> Furthermore, while this characteristic shows little relationship to most school factors, it is related, for Negroes, to the proportion of whites in the schools. Those Negroes in schools with a higher proportion of whites have a greater sense of control. This finding suggests that the direction

> such an attitude takes may be associated with the pupil's school experience as well as his experience in the larger community.

The three agree-disagree items on which the score for sense of control was based are:

> Good luck is more important than hard work for success.
> Every time I try to get ahead, something or somebody stops me.
> People like me don't have much of a chance to be successful in life.

The theme is obviously the same as that of Rotter's I-E scale discussed above. As the researchers of the study observe: "There is an objective basis for this difference in feelings of control, since these minority children have less chance to control their environment than do the majority whites." For a slum Negro child, agreement with each of these items is likely to be the "right answer." The relatively powerful correlation of these reality-based attitudes with educational achievement within each ethnic group is impressive, though the findings of course suffer from the inherent causal ambiguity of all correlational data.

The Problem of Transcultural Relevance

If the cogency of our formulation of the competent self be granted, what of its general relevance? Is this only another projection of middle-class values reflecting culture-bound bias? My suggestion is that while different cultures would indeed value the competence syndrome differently, in principle it has transcultural relevance, as the content of specific goals and the knowledge and skill required to achieve them do not.

Surely the competence syndrome has special relevance for modern technical society where particular knowledge and skill is rapidly obsolescent — the more so to the extent that individualistic values prevail. If modern society is to remain viable as an open, free society, its major roles need to be adequately manned by persons sufficiently endowed with the qualities that we have been discussing. Persons who are seriously lacking in these qualities tend to be barred from effective participation. This is the problem of the ghetto minorities. When a conspicuous number of young people from elite groups in the society also show signs of a failure of hope, a loss of sense of efficacy, and withdraw hippie-style into passive noncommitment or explode in symbolic protest, there is indeed occasion for alarm at the dawning crisis of confidence that is implied. The context in which the agenda for this chapter is framed takes for granted that the fostering of competent selves is now an urgent social need.

What of traditional folk societies? Contemporary wisdom tells us to emphasize their variety, not their sameness. Nevertheless, the sharp contrast with our unique modern situation permits some things to be said. The traditional world was a small, parochial one in which the dramatis personae of hamlet and village could be well known to each of the players. The compass of daily life was finite and familiar, though it was surrounded by a great Unknown of fearsome natural forces and dangerous strangers. The ritual life of the community supported the individual in a sense of significance and worth. Given his embeddedness in traditional communal life, the individual was probably less saliently aware of his isolated selfhood than he is in the fluid modern world. Yet in the limited sphere within his purview, in social life and in agriculture and the associated crafts, he could earn honest feelings of efficacy; very likely he could know his effectiveness with less ambiguity than is characteristic in complex modern society, since the feedback was direct and the criteria were intrinsic or traditional. Cultural elaborations in the creative arts attest to the prevalence of motivation toward excellence beyond the requirements of mere conformity or survival.

Within a framework of scarce cognitive and technical resources that in fact imposed narrow limits on people's ability to master their environment and control their own lives, people could nevertheless develop a sense of self-respect and efficacy. The stable round of events in the life cycle gave a basis for hope. Outside the limits within which competence could be real and unambiguous, the fatalistic beliefs and propitiatory or controlling ritual and magic provided by the culture relieved the individual of some of the burden of inventing his own neurotic defenses against the anxieties of living in a world where so much was beyond his understanding and control.

This generalized and no doubt idealized picture ignores dramatic intercultural variation that clearly has a bearing on the prevalence of competent selfhood. One has only to read a perceptive ethnographic and psychological report like DuBois' account of *The People of Alor* (1944) to recognize that traditional societies can sustain themselves in persisting culture patterns that entail a very high cost to individual selves. DuBois' Alorese seem so hag-ridden by anxieties and so preoccupied with cultural and individual defenses against them, at the expense of effective coping, that one is forced to conjecture that the society could endure only in a remarkably protected environment.

It is thus germane to inquire about the extent to which conditions that prevail in traditional societies are compatible with the development of competent selves, even though the questions arise from concerns that are part of our own social predicament. When we turn to instances of disintegrating culture at the margins of modern life, as depicted in Oscar Lewis' accounts of the "culture of poverty" (for example, 1959), the relevance of our conception is unmistakable. What is dramatically evident is the absence of the competence syndrome, the presence of the vicious circle. For life to be at all endurable in the mutually exploitative jungle world at a nearly "animal" level of existence, where trust would be folly and self-respect is unattainable, people *have to* adopt a fatalistic view. They *have to* seize upon such fleeting gratifications as come their way. And the very adaptations that make a bad life minimally supportable trap people in "the life." From within this system there is little chance of escape.

If further grounds are needed for regarding our approach to competence as transculturally relevant, they may be found in the fruitful use of the closely related concept of *civic competence* in Almond and Verba's (1963) comparative study of political culture in five countries. Almond and Verba's concept is a direct equivalent of the one developed here, as focused on the more restricted sphere of political attitudes and action. The authors find striking national differences, to which they give a major role in interpreting the functioning of the formally democratic political systems in these countries, in people's actual political competence — their ability and readiness to take the initiative in influencing political decisions that affect them — and in their *sense* of civic competence — their belief that they can exert such influence. The data of their study do not settle whether civic competence is most usefully regarded as part of a general competence syndrome or may be so much influenced by special features of national political systems as to require separate assessment. As one of the most fertile recent studies of comparative politics, however, this work is testimony to the cross-national relevance of competence as a strategic variable.

Akin to the question of cross-cultural relevance of competence is that of the relevance of competence to the two sexes. As the cross-cultural data reported by Barry, Bacon, and Child (1957) for 110 cultures make clear, there is a widespread pattern, corresponding to what prevails in our own society, according to which there is greater pressure toward self-reliance and striving for achievement in boys, toward nurturance, obedience, and responsibility in girls. Any measure of the competence syndrome is likely not to be "fair" to girls — but neither are the traditional cultures of the world in this respect. Our concept appears relevant to both sexes, though it will be important to examine how the antecedents of competence are structured differently for boys and girls, and how competence strivings may be channeled in girls and women under cultural circumstances that limit their direct expression.

THE EARLY DEVELOPMENT OF COMPETENCE

The competent self, as we have examined the concept in the first section of this chapter, is planted squarely in the midstream of socialization and personality development, after the important achievements underlying selfhood have already occurred but leading, under favorable circumstances, to productive spirals of further growth. What are the precursors of competent selfhood? By what processes and subject to what essential conditions does the baby human animal get set on a trajectory that creates the grounds for its favorable further development? Recent research on infancy and early childhood identifies some of the possibilities and allows us to formulate questions that could not have been posed only a few years ago. But it still does not provide the answers that we need. Wise social policy must still hedge its bets while entertaining alternative views of what is strategic in the course of development. Meanwhile, further research is urgently needed, and profitable directions for it to pursue are reasonably clear. For good reason this is currently a field of very active investigation.

White's initial article (1959) in which his concept of competence was introduced reviewed a variety of evidence from research on animals and infants that cast serious doubt upon the then still current, though shaken, assumption that the organism's reaching out to the environment in curiosity, exploration, and manipulativeness could be accounted for in terms of learned by-products of biological drives, based on tissue needs, directed toward end-states of quiescence. His negative argument, questioning the inclusive adequacy of motivational theory rooted in tension reduction, was persuasive to many readers. But his positive case, for a special category of biologically given motivation toward the production of effects in the environment, was less satisfying.

As an interim schema that frees the imagination to consider possibilities ruled out by prevailing orthodoxies in motivational theory, it undoubtedly made a major contribution. But it left open the question of what *sort* of effects would lead to intrinsically rewarding feedback, and indeed left the details of effectance or competence motivation and its development essentially unspecified. His subsequent monograph (1963), an epistle to the gentiles of psychoanalytic persuasion, did not help matters in its gratuitous assumption of "independent ego energies" to account for competence motivation, though it added a rich and provocative discussion of the part played by competence motivation in later ego development. The time for motivational theories based on the energy metaphor that Freud adopted from Helmholtz had already past; too much was being discovered in modern neurophysiology to which the energy metaphor with its associated hydraulics was not at all relevant, and it was beginning to appear equally misleading in regard to the facts of behavior. White leaves us, then, with the assumption that man's active commerce with the environment has a biological basis other than the satisfaction of tissue drives. The job of clarifying what that basis might be essentially remains.

Mammalian Precursors of Competence

A good empirical starting point for us is provided by the results of a major program of research on the behavior of captive white-footed mice, reported by Kavanau (1967) since the appearance of White's papers. Psychologists have a predilection for rats and mice, but unfortunately they have found it convenient to work mostly with domesticated strains that are uninformative about the behavior traits that have emerged as products of mammalian evolution — and hence about the biological endowment of man as a domesticating but still (genetically) undomesticated animal. Not only have they preferred to study creatures that have had much of the native behavior repertory of the wild species bred out of them, but they have also chosen to investigate the animals' behavior in very restricted settings such as Skinner boxes and discrimination apparatuses. The zoologist Kavanau follows a wiser strategy with richly rewarding results. He has placed members of a wild species in an ingeniously constructed artificial environment with many potentialities for variation under the experimenter's or under the animal's control: a special cage with nest box and activity wheels for running under free and motor-driven conditions, provided with switches by which, when the experimenter wishes it, the animal can itself control major features of its environment (illumination, motor-drive for the wheel, and the like). Many aspects of the animal's behavior are automatically recorded.

What do the white-footed mice tell us about one variant of mammalian behavior? Here are some excerpts from Kavanau's summary of his detailed findings from a six-year program of research.

> Confined animals are likely to seize upon and repeatedly exercise virtually any opportunities to modify (and alter their relationships with) their surroundings. In addition they have a strong tendency to counteract nonvolitional and "unexpected" deviations from the status quo. As a result, their responses do not bear an immutable relationship to the nature of the stimulus or other variable being modified; stimuli and activities that are rewarding in certain circumstances are avoided in others. These aspects of behavior have been illustrated by studies of nest occupancy, running in motor-driven wheels, and control of intensity of illumination. (p. 1638)

Thus, mice will frequently leave the nest when the experimental enclosure is disturbed during the day. Sometimes they will immediately return to the nest; sometimes not. But if they are put back in the nest by hand, they will dependably leave it immediately, no matter how many times they are put back. So much like men! "In this relatively clear-cut case, an act or situation which is rewarding when carried out volitionally is avoided when initiated by force — the animal responds by doing the opposite."

Similarly with the motor-driven wheel. If the experimenter starts the motor while the mouse is in the wheel and the mouse can turn it off by a lever, it does so promptly, no matter what the speed or how experienced the mouse may be with motor-driven running. But if the mouse itself starts the motor-driven wheel and the experimenter turns it off, the mouse predictably and promptly turns it back on again.

> The results of the control-of-illumination studies suggest the complex interplay of tendencies to modify features of the environment, to avoid conditions imposed compulsorily, and to select preferred levels of illumination. (p. 1638)

By ingenious experimental variations Kavanau has shown independent tendencies in this nocturnal animal to prefer low illumination, but also to initiate change in illumination apparently for its own sake, yet to resist change imposed by the experimenter (though, of course, from the mouse's point of view the imposed change just happens; the experimenter does not figure in the mouse's world).

Still other studies showed that under training regimens that give the mice experience with a variety of running wheels, some requiring split-second timing and quick reflex action (for example, square "wheels" and wheels with hurdles), the mice prefer these more "challenging" tasks to running in plain round wheels.

Kavanau further reports:

> White-footed mice readily master complex regimes in which several different levers and shutters must be pressed or rotated in certain sequences within seconds for different rewards. They quickly learn to traverse mazes containing hundreds of blind alleys and do so frequently without extrinsic reward. It is unlikely that these remarkable learning performances even begin to approach the capacities of the animals. (p. 1638)

One can share Kavanau's enthusiasm for these attractive little creatures, for they provide more cogent evidence in regard to White's thesis than any animal research that was available for him to cite. For the types of capitive mouse behavior that we have sampled, the rules appear to be these:

(1) If things stay the same for very long, change them if you can.

(2) To the extent that you can resist imposed change, do so.

(3) All the same, there will be some environmental conditions that suit you better than others. Pick those conditions, unless rules 1 and 2 supervene.

(4) When you are out for exercise, use your skills and capacities to the hilt.

"Effectance" describes what these mice are up to, but it is a pallid summary. They also show both autonomy and need for variety (Fiske and

Maddi, 1961), as well as relatively stable preferences for certain environmental states over others. The gratifications of self-initiated action and the aversive quality of imposed environmental change are clearly evident.

Psychologists have sometimes written as though a fact about people cannot be regarded as legitimate unless it can also be demonstrated in lower animals. No such odd reasoning is intended here, of course. I have no doubt that children show curiosity and negativism and test their capacities in play. What is at issue is whether they do so as part of their evolutionary heritage as mammals. Even the most careful study of one species cannot settle the matter, but Kavanau's research in conjunction with other recent work, especially on primates, creates a strong presumption that these precursors of the competence syndrome have a biological basis. Certainly the behaviors that he describes should yield an evolutionary advantage.

The Emergence of Intrinsic Motivation

How, then, are we to conceive of the human infant's active involvement with the world? Piaget, whose ingenious and detailed observations of the behavior of his own children as infants (1952) undoubtedly provided the most important single stimulus to current research interest in early development, took the motivational aspect of this involvement for granted. We simply find the infant engrossed in the process of actively constructing his world, building "schemata" — cognitive-behavioral structures — to which he *assimilates* the presenting stimulation at the same time that he *accommodates* to its refractoriness. During the sensorimotor period of infancy, these schemata are pre-symbolic action-patterns, the achievement of which involves mastery of the instrumental resources of the body and stabilization of a world of objects as two sides of the same coin. Attainment of the schema of directed grasping, for example, establishes for the infant the primitive reality of the object grasped as implied in the complex pattern of sensorimotor coordination. In his waking hours, the infant is constantly busy practicing and applying his existing repertory of schemata, and with increasing maturity, trying out new ones that when perfected increase his cognitive and behavioral command over an ever widening world. Paradoxically, the infant gains in real power over the world to the extent that his emerging cognitive structures provide a coherent formulation of its existence and structural properties as relatively independent of his own actions. The infant comes to construe the world in polar relation to the self and discovers its properties in an endless program of behavioral "experimentation" as it shapes the consequences of his actions.

Given Piaget's enduring preoccupations with developmental epistemology, it is only natural that he has left the motivational aspect of cognitive development implicit in his formulations. The closest that he comes to its explicit recognition is in his metaphorical reference to schemata as feeding upon (receiving "aliment" from) the experience that is assimilated to them. Yet the motivational relevance of his account is obvious, and White (1959) found some of his most persuasive illustrations in Piaget's descriptions of infant behavior.

J. McV. Hunt, who had previously (1961) examined in detail the bearing of Piaget's research and theories on the very American question (in which Piaget himself was little interested) of how to promote and accelerate intellectual development, has recently (1963, 1965) turned his attention to explicating their motivational implications, grounding his reinterpretation of Piaget in recent research and theory about arousal, attentional processes, curiosity, and exploratory behavior. With White, Hunt sees in Piaget's descriptions evidence for intrinsic motivation, which he spells out as "motivation inherent in information processing and action." Reflecting his background in positivistic behavior studies, he is critical of formulations that give an illusory appearance of dealing adequately with motives by naming them — a fault that he finds in White's "effectance" — or that bypass the problem by postulating spontaneous activity. The details of how Hunt seeks to avoid these errors by recourse to mechanisms and relationships currently entertained in neurophysiologically oriented accounts of motivation need not concern us. But the essentials of his explication and simplification of Piaget are worth considering, as pointing to an epigenetic sequence which, if firmly established, would provide a framework within which social influences on the development of intrinsic motivation might be studied.

Hunt draws upon the idea, put forth by McClelland *et al.* (1953) among others, that the affective value of informational input to the organism — pleasant and reinforcing or unpleasant and aversive — depends on its relation to the organism's then-existing adaptation level. Small discrepancies between a characteristic of input and the adaptation level of the organism for that particular characteristic and modality of input arouse pleasant affect; large discrepancies arouse distressing affect. Affective arousal, according to this view, underlies the development of persisting motives. But the very young infant has yet to establish internal standards of reference. During the first four or five months, in Hunt's first stage which corresponds to Piaget's first two, the infant is reactive, a captive of his field of stimulation. Change in this field evokes from him the "orienting response," which is followed by reduction of tension and arousal.

> In this first stage of intrinsic motivation, the standard of reference against which new receptor inputs become incongruous is the ongoing input of the moment. . . . This responsiveness to change in input, especially through the eyes and ears, indicates that a basis for motivation

> inherent in the infant's informational interaction with his circumstances exists, ready-made, even at birth. (1965, p. 232)

Since the neonate's only standard that governs affective arousal in informational interaction is that of ongoing input, the absence of change — as in neglectful orphanage environments in which input is relatively homogeneous — means the absence of intrinsic motivation, which in the short run means apathy and in the long run should lead to retardation.

This view of the motivational aspects of informational commerce with the environment puts a different interpretation on the often-cited observations of Spitz (1945), who attributed the depression and retardation of orphanage foundlings to the lack of mothering. The new view is congruent with increasing skepticism among careful students concerning the consequences of maternal deprivation as such (Yarrow, 1964). Also working with institutionalized infants, B. White and Held (1966) have since provided decisive evidence that enriched opportunities in the world of the institutional crib have striking effects on the development of the infant's capacities for attention and prehension. At the Puerto Rico Conference, White voiced the conviction that these measurable specific effects were accompanied by a generally more positive engagement with the world, which looked like a precursor of competence.

Hunt's second stage appears when the infant begins acting to regain perceptual contact with various kinds of receptor inputs as "interesting spectacles" — in Piaget's phrasing. No longer merely responsive and also commanding a more efficient motor apparatus, the infant can now be said to show intentional activity, in that the instigation of his actions is based on discrepancy from an internal standard. He acts to reestablish sights and happenings to which he has become emotionally attached during the process of increasing familiarization. (Hunt leaves open the question as to whether familiarization as such leads to the attachment or whether it follows upon changes in input that are contingent on the infant's own actions — a theme we remember from the work with white-footed mice.)

Some time in the first year, the infant's cognitive world becomes sufficiently furnished that the familiar loses some of its appeal, and the infant is attracted more to novelty as such. Much remains to be clarified in this formulation, because as Hunt notes, this third stage is also the time at which really serious attachments to persons and places begin with concomitant fear of the strange. It is at this period that Hunt thinks that R. W. White's conceptions of competence motivation toward original constructive activity become relevant.

Some of the other puzzles not resolved by this provisional formulation may be noted briefly. What *are* the characteristics of the stimulus environment that attract the infant's attention, engage his awakening curiosity, draw him outward in cognitive involvement with the world? Novelty and discrepancy from expectation are a first approximation, but what of complexity, what of innately attractive figural properties, like the simple bull's-eye that predictably draws an infant's attention? To what extent is it critical that the infant produce the changes in stimulation by his own actions? Bower (1966) has shown that three-month-old infants acquire the capacity to perceive visual depth through response to the relative motion within the visual field — "motion parallax" — that results from their gross head movements. That their own self-induced movements are crucial is suggested by the research of Held and Hein (1963) on kittens, who found that self-induced movement was essential for normal visual-motor development, and externally-produced movement in the presence of a dependable surround was insufficient.

Is the relationship between early stimulation and the development of intellective competence and intrinsic motivation a continuous function — the more the better? Or a curvilinear one? We no longer hear warnings about over-stimulation, but that is not because the facts are clear. Amid the current excitement about the potential benefits from early stimulation, a note of caution is in order. The possibility that there may be such a thing as over-stimulation is suggested by the observation of White and Held (1966), in their study of institutionalized infants already cited, that the introduction of an enriched visual surround when the infants were about five weeks old did not immediately produce favorable effects. Rather, the group with visual enrichment actually exhibited *less* visual attention during the first five weeks of exposure, and the investigators reported their impression that during this period the infants engaged in much more crying than the control group. Favorable effects began only at about ten weeks of age. Timing would seem to be critical. The possibility that there is some minimal level of stimulus variation needed for normal development, beyond which additional dosage makes less difference, also needs to be explored.

What, for that matter, is the interplay between emergent intrinsic motivation, as emphasized by Hunt, and the sense of well-being that presumably arises from the contact comforts of good mothering? Until about 1960, mothering was evidently made to carry too heavy and exclusive a developmental burden. (In his critical review of professional advice to parents over forty years, Brim [1959] found that virtually no attention was given to cognitive development.) But even though some of the consequences previously ascribed to inadequate mothering can now be interpreted more plausibly in terms of the lack of stimulating interplay with the environment (of which the mother is usually a salient component), it would be foolish to assume that mothering makes no difference. Perhaps contact comfort is necessary from the beginning, and an emotional relationship with a stable, affectionate caretaker becomes important in Hunt's third stage? In our enthusiasm for progress in understanding cognitive development, we might wisely dampen any pendulum swing away from recognition of the probable importance of maternal love.

Unfortunately, different sorts of investigators are likely to care about these two topics, and in general research and theory have not been directed toward knitting them together, as an adequate account of the Anlagen of the competent self in infancy would seem to require. We need to know more about how mothering or its lack affects the infant's readiness for active exploration, as is suggested by Mary Ainsworth's finding (Ainsworth and Wittig, in press) that one-year-old infants (like baby chimpanzees) engage in much more active environmental exploration in the presence of their mothers than when with a stranger. The present stage of research and theory opens up many important questions but does not settle them. I recently heard a prominent child psychiatrist assert with some assurance that whether or not a child will ever attain self-respect is probably decided by the time he is two — and that maternal love versus deprivation makes the difference. Fortunately, our present knowledge radically undercuts that assurance, but it does not yet provide the needed answers.

Hunt's version of Piaget has provocative implications for the impact of social structure on socialization for competence. The extent to which slum children actually do suffer the effects of deprivation in infancy is a matter for debate, as their subsequent deficit is not, but the foregoing account helps to focus our inquiry about likely causes of deficit. For one thing, the untidy confusion of a crowded tenement flat certainly does not deprive the young infant of varied stimulation unless he is parked unattended in a convenient crib. Nor, as the infant construes his world, is the chaos that appalls the middle-class visitor necessarily so chaotic from the perspective of the burgeoning schemata of later infancy. Things are things, whatever their disarray, and the baby on the floor has as good a chance as his middle-class counterpart to explore their properties. If he is left in a crib for the convenience of mother or granny, he *may* indeed be deprived, but such deprivation is hardly specific to the slum. One is led to conjecture that before major handicaps appear as the child enters the symbolic world of language, the main liabilities are to be looked for in instability of temporal scheduling (conceivably relevant throughout infancy) and in such social factors (presumably most relevant in later infancy) as erratic scheduling of social reinforcement and instability of relationships with caretakers — items that do not figure prominently in the cognitively focused account of development we have just reviewed.

Continuity versus Discontinuity between Infancy and Early Childhood

By the time the infant is a year old, the terminology of competence seems to fit very well the coherent ways in which infants differ from one another. This impression is supported by evidence in Wenar's study of "competence at one" (1964). Defining "executive competence" as "the child's ability to initiate and sustain locomotor, manipulative, and visually regarding activities at a given level of complexity and intensity, and with a given degree of self-sufficiency" (p. 336), he found a significant tendency for indices of his proposed components of competence to vary together, with the exception of self-sufficiency. What remains in doubt, and this is an area of uncertainty where research is most badly needed, is the linkage between competence in infancy and in early childhood.

At about two years of age, the preschool child emerges out of babyhood. He begins to talk, not with faltering words, but using language as a major channel of increasingly efficient communication with other human beings, at the beginning principally his parents. With language goes a new level of organization of his mental life.

Once, psychologists were wont to assume that the symbolic tokens of language and of thought as inner speech, acquired from the culture, transformed the young child's capacities for problem-solving, for future orientation, and for self-regard; a single causal direction was assumed from language to thought, fitting the now discredited view of the infant mind as *tabula rasa*. Better contemporary understanding of the constructive aspects of language learning (for example, Lenneberg, 1967) now suggests that only after the child has already grown into capacities for symbolization and for the induction and creative application of sentence-producing rules (a process that cannot be explained by passive imitation) — only after his thought is already in the process of being transformed — can he conceivably display the creative, productive use of language that is characteristic even of beginners. We must now give much more weight to the maturing capacities and cognitive dispositions that underlie the onset of language. But once the child can talk and understand, language becomes the preeminent tool for further cognitive elaboration in development.

Piaget labels the distinction between infancy and the preschool years as that between the sensory-motor and the "pre-operational" periods. Though Piaget is less interested in this aspect of development, reflective selfhood (Mead, 1934) emerges along with symbolization and language. In spite of the apparent sharp discontinuity between infancy and childhood, does favorable development in infancy predict competence in childhood and later? The evidence is slim. Flavell (1963, p. 150) cites

Piaget as noting that the period from two to four years is the least investigated period in the entire developmental span.

The issue of predictive continuity or discontinuity across this little known boundary makes a considerable difference for social policy. It is considered in Hunt's discussion of the development of intellectual capacities, in particular how their further development might best be stimulated (1961, p. 314). Citing Bayley (1940) on the high reliability but absent predictive validity of infant mental tests, Hunt argues that "predictive validity could be expected only by assuming fixed intelligence and predetermined development" (which Hunt denies); low predictive validity in relation to later childhood and adulthood does not discredit the validity of the tests as reflecting the intellectual attainments of infancy. On the same page, however, we find him also arguing that "inasmuch as developmental rates are most rapid, in absolute terms, during the early months and the first couple of years, this is probably the period of most importance for maximizing intellectual potential" — an argument that is currently reaching the popular literature with little more empirical evidence to back it up than was at Hunt's disposal. (We may be at the point of overemphasizing the early years in the cognitive realm before the evidence is in, just as the Freudian revolution led an earlier generation of parent advisors to overemphasize them in the emotional realm.) But note the logical problem in joining the two statements. *If* what happens in the first two years is so important for later intellectual attainment, *why* is measured intellectual status near the end of that period so poor a predictor of later intelligence? If the linkage between infant and childhood intelligence is as feeble as the empirical correlations indicate, what grounds do we have for believing that stimulating infant intelligence can produce gains that will be preserved in childhood and later? Major decisions on the ages at which social investment should be made in remedying incompetence and promoting competence hinge — or ought to hinge — on how this issue is resolved.

Bayley (1966) has recently summarized a variety of evidence from the Berkeley Growth Study, concerning not only the stability and predictive value of intelligence-test scores but also the changing nature of correlations between mental scores and a variety of other behaviors and conditions, which sharpens the case for a substantial realignment of mental functions in the two-year-old. But perhaps there is reason to expect continuities in intrinsic motivation even if there is discontinuity in the organization of intellective functions. Intuitively such continuity makes sense.

There is at least some empirical evidence for motivational continuity across the infancy-childhood barrier, in the longitudinal correlations of the Menninger "coping" study (Murphy, 1962). For this small, intensively studied sample, infancy ratings on protest, termination, and resistance in the feeding situation — which might be interpreted as precursors of autonomous mastery — were substantially correlated, among the boys, with such preschool variables belonging to the competence cluster as impulse control, reality testing, overall ability, clarity regarding own identity, persistence in the face of failure, ability to restructure the environment, determination, drive for mastery, sense of importance, and problem-solving attitude toward life. Bearing on my earlier plea for the integrated study of the consequences of good or poor mothering together with those of productive interplay with the environment, Murphy further reports substantial positive correlations (also for boys) between "oral gratification" in infancy — which sounds like a reflection of good mothering — and a number of competence-related preschool variables: clarity of perception, sense of self-worth, strength of interest, ability to control the impact of the environment, and reality level. The negative correlations with depreciation of others, loss of perceptual clarity under stress, and tendency to get fatigued are equally pertinent and interesting. Given the limitations of this exploratory study, these relationships have to be regarded as suggestive rather than conclusive. On the side of discontinuity are the Kagan and Moss (1962) findings, in the Fels longitudinal study, that ratings of achievement behavior in the first three years show low negative correlations with comparable ratings in later childhood, in spite of evidence for substantial continuity between later childhood and adulthood in this motivational area. Better evidence in regard to continuity versus discontinuity of both intellective and motivational functions is badly needed, especially in regard to the persistent effects of interventions intended to improve the course of development.

Pending new light on this question, we may nevertheless be sure that the onset of talking creates new opportunities and challenges for some children, and begins or accentuates a cycle of intellectual handicap and failure for others. To the extent that children from the Negro slums learn as their native tongue a "substandard" dialect that makes them foreigners when they come to school, they are handicapped at least in regard to communication with teachers and possibly in social contacts with other children. Beyond this de facto disadvantage, however, patterns of language usage in the lower class may entail intrinsic intellective handicaps to the child who acquires them. In his sociolinguistic studies of the English middle and working classes, Bernstein (1964) proposes that speech is, indeed, "the major means through which the social structure becomes part of individual experience." As compared with the "elaborated code" of middle-class speech, the working class communicate by a "restricted code" in which meaning is organized via selection among a severely limited range of alternatives. Bernstein holds that the two modes of speech "elicit and sustain particular forms of relationships to the environment and so establish different orders of learning and relevance" (p. 258). The restricted code, with its limited structural organization and lexicon, is adapted to solidary communication about a limited stock of culturally shared referents. Within this framework, concrete, global, descriptive relationships are expressed at a low level of conceptualization. Communication of subjective intent is typically not well elaborated. As Bernstein puts it, the restricted code "signals the normative arrangements of a group rather than the individuated experience of its members" (p. 255). While warm solidarity is promoted, so is passivity and projectivity. Bernstein suggests that children reared to the restricted code may not progress in cognitive development from concrete to formal operations in Piaget's terms.

The Chicago studies by Hess and his colleagues (for example, Hess and Shipman, 1965) provide systematic evidence in support of these plausible hypotheses. These investigators observed Negro mothers, drawn from contrasting levels of social status, in interviews and in interaction with their four-year-old children as the children worked at various tasks. Mothers from the lower strata indeed used speech in a restricted way, which tends to foreclose the need for reflective weighing of alternatives and consequences. But Hess, though he follows Bernstein's analysis of speech patterns, is more interested in the entire teaching style that mothers use with their children, and how different styles of teaching shape the children's learning styles and information-processing strategies. As Hess and Shipman summarize the import of their research:

> The picture that is beginning to emerge is that the meaning of deprivation is a deprivation of meaning — a cognitive environment in which behavior is controlled by status rules rather than by attention to the individual characteristics of a specific situation and one in which behavior is not mediated by verbal cues or by teaching that relates events to one another and the present to the future. This environment produces a child who relates to authority rather than to rationale, who, although often compliant, is not reflective in his behavior, and for whom the consequences of an act are largely considered in terms of immediate punishment or reward rather than future effects and long-range goals. (p. 885)

These considerations carry us beyond the impact of class-related speech patterns as such, to issues with which we will be concerned in the next major section of the chapter. Research now in progress in the presently very lively field of sociolinguistics should throw further light on the channel that language provides for the transmission and perpetuation of class-linked aspects of competence. The period from one to three years old, before most children become readily accessible to observation in the nursery school, would seem to be a particularly strategic phase of development to study, crossing as it does the apparent major discontinuity in the development of intelligence and including the major steps in the development of language.

Competence and Emerging Selfhood

With language comes selfhood, and we make contact with our starting point in this chapter: the *person* as possessing attributes of competence or incompetence. From this point on, to speak of the "organism" reflects a deliberately partial perspective. Our earlier discussion has already made a case for assuming that once the child attains the level of communicative social participation as a conscious self, the motives and attitudes in which we are interested are organized around or channeled through the self as reflexive object and enduring structure.

Apart from the diffuse background of bodily awareness, the child's sense of self would appear to have its origins in two distinguishable sorts of input, only one of which has been emphasized in the major line of social-psychological theorizing. One is the feedback that the child gets about the effects of his actions on the world of physical objects and people, as stressed by White (1959) and throughout this chapter. The other is feedback from the mirror of social response and appraisal, as emphasized by the great names in the symbolic-interactionist tradition. Both sorts of ingredients, I propose, are necessarily involved in the constitution of the self. How they are integrated in the self as it becomes stabilized as an established structure is a matter of decisive importance for the child's orientation toward the world, since the self continues to be the vehicle both for approval-seeking motivation guided by social comparison and for intrinsic competence motivation toward the production of valued effects. The interplay between these motivational aspects of selfhood will be examined in more detail in the next section.

The development of these two aspects of the self requires description in different terms, and different social factors emerge as likely to be influential in the development of each. Consider first the component of reflected social appraisal, as initially suggested by James, Baldwin, and Cooley and brought to its most sophisticated statement by Mead (1934) in his formulation that reflective self-awareness depends upon adopting toward one's own attributes and actions the perspective of people at large, generalizing across the various particular role relationships in which one is in communicative interaction. From this vantage point, development of the self depends upon the ever-widening and more complexly organized sets of role relationships in which the child is involved, starting with the mother-child pair, extending to the more complicated role system of the immediate family, and, beginning with the school years, broadening to include the peer group, extra-familial adult authorities, and, progressively, the entire complex structure of society at large as the individual is related to it. As the "generalized other" whose perspective the child adopts becomes progressively *more* generalized, his reflected view of himself becomes more "objective" — less dependent upon the contingencies of particular role relationships — at the same time that he becomes equipped with the role repertory to participate effectively in the full range of social life.

Throughout this course of development, the theme of reflected *appraisal* calls our attention to how the child is evaluated by the various "significant others" and to the categories of people that enter his world of relationships, as primary determinants of his emerging self-evaluation. It is through who these others are and how they treat him that the social structure has its impact on his feelings of worth — a theme introduced by neo-Meadians under the influence of Sullivan (1953). Since the generalized other of the preschool child is restricted to the immediate family, it is how the child perceives their feelings about him that makes the most difference to this aspect of the beginnings of selfhood.

This is the familiar social-psychological account of the development of the self, and while it would seem to be correct and useful so far as it goes, it is clearly one-sided. Along with interactionist role theory generally, it looks like the theory that Riesman's "other-directed man" (Riesman, 1950) would naturally invent to give an account of himself. It needs to be balanced by attention to those aspects of the self that continue to channel intrinsic motivation.

It is clear that intrinsic motivation *does* become channeled in the course of development. The infant, like the captive white-footed mouse, may seek his effects from the environment in rather randomly selected directions; not so the older child nor, of course, the adult. Just any effect won't do. The developing person comes to specialize in seeking environmental effects in particular realms, and he acquires values or standards against which he measures the adequacy of the effects that he has produced. Progressive definition of one's sense of identity is in good part a matter of such limitation and specification of one's claims on life.

One aspect of this process of progressive motivational differentiation was given an early formulation by Gardner Murphy (1947) in his concept of *canalization* — the tendency to seek gratification in the particular modes and from the particular activities that previously have been found gratifying; that is, one's areas of success point the direction for focusing one's further efforts. But this idea, which is really a variant of commonplace concepts of reinforcement, does better as an account of the differentiation, say, of the general biological hunger drive into a set of culturally specific food preferences and appetites than it does as a formulation for the development of elaborating, self-feeding, insatiable interests and endeavors that are intrinsically motivating to the mature person. In his discussion of *propriate* (self-related) striving, Allport (1961) captures descriptively this aspect of motivation as involving the person's self-directed intentions.

With the development of the self, then, the person's initial diffuse orientation toward effective engagement with the environment becomes *differentiated* and specialized. At the same time, however, his self-conceptions and self-attitudes, formed in the light of feedback from effects achieved *and* from social appraisal, provide the basis for *generalized* orientations of competence or incompetence, relatively stable across the vicissitudes of particular transactional encounters or role relationships. It is the dialectic interplay of trends toward generalization *and* differentiation that gives rise to the integrated organization of personality structure.

SOCIAL APPROVAL, SOCIAL COMPARISON, AND INTRINSIC MOTIVATION

Some Interrelations

But the developmental sequences involving the results of reflected appraisals of the child's qualities and performances, on the one hand, and the intrinsic effects of his own self-initiated activities, on the other, do not proceed independently of one another. The distinction is analytic and does not at all correspond to neatly separable aspects of personality development or structure. Thus, the two sorts of motivation can run parallel and fuse, as when parents or teachers bestow their approval on the child for performances that are also intrinsically rewarding. Gratifications from social effectance can supplant and substitute for those of social approval when the latter are not to be had — as when the "bad" child settles on getting a rise out of adults whose approval he has no hope of receiving (at the same time probably reaping social rewards from his peers). Or — one suspects more commonly with the middle-class child — extrinsic rewards of approval, grades, and, later, money may come eventually to replace intrinsic satisfactions, at heavy cost to the person's zest, creativity, and sense of meaningfulness.

I want to avoid giving the impression that intrinsic motivation is uniformly good and social-reinforcement motivation bad in socialization and personality development or that it makes any sense to conceive of the individual as unfolding autonomously under the guidance of pure effectance. Children and people generally need to feel well regarded by the others they care about, and if they do not, they are thrown into all manner of defensive maneuvers. Some sense of goodness coming from benign reflected appraisal is probably essential if the person is to be free to cope. Then, too, the child has to acquire some routine skills — for example, the "times tables" — that depend on rote practice under extrinsic reward, intrinsic rewards during their acquisition being notably lacking.[3] Moreover, often the standards by which a person can recognize an effective performance that is intrinsically rewarding are not themselves given intrinsically. Social convention defines the good performance in football and in banking, to a greater extent than in felling a tree or weaving a robe, but that does not eliminate the joys of effectance in playing the game. In large areas of personal and social behavior, as Festinger (1954) has emphasized, one can evaluate one's attributes and performances only through some process of social comparison. People appropriately turn to others to know how they stand when directly informative feedback from the results of their actions is unavailable.

The clear separation of what is extrinsic and what is intrinsic becomes the more difficult because, as Allport (1961) liked to stress, the motivational basis of particular activities does not stay put. Something that is not initially rewarding for its own sake becomes intrinsically rewarding as one achieves skill — whether playing the piano, dancing, or doing a problem in calculus. Conversely, something that was rewarding may cease to be so once mastered, especially if it is not highly valued by others. Socially derived values assist in defining what tasks are worth working on, what kinds of mastery worth pursuing. Moreover, since different segments of the social structure entail diverse definitions of worthwhile activities and tasks, social factors undoubtedly contribute to the channeling of competence, to the focusing of intrinsic motivation.

Despite the fact that the intrinsic and extrinsic, the personal and the social, strands become inextricably entangled, we must pursue the fate of intrinsic motivation. We must be particularly interested in identifying approaches to socialization that dampen intrinsic motivation and replace it by motivation for social approval and preemptive orientation toward extrinsic rewards. The procedures of our educational institutions invite examination from this perspective. The late president of Vassar, Sarah Blanding, told of a dewey-eyed freshman who approached her at the President's Reception to pronounce solemnly, "Miss Blanding, I think every young student has a spark of genius somewhere within her . . . and it is the duty of the faculty to *water* that spark." What in the educational process is likely to water the spark of intrinsic motivation, producing results that are familiar to saddened teachers and discouraged parents?

[3] O. K. Moore's electronically controlled "responsive environment," described in Hunt (1965), manages to enlist intrinsic motivation even in the service of rote learning; hence its appeal and efficiency as a teaching device.

One obviously unfavorable factor, which is critically important in the lives of many children, is a consistent history of failure and disapproval attending their independent efforts. Using a Reinforcement History Questionnaire that inquired about characteristic parental reactions in a variety of situations of effort, success, and failure on the part of the child, Katz (1967) found that among Negro boys (though not among girls) low school achievement, anxiety, and a propensity for self-devaluation, which as we might expect were all interrelated, were each in turn related to the predominance of negative reinforcements from parents — reports of low parental interest and acceptance and high parental punitiveness. When a discouraging start at home is followed by disparagement and ego-assault at school, the damage is only compounded. In *Death at an Early Age*, Kozol (1967) gives a poignant account of such factors as they impinge on Negro children in a segregated Boston school. Intrinsic motivation is bound to be quenched in settings where effort is predictably followed by failure (no intrinsic satisfactions) and accompanied by social indifference or disapproval (no extrinsic ones, either).

But let us assume well-intentioned parents and teachers, and more fortunate children. Good teaching by the agents of socialization, whether parents or teachers, would often seem to require more skill and forbearance than these people possess. It is easier to lecture than to develop a collaborative teaching relationship in which the child is encouraged to take the initiative. It is easier to lay out the facts for rote learning, necessarily sustained by extrinsic reinforcements, than it is to arrange curricular experiences in which knowledge and skills are seen by the child as instrumental to his own problem-solving efforts. It is easier to help the child who is in difficulty by giving him the "right" answer, the "right" method, than it is to point his attention in directions that support him in making the discovery for himself. How to give the right amount of the right kind of help at the right time, and not too much? It is easier to lay down rules by fiat than to go into the reasons for behavioral requests and on occasion to modify a request when the child has good countervailing reasons of his own. Educational theory since the days of Dewey has recognized the importance of building upon the child's active participation in the learning process, but realization of this aim in crowded classes led by teachers who, as the products of traditional educational experiences are themselves far from ideal models of competence, is another matter. The spark gets watered.

Achievement Motivation and Competence

At the Puerto Rico Conference, some of the most provocative talk about intrinsic versus extrinsic motivation in socialization for competence centered on the need for achievement — a concept that at first blush appears to have much in common with White's concept of competence. For McClelland *et al.* (1953), the concept meant striving to attain standards of excellence. They carried out an exemplary program of research on its antecedents and results based on scoring for achievement motivation imaginative stories told by subjects about a standard set of pictures — an adaptation of the Thematic Apperception Test (TAT) technique. The scoring system was derived empirically by noting the categories of content that distinguished the stories of students whose achievement motive had supposedly been aroused, as compared with stories written in a "neutral" condition. For the condition in which achievement motivation was to be aroused, subjects were given a difficult prior task — just before writing their stories — which was presented to them as a test of intelligence, a trait that most students can be assumed to want to excel in. Subsequent research (summarized most recently in Atkinson and Feather, 1966) has found high need for achievement to be associated with achievement training by both parents and independence training by the father. Warm but dominating mothers who are much concerned with their sons' performance contribute to high need for achievement in sons; dominating fathers, to low achievement motivation. A central influence in the learning of achievement motivation is the parents' conditional approval.

There are a good many difficulties with the concept of achievement motivation as embodied in this fantasy-based measure, most of which are reviewed by Katz (1967). There are questions about its generality, its applicability to women, its openness to influences that contaminate its value as a measure of motivation. The findings in regard to its relationships to achievement-oriented behavior have been ambiguous, except as a predictor of entrepreneurial striving in business men. Given this less than encouraging record, one suspects that there has been slippage between the theoretical definition of the motive and what has actually been captured in the measurements.

The technique of arousal that was employed in developing the scoring system did not directly arouse "standards of excellence"; rather, subjects were led to be concerned about their competitive standing in a quality that was important to them: intelligence. Perhaps, after all, the motive thus imperfectly tapped has more to do with competitive striving in a context of social comparison than with intrinsic effort toward excellence. Atkinson and Feather entertain this possibility: "Under some conditions thematic apperceptive n Ach scores may reflect *extrinsic* motivation in-instead of, or in addition to, achievement motivation. The possibility is sufficiently important to make this one of the most significant problems for future study" (1966, p. 350). Evidence in support of this conjecture is provided in Skolnick's finding (1966) that, for men, McClelland-style fantasy scores for achievement correlate more highly with the California Psychological Inventory scale for *Achievement via conformance* than with that for *Achievement via independence* (contrary findings for women perhaps being explicable in terms of the culturally prescribed feminine sex role, according to which competitive achievement striving, as deviant, requires independence of prevailing norms).

If we give weight to these misgivings and to the emphasis on conditional approval in the antecedents of achievement motivation, the apparent similarity between *n Ach* and our competence syndrome is dispelled. Achievement motivation would seem at root to involve performance for the sake of social approval; competence motivation involves being able to risk disapproval in order to master a task on one's own terms. No doubt, effective performance is often for the sake of approval; but at what psychological cost?

A congruence seems apparent between achievement motivation and the approach of the "traditional" school with its competition and grades, its reliance on extrinsic motivation to power the learning of facts and specific skills. More congruent with the development of competent selves is the "modern" orientation according to which the school tries to build on the child's native and intrinsic curiosity, on his active initiative in the learning process. In such schools, intellectual mastery in terms of the child's own organization of knowledge is valued rather than the level of factual attainment. The child is helped to discover the self-relevance of what he learns; interplay between the subjective and objective is encouraged.

But the value question that brings heat to arguments about humanistic child rearing and progressive education remains: Is the development of strong need for achievement an asset or a liability? American society obviously thrived when it was manned by a middle class that was competitively oriented toward achievement — at a toll for the individual. If the school and the home train children so as to maximize their sense of competence and autonomy, they will not want to do all the things that society calls upon them to do; they may not choose to do things that society needs to have done, including things that later on they may themselves wish they had chosen to do. One can imagine supporters of traditional education, competitive achievement motivation, and the associated values of the Protestant ethic putting up a strong argument for the older way. At root, a choice of values is at issue.

These issues are beginning to become clarified in recent research on the child-rearing antecedents of competence-related behavior. Two studies that are interesting to compare in this regard share as a valuable common feature the collection of systematic data on parent-child interaction in a standard situation. In the classic study of the antecedents of achievement motivation, Rosen and D'Andrade (1959) found that mothers of boys who scored high in need for achievement were distinctive in being more intrusive, setting high standards for their boys' performance, and insisting on a superior performance. They did not allow the child much autonomy in decision making. Helen Bee (1967) reports a contrasting pattern of behavior for parents of nine-year-old children of both sexes who had been selected for their ability to resist distraction, a feature of inner control that would seem to belong to our competence syndrome and should certainly contribute to effective performance in many settings. Bee found that in comparison with parents of distractible children, parents of non-distractible children give less specific suggestions about how to accomplish the task, give more positive encouragement, pay more attention to their child's contributions in decision-making interaction, and make relatively more evaluative comments than suggestions. They seem to be concerned that the child's achievement be his own. In congruence with Wenar's (1965) finding that self-sufficiency did not cohere with other indices of infant competence, Bee reports that contrary to expectation, non-distractible children make more bids for help, but they also reject help more often. Perhaps what is relevant to competence is not so much self-sufficiency as the ability and disposition to make use of others' help on one's own terms.

Diana Baumrind has recently contributed evidence that bears more directly on the parental practices associated with competence in nursery school children. In one study (1967), she identified for comparison three groups of children selected on the basis of their behavior in nursery school: a competent group who were assertive, self-reliant, self-controlled, buoyant, and affiliative; another group who were discontented, withdrawn, and distrustful; and a third group who had little self-control or self-reliance and tended to retreat from novel experiences. Parents of the competent group tended to be controlling, demanding, communicative, and loving; parents of the unhappy and disaffiliated group were relatively controlling and detached; and parents of the least self-reliant and self-controlled group of children were noncontrolling, nondemanding, and relatively warm. A second study (Baumrind and Black, 1967) examined the relations among parent behaviors, parent attitudes, and child behavior in an unselected sample. While the results of this research show important sex differences in relationships that are too complex for ready summarizing, the findings again suggest:

> Parental practices which are intellectually stimulating and to some extent tension-producing (socialization and maturity demands, punitiveness, firmness in disciplinary matters) are associated in the young child

> with various aspects of competence. Techniques which fostered self-reliance, whether by placing demands upon the child for self-control and high level performance or by encouraging independent action and decision-making, facilitated responsible, independent behavior. Firm discipline in the home did not produce conforming or dependent behavior in the nursery school. (p. 325)

For engendering competence, it is clear, love is not enough, though it matters. Challenge, respect for the child, perhaps even some abrasiveness in relations with the child that provokes his assertiveness, good communication with an emphasis on the reasons for directives — these would seem important too, and are supported by convergent evidence. Baumrind's particular stress on high parental demands, firmness, and even punitiveness remains controversial, and no conclusion can be drawn about competence versus need for achievement when the relatively few relevant studies available employ different criteria and measures and draw their observations from different populations.

Our discussion has carried us rather far from the topic of achievement motivation, as treated in the work of the McClelland-Atkinson group. Achievement motivation can of course be studied by methods other than fantasy-based measures; other investigators have sought to save the concept by introducing differentiations that take into account some of the criticisms we have noted. For example, Veroff (1967), in the recent paper that also reviews an impressive program of related research done with his students, contrasts *autonomous* achievement motivation, which brings internalized personal standards into play, with *social* achievement motivation, in which the standards of excellence are based on social comparison. He offers a conjectural developmental sequence with three stages: an early one in which autonomous motivation predominates, a second stage in which social comparison is central (in the early school years), and finally a third one in which these components of achievement motivation are effectively integrated. He interprets various defects in the development of achievement motivation in terms of deficiencies in motive acquisition at the several stages. His data very broadly accord with the scheme, without giving it compelling support. But they do not answer the question of whether we are indeed dealing with an intrinsic sequence or instead with the consequences of dumping curious and autonomous youngsters into conventional, competitive schools. Nor is his concept of the integrated stage well developed. Rather, the question would seem to be: *how* are the autonomous and social components put together?

Katz (1967), whose paper we have already cited, is concerned with the much more specific problem of accounting for the motivational aspect of Negro deficit in school achievement and in this context finds the McClelland-Atkinson approach wanting, as focusing exclusively on motive strength while providing no useful information about the inferred self-regulatory behaviors that are supposedly involved. His decision to bring the children's normally covert responses of self-approval and self-disapproval under direct observation in an ingeniously contrived situation nicely complements the studies of Rotter (1966), Coleman *et al.* (1966), and Crandall, Katkovsky, and Crandall (1965) on children's beliefs in their own control of reinforcements in achievement situations. Rather than focus on their *beliefs* that reinforcing outcomes are under their own control, Katz studied how they actually administer reinforcements of approval or disapproval to themselves, while performing simple standard tasks.

He found that under conditions of supposed privacy, low achieving boys were more likely than relatively high achievers to indicate disapproval of their own performances, actual quality of performance being equivalent for the groups. The relationship does not hold for girls, a finding of sex differences that recurs throughout the complex literature of achievement research and cannot be pursued here, though with clarification of their basis should come much better understanding of the socialization antecedents of achievement motivation and behavior. If we hold in abeyance Katz's interpretation of his data in terms of internalized processes of covert reinforcement or their lack, on the surface his findings portray the low achievers' generalized unfavorable view of their own performance, which carries over even to situations in which the performance is not deficient. This discouraged outlook is entirely compatible with their giving voice to unrealistically high goals. Indeed, as Katz plausibly suggests, verbal subscription to high goals can substitute for constructive action toward achieving them.

This foray into recent research and theory about achievement motivation cannot produce tidy solutions from a field that is not yet ready for them. Hopefully, it may have sensitized the reader, as it has the author, to the complexity and difficulties of conceptualization and measurement that hamper attempts to disentangle intrinsic and extrinsic motivation in regard to a person's tendencies to engage constructively with the world.

Anxiety and Need for Approval

We may close this section by brief attention to some motivational dispositions that are clearly incompatible with intrinsically motivated competence. The first to be considered, need for approval as studied by Marlowe and Crowne (1964), sounds like the concern with social appraisal that we have been discussing. However, their method of assessing individual differences singles out as high scorers persons whose need to be well regarded by others is in defense of a very vulnerable self-regarding sentiment. The social desirability scale that Marlowe and Crowne use in their research allows people to endorse statements — outside the realm of psychopathology — that are commonly regarded as desirable attributes but are usually false. It thus identifies, at the high end, people who will go to considerable lengths to make a favorable impression. If the straightforward desire to be liked and receive social reinforcement can sometimes interfere with competence motivation, its defensive equivalent is unquestionably disadvantageous. Marlowe and Crowne present evidence that is generally consistent with this view, showing that while high scorers learn well under conditions of social reinforcement, they are dependent and compliant, and show themselves as defensive and avoidant in psychotherapy. But it is not clear whether it is their underlying low self-esteem that is incompatible with the competence syndrome, or, on the other hand, the defensive posture that they have adopted in order to bolster it.

In common psychodynamic theory, defensiveness is linked to anxiety. Anxiety as a momentary state may energize the person toward emergency action, but as an enduring trait the evidence shows according to expectation that it generally goes with low competence. This is not the place to consider the technicalities of pencil-and-paper anxiety scales and their use in research, which have been reviewed by I. G. Sarason (1960) and by Ruebush (1963). The most thorough work relating anxiety to achievement and competence in children has been that of S. B. Sarason and his colleagues (for example, Sarason, Davidson, Lighthall, Waite, and Ruebush, 1960; Hill and Sarason, 1966), who focused on a measure of test anxiety. Test anxiety tends to lead to poor school achievement, and in its antecedents and correlates is clearly part of the incompetence cluster.

SOCIAL STRUCTURE AND COMPETENCE

At scattered points throughout the chapter, we have noted ways in which factors of social structure — especially social class and ghetto status [4] — impinge on the development of competence. Having looked at its sources in infancy and tried with only partial success to disentangle some of the motivational factors that affect competent functioning in childhood and later, it is time for us to return to our provisional model of the competent self, established in benign circles of productive engagement with the environment, and its incompetent counterpart, mired in vicious circles of self-defeat. To expand our view of the self-sustaining system we can

[4] An excellent integration of research findings concerning child rearing and family-life patterns associated with poverty, with implications for action programs, has been recently provided by Chilman (1966).

now look for strategic factors of social structure that gear into these vicious or benign circles. In the personal system centering on the self, I suggested that attitudes of hope and of self-respect are at the crux of competence. Are there corresponding features of a person's location in the social system that play an equally strategic role?

Power, Respect, and Opportunity

I think there are such strategic aspects of location in the social structure: *opportunity*, *respect*, and *power*. Opportunity corresponds to hope and provides its warrant. Respect by others — more important in this regard than love or approval — provides the social ground for respect of self. And power is the kingpin of the system. Power receives respect and guarantees access to opportunity.

Restriction of opportunity not only blights hope; it excludes the person from the chance to acquire the knowledge and skill that would in turn enable him to surmount the barriers to effectiveness. Contempt and withheld respect may lead to "self-hatred" (Lewin, 1948) and may necessitate debilitating postures of self-defense. Absence of power entails general vulnerability and creates dependence. When opportunities are offered without a sharing of power, we have paternalism, which undercuts respect, accentuates dependence, and breeds a lurking resentment that the powerful are likely to condemn in righteousness as ingratitude.

The current world has fully displayed the inadequacy of paternalism and resounds with the claims of the powerless. Former colonial peoples, American Negroes, college students and other youth — all are engaged in strident power claims. And the prophets, the apologists, the critics of Black Power have almost succeeded, among them, in washing out all stable meaning from the term. Yet fundamentally the prophets and apologists are right, since power is objective control over what affects one's destiny.

As many commentators have noted, the currently escalating power claims by the disadvantaged are not to be explained by their extreme deprivation; rather, the contrary. The fact that these claims can be made at all is a sign of growing competence among people who before were fatalistically adapted to their powerless positions as apathetic students, colonials, or Uncle Toms. Loosened bonds of paternalistic authority, expanding opportunities, and instant mass communication across classes and countries and from campus to campus lead to rising expectations in an affluent society and modernizing world — the glimmerings of hope — and as the movement gathers momentum, models, which the still powerless and incompetent can identify with to gain vicarious strength, become available. The unreasonableness and unrealism of the claims to power, the frequently self-defeating tactics are understandable as stigmata of the persisting incompetence produced by powerlessness. Given unrealistic and insecure hopes that are bound to be frustrated, given competition among the leadership elite in the outrageousness of their claims, and given the predictable "backlash" from whoever constitute the relevant Establishment, the potentialities for continued explosive violence are very great indeed.

If social chaos can somehow be avoided, even spurious compensatory claims to respect and power have their value in what we must hope will be a transition to more fully shared power and greater competence for the presently deprived. The problem here is not the powerlessness and incompetence of individuals but that of massive social groups with shared, mutually reinforcing sentiments about self and world. Even flagrant reversals of white racist values, even transparent fabrications of a glorious history can help people who have little basis for realistic hope to develop the beginnings of a sense of worth and a feeling that they can have important effects in this world. The models furnished by conspicuous leaders provide a vicarious basis for the feeling of competence. In this regard, sinners like Adam Clayton Powell and Kwame Nkrumah may make more difference than saints like Martin Luther King. They are closer to their followers and more understandable.

Of course, extreme power claims by all social groups can never be simultaneously satisfied. The logical end point of pressing these claims would be a war of all against all — the Hobbesian "state of nature" that still exists in principle among nations. We may hope that as the powerless gain in real power and in both the feeling and the fact of competence, they may abate their more extreme claims, while the holders of power relax their resistance. The resulting state of shared power and accompanying responsibility, as and if it is approximated, could create a community fit for competent selves.

In this excursion about power and competence, I have neglected the asymmetrical power relationship that is most germane to socialization — that between parent and child, socialization agent and socializee (let us regard college students as quasi-adults). Age grading is itself a fact of social structure. Do the same considerations apply here? Yes, I think, with a difference. The difference is that the asymmetry in real power and competence is inherent, and hence some variant of paternalism — call it parentalism? — can hardly be avoided. And the attempt to disguise it can amount to an abdication of responsibility or can undermine the honesty of the relationship.

But with this important qualification, I think the fundamental relationships between power and competence hold. The authoritarian parent who uses his age-status for the naked assertion of power over his children gets dependence and passive resistance; maybe, if he is lucky, revolt. The wise nurture of competence in the young would seem to call for a deliberate progressive sharing of power and responsibility as the growing competence of the child enables him to use it. A little faster, perhaps, than is securely warranted by what the child can do: good "parentalism," unlike conventional paternalism, sees to it that the child has real problems and challenges to face, and that his solutions are his own.

Deviant Forms of Competence

Throughout this discussion I have knowingly overdrawn the picture of incompetence that goes with powerlessness and hopelessness, especially in the urban ghetto, so as to lay forth as clearly as possible an interpretative perspective which, though conjectural, seems to me to make a variety of salient current developments intelligible. True, the incompetence is there (along with remarkable instances of competence in spite of great handicap), and much deviant and problematic behavior can be interpreted as an attempt to seek escape from self and world, or to gain a short-circuited, illusory sense of efficacy — thus drug use and the search for kicks. Much, but not all. Some antisocial behavior, deviant from the point of view of the environing and superordinate society, may in part be directed toward alternative modes of competence that remain available and indeed become normative in the ghetto subculture when legitimate channels of effectance are closed off. The combative prowess of the gang leader and member, virtuosity in aggressive "mother talk," audacity in sexual exploits, and competence in the risky skills of the hustler belong under this heading, though these directions of activity obviously also yield extrinsic rewards. The larger society will regard these directions of activity as bad, but those who plan and direct rehabilitation programs will do well to remember that for many slum youth, all of their resources of competence motivation get channeled in these deviant directions. A lot of self is invested in them.

Small wonder that when youths from the slums are asked to give up these known avenues for intrinsic motivation for the sake of the uncertain benefits of a square world to which they have no commitment, they often "blot out" in some disastrous act which rescues them, at the very brink of successful rehabilitation, from the dangers of this fate. (This pattern was described in the conference paper by Nathan Caplan.) Such unsuccessful outcomes are the more likely to represent "healthy" strivings toward competence and autonomy when rehabilitation programs can still appear to the clients to be aimed mainly at satisfying the social workers' needs for achievement, not the clients' autonomous desires.

Even the "floating" that characterizes many slum boys, a manifestly incompetent pattern of behavior, testifies to residual effectance motivation under conditions that exclude true effectiveness. Observations that

Caplan reported in connection with street club work identified two distinct recurrent patterns of daily activity. On the one hand were boys who did not get into trouble, whose sequence of activities seemed highly organized along culturally approved lines. Interviews suggested that for many of these boys achievement was primarily a matter of cultural conformity. The "floaters," on the other hand, spent much of their time trying to find something to do by exploring their environment. They spoke of "hanging around," "messing around," or "roaming." When asked for a more definite description of their behavior, they were at a loss to give a more precise account except in terms of looking or waiting for something to do or happen.

Very likely some of the most promising talent in the slums is channeled in socially deviant directions. If the planners of rehabilitation programs hope to be effective, they will have to find ways of building on this competence and redirecting it, not quelling it.

There should be no summary to this chapter, which, as we end with the social concerns that stimulated the Committee's initial interest in the socialization of competence, closes in a neater pattern than the state of research-based knowledge really justifies. We have encountered many issues that call for better theory and further investigation. Characteristically, it has been easier to write coherently and "wisely" about those subjects, near the head and tail of the chapter, for which the facts are thinnest — and most malleable. The somewhat more rigorously worked areas of early development and achievement motivation are also the hardest to bring into focus.

References

Ainsworth, Mary D. Salter, and Wittig, Barbara A. Attachment and exploratory behavior of one-year-olds in a strange situation. In B. M. Foss (Ed.), *Determinants of Infant Behaviour*. Vol. 4. London: Methuen; New York: John Wiley & Sons. (In press)

Allport, G. W. *Pattern and Growth in Personality*. New York: Holt, Rinehart & Winston, 1961.

Almond, G. A., and Verba, S. *The Civic Culture. Political Attitudes and Democracy in Five Nations*. Princeton, N.J.: Princeton University Press, 1963.

Atkinson, J. W. *An Introduction to Motivation*. Princeton, N.J.: D. Van Nostrand Co., 1964.

Atkinson, J. W., and Feather, N. T. *A Theory of Achievement Motivation*. New York: John Wiley & Sons, 1966.

Barron, F. *Creativity and Psychological Health*. Princeton, N.J.: D. Van Nostrand Co., 1963.

Barry III, H. A., Bacon, Margaret K., and Child, I. L. A cross-cultural survey of some sex differences in socialization. *Journal of Abnormal and Social Psychology,* 1957, 55, 327–32.

Baumrind, Diana. Child care practices anteceding three patterns of preschool behavior. *Genetic Psychological Monographs,* 1967, 75, 43–88.

Baumrind, Diana, and Black, A. E. Socialization practices associated with dimensions of competence in preschool boys and girls. *Child Development,* 1967, 38, 291–327.

Bayley, Nancy. Mental growth in young children. *Yearbook of the National Society for the Study of Education,* 1940, 39, No. 2, 11–47.

Bayley, Nancy. *The Two Year Old.* Durham, N.C.: The Durham Education Improvement Program, 1966.

Bee, Helen L. Parent-child interaction and distractibility in 9-year-old children. *Merrill-Palmer Quarterly,* 1967, *13,* 175–90.

Bernstein, B. Aspects of language and learning in the genesis of the social process. In D. Hymes (Ed.), *Language in Culture and Society. A Reader in Linguistics and Anthropology.* New York: Harper & Row, 1964. Pp. 251–63.

Bower, T. G. R. The visual world of infants. *Scientific American,* 1966, *215,* 80–92.

Brim, O. G., Jr. *Education for Child Rearing.* New York: Russell Sage Foundation, 1959.

Chilman, Catherine S. *Growing Up Poor. An Over-View and Analysis of Child-Rearing and Family Life Patterns Associated with Poverty.* Washington, D.C.: Division of Research, Welfare Administration, U.S. Department of Health, Education, and Welfare, 1966.

Coleman, J. S., Campbell, E. Q., Hobson, Carol J., McPartland, J., Mood, A. M., Weinfeld, F. D., and York, R. L. *Equality of Educational Opportunity.* Washington, D.C.: U. S. Office of Education (Superintendent of Documents Catalog No. FS5.238.38001), 1966.

Colson, Elizabeth. Competence and incompetence in the context of independence. *Current Anthropology,* 1967, 8, 92–111.

Coopersmith, S. *The Antecedents of Self-Esteem.* San Francisco: W. H. Freeman & Co., 1967.

Crandall, Virginia, Katkovsky, W., and Crandall, V. J. Children's beliefs in their own control of reinforcement in intellectual-academic achievement situations. *Child Development,* 1965, *36,* 91–109.

Du Bois, Cora. *The People of Alor.* Minneapolis: University of Minnesota Press, 1944.

Erikson, E. Identity and the life cycle. *Psychological Issues,* 1959, *1,* No. 1.

Ezekiel, R. S. The personal future and Peace Corps competence. *Journal of Personality and Social Psychology, Monograph Supplement,* 1968, 8, No. 2 (Part 2).

Festinger, L. A theory of social comparison processes. *Human Relations,* 1954, 7, 117–40.

Fiske, D. W., and Maddi, S. R. *Functions of Varied Experience.* Homewood, Ill.: The Dorsey Press, 1961.

Flavell, J. H. *The Developmental Psychology of Jean Piaget.* Princeton, N.J.: D. Van Nostrand Co., 1963.

Foote, N. N., and Cottrell, L. S., Jr. *Identity and Interpersonal Competence. A New Direction in Family Research.* Chicago: University of Chicago Press, 1955.

Gladwin, T. Social competence and clinical practice. *Psychiatry,* 1967, 30, 30–43.

Goffman, E. *The Presentation of Self in Everyday Life*. Garden City, N.Y.: Doubleday Anchor Books, 1959.

Gross, N., Mason, W. S., and McEachern, A. W. *Explorations in Role Analysis*. New York: John Wiley & Sons, 1958.

Haan, Norma. A proposed model of ego functioning: coping and defense mechanisms in relationship to IQ change. *Psychological Monographs*, 1963, 77, No. 8 (whole No. 571).

Hartmann, H. *Ego Psychology and the Problem of Adaptation*. New York: International Universities Press, 1958.

Held, R., and Hein, A. Movement-produced stimulation in the development of visually guided behavior. *Journal of Comparative and Physiological Psychology*, 1963, 56, 872–76.

Hess, R. D., and Shipman, Virginia C. Early experience and the socialization of cognitive modes in children. *Child Development*, 1965, 36, 869–86.

Hill, K. T., and Sarason, S. B. The relation of test anxiety and defensiveness to test and school performance over the elementary-school years: a further longitudinal study. *Child Development Monographs*, 1966, *31*, No. 2 (whole No. 104).

Hunt, J. McV. *Intelligence and Experience*. New York: The Ronald Press Co., 1961.

Hunt, J. McV. Intrinsic motivation and its role in psychological development. In D. Levine (Ed.), *Nebraska Symposium on Motivation 1965*. Lincoln: University of Nebraska Press, 1965. Pp. 189–282.

Hunt, J. McV. Motivation inherent in information processing and action. In O. J. Harvey (Ed.), *Motivation and Social Interaction: Cognitive Determinants*. New York: The Ronald Press Co., 1963. Pp. 35–94.

Inkeles, A. Social structure and the socialization of competence. *Harvard Educational Review*, 1966, 36, 265–83.

Jahoda, Marie. *Current Conceptions of Positive Mental Health*. New York: Basic Books, 1958.

Kagan, J., and Moss, H. A. *Birth to Maturity. A Study in Psychological Development*. New York: John Wiley & Sons, 1962.

Katz, I. The socialization of academic motivation in minority group children. In D. Levine (Ed.), *Nebraska Symposium on Motivation 1967*. Lincoln: University of Nebraska Press, 1967. Pp. 133–91.

Kavanau, J. L. Behavior of captive white-footed mice. *Science*, 1967, *155*, 1623–39.

Kozol, J. *Death at an Early Age. The Destruction of the Hearts and Minds of Negro Children in the Boston Public Schools*. Boston: Houghton Mifflin Co., 1967.

Lefcourt, H. M. Internal versus external control of reinforcement, *Psychological Bulletin*, 1966, *65*, 206–20.

Lenneberg, E. H. *Biological Foundations of Language*. New York: John Wiley & Sons, 1967.

Lewin, K. Self-hatred among Jews. In K. Lewin (Gertrud W. Lewin, Ed.), *Resolving Social Conflicts*. New York: Harper, 1948. Pp. 186–200.

Lewin, K., Dembo, Tamara, Festinger, L., and Sears, Pauline S. Level of aspiration. In J. McV. Hunt (Ed.), *Personality and the Behavior Disorders*. Vol. I. New York: The Ronald Press Co., 1944. Pp. 333–78.

Lewis, O. *Five Families. Mexican Case Studies in the Culture of Poverty*. New York: Basic Books, 1959.

Linton, R. *The Study of Man*. New York: Appleton-Century, 1936.

Loevinger, Jane. The meaning and measurement of ego development. *American Psychologist*, 1966, *21*, 195–206.
Maccoby, Eleanor E., Dowley, Edith M., Hagen, J. W., and Degerman, R. Activity level and intellectual functioning in normal preschool children. *Child Development*, 1965, *36*, 761–70.
Marlowe, D., and Crowne, D. *The Approval Motive*. New York: John Wiley & Sons, 1964.
McClelland, D., Atkinson, J. W., Clark, R. A., and Lowell, E. L. *The Achievement Motive*. New York: Appleton-Century-Crofts, 1953.
McDougall, W. *An Introduction to Social Psychology*. 14th ed. Boston: John W. Luce, 1921.
Mead, G. H. *Mind, Self, and Society*. Chicago: University of Chicago Press, 1934
Mischel, W. Theory and research on the antecedents of self-imposed delay of reward. In B. Maher (Ed.), *Progress in Experimental Personality Research*, Vol. 3. New York: Academic Press, 1966. Pp. 85–132.
Murphy, G. *Personality: A Biosocial Approach to Origins and Structure*. New York: Harper, 1947.
Murphy, Lois, *et al. The Widening World of Childhood. Paths Toward Mastery*. New York: Basic Books, 1962.
Myrdal, G. A methodological note on the principle of cumulation. In G. Myrdal, with R. Sterner and A. Rose, *An American Dilemma. The Negro Problem and Modern Democracy*. Vol. 2. New York and London: Harper & Brothers, 1944. Pp. 1065–70.
Osgood, C. E., Suci, G. J., and Tannenbaum, P. H. *The Measurement of Meaning*. Urbana: University of Illinois Press, 1957.
Piaget, J. *The Origins of Intelligence in Children*. New York: International Universities Press, 1952.
Rae-Grant, Q. A. F., Gladwin T., and Bower, E.M. Mental health, social competence and the war on poverty. *American Journal of Orthopsychiatry*, 1966, *36*, 652–64.
Riesman, D. *The Lonely Crowd*. New Haven: Yale University Press, 1950.
Rosen, B. C., and D'Andrade, R. The psychosocial origins of achievement motivation. *Sociometry*, 1959, *22*, 185–218.
Rosenberg, M. *Society and the Adolescent Self-Image*. Princeton, N.J.: Princeton University Press, 1965.
Rotter, J. B. Generalized expectancies for internal versus external control of reinforcement. *Psychological Monographs*, 1966, *80*, No. 1 (whole No. 609), 1–28.
Rotter, J. B. *Social Learning and Clinical Psychology*. Englewood Cliffs, N.J.: Prentice-Hall, 1954.
Ruebush, B. K. Anxiety. *Yearbook. National Society for the Study of Education*, 1963, *62*, No. 1, 460–516.
Sarason, I. G. Empirical findings and theoretical problems in the use of anxiety scales. *Psychological Bulletin*, 1960, *57*, 403–15.
Sarason, S. B., Davidson, K. S., Lighthall, F. F., Waite, R. R., and Ruebush, B. K. *Anxiety in Elementary School Children*. New York: John Wiley & Sons, 1960.
Sarbin, T. R. Role theory. In G. Lindzey (Ed.), *Handbook of Social Psychology*. Vol. 1. Cambridge, Mass.: Addison-Wesley Publishing Co., 1954. Pp. 223–58.
Seeman, M. On the meaning of alienation. *American Sociological Review*, 1959, *24*, 782–91.

Skolnick, Arlene. Motivational imagery and behavior over twenty years. *Journal of Consulting Psychology*, 1966, *30*, 463–78.
Smith, M. B. Competence and "mental health": problems in conceptualizing human effectiveness. In S. B. Sells (Ed.), *The Definition and Measurement of Mental Health: A Symposium*. (In press)
Smith, M. B. Explorations in competence: a study of Peace Corps Teachers in Ghana. *American Psychologist*, 1966, *21*, 555–66.
Smith, M. B. "Mental health" reconsidered: a special case of the problem of values in psychology. *American Psychologist*, 1961, *16*, 299–306.
Smith, M. B. Socialization for competence. *Items*, 1965, *19*, 17–23.
Spitz, R. A. Hospitalism: an inquiry into the genesis of psychiatric conditions of early childhood. *Psychoanalytic Study of the Child*, 1945, *1*, 53–74.
Sullivan, H. S. *Conceptions of Modern Psychiatry*. 2nd ed. New York: W. W. Norton & Co., 1953.
Veroff, J. Social comparison and the development of achievement motivation. Paper presented at the conference on Development of Achievement-Related Motives and Self-Esteem, Graduate Center, City University of New York, October 1967.
Wenar, C. Competence at one. *Merrill-Palmer Quarterly*, 1964, *10*, 329–42.
White, B. L., and Held, R. Plasticity of sensorimotor development in the human infant. In Judith Rosenblith and W. Allinsmith (Eds.), *The Causes of Behavior: Readings in Child Development and Educational Psychology*. 2nd ed. Boston: Allyn & Bacon, 1966. Pp. 60–70.
White, R. W. Competence and the psychosexual stages of development. In M. Jones (Ed.), *Nebraska Symposium on Motivation 1960*. Lincoln: University of Nebraska Press, 1960. Pp. 97–141.
White, R. W. Ego and reality in psychoanalytic theory. A proposal for independent ego energies. *Psychological Issues*, 1963, *3*, No. 3.
White, R. W. Motivation reconsidered: the concept of competence. *Psychological Review*, 1959, *66*, 297–333.
Witkin, H. A., Lewis, Helen B., Hertzman, M., Machover, Karen, Meissner, Pearl B., and Wapner, S. *Personality Through Perception*. New York: Harper, 1954.
Wylie, Ruth C. *The Self Concept*. Lincoln: University of Nebraska Press, 1961.
Yarrow, L. J. Separation from parents during early childhood. In M. L. Hoffman and Lois W. Hoffman (Eds.), *Review of Child Development Research*. Vol. 1. New York: Russell Sage Foundation, 1964. Pp. 89–136.
Young, D. Memorandum of suggestions for research in the field of social adjustment. *American Journal of Sociology*, 1941, *46*, 873–86.

RONALD LIPPITT

EIGHT *Improving the Socialization Process*

CONTENTS

Basic, systematic knowledge about the socialization process and its patterning in society is an important area of scientific curiosity. This knowledge is also a resource much needed by many participants in the society whom we will call socialization agents and agencies.

The preceding chapters have reviewed the current status of core areas of knowledge about the socialization process and have organized it conceptually so that we can comprehend more adequately the complexities and dimensions of this area of research and theory. But the achievement of comprehensibility does not guarantee the utilization of this body of knowledge as a resource to improve the process of socialization and resocialization of children and adults.

Utilizing theory and research about socialization poses quite new and different problems from those of research productivity, methodological rigor, and conceptual sophistication. We have to focus on a series of engineering and policy problems, such as:

(1) How do we identify the situations and phenomena where improvement is needed?

(2) Who are the socialization agents and agencies whose performance must be improved?

(3) What are the problems of change and resistance to change of socialization situations and agents?

(4) What are some of the models for innovating change in socialization goals and procedures, and in the roles of socialization agents?

Coping with these questions requires utilization of knowledge from fields other than socialization research and theory; for example, social-value theory, research and theory on social change, intervention theory and technology, and research on education and re-education. This chapter can only make illustrative probes into this complex area of socialization engineering. Another volume of the same scope as the present one would be required to encompass the major dimensions of

This chapter was prepared with the assistance of Dodd Bogart.

the task of changing and improving the socialization structures and processes of the society.

The posture of the socialization agent must be quite different from that of the socialization researcher. The agent must always face the fact of taking action with incomplete knowledge. He must blend tentative-mindedness with decision-confidence; he must feel free to act without inhibition, but also without dogmatism. Scientists, free from the pressure and responsibility to act, feel constrained to "wait until we have better data." This often means that the socialization agent is deprived of "the best that is known right now" and must act on even less adequate resources.

This chapter focuses primarily on the improvement of the socialization of children rather than the resocialization of adults. We do consider a special case of adult resocialization — that of changing the performance of the adult socialization agents. This is not a shift to a new occupational role, as illustrated in some of Brim's examples, but rather a change in orientation and performance of the same role, for example, of teacher or parent.

Our first step of analysis is to identify a variety of socialization phenomena, typical decisions of socialization agents, and socialization consequences. The illustrations include actions of individual persons as socialization agents and also the behavior of groups or organizations acting as agents.

SOCIALIZATION AGENTS AND AGENCIES IN ACTION

Each of the following episodes presents very briefly the activity of a socialization agent or agency. Each activity is described in terms of a socialization decision, a socialization action or intervention, and a socialization consequence.

Parent and Child

Socialization decisions: Laura and Jack Martins are in their dressing room about 11:00 P.M. talking about their fourteen-year-old daughter, Jean. Laura says to her husband, "I just don't like the idea of Jean's hanging around with those friends of hers instead of coming home after school. I never see her anymore until about 5:30 or 6:00, and she is very evasive about who she's been with and what she's been doing. I wish you'd speak to her and get her straightened out about the kind of friends she has and what she does with them." Jack replies with a frown, "You know I'm not around to follow through on a thing like that, and anyway, I don't see that you have any facts to support the idea that she is doing anything wrong. We certainly can't control who she picks for friends, and it seems to me that she's too old for us to be making her come home after school when they have so many activities around school these days." Laura replies angrily, "Well, I don't believe we have any right to neglect our daughter and her welfare this way. She's not old enough to take care of herself with all those older boys around the school. If you won't do anything, I will. I am going to lay down the law about her getting home after school." After a pause, Jack comments, "It seems to me you are being overprotective because the other two are off to college and Jean is the last and only one at home. It seems to me it would be worthwhile for you to find something to do — like a job — where you could develop new interests and use your energy instead of fretting about Jean."

Socialization action: The next morning at breakfast Jean's mother gives her firm instructions about coming home from school and clearly communicates her disapproval and distrust of Jean's after-school time. Jean perceptively notices that her father says nothing and gives her a friendly pat on the back as she starts off for school.

Socialization consequence: Very angry at her mother and determined somehow to get around her restrictions, Jean walks to school. She knows, without articulating it to herself, that her mother and father are not in agreement, and she knows that when she defies her mother she can expect some kind of sympathy and support from her father.

Teacher and Classroom Group

Socialization decisions: Miss Frank is sitting home in the evening thinking about her third-grade classroom group. She is particularly concerned about the language-communication period in which the children do composition, reading, and preparation of reports. Some of the children get through very quickly and seem bored and unchallenged, while others seem to be struggling beyond their depth and need a lot more help than they are getting. She decides that, starting tomorrow, she will place the children into three ability groupings on the basis of their facility in reading and expression, and will spend more time working with the less articulate group, giving the more advanced group extra assignments to do.

Socialization action: The next morning Miss Frank reads off the names of the members of the three new groups for the communication period and asks them to regroup themselves and make separate clusters of seats in three parts of the room. She says this is to make it easier and more fun for everybody to work on reading and making reports.

Socialization consequences: As the children are shifting their seats, Nancy says to her friend Jane, "Well, I guess she is putting me in the dummy group. I wish I could spell as well as you do, so we could be in the same group." Jim says to his friend Jack, "I wish I was going to be in the same group you are. She is putting me in the fast group. That means we will get a lot of extra work. I don't like that. And the group is mostly girls which I don't like either." Jack replies, "That's what you get for being smart."

Policeman and Boy

Resocialization decision and action: Lieutenant Scott, sitting at his desk in the Juvenile Bureau facing fifteen-year-old Larry Olds, who is in for his third offense in the past four months, says, "What's the trouble with you, Larry? What's come over you this year?" Larry sullenly replies, "I don't know. It seems that every time I do something to have a little fun with the fellows, some cop is around and picks me up. I don't know why they pick on me. They don't do anything to most of the rest of the fellows. And they all do the same things." Lieutenant Scott responds, "Well, I'm going to give you just one more chance. And if you get into trouble again, you are going to court. The big trouble is the older fellows you are hanging around with. You have got to stay away from them. So I want you to come into the Juvenile Bureau every afternoon after school. Bring some books so you can study. If you can stay away from your buddies and get some school work done, maybe it will help you straighten out."

Resocialization consequence: In the hall at school the next day, Jerry speaks to Larry, "What did old Scott have to say? What did he do to you?" Larry, grinning and shrugging his shoulders, replies, "Aw, he gave me a bawling out and said I have to come in to study every day after school so I won't get in trouble with all my bad friends." Jerry, laughing, says, "What a screwball he is . . . a sourpuss when a fellow tries to have a little fun. The fellows are going to meet at the drive-in tonight. I'll pick you up. Dick and I were thinking it would be fun to skip school sometime next week and see if we can catch a freight over to the city and back. See if we can make it all in one day with no money. How about that for some fun?" Larry replies enthusiastically, "That's a real brainy idea. You can count on me."

Older Brother and Younger Brother

Socialization decision: Jim says to his eighth-grade classmate Bob, at the lunch period, "A bunch of us are going to have a skateboard rodeo after school at the new cement parking lot on Forest Hill. How about coming along?" Bob answers enthusiastically, "That's tremendous. We could really set up a good obstacle course over there. How about coming by after school, and we can go over together." Jim somewhat hesitantly adds, "But let's not take Barry (Bob's sixth-grade brother) along, huh?

Bob feelingly replies, "I'm with you on that. He's my brother and all that, but he is just too young for our gang."

Socialization action: It's after school, and Bob is coming down the stairway of his home, from his bedroom, with his much prized skateboard under his arm. His brother Barry sees him from the kitchen and shouts, "Where are you going?" Bob replies, "Just out with some of the fellows." Barry shouts, "Just a second, I'll be right with you. I've got my board out back." Bob, feeling irritated and guilty, responds, "Naw, it's just a little bunch of fellows, and they invited me, but they didn't invite you." Barry continues persistently, "Aw, that's all right, they won't mind. I'm just as good as any of them on the board." Bob shouts angrily, "Listen, squirt, this is my gang, and they don't want you, see. It's just for us older fellows."

Socialization consequences: Barry is gazing dejectedly after his older brother who is running down the front walk to meet Jim. He is thinking to himself, "Why are the Junior High kids always down on me? I can do things just as well as they can. My brother is the meanest of all. Wait till I get to be his age. I'll show him. It's no fun to be a sixth grader. I wish I was older."

Best Friend

Socialization decision and action: High schooler Sue Ann wants "desperately" to see the movie and has just gotten permission from her mother to take the evening off. But she certainly doesn't want to go alone. Her best friend, Marion, just "must" go. It would be such fun to see it together and have a pizza and talk about it afterwards. She calls Marion and enthusiastically invites her. There is a pause, and Marion says, "Gee, Sue, I've got all that math he gave us today. You don't have it done, do you?" Sue Ann answers, "No, of course not. But this is the last night of the show, and we can tell him we lost our assignment, or we can get Sally to give it to us in study hall in the morning. She will have it all done, and it will all be correct." Marion hesitantly responds, "Well, I don't know. He will be pretty mad if we don't hand it in. But if you think Sally will help us . . ." Sue Ann eagerly says, "Sure she will. She is one of my best friends. She wouldn't say no. And I helped her once. Anyway, school work is not the most important thing in this world." Marion adds hastily, "You're darn right it isn't. Let's go and have a little fun. And to heck with it. I've been studying too hard anyway."

Socialization consequence: The next morning at school at the beginning of the second period Sue Ann meets Marion at the study-hall door and states, "I've got Sally's paper. Here it is. She was a little mad about it. But it's OK. I fixed it up. But she says we have to each get one problem wrong so as not to do it just like she did. Let's each make it a different problem. That ought to fool him, OK?" Marion laughs and replies, "That's a tricky idea. Anyway, who cares whether we get a B instead of an A. Like you said, school's not so important. There are other things in this world."

Employer and Worker

Resocialization decision: Jack Simpson, president of a small but flourishing company, is talking with Cox, supervisor of the records section. Simpson states, "They promised us they'd have the machines in in two months. Then you can have one of the best records systems in the business. We will really be on top of inventory and sales as well as accounts." Bert Cox replies with anxious concern, "Well, you know I'm going to need about four less fellows to handle the operation. What are we going to do about them? Most of them have been with us for quite a while." The president replies, "We'll just have to do the best we can for them. If they can fit in someplace else we ought to use them; otherwise I'll ask personnel to help them look around for other opportunities. We are expanding our sales force. Let's offer them a chance to take sales training and see if they can make out on the road. Maybe they've got some real hidden talent. We'll pay them their regular wages during the training period. They ought to appreciate that."

Resocialization action: Wally Jenson, one of Bert Cox's records staff, was told about the impending change and was offered the opportunity to take the two-week sales course. He had to have a trial period to see how the course would work out. Wally responded without too much hesitation, and has begun the course sessions. He is feeling somewhat uncomfortable, surrounded by younger, quite assertive fellow class members. The readings and lectures on salesmanship seem to reveal a rather foreign land. In the role-playing session this morning he felt rather depressed by his fellow students' critique that he hadn't sounded like he really wanted to sell the client the product because he seemed so hesitant to "push it across."

Resocialization consequences: Wally Jenson is beginning to realize from his resocialization experiences in the retraining course that he is really on the threshold of a rather major change in his conception of himself, his style of life, and his family role as husband and father. He is beginning to feel tense and quite uncertain about this whole potential "change of life" situation. He is beginning to feel hostile toward the company, uncertain about himself, and guilty about what is going to happen to his family life as he moves into the role of traveling salesman.

Husband and Wife

Resocialization decision: Harry Inglis is driving home from work along the freeway. His mind is wandering a bit. There is a sense of pride as he thinks of his oldest daughter, Jennifer, finishing her first year of teaching and planning to be married next summer to a very fine, young pediatrician. Then his mind moves to his son Harvey, who, in the middle of his junior year at the state university, is doing very well, and has just made the decision to go into business administration. Then, rather painfully, his thoughts flow to his wife Ruth at home, a few miles ahead, alone in their good-sized suburban home, maybe two cocktails ahead of him, feeling a bit neglected. Ruth just wasn't so much fun, for herself or for him, these days. It was high time he pushed harder on the idea of her beginning to take some classes at the community college and exploring job possibilities that would give her some focal interest outside of herself and the empty house. The spasmodic interludes of bowling, women's club, and volunteer work were certainly not resulting in any significant commitment or sense of meaningful activity.

Resocialization action: Over a second drink, Ruth is babbling on, "And Suzanne was telling me this morning that the Sheraton girl is pregnant. I just couldn't believe it. They seem like such a nice family. But then I did hear that Jim (her father) has taken to staying in the city several nights a week to work at the office and that doesn't look very good to me." Harry interrupts, "Listen, Ruth, you know I couldn't care less about all this gossip and stuff, but I do care that this seems to be all there is for you to think about and be interested in. Why don't you agree right now to start with that course in social service over at the college and talk to the employment office about interesting jobs. I hear they have some very interesting things to do in the antipoverty program." Ruth lightly replies, "So you want to get rid of me, huh? Time for old mama to get out in the big world." Harry answers, "You know that's not it. I'm just concerned that there's not much to do around the house anymore, and without the kids you need a new interest or things will just go from bad to worse." After a long pause Ruth says, "I guess you are right. I'll go down and see them tomorrow. I just can't think of anything that seems very interesting to do."

Resocialization consequences: Ruth meets her husband at the door looking younger and very much alive. "It looks like I may be getting a part-time job over at the new neighborhood center. They need someone to go and visit the mothers of the preschool children they are working with. I've only had the one social service course, but they are putting on a special training program and they think I will be qualified to tackle it. And do you know that in half of those homes, there is no father at all. . . ."

Downtown Church

Socialization decision: The big, downtown church is located in what has now become a typical central-city neighborhood. Reverend Peterson, meeting with his board of directors, says, "As you know there is a great lack of resources for the leisure-time activities of young people in this neighborhood. A lot of them have gotten into serious difficulties, or will, if they don't get additional help. Some of them are dropouts, and most of them are pretty seriously alienated from school and also from their parents. A lot of them, of course, come from broken families. We know we just can't open our doors and expect that they will come in to use our facilities. They are suspicious, and they don't have any experience or skills in developing programs for themselves. We'll have to make what they call 'an outreach effort' if we really want to be of service, and we've got to be prepared for rebuffs and suspicion. It takes time and patience to prove to these young people that you are not down on them and plotting to 'do something to them.'" After a lengthy discussion the board agrees that the church should take the initiative with an outreach program and agrees with Reverend Peterson that he should try to recruit the interests of some of the younger men and women in the church to spend some volunteer time, and should use some financial resources to get one or more experts to hold some training sessions for the volunteers and to purchase whatever modest program materials and food might be needed to start a pilot program.

Socialization action: Four young men — two married and two unmarried — and six women — four of them unmarried — responded to the call for volunteers and are participating in a series of five seminar sessions to acquaint themselves with the facts about poverty, alienated young people, and the neighborhood in which they will be working. They have each committed themselves to the following tasks: finding out how many young people are living in particular blocks, making personal contact and extending personal invitations to several girls and boys to get them to attend an initial, get-acquainted social affair, and discussing their interest in forming one or more groups for a discussion and activity program where their ideas would be used as much as possible.

Socialization consequences: Most of the members of the board are satisfied and say to their colleagues in private that the church is taking some initiative instead of "sitting by." The volunteers themselves are having trouble initiating contact with their would-be clients, are convinced that it is an important thing to do, feel quite uncertain about their own skills and resources, and are wishing they had had more training for this kind of work. Some of the neighborhood young people have been very cautious in their contacts and noncommital in response to the invitation to come to a meeting; others have walked by the church building several times wondering what it's like inside; others are feeling quite secure about the idea of going together to look it over and see what it is like. Neither the leaders nor the youths have had any basic confrontations yet of the differences in their backgrounds, value systems, and potentialities for educating each other.

The Board of Education

Socialization decision: The board of education is listening to the superintendent present a recommendation that the board allot certain funds, to be supplemented by antipoverty funds, for the recruiting, training, and employment of a group of teacher's aides who would be assigned to work with elementary school teachers in the schools and classrooms where there is the greatest need for educational help and the greatest range of ability in motivation within the classroom group. One of the board members queries, "Is this mostly just to give more manpower to keep the kids in order?" The superintendent replies, "No, that's not the idea we have in mind. This has been the approach in some of the other programs, but my conviction is that in the long run each teacher should have two or three educational aides who are working under her supervision to do significant professional work in assisting the learning activities of individuals or small groups of children within the room. This would be a pilot start in that direction to see what types of persons can be recruited and how much we can do to give them careful training as sub-professionals." The board approves the recommendation for the new program.

Socialization action: At the level of the adults, a variety of women in the community — middle-aged, former teachers who have been raising their own children for the past fifteen or twenty years, a number of young married women with no children, and a number of single girls who must work while going to night school — find themselves involved in a new and challenging occupational role, and the regular classroom teachers find themselves coping with quite a new role as classroom managers. At the level of the children, many of them begin to find it possible to have some continuity of contact with an adult during the classroom day when they need help, and they find themselves working in smaller classroom groupings where there is invitation and opportunity to express themselves even though their ideas may not be the best and may not come out the fastest.

Socialization consequences: Some of the educational aides are finding it quite difficult, in contrast to their years as parent with their own child, or their relations to younger sisters as older sibs, to take a professional attitude and role with the children. Others are finding the opportunity tremendously challenging and are already planning for further professional training with the idea of becoming certified teachers. Some of the regular classroom teachers are finding themselves very threatened by the way in which things have changed so that they are no longer *the* central figure for all the children at all times. Some of the children clearly are identifying with the classroom aide, and she is showing remarkable competence, somewhat threatening, for "an untrained person." Some of the children are finding it an interesting game to play off one grown-up against the other to get their way more often and more efficiently; others are finding a great release in the opportunity to get more support and help, to be noticed, to receive feedback about their achievement efforts, and to relate to someone who seems to be able to "be a little closer to them."

Council of Social Agencies

Socialization decision: At the weekly staff meeting, several members have brought up the fact that there is an increasing variety of demands and needs for volunteer manpower which seems to go beyond the resources and training plans of the various individual agencies. In addition, one of the staff members has cited a recent report of the great value which seemed to emerge from a central training program that gave basic training to volunteers from a variety of agencies. Evidently it had been possible to provide a more professional level of training, and also the workers from the different agencies seemed to gain a great deal from their contact with each other and the perspective they could give from the background of their various programs. At the end of an hour's discussion, the staff agreed that the council ought to provide cross-agency training programs for volunteers and sub-professionals and seminars for professionals on a regular basis.

Socialization action: The council announced these new training opportunities and initiated a training program for volunteer youth workers and a seminar for professional youth workers from all types of educational, recreation, leisure-time, and religious-education agencies.

Socialization consequences: They received a great deal of negative feedback from some agencies and very positive response from others. The workers from the agencies which did participate began to discover many potentialities for collaboration and cross-referral, were able to profit a great deal from sharing types of group work practices from one setting to another, and began to identify many omissions and duplications in the program opportunities available to various age groups, sex groups, and children from different neighborhoods.

City Council

Socialization decision: The city council has before it a proposal from two of the council members to establish a city youth council which would have on it representatives from all youth-serving programs including agencies, school systems, churches, etc. It was also proposed that the chairman of the youth council should sit ex officio on the city council as a linkage or liaison between "youth affairs" and "city affairs." After much wrangling and hassling, the idea was changed considerably to an invitation to all student councils and other youth groups to send representatives as observers to city council meetings to "learn how the city does its work" so that they could help the young people understand city affairs.

Socialization action: A letter from the mayor went to all the appropriate organized youth units in the community.

Socialization consequences: The discussions in most of the groups were quite desultory, and the members seemed uninterested. In a few groups there were active discussions which usually focused on the theme "Who wants to sit and be an observer? Why don't they trust us to meet and think about what ought to be done to improve things like delinquency and drinking in town and to make recommendations to the city council for things that ought to be done?" Very few representatives turned up as observers at the council meetings. A few council members noted this circumstance and felt it confirmed their belief that "the young people aren't interested in this kind of thing." Others didn't even remember the invitation.

These brief illustrations remind us of the great variety and continuous flow of policy decisions, intervention actions, and consequent reactions making up the complex network of socialization events which provide the context for the lives of children, youth, and adults in every community. These symptoms of fragmentation, discontinuity, lack of coordination, and poor communication provide a basis for dis-ease about the quality and effectiveness of the socialization process. Let us look more carefully at who the socialization agents and agencies are and the problems they have in carrying out their functions.

THE SOCIALIZATION AGENTS

Who Are the Socialization Agents and Agencies?

The daily socialization mazeway of the child and youth is indeed a medley of intervention. Many of the inputs are competing for attention and time; some are conflicting in their messages; there are great variations in the type of relationship offered by, and expected with, the socialization agents.

Our typical child starts the day with some brief, but often intensive and conflicting, input from two parents, which often deals with expectations about getting up, dressing, eating behavior, school homework commitments, after-school schedule, etc. In addition the child may observe an older sibling's behavior or may react to expectations of a younger sibling. On the way to school there may be social-control inductions from a school bus driver, a street-corner citizen traffic aide, or a policeman alert to the deviant behavior of youthful bicyclists, pedestrians, scooter drivers, and secondhand car navigators. At school a variety of teachers compete for priority, provide very different relationship models, and articulate quite varied standards about work, independence, cooperation, competition, and definitions of legitimate and illegitimate relations with fellow students. There is opportunity to observe and experiment with modeling after the behavior of older students and status figures within one's own age group. At noon the cafeteria supervisor or lunchroom manager is in watchful waiting. After school there may be extracurricular activities led by the same adults who have been teachers during the classroom day but who are attempting to play a different role in these volunteer groupings. For some there may be a club meeting led by a volunteer adult sponsored by one of the leisure-time program agencies. The proprietor of the drug store has a watchful eye as the young one thumbs through items on the newsstand. His posture of distrust and disapproval blends with the hurriedly thumbed-through pictures and messages which carry a set of messages quite different from those coming from the volunteer leader and curriculum materials of the weekly Sunday school class or youth fellowship group.

Back at home again the TV set adds its input of messages from the commercials and programs aimed at the young ones, or aimed at uneducated adults and timed for the young ones to observe. Siblings and parents become a part of the end-of-the-day input along with a couple of telephone calls from friends which support the collusive collaboration of the peer culture to avoid, or make as easy as possible, some of the work demands and schedule demands of the adult subcultures. All in all it has been a day full of many demands and conflicting messages.

The Segments of the Socialization Community

Most frequently, perhaps, we think of the community as an economic community, a political community, or a physical community. But it is just as valid, and for our purposes more important, to think of the community as a *socialization community*. In our studies of community functionings, we have identified a number of clusters of personnel that have a vested interest in influencing the behavior and values of children and youth. Each of the following clusters has a program of socialization, more or less planned, and more or less formally presented as a program to influence the growth and development of information, attitudes, values, and behavior of the younger members of the community.

(1) The formal education system, public and private.
(2) The churches with their programs for children and youths.
(3) The leisure-time agencies with their recreational, cultural, and character education programs.
(4) The social control and protection agencies such as the police, courts, traffic-safety agents, etc.
(5) The therapeutic, special correction, and resocialization services such as counselors, remedial clinics, and programs for the handicapped.
(6) Employment offices and work supervisors who hire the young and supervise them on their paid jobs.
(7) Political leaders who have an interest in involving the young in political activities such as civil rights protests.

In addition to these seven personnel clusters which have more or less articulated programs and professionalized socialization agents, there are the following two additional populations of agents:

(8) The subculture of parents.
(9) The subculture of like-age and older peers.

And in addition to these populations of "direct agents" there is the population of agents who control and distribute the socialization interventions of the mass media — the TV programs, the radio programs, newspaper stories, and newsstand materials. These ten vested interest clusters we will call the segments of the socialization community. Let us look at their structure and functioning a little more carefully.

The Structure of the Socialization Community

Many of the key socialization agents of the community never come in contact with the socializees, except perhaps in their role as parents. Within each socialization segment there is a variety of agencies or institutions with socialization objectives. Usually there is a policy-making board of directors made up of laymen or professionals or both (for example, the board of education, committee on religious education, agency board, company-management committee, etc.) Under this board there are typically program administrators and program designers who both prepare the materials that carry the messages of the socialization programs and plan the procedures for reaching the young ones or adults who are the targets and clients of the program effort. Under the administrators and programmers are the professional direct workers (for example, teachers, group workers, counselors, policemen, etc.) or volunteer workers (for example, scoutmasters, big brothers, Sunday school teachers, and club leaders) who receive training and supervision from professional workers.

Another way to look at the components of the socialization structure is to differentiate those agents which assume an informal role of agent without official delegation and sanction by the community, such as older peers, sibs, high-status peer-group members, neighbors, storekeepers, etc., from those agents who are delegated to take a socialization responsibility as representatives of some segment of society or of the total society. In this group of formally delegated agents we can differentiate between the nonprofessional and the professional or sub-professional agents. The nonprofessional agents would include parents, babysitters, and other parent substitutes, volunteer recreational group leaders, Sunday school teachers, political leaders, and in some degree, employers. The professional and sub-professional agents include teachers, recreation specialists, social group workers, policemen, counselors, reading and speech correction specialists, etc.

We can also think of the socialization agents as either direct or indirect agents. Most of the policy makers and program designers have no direct contact with the young ones. They work indirectly through the population of direct workers. This is also true of those who exert their influence through the mass media. Finally we must remember that the term *socialization agent* does not necessarily denote an individual. It may refer to a group, or even an agency or institution which plans and initiates interventions.

PROBLEMS OF THE SOCIALIZERS: GOALS AND VALUES

If we are to derive and develop ideas for the improvement of socialization, we must identify the key problems facing the agents. Some of these problems are ones of value criteria, that is, formulating socialization objectives; others are of quality of performance; still others are of collaboration and coordination between agents and agencies. Our brief selection of priority problems follows.

Formulating Articulate Socialization Goals

If we interview parents, teachers, or other socialization agents about what they believe is expected of them in the way of products of their socialization effort, we usually get a variety of vague and often inconsistent formulations of what they hope children and youth will become as a consequence of their socializing efforts. Parents, of course, have received very little in the way of orientation to socialization goals or expectations, but even the volunteers and professionals who have received agency training and supervision can speak easily about activities, fairly articulately about methods, but only haltingly about goals or desired outcomes. They can talk about desirable learning activities but are quite unclear as to whether the desired end product of these activities is a certain state of information in the child, a certain attitude toward learning, certain skills at learning activity, or certain resultant values. In most cases there seems to be a combination of lack of communication of outcome expectations, ambiguity about what expectations are communicated, and a lack of connecting ideas about how ideal outcomes relate to the concrete material about methods and activities which usually is communicated in the training activities.

A second problem one quickly discovers in discussions with teachers about goals and methods is that they are confused about the conflicting messages they have received from such "authoritative sources" as various professors of education, statements of the board of education, the dictates of their administrators, the consultative advice of their supervisors, and the input from parents. One message says that the student's academic achievement is the primary desired outcome and that a rigorous program of work with high standards is the method; another message agrees that achievement is a primary value but stresses that a permissive program of stimulation of self-inquiry and a dependence on the development of self-motivation is the method; another message says that learning how to learn and the methods of solving problems, rather than any particular subject-matter mastery, is the major outcome objective; and a fourth message says that the social emotional adjustment, the mental health, and the personality growth of the child is the primary outcome value requiring individualized concern about success experience and the development of social relation skills and positive self-evaluation. These competing and conflicting inductions from the experts and the power figures confuse the conscientious socialization agents, and they receive very little help in thinking through the problems involved in arriving at their own professional judgment.

Projecting Personal Needs as Socialization Goals

With all this lack of agreement about goals and the lack of professionalization of goal orientations, it is no wonder that much of the goal orientation of many socialization agents seems to be primarily a projection of their own personal needs derived from the background of their own socialization experiences and their reactions to them. One study has indicated that a large proportion of the volunteers and professionals providing group leadership of children and youth perceive themselves as having to substitute for inadequate parents, with consequent attitudes of hostility towards the parents and competitive efforts to "win the children." Some teachers find, when they are faced with the situation of team teaching, practice teachers, or classroom aides that they are quite threatened by someone else's "getting close to the children" or dividing up the teaching activity by relating to different subgroups. The fact is that their major source of personal satisfaction is the positive dependency relationship of all the young ones. Becoming a manager rather than a direct controller of the socialization experience program of the children is unsatisfying because their major personal need is to be the central figure for each child.

Many socialization agents project into the desired socialization outcome of "becoming a good citizen" the meaning of teaching children obedience and conformity to what is expected of them. From this conception they easily rationalize a basis for satisfying their own authoritarian control needs by operating a socialization regime which expects and demands grateful submissiveness and dependency. There is often wrathful indignation when the young ones demonstrate ingratitude "for all I've done for them."

Another frequent projection of personal need is manifested by the socialization agent who tries to "become one of the kids" and vigorously projects goals of "keeping hands off and letting every child become himself" or of "they'll be growing all right if they are having fun." This type of projection is often based on a personal anti-authority posture in which the socialization agent is implicitly ganging up with the kids against the grown-ups, so that he not only abrogates his responsibility of representing adult socialization goals but often actively joins collusively in trying to subvert the efforts of other societal agents. This discussion is just a small sample of the complex motivational issues which underlie to some degree the socialization ideology of all agents. It points to the great need both for active programs of training which place emphasis on the clarification and operationalization of socialization goals and for the attainment of self-awareness as an important step in achieving responsible role taking as a parent, teacher, club leader, counselor, employer, or any other significant socialization role.

Linking the Goals of Society and the Values of the Socializee

The problem of formulating and pursuing appropriate socialization goals is made even more complex by the fact that the child or youth is continuously in the process of formulating a set of personal goals and values which are emergent from his coping with and using the input from the great variety of experiences with all socialization agents and also from his coping with his own internal experience of maturation and problem-solving experimentation. So the young one develops his own expectations, hopes, and demands as he interacts with socialization agents. He initiates input as well as receives it. The sensitive socialization agent must accept and support this development of personalized initiative and identity as well as take responsibility for representing the values and expectations of the larger society. This dual loyalty-responsibility of being a two-way linking agent is one of the most central and challenging aspects of the role of socialization agent. The detached gang worker must represent some of the needs and interests of the delinquent gang to his agency and must represent the agencies' norms and values to the gang; the effective classroom teacher must sometimes negotiate with the principal or the parents in the interests of her classroom group as well as influence the development of norms and expectations within the classroom group. The parent is faced with the difficult problem of being a sensitive linkage between the angry neighbor and her child, or the juvenile officer and her teen-ager. By and large the skills of creative compromise ending in negotiation are not part of the training and value orientation of the socialization agent. This is a serious omission.

Value Problems of Intervention Policy

The question of when to intervene and when to leave the socializee on his own to generate his own initiative toward growth and development is the most important value judgment which socialization agents must continuously make. One of the issues which frequently comes up in this decision situation is whether a permissive "leave him on his own" policy will in fact be a supportive opportunity or will be experienced as neglect and rejection by the young one. Much permissive behavior of socialization agents is the result of avoiding decision making rather than making a thoughtful decision in the interests of the socializee. Another decision problem emerges from the fear of indoctrinating the young one with one's own particular values or of competing with the values of some other more centrally responsible agent such as the parents. A third illustrative problem is the issue of whether or not to step in vigorously and often forcibly in order to protect the child from doing himself or society harm. The consequences of following the policy of "letting him learn his own lesson" are often more destructive than instructive. But this is not always so. Skilled decision making is needed.

Substantive Content Goals versus Methodological Process Goals

"Should we teach him *what* he should believe or *how he should decide* what to believe?" This question represents one of the most challenging dilemmas for all types of socialization agents working with children, youth, or adults on problems of socialization or resocialization. Research seems to indicate that the way in which the socialization agent answers this question will determine whether the young one learns his values as rigid, unchanging guides or whether he achieves criteria for value judgment which permit him to examine and change his values as he changes and as his society changes. Currently there is much interest in the field of education in formulating an educational program which will stimulate learning to learn rather than focus on specific information acquisition. But certainly a great deal of content must be learned, and learned in such a way that it is quickly and flexibly available as a resource for action and for further learning. The socialization agent must find a creative blend for these two policy orientations.

The Lack of Dialogue about Socialization Goals

Why is there such a lack of dialogue about socialization goals, both within and between the segments of the socialization community? This seems to be one of the most serious problems affecting the performance and the formulation of objectives of all socialization agents.

One major inhibition of dialogue seems to be the fact that at some level of awareness most socialization agents feel guilty or anxious because they are not accomplishing as much with the young ones as they either would like to or feel they are expected to. Thus to get into dialogue about the problem would be to expose themselves to the negative evaluation of others and also to confront themselves with the problem. Of course part of the reason for the discrepancy between ideal and actual achievement derives from the ambiguity and vagueness about goals and therefore the lack of opportunity to get any realistic feedback about the degree of success.

Another problem is that most socialization agents, both professional and nonprofessional, seem to feel apologetic about being "philosophical" or "idealistic" or "theoretical." Somehow these are the opposite of being practical and realistic. It has been our discovery that once a sharing of personal values about goals has been legitimized there is a great flow of enthusiastic and very meaningful dialogue. But the assumption that "everybody else would raise their eyebrows if I talked about these things" seems to be an effective barrier to initiating significant professional conversation about goals and values.

A third posture that inhibits dialogue seems to be an attitude about autonomy and compromise. What I do with my children or my class or my club is my own private business and not open to inspection. It is part of my integrity as a person, part of my autonomy, to do things the way I do them with the young ones under my supervision. If I expose my values and my practices to others, they might influence me, they might induce me to compromise in a dialogue between me and them, and to compromise is bad. It means giving up the best for something that is less good. This peculiarly dysfunctional attitude about compromise is a deeply ingrained part of American character structure. It is quite a personal revolution to take the posture that compromise represents the potentiality for creative blending of the insights of self and others to achieve a more complete understanding, a more adequate policy, or a more skillful practice.

A fourth barrier to active dialogue about goals probably derives from our buck-passing orientation about socialization responsibilities. One way to avoid feeling too overloaded, too weighed down, by one's responsibility as a socialization client or agency is to place the core responsibility elsewhere. The school person can say, "We have to focus on his academic achievement, but that's obviously just a small part of the job." The leisure-time agency leader can say, "Our job is to provide fun and recreation, and, of course, he'll learn some things from our activities, but this isn't the serious part of growing up." And the parent is usually saying, "I'm not the expert on what he needs. I just do the best I can." A change to a posture of collaborative sharing of the responsibility is needed, but it will come only if these various barriers to active dialogue can be coped with.

PROBLEMS OF THE SOCIALIZERS: ROLES AND ACTION

Assuming we have, or could get, reasonable clarity on the policies and objectives of socialization and resocialization, there still is the critical problem of action. Good intentions may be appropriate and sophisticated, but performance still may be ineffective or lacking. We briefly review here a few of the problems of lack of action, or poor-quality action, and ineffective impact.

Derivation of the Socialization Action Strategy

Once socialization goals have been clarified, it is potentially possible to scan relevant research and theory in order to derive appropriate action designs. This kind of retrieval of knowledge to create appropriate educational engineering designs is seldom practiced. The socialization agent may feel sure that what is wanted in the socializee is a change of attitude rather than the acquisition of new information. A review of relevant research would indicate some of the necessary conditions for bringing about attitude change as contrasted to informational change. But because this type of derivation is not made, the techniques used by parents, teacher, or group leader are quite likely to be designed to bring about an increase in information but no change in attitude. For example, our studies of interpersonal dynamics in the classroom have revealed the important relationship between the child's status in the interpersonal peer-group structure of the classroom and his motivation and performance as an academic achiever. From such research information, it would be possible for socialization agents with a major objective of producing academic achievement in the child to derive some of the necessary aspects of the role of teacher as a facilitator of healthy intragroup relations as an important means toward the improvement of achievement. Such derivations are typically not made, and so the role definition of the socialization agent tends to remain relatively static and undifferentiated in spite of the growth of important relevant knowledge.

Allocation of Responsibility

As we have indicated earlier, research analyses reveal that most socialization agencies allocate a major responsibility to the parents for the early socialization of the child. But in spite of this, very few resources have been allocated to provide support and development of the parental role. Very few agencies and agents define their socialization functions in terms of its complementarity to the parental function or in terms of collaboration with parents or training of parents.

Another illustration of a lack of initiative and responsibility for defining division of labor in the raising of children is the posture typically taken by school systems that the role of the school, as a community socialization agency, must be independent of, and quite unrelated to, that of the other socialization agencies who share in making a daily impact on the child. Parents perceive school personnel as wanting and expecting them to keep their distance from the program, and interviews with teachers typically indicate their perception of parents as unqualified amateurs who are likely to create problems in the carrying out of an effective school curriculum.

Inhibitions to Manpower Utilization

The distance and distrust of the "amateurs" by the professionals in the field of socialization result in a serious lack of the development of socialization manpower to meet the tremendous and varied needs of child rearing, youth development, and resocialization. The professional change agents tend to remain blind to the very high influence exerted by nonprofessional agents in the socialization system, for example, parents, older peers, sibs, best friends, peer group, etc. As the result, there is a lack of collaboration with, and training of, key socialization resources. In addition, teachers and social workers have been slow to support the development of the variety of sub-professional social service and educational roles which are now emerging, particularly in the antipoverty program. The recruiting and training of adults and older youths, used as sub-professional educational aides in the classroom and in the community, are going to be major action strategy developments of the next decade. Appropriately recruiting and adequately utilizing this manpower will be a major responsibility of the professional workers.

Another major problem of inhibition of socialization initiative is dramatically highlighted in newspaper accounts of the lack of sense of responsibility children, youth, and adults have today for "being their brother's keepers." Several studies reinforce the newspaper reports of individuals hesitating to become involved in any way in someone else's deviancy or problems. The mother hesitates to get involved in disciplining her neighbor's child, witnesses refuse to "see" or report delinquent behavior, and the person who attempts to intervene in support of a scapegoat tends to be perceived as a "sucker" rather than to be identified as a spokesman for the rest of us, one toward whom we feel grateful for the intervention initiative. So in addition to the lack of clarity of role definition among the professionals, and the resistance to the development of sub-professional roles, we find serious restraints against assuming the role responsibility of socialization agent within the peer culture of socializees and the larger community, which has basically a keen vested interest in the fate of the socialization process but avoids perceiving and acting in terms of this basic interest.

The Quality of the Role Performance of Socializers

Because of the crucial role they play in the maintenance and development of the society, one would assume that a major effort would be made to upgrade the quality of the performance of socialization agents. It is true that we find the community highly sensitive and often irrationally outraged at some symptoms of deviancy in the performance of a socialization agent. Although this would seem to suggest that the community is concerned with the attainment of models of perfection in the role taking of its socialization agents, in reality there is very little knowledge of, or concern about, the actual interactions that take place between socialization agents and socializees. As long as "things seem to be going along OK" little attempt is made to get evaluative feedback about the success of socialization efforts or to initiate continuing programs of in-service training which would provide the basis for the development of a high-quality socialization process. In the crucial areas of nonprofessional socialization — for example, baby-sitters, older sibs, older peers, volunteer workers, and even parents — there is a lack of orientation toward training the socialization agents. The assumption seems to be that good will is enough or that care taking rather than skilled socialization agentry is all that is desired. Experimental seminars with older elementary school children on "ways of helping the youngers" have indicated a great responsiveness and eagerness to learn, and a great shift in values and behavior patterns as a result of a brief training program.

Another problem is that the training courses for both volunteers and professionals tend to emphasize cognitive, conceptual learning, without a linking of this to effective skill development. Recent studies have shown remarkably little correlation between a teacher's knowledge about child development, educational methods, or sophistication of goals and her actual performance on the job in interacting with children. These agents may be very clear on their role definition and the expectations of the society but very ineffective in role actualization.

Coordination of Role Performance

Much of the efficacy of the socialization impact on the child, youth, or adult of the various socialization agencies depends on the type of communication and coordination that takes place between agents and agencies. We have already noted this problem of coordination in the previous section on goals and values. The same basic issues are just as relevant here in terms of actual patterns of interaction with the socializee. As we have noted this may be a lack of "horizontal collaboration" between agents in the same socialization segment, such as mother and father, or between socialization segments such as parents and teachers; or it may be a lack of coordination vertically between the policy leaders, program designers, and direct workers within a given socialization segment, such as the school system, a church program, or a recreation agency. The problems for the child may be problems of competitive demands for time, incompatible models of appropriate behavior, or inconsistent behavioral styles of intervention along such dimensions as autocracy–laissez faire, formality-informality, or neglect through buck-passing by the various agencies.

There is another problem of coordination that impinges more indirectly on the socializees. This results from the lack of communication and sharing of the goals of socialization between those segments of the community which have socialization as a major concern and those segments which have a major concern for the control and management of the economic, political, and physical aspects of community life. A lack of policy support for important aspects of an educational, leisure-time, or occupational-training program in the community may result in a lack of certain important socialization roles in the development of a child or a very low quality of role taking because of the lack of resources to employ and train adequate manpower.

PROBLEMS OF APATHY, RESISTANCE, AND COUNTERACTION OF SOCIALIZEES

One of the frequent action problems of socialization agents and agencies is the lack of responsive collaboration of the young ones. Sometimes they seem to be engaged in a collusive "slow-down" or in a wildcat strike to stay away. Other times they are very much present and actively testing the authority of the would-be adult helper or teacher. Many a teacher and parent has discovered that planning to provide a new opportunity (for example, new curriculum materials) does not necessarily result in voluntary utilization of the opportunity by the children. At this point, many socialization agents react with righteous indignation and diagnoses of resistance, ignorance, ingratitude, and other evaluations. The challenge at this point is to look at the situation through the eyes of the socializee. This is crucial if we want to improve the socialization process in our society.

The effectiveness of the influence of the socialization agent does not only depend on his goals and skills but also to a high degree on the readiness and responsiveness of the socializees — the children and youths who are targets of the socializing efforts. As the young ones interact with the parent, teacher, policeman, church fellowship leader, or detached worker, they are not reacting as individuals. They are imbedded in, and highly responsive to, like-age peer groups, older peers, cross-sex associations, cross-class and cross-racial associations, etc. They are almost always coping with multiple loyalty situations as well as with the continuity or discontinuity of flow of experience from one situation and agent to another. Although young people are not officially organized into a "National Association for the Improvement of Parents and Teachers," they frequently use the techniques of slow-down, boycott, and sit-in.

Probably their single biggest problem is their lack of involvement in, or commitment to, socialization goals and a meaningful time perspective. In only rare cases do socialization agents and agencies set up collaborative structures and procedures to include the socializees in the goals and plans for their own development. Lack of involvement of the socializee ensures apathy, resentment, and conformity instead of creativity; dependency or rebellion rather than interdependence. These problems begin at a very early age level.

Coping with Inconsistent Socialization Influences

Another major issue is the discontinuities and inconsistencies of the input of the various socialization agents. The young ones may experience similarity or dissimilarity in the influences from mother, father, teacher and other agents — dissimilarity, for example, in the expectations and values held for the child's behavior.

Differences in acceptance and rejection, or evaluations of success and failure, by the different agents provide the child with many dilemmas as he moves from one socialization situation to another. Also the young one perceives with great sensitivity the degree of agreement or disagreement between mother and father, or parents and teachers. These perceptions of harmony or disagreement in the orientations of the important agents is an important determiner of the problems created for the socializee as he copes with the problems of responding to the varied sources of influence.

We have been able to differentiate at least five patterns of problem solving adopted by pupils in coping with the differences in expectations, pressures, and needs from parents, teachers, peers, and the self. We examine them briefly below. The same child may, of course, adopt several of these patterns in coping with different decision and action situations.

COMPARTMENTALIZED LOYALTY

One tempting and frequently used way to avoid the stress of conflicting loyalty pressures is to avoid the confrontation, to deny that there is an issue of conflict. Although sometimes this method requires a great deal of psychological energy, some children are remarkably successful in keeping their relationships in separate compartments of the self. When they are with their parents, their teachers and peer associates do not exist. And likewise when they are with their teacher, their parents have no psychological existence. This type of situational and relationship opportunism can be carried to remarkable lengths to avoid internal confrontation and conflict. One consequence is certainly a delay in the development of an integrated personal identity which emerges from personal decision making and from the confrontation, internalization, and integration of the many socialization influences.

THE PERVASIVE DOMINANT LOYALTY

Another way to simplify life in resolving the complexities of conflicting socialization influences is to make one of the reference sources the psychologically dominant one, providing guidance in all situations. By making loyalty to a mother or to a best peer friend the dominant loyalty, it is possible to avoid a great deal of discomfort in decision making. One can think of the other voices as irrelevant and thus stop listening to them, or can quickly and easily reject the competing messages as incorrect or misleading. In many situations of conflict between the voices of the peer group and the voices of the grown-ups, the child adopts the policy of listening to one and rationalizing a rejection of the other in order to make the decision situation easier and to avoid the pain of the "working-through" process which would be required. One of the consequences of selecting a dominant external voice among the various referent sources is that the child tends to inhibit the development and use of his own internal voice as a legitimate guide.

REJECTING THE REFERENCES

This third solution is often chosen by both young and old. It might be called "the plague on both your houses" solution. The sense of irritation and confusion which results from being exposed to inconsistent and competing demands and expectations is reacted to, in this case, by a psychological response which in effect says, "If you can't agree, then there are no authoritative standards, and I am free to do what seems most attractive to me." This resolution receives support from the child's needs for autonomy and the attractiveness of the pleasure-seeking impulse which is one of the inner voices in most decision situations. The child's experience with the inconsistencies between demands and expectations of parents, teachers, and others can easily provide the context and motivation for this "autonomy resolution."

STRIKING A BALANCE

Many children try conscientiously and anxiously to listen to all the voices and to arrive at some kind of compromise that will somehow please everybody. More frequently than not this attempt to balance all the voices in the situation results in dissatisfaction and discontent. And there is very little gain in the development of self-identity from this posture of mechanical compromise or "striking an average." This is, however, one of the most natural first attempts at resolution of the problem of the medley of voices, and usually it is the experience of lack of success in dealing with this kind of complexity which pushes the child toward finding a simpler resolution, such as the three already described.

INTEGRATION AND RECIPROCAL INFLUENCE

In this fifth pattern the child has learned that the decision and the action genuinely "belong to him" but that he has the responsibility and opportunity to listen to, and to seek out, the ideas of the others as resource material *for himself*. A second thing he has learned is that he is not just a target of influence pressure from others but that he is in a reciprocal relationship with others and has the right and responsibility to attempt to influence them and the direction of their influence attempts on him. Mental health and intellectual development flow from the pupil's discovery and development of the possibility of this basic posture of interdependence (as contrasted to independence or dependence) in interpersonal decision making and interaction. One of the basic goals of socialization is to help the pupil discover and achieve this problem solving, reciprocal-influence orientation.

The child's relationship to his peer group determines in a crucial way his response to the adult socialization agents. In a large number of classrooms the majority of the students believe that a majority of their classmates disapprove of active participation in classroom activities or of asking the teacher for help. Usually a majority of the children say that they personally do not feel this way but that most of the others do. Their behavior is guided to a high degree by perceived group norms. Students tend to perceive teachers as feeling more critical than positive toward them, and the students reciprocate by feeling negative toward, and rejecting or ignoring, the influence efforts of the teacher.

Typically the socializee has a self-conception of having a very low potency to influence socialization agents with his needs and interests. And as a consumer of socialization opportunities, he has received very little consumer training in the goals and skills of learning from adults or seeking out and using resources needed in initiating self-socialization actions. We will return to this point later.

RESOCIALIZATION OF THE SOCIALIZATION AGENTS

In the sections above we have reviewed some of the problems faced by socialization agents and agencies in coping with their crucial responsibility of rearing, educating, and guiding the young toward well-functioning adulthood. As indicated earlier we have not tried to deal with the analysis of adult resocialization at the same time. But at this point we are ready to analyze the special case of resocialization of socialization agents.

As we think about the job of training or retraining the socialization agents, what problems of effectively inducing changes in the values, attitudes, knowledge, and performance skills of these agents confront us? What problems of learning and using new knowledge and skills do the agents face? After reviewing these problems of resocialization, we will be ready to look at some concrete models of procedures for improving socialization practice.

Basically, the process of resocialization involves the mobilization and use of three types of resources: (1) resources of knowledge and practice from "outside," that is, from university centers, centers of innovation of new practice; (2) resources from one's own interpersonal work setting, from evaluation of present practice, diagnosis of readiness for change; and (3) resources from within the self, that is, linkages between new ideas and action commitments, between changes in personal value and behavior. Let us look briefly at some of the problems involved in making changes in socialization roles.

Linking Research and Development to Performance

The conception of educational engineering as an applied discipline linking basic research to educational practice has been developed to a very meager degree; and the same holds true to even a greater degree in the other areas of socialization such as social work, recreation and leisure-time programs, religious-education programs, etc. Because of the lack of socialization engineers with good scientific training, there has been very little blending of the value concerns and intervention issues of the practitioner, on the one hand, and the systematic knowledge about the process of development, of learning, and of planned change on the other hand. This lack of conceptual and operational linkage between basic research and the decisions and actions of socialization agents is a major block to the improvement of socialization practices, on the part of professionals (for example, teachers, youth workers), sub-professionals (homemaking aides, classroom aides), and nonprofessionals (parents). It seems clear from the evidence that new knowledge alone will not exert much push toward change in the performance of socialization agents. The internalization and use of new knowledge require a much more active process of interaction and confrontation than is required in such fields as agriculture and medicine.

Sharing Social Practice Inventions

If one interviews a group of parents or teachers or other socialization agents about where they get their practices from and what kind of developmental work they are doing on the improvement of practice, one learns very quickly that there is really no concept of social invention or of the systematic development and testing of innovation. Many creative practitioners are doing so many creative frontier things. But because the notion of social invention is missing from their orientation to their own role and their own field of practice, very little effort is made to document or to evaluate their practice innovations. In fact, there seem to be real inhibitions to doing so. As we probe socialization agents about why they have not shared their particular techniques with others, we discover they typically have an image of raised eyebrows on the part of colleagues — an image of "they'd think I was just blowing my horn" at the idea of sharing technical discoveries in the area of socialization practices. We find the colleagues of creative inventors also quite inhibited in seeking to get information — inhibited by the notion that their peers and supervisors expect them to be their own inventors and would negatively evaluate "imitating somebody else." So we have a great volume of creative socialization practices which remain invisible and inaccessible to review and consideration, and we also sometimes have the faddish, uncritical adoption of non-validated practices that have been poorly conceived and poorly described but that seem to be solving an important problem. These first two problems have been problems of linkage to external resources. The next two are problems of resource mobilization and use inside the system.

The Lack of Feedback

Our frequent impatience with socialization agents for their lack of effort to improve the quality of their performance must be tempered by the recognition that most socialization agents get very little feedback about whether their current practices are highly successful, moderately successful, or failing. The farmer knows quickly how much corn per acre is being produced by the hybrid corn; the doctor gets quick feedback as to whether his intervention has reduced the infection and fever; and the physical engineer receives objective records about the output of the machine. But the socialization agent typically lacks standards and criteria — standards for his performance and criteria for the effectiveness of his efforts — and also typically lacks the tools for making this type of check. So, on the one hand, there is little basis for feeling successful and rewarded, but on the other hand there are few data to indicate that certain goals are not being achieved and that efforts are needed to improve one's practice. Therefore, the agent receives little stimulus for taking the risks of searching for and utilizing new resources. His performance remains relatively invisible to peers, colleagues, and supervisors. There is neither competitive challenge nor good communication channels to stimulate sharing and improving practice. In addition, there often tends to be quite a high sensitivity to the potential negative reaction of others "if they had a chance to see what I am doing." Internal feedback should be both the greatest indicator of need for change and the stimulus to retrieve external resources.

The Collusive Cycle of Resistance to Change

When a farmer decides to change his farming technique by using a new seed, fertilizer, or farm implement, he does not have to be very concerned about how the soil or the tool will react to his change of concept and practice. But in the field of human affairs, every socialization agent's behavior patterns are embedded in a set of mutual interpersonal expectations and reciprocal adaptations. A great deal of security is derived from the predictability of the behavior of others. The typical socialization agent has reciprocal expectations and adaptations in relation to supervisors, peers, and socializees, as well as in relation to himself and his own self-concepts. For example, socialization agents and their supervisors fairly typically have arrived at a mutual adaptation where there is a verbal exchange of information and counseling about what the socialization agent is doing rather than any actual observation of behavior, so that the agent avoids the threat of direct observation and the supervisor avoids both the inconvenience of scheduling direct observations and some of the embarrassments of evaluative feedback.

In a similar fashion, colleagues (that is, fellow teachers, fellow Sunday school teachers, neighboring parents, etc.) usually carefully avoid observing each other at work and also frequently hesitate to innovate new types of practices because they assume that their deviancy would be negatively evaluated by their peers. We have found a number of situations where colleagues were all inhibiting themselves because they assumed that what they would like to do would be considered deviant, when, in fact, all their colleagues were feeling the same way but were maintaining a collusion of ignorance and an inhibition to changing the socialization practices.

The mutual adaptations between the socialization agents and the socializees are also an important basis of resistance to change. In a classroom the unspoken agreement often seems to go something like this: "Don't ask us to do too much, or set too high standards, and we will give you pleasant feedback to the effect that you are regarded as a good teacher." Frequently the unspoken agreement between teen-agers and their socialization agents seems to be "Don't spring anything new and extra on us, and we won't rock the boat concerning your job with us."

In discussions with parents, teachers, club leaders, and other socialization agents who are trying out new approaches, we also find evidence of the importance of the internal feedback cycle in relation to one's own conception of one's role on the job. Frequently the reluctance to try new behavior patterns is expressed in terms of feelings of awkwardness or inadequacy in the new pattern of interaction with the young ones. There is a danger of diminishment of the perception of self as competent and able to handle whatever comes up in the relationship with the child or children. These cycles of mutual expectation and adaptation are one of the strongest bases of resistance to change, even though both parties are discontented with the way things are and would be eager to have the change come about. They would discover this quickly if they were in communication with each other.

The Need for Deeper Intrapersonal Changes

Another important fact about change in performance as a socialization agent is that what must be changed is a behavior pattern and the internal supports for this pattern in contrast to the typical process of change in the fields of biological and physical technology in which the human agent does something differently with a physical thing, such as a tool, drug, seed, or chemical. Changing a behavior pattern usually implies a change of some depth in the values, attitudes, and skills of the agent.

This requires a deeper personal involvement in the adopting of the new practice, and therefore there are more problems of relearning and internal resistance to change. One of the implications of this fact is that new socialization practices cannot be successfully transmitted by simple written discussions. Such new information is only a first step in a complicated process of relearning which requires careful support and guidance to be successful. Relatively superficial, cognitive changes will be significant guides to change only if supported by deeper processes of value change, decision commitments, and goal setting.

Internalization of Change: Adaptation Rather than Adoption

If a mother is to learn to discipline her child differently or an employer is to learn how to stimulate his employees to become motivated to change their jobs or performance level, then, as we have noted, a rather basic change in behavior pattern is required. The particular behavioral style of one successful socialization agent may not be the one which will be most compatible or successful for a second agent. This does not mean that they cannot learn from each other through the sharing of practices or from the same research. It does mean that learning from someone else is a process of internalizing and adapting the new practice rather than imitatively trying to adopt the exact behavior pattern. This type of adaptive behavior requires a deeper understanding of the principles underlying the particular practice than is needed for imitative adoption in agriculture, industry, medicine, etc.

All these observations and illustrations lead us to conclude that the job of training or retraining socialization agents is a different and much more complex process than the training of change agents in the fields of biological and physical technology. And in spite of this fact of greater difficulty, the field of socialization practices is nowhere near as well developed or sophisticated as these other biological and physical engineering fields where networks of linking agents, diffusion procedures, and specialized manpower provide links between basic and applied research and provide active programs of in-service training to maintain the upgrading of the quality of practice. With this background, we turn next to the opportunities and potentialities for upgrading the quality of the performance of the great variety of socialization agents and agencies.

MODELS FOR THE IMPROVEMENT OF SOCIALIZATION PRACTICE

In view of the foregoing discussion of the complexities of the role of the socialization agent and the basis for resistance to change, what hope can we have for major significant improvements in the socialization of our young ones? Probably never before have the major forces in our society been so sensitive to, and oriented toward, the improvement of practices of raising and educating children and preparing young people for adult roles in a rapidly changing social order. Teachers, parents, church leaders, social workers, employers, and many others are sensing this priority and making efforts to examine and to improve the efficacy of their effort. The symptoms of failure with many young ones — for example, school drop-outs, teen-age suicide, pre-marital pregnancy, drug addiction, aggressive delinquency, withdrawal from interaction with the older generation — are creating a sense of alarm about the adequacy of our understanding of, and approach to, the socialization task. Some increase in financial reward and status recognition for professional and sub-professional workers has emerged; very large increases in funds for research and program development are providing stimulus; and the quality of professional training programs is being improved. What evidence do we have that the concepts and designs are available to provide the type of help which is needed, once a socialization agency or agent has become sensitive to the need for improvement?

We have identified two major approaches to the improvement of the performance of socialization agents. One approach includes a variety of designs for retrieving and mobilizing external resources — that is, external to the agency or the agent — in order to improve practice. The second approach includes a variety of techniques for mobilizing and organizing the resources within the system as the basis for resocialization of the socialization agents. By "resources" we mean research-based theory and knowledge, inquiry methodology, and innovated practices which have been validated by systematic evaluation and documentation efforts.

Mobilizing External Resources

PROBLEM-CENTERED RETRIEVAL OF THEORY AND RESEARCH

If basic research and theory about child development and social change are to have any impact on the improvement of socialization practices, then it is crucial that the accumulated theory and knowledge be retrieved and organized in such a way as to be relevant to particular problems of socialization and to provide the basis for deriving rational action designs for the performance of socialization agents and the program of the agencies.

One example of this is the retrieval-and-derivation conference procedure. A group of school administrators and teachers had become very sensitive to the need to do something more about their problem of the "in-betweeners," that is, older elementary school boys who were too disruptive to be acceptable in the regular classroom but not yet deviant enough to become the responsibility of the police and the court. A small team of research workers and educators were convened. During the first period of the day the main responsibility of formulating a series of research generalizations which seemed to have relevance to the problem phenomenon and which were based on good research and theory fell to the scientists. During a two-hour period quite a number of generalizations which seemed to have relevance to the problem presented by the socialization agents were brought forth. During a second period of the conference the scientists and educators worked together to formulate "implication statements" which seemed to follow from the research generalizations as possible directions for action in dealing with concepts, variables, and causal relationships identified in the generalizations. These implication statements were then used as a basis for attempting to project specific action steps and program designs. During a final phase of the conference the discussion focused on the feasibility of the various action ideas and the most effective mixture of action ideas which might constitute a total program design. The design which emerged was quite different from anything the educators or researchers had expected. The steps of research retrieval and derivation developed at this conference are illustrated in Table 1. The innovations were tested for a year in two school buildings. The evaluation research indicated the superiority of the design over previous efforts and revealed a number of next steps for improvement in this resocialization program. The important point here is that a "linking agent" oriented to practice but trained as a scientist provided a basis for bridging the needs of socialization agents to the resources of the scientist in order to develop a systematic action design for the improvement of practice. The design required a good deal of reorienting and retraining of the socialization agent to meet the requirements of the derived action plan.

ACCESS TO DEVELOPED AND TESTED MODELS OF PRACTICE

The demonstrated model, available for observation and adoption, is one of the most common approaches to the improvement of practice in such fields as agricultural, medical, and industrial technology. As we have noted previously, there has been considerable resistance to making one's performance as a social practitioner available for observation and documentation. But during the past few years the idea of a demonstration project has become quite a familiar idea in social practice, for example, in community antipoverty projects, delinquency control programs, etc. But most frequently the demonstration is not documented in a systematic, detailed way, and the opportunity for observation is not made available in a meaningful way. The communication of the demonstration seems frequently to be designed to communicate "see how well we have done" rather than a blow-by-blow description of how something has been accomplished, the problems that were encountered, the interpretations of difficulties encountered, and evaluation research findings. The "cross-age demonstration" will illustrate some of the details necessary to the demonstration procedure as a technique of providing outside resource experience in order to promote the improvement of socialization practices.

A university-based research team, from their field observations and their theorizing about the process of socialization, had developed the idea that use of older peers as socialization agents was neglected, and represented an important potential in the educational program of young children, particularly children from underprivileged backgrounds and children manifesting psychological alienation from teachers and other adults. Working with a cooperating school-system field site, they developed a design for recruiting and training sixth-grade children to function as educational aides in the first, second, and third grades. The first model of the design was worked out and conducted by a demonstration teacher on the action-research team; a number of teachers in the school building participated as observers. The evaluation research validated the feasibility and educational significance of this particular innovation in educational practice. The work of the demonstration teacher was photographed and taped. An audio-visual presentation of the demonstration was developed and shown to teachers in another building. It was discovered that this audio-visual presentation provided an excellent stimulus for motivation to try out the new practice but did not adequately communicate skills and some of the traps involved in successful adoption of the procedure. Additional consultation and skill practice were required. As a result the next diffusion effort was to train someone within the school building to use the demonstration package and to develop adequate supplementary training experiences to make adoption and adaptation of the model a successful experience for most interested teachers. A great deal of work remains to be done in discovering the most efficient combination of participant observations, written records, tapes, and audio-visual presentations to permit the successful high-quality adoption of the discoveries of demonstration projects. A very promising experiment is underway in providing opportunities for parents to observe parental child-rearing practices of other parents.

CROSS-PEER OR CROSS-AGENCY SHARING OF PROMISING PRACTICES

A third procedure for stimulating the "importing" of new socialization practices into the repertoire of the agent or agency is the promotion of procedures for sharing experience with promising practices between practitioners, that is, between parents, between teachers, between employers, etc. As we have indicated previously, there is a great deal of

TABLE 1

Illustration of a Research-Derivation Process

RESEARCH GENERALIZATIONS	IMPLICATION DERIVATIONS	ACTION DERIVATIONS
1. *Finding:* The regular teacher is perceived more negatively by boys who later become delinquent than by boys matched with identical I.Q. who do not get into trouble.	1a. Need to experience a positive relationship with a teacher.	A. Special Classroom (1a, 2a, 2b, 7a, 8a, 9a) . . . eight "in-betweener" children together for a half-day . . . focus on academic fundamentals and behavioral interaction . . . weekly training consultant for teacher
2. *Finding:* The socially handicapped pupil has often given up aspirations of competence in his studies and therefore rejects the value of becoming successful in school work.	2a. Change in values of self and of competence need to precede acceptance of school subjects. 2b. Project-oriented school experiences are most likely to provide necessary success in initial approach to academic work.	B. Visiting Teacher (2a, 5a, 6a) . . . meets weekly with each child . . . meets weekly with parents of child
3. *Finding:* The students in the classroom are crucial definers of what competencies and behaviors are accepted and rewarded.	3a. Need acceptance by, and integration into, the socialized peer culture.	C. Regular Classroom Human Relation Training (3a, 4a, 7a, 8a, 9a) . . . consultant-demonstrator works in same classroom . . . teachers and consultant meet weekly as a resource team to each other on problem solving and developing classroom innovations
4. *Finding:* The socially handicapped children tend to be rejected, and feel rejected, by the "pro-school" and "pro-teacher" peers and form an "anti-teacher," "anti-school" subgroup.	4a. Individual values and norms are best modified by pro-teacher, pro-school peers.	D. After-School Activities Clubs (3a, 2a, 4a, 9a) . . . "in-betweener" children with well-adjusted peers . . . consultant-demonstrator leads some clubs . . . consultant meets weekly with adult leader
5. *Finding:* In relationship with his parents, the socially handicapped child	5a. Work with parents on relations with their children and	E. Child in Regular School Program Half-Day (8a, 9a)

has less interaction and more negative attitudes, with father role most potent, then other children; and these attitudes are reciprocated by parents.	the school should result in improved school adjustment of child.	F. Case Conferences (8a, 9a) . . . semimonthly for involved school staff and clinicians G. Policy Committee Meetings (9a) . . . annual meeting for evaluative reporting and policy review
6. *Finding:* The underachieving child perceives that his parents have less interest in his life at school and his standards of work and learning than the parents of other children.	6a. Work with child on relations with parents should improve school adjustment.	H. Evaluation Team (9a) . . . action-research team relates to program personnel as indicated above . . . conducts data analysis and reports results
7. *Finding:* The socially handicapped child typically gives the false impression of basic low capacity because of deprived cultural background, low language facilities, poor social skills, low motivation to perform, and rejection of self as adequate.	7a. Interesting projects need to be planned providing basic skill practice and success experience for self-re-evaluation.	
8. *Finding:* There tends to be very little transfer of human relation learning, scholarship, and attitudes from the training setting to other classrooms unless transfer is directly worked on and continuing opportunities for practice are offered.	8a. Continuity with regular school program should be maintained.	
9. *Finding:* The various sources of influence on the individual's world — for example, teachers, peers, parents, and other reference groups — are so interdependent that change in the child can best be effected by simultaneous "multiple entry" through the different sources of influence. A "single entry" effort often has the negative effect of mobilizing resistance and rejection in other areas.	9a. Multiple-entry approach of programming in several areas should be applied.	

resistance to initiating professional dialogue about one's own practices or the practices of one's peers. And what communication does exist tends to be highly distorted so that one presents oneself as competent and successful in raising one's children or reeducating one's workers. Two examples of cross-peer models will illustrate some of the potentialities in this area.

In one city an interdisciplinary university team invited socialization agents from all kinds of agencies in the community that worked directly with youths to participate in a seminar. In the early stages of the seminar, discussion about practices tended to be general or to be focused on case material brought in by the seminar staff. But probing discussion about critical issues of performance was legitimized, and a climate of trust developed in the group; the workers began to share their problems and their successes of socialization practice. They discussed the issues involved in deciding what to do, began to describe and then to role-play for demonstration purposes the actual behaviors they used, and began to analyze critically the consequences of their efforts. They arrived at the realization that they could not trust themselves to describe what they actually did in interacting with socializees or to evaluate their own efforts. They began to invite visitors and also developed an interview schedule which they could use with each other to get concrete objective descriptions of their most successful practices. They developed a looseleaf notebook of "promising practices" and reported achieving a great many insights about their own practices and the outlook of the young ones from this exchange process.

In the second illustration, a university consultant worked with a school-system team to design and sponsor a "sharing our teaching" day. After a brief opening presentation on the importance and difficulties of sharing teaching practices as a resource, grade-level meetings convened in which the teachers made a census, recorded on a ditto master, of the factors they found within themselves and their situations which inhibited and facilitated exchange of information about their teaching practices. Their census of problems was reproduced and available for reading by everyone during the lunch period. In the afternoon the grade-level meetings convened again. With the help of a group convener the teachers formed circles (about twelve in each group), and each teacher had an opportunity to identify in one minute or less a teaching practice of his or her own which might be a helpful resource for others. The group then had to develop criteria to select the four practices which they wanted to focus on for the rest of the afternoon. They were provided with a group interview schedule to use in probing in detail each of the four group members who had now become informants about their own practice. The detailed descriptions which were elicited were recorded on ditto masters by a group recorder and were immediately dittoed and made available as a professional workbook of promising practices generated by the exchange process of the day. This experience was evaluated very highly by the participants who planned further sessions following this general design.

Probably none of these illustrations have been detailed enough to clarify the three stages common to all these learning situations. In one way or another the learning or relearning experience of the socialization agent seems to go through an initial phase where the acceptability of recognizing and sharing problems of understanding and performing the socialization job is legitimized. In the second phase some clarity of understanding of a design for action or of a performance model developed by someone else in another setting is achieved. In the third phase the agent must internalize the model sufficiently so that he can face the value issues and skill problems involved in actually making the commitments and carrying out the actions which will change his performance as an agent in the socialization process.

Mobilizing Internal Resources

In all the illustrations reported above, the attempt has been to improve the socialization practices by the communication and utilization of knowledge developed in other settings through work with other socializees. There is always the problem of the applicability of such resources to the particular problem, capabilities, and types of socializees being worked with. Even if the designs and practices are highly relevant, the particular socialization agent may not perceive the relevance or may mobilize the idea of non-relevance as a defense. The parent may say, "My child is not like those children," or "Our family is not like theirs." The teacher may say, "My class is quite different," or "I worked with fifth-graders, but I'm working with fourth-graders now." Or the leaders of a particular community may say, "That kind of delinquency prevention program is possible and might work all right in city X, but we don't have the same facilities and budget they do." For these reasons very often the most effective approach to inducing change in the goals and performances of socialization agents and agencies is to generate specific and diagnostic study of the particular action context and to attempt to utilize the data from such diagnosis as a basis for commitment and action toward change. Four models of procedures for generating change in this way are illustrated below.

DIAGNOSTIC STUDY WITH FEEDBACK

In one experimental program the university-based team worked with thirty collaborating elementary and secondary school teachers. They collected extensive interview material from each teacher about her teaching philosophy, operating objectives, and her relations with her colleagues and her pupils. Data were collected from all the children in the classroom about their relations with each other, their perception of the teacher and their relationship with her, their attitudes toward school and school work, their achievement motivation and their actual achievement. Ten of these teachers received a tape from the research team summarizing the data collected from herself and her classroom and an interpretation of problems revealed by the data and recommendations for possible directions of change to improve the effectiveness of the classroom learning climate. Ten other teachers participated personally in two feedback sessions in which they had a chance to review the data with the university consultants, to generate some interpretations of their own, and to participate in discussions about ideas for improvement in their teaching practices. They also had an opportunity to request further consultation as needed, and quite a bit of use was made of this opportunity. The other ten teachers had an opportunity to participate in an intensive four-week summer workshop in which they took part in the analysis of the data from their classroom, received presentations on the conceptualizations of the dynamics underlying the teaching-learning process, had an opportunity for consultation on plans for initiating change in their teaching practices, and had an opportunity to practice changed performance patterns with a special group of children who were available to provide practice opportunities which were not "playing for keeps." A follow-up during the next academic year revealed that all of the ten teachers in the intensive feedback and consultation program made significant changes in their performance, while only a few of the other teachers showed major changes and some teachers showed no change at all in their performance pattern as socialization agents.

Another interesting illustration of the diagnosis and feedback process is a study in which questionnaires from a large number of classrooms revealed that in many of the classrooms the majority of the pupils believed that the majority of fellow pupils were against too active participation in classroom discussion and doing extra homework. Actually a majority of the pupils in these classes indicated privately on their questionnaires that they would like to relate to the teacher more actively in learning activities. A feedback of these data to the classroom group created a great deal of surprise and legitimized a release of participation and activity inhibited by the state of pluralistic ignorance maintained by the noncommunication within the classroom. Informational feedback is adequate to create a good deal of change in such situations where the inhibition to change in the behavior of socialization agents and socializees is maintained by ignorance rather than by certain satisfactions with "the way things are now."

Other examples of programs of data collection and feedback to parents and to volunteer and professional group leaders reveal that generally the feedback generates an awareness of the need for changing one's practices but usually also generates defensiveness and anxiety about the risks of change. As a result there is often very little change of performance unless there is an additional program of effort to support the setting of change objectives and the initiating of change attempts as an aftermath of the feedback program.

INTERNAL ACTION RESEARCH WITH "WORKING-THROUGH" PROCESS

In the illustrations given above, the diagnostic data were collected by outsiders and fed back to the insiders after a certain amount of analysis and interpretation. Another type of internal action-research process involves the socialization agents, and perhaps the socializees, in the actual diagnostic process of collecting data, processing it, and interpreting the findings and the implications of these findings. It is usually assumed that this type of process increases the probability that the potential consumers of the knowledge will accept the validity of the data and will become more committed to utilizing the knowledge which they have participated in generating.

This type of process is illustrated by a junior high school project in which parents, teachers, and students were all interviewed about their perceptions of the expectations of the others, their evaluation of the behavior of the others. The data were collected from parents by an interviewing team of parents trained by the university consultants to conduct the interviews with valid methodology. The data were collected from teachers by a teacher team, and a team of student-council members were trained to conduct the interviews with fellow students. The research committees participated in the analysis process, and "feedback teams" of pupils, teachers, and parents were trained to present and discuss the findings at PTA meetings, teachers' meetings, and student gatherings.

In a larger program about two hundred community citizens were carefully trained to conduct interviews with samples of youth, parents, and professional socialization agents about the problems of youth deviancy and youth development in the community. The fact that the data were collected locally seemed to help the community leaders considerably to accept the validity of some of the rather threatening material, but there was no great gain in the involvement of key power figures in utilizing the knowledge, because they themselves had not been involved in doing the interviewing. The internal process helped to make the data more valid in their view but did not create a greater sense of relevance and of commitment to do something about it.

Internal Linkage of Parts of the Socialization Agency or System

The lack of congruence of goals and actions of the socialization agents has been identified earlier as a major problem. The internal resources of the system need to be linked effectively if the socialization effort is to be more significant. Two examples of such linkage designs will illustrate this concept.

A nomination procedure, using informants from all segments of the socialization community, identified the key socialization power figures of the community — the key influentials in the programs of formal education, religious education, social control, leisure-time programs, employment, rehabilitation, and family education. These leaders were interviewed about their perceptions of socialization goals, desirable "products" (that is, types of children and youth), attribution of the causes of desirable and undesirable development, perceptions of the goals and practices of each others' programs, and amount and type of communication between these key figures. These leaders were then convened in a community socialization leaders' seminar to receive feedback from the diagnosis. There were many surprises about differing values, different perceptions of program purposes, disagreements about responsibility, and identification of buck-passing of programs for deviants and underprivileged children. Significant efforts toward collaboration and consistency were motivated.

In a similar model, at a different level, youths nominated the significant adult figures in their life space. These key socialization agents were convened to discuss their perceptions of the socializees, their conceptions of needed help, and their reactions to each others' ideas, and to explore more meaningful congruence of helping efforts. This design was reported to have very powerful resocialization impact for working with older teen-agers.

Internal Linkage within the Socialization Agent

It was noted earlier that there is frequently a serious lack of linkage between the knowledge or intentions of a teacher or parent and his actual behavior. The internal gaps between knowledge, goal, commitment, and performance are typically serious blocks to the utilization of new knowledge. The techniques of inducing such linkages within the person have been the major concern of learning laboratories such as those conducted by the National Training Laboratories. A typical program for socialization agents is the State of Michigan Laboratory for Youth Workers and Educational Leaders. This laboratory, conducted twice a year, is cosponsored by twenty socialization agencies and three state universities.

The eight-day laboratory is conducted by an inter-university faculty team with interdisciplinary scientific training and certification as human relations trainers. The design of the training experience includes conceptualization sessions on various aspects of socialization, sensitivity training sessions focused on achievement of self-insight and effect of own behavior on others, skill practice exercises focused on connecting intentions to action skills as socialization agents, and consultation periods providing an opportunity to diagnose needs for change and plans for change in one's own operating situation as a teacher or professional worker with youth in other agency contexts. This type of educational design stresses that the learning of concepts and information tends to remain remarkably divorced from basic attitudes and behavior patterns unless there are carefully planned opportunities for self-confrontation and emotional support for the receiving and utilizing of feedback about one's own behavior as a socialization agent.

In summarizing these sections on models for mobilizing resources to improve socialization practice, we may generalize that there are basically four possible ways to improve socialization practices:

(1) Improve the quality of the program and the performance of existing socialization agents.

(2) Increase the collaboration between existing agents and maximize the congruence of their input.

(3) Add new socialization agents and experiences.

(4) Teach the socializee to be active and selective in making self-socialization efforts.

We have seen illustrations of the first, second, and third of these patterns in the previous sections. The fourth pattern is the most neglected and, in a pluralistic, urban society, probably the most crucial. The next section presents illustrations of this improvement model.

Training the Socializees to Take Self-socialization Initiative

A colleague, reviewing the various problems of improving the socialization process, exclaimed, "I don't see any real solution except to have a powerful community coordinator of socialization to bring about more consistency in the behavior of the socialization agents." But this is a pluralistic society, where diversity of values and programs is a strength as well as a weakness. We must try to develop more creative and effective ways of getting voluntary collaboration of the parents, teachers, and others. Probably the greatest single possibility of improving the socialization experience of the young ones is to educate them directly to be more sophisticated and skillful utilizers and creators of their socialization experiences. They are the ones in the best position to be integrative and selective in dealing with the pluralism of input from the many socialization influences — peers, adults, mass media. Four models of training for self-socialization will illustrate briefly the great potentialities of this approach.

A sample of socialization agents from all types of agencies in the city were asked to nominate the most influential teen-agers they knew, ones who in their opinion exerted both negative and positive influence. From the two hundred nominees the project team selected thirty boys and girls — Negro and white, middle class and lower class, "positive" and "negative" leaders. They were invited to form a seminar of teen leaders. Through discussion, role playing, and other inquiry procedures, they focused on two problems: intergroup hostilities within the teen culture, and problems of communication between the generations. They organized a weekend human relations lab with their consultants to work on interracial and inter-social class relations. They organized and conducted a series of teacher and parent-education evenings. Their invitations to teachers and parents were accepted — no problems of attendance. Typically, they started the evening with a sociodrama of a teen-parent or teen-teacher relationship problem, with the observers organized as diagnostic teams composed of teens, parents, and teachers. The discussions focused on "What happened? Why did they behave the way they did? Would it have been better to behave in different ways? Why?" Often diagnostic teams would complete their analysis with a demonstration of their version of improved communication and consequences. The teen steering committee wrote a pamphlet about problems of communication between the generations. They used the evaluation data they collected at each session. They were the active inquirers, the initiators of the confrontations and dialogues with their socialization agents.

A fourth-grade social studies teacher, with help from a university consultant, developed a study unit entitled "Learning from Grown-ups" in which the pupils studied a sample of "behavior specimens" of teacher-pupil interaction. They observed and analysed the different ways in which teacher and pupils interact, the problems of communication, of influence, of motivation to learn. They conducted an inquiry into why adults are needed as learning resources and engaged in skill practice exercises on how to use adults effectively as resources and how to give adults feedback about ineffective behavior. The teacher and scientist observed major changes in motivation and initiative.

A "cross-age socialization project" developed a program of training older students to function as educational helpers in the classrooms of younger pupils. Sixth-graders worked in the first and second grades; junior high students worked in the fourth and fifth grades; high school students worked in junior high and elementary school. To prepare themselves, the olders participated in seminars where they studied the needs and attitudes of young learners, the techniques of helping, the ways to get briefing from the teachers. They were of course working on their own problems of learning and of relations to adults at the same time. Their attitudes and behaviors toward teachers changed dramatically as they became trusted collaborators and achieved competence through training.

A social science laboratory course for upper elementary grades conducts laboratory study units such as "Being and Becoming," "Deciding and Doing," and "Social Influence" in which the pupils study the phenomena of their own development and behavior, and their relations to peers, parents, teachers, and other roles in their world. They read what child psychologists and other scientists have discovered about these phenomena and work on applying their learnings to their own performance in growing up and interacting with adults.

There are, of course, hundreds of examples of the growing efforts to help children and youth explore greater areas of freedom and responsibility. But on the whole these fall far short of their potential and are often self-defeating because the young ones do not receive help in confronting the value issues, the knowledge resources, and the skills they need to become competent consumers of self-socialization opportunities.

PROBLEMS AND CHALLENGES OF THE RESOCIALIZATION AGENT

From our observations, the reeducator of socialization agents faces certain general decision and action problems, whether he is training volunteers, such as scoutmasters; or "delegated amateurs," such as parents; or professional workers, such as teachers and probation officers. Some of the major problems are summarized below.

How Much Initiative? When? With What Focus?

The trainer must always be facing the question of how actively to intervene in the relearning activities of the trainees. The objective is to achieve some type of internalized self-direction of new patterns, through which initiative for continuing development will be taken by the trainees. To appropriately support this process of internalization and, at the same time, to introduce the necessary cognitive and affective learnings are the crucial and continuing responsibilities of the trainer. The change agent must find behavior techniques for providing necessary emotional support and conceptual perspectives without coercively controlling the learning of the trainee. He must find ways of giving direction to thinking and behavior while, at the same time, leaving — in fact, encouraging — freedom to make decisions. He must provide behavioral models and demonstrations without limiting the freedom to consider alternatives. He must be able to share what he has learned and believes with the learners without creating an external guidebook for thinking and behavior.

It is important to help socialization agents raise the important question of what right they have to initiate intervention, to give direction to the growth of someone else, even a child. It is important that every socialization agent be helped to face this question squarely for himself, and the staff and board of every socialization agency should regard this as a major policy question. An illustration of what may emerge from this thinking-through process is reflected in the work of a small group of teachers who were helped to pose this question in an in-service training program where they were developing a design for doing something about the rejected and withdrawn pupils in their classrooms. They were planning to initiate a special therapeutic training program for these young ones. They asked themselves, "What right do we have to intervene when the pupils are not asking us for help?" After much discussion they concluded that there were four bases for the value judgment that they should take initiative to intervene. Firstly, it was evident that even though at the verbal level the children were not able to formulate a request for help, they were suffering psychological, emotional pain which they could not handle and that in many of their behaviors they were reaching out for help. A second basis for intervention derived from the clear evidence that the psychological state of these children was preventing them from engaging freely and efficiently in academic learning activities, and that the teachers accepted the fact that they had been delegated by society, through the school board and their supervisors, to conduct an efficient program of learning activity for the pupils. A third basis for intervention, they concluded, derived from the fact that these alienated, peripheral members of the classroom group were damaging the learning opportunities of the other members of the group, either by their disruptive behavior or by their withdrawnness, which represented a withholding of the resources they had to offer the rest of the group. A fourth basis for intervention derived from the evidence that the type of vicious circles of maladjustment in which these children were enmeshed had a good probability of becoming more serious with succeeding years, culminating in potentially serious harm and cost to society, for example, the harm of destructive delinquency and criminal activities or the costs of hospitalization.

Adequate Input

Too many socialization agents — parents and professionals — have been inappropriately induced to try something new or different and have been burned by the failure of the experience. Usually they have been induced to try something which could not succeed because it represented a single entry into the child's life space where a multiple-entry program was necessary to support a significant change. For example, the PTA program induced a mother to try something different in her approach to the feeding of four-year-old Johnny without inducing the father or older sib to make a similar change in approach. Very often the individual socializee is not the appropriate target for the effort of the socialization agent. Socialization agents must learn this. The more appropriate and necessary target may be a group of which the child is a member, or the organizational co-worker context of the worker, or a set of individuals who are strategically related to the socializee. Just as children become cynically inoculated against the inconsistent inputs of socialization agents, so do socialization agents become cautious and inhibited because of their unsuccessful involvement in influence attempts based on poor understanding and inadequate strategy. They become appropriately resistant to efforts to change their performance as socialization agents.

Inside Trainer or Outside Consultant?

Husbands are probably in a poor position to function as parent educators of their wives. School principals have difficulty functioning as in-service trainers of the teachers under their supervision. But outside consultants have difficulties achieving an adequate diagnostic understanding of the continuing needs and problems of the socialization agent in a particular agency or context, and have difficulty providing the continuity of support and feedback needed to maintain the growth and development of most socialization agents. Perhaps one of the most effective solutions is illustrated by the functioning of educational improvement teams in the following two projects. In one project each school building had a teaching improvement team composed of the principal, a high-status sociometrically accepted classroom teacher, and a university-based consultant. The three of them worked together to identify improvement needs, design in-service training activities, and to take initiative in inviting participation of outside resources. In another project there were school system-wide committees composed of a representative of top administration, a curriculum specialist, high-status elementary and secondary school principals and two or three creative elementary and secondary school teachers, and a university-based consultant. This team worked together to sponsor diagnostic activity, and to design and implement in-service training programs. The importance of achieving the appropriate social-emotional distance is also illustrated by the success of a resocialization program for family units, each with a seriously recidivist delinquent son. The most effective design for helping the family members move toward meaningful communication with each other was found to be group-therapy sessions composed of mothers, fathers, and sons, but no one from the same family. Thus they were "outsiders" to each other, but at the same time were "insiders," in the sense of having similar problems and being in familiar role relations of mothers, fathers, and sons. Probably the most creative designs for the training of socialization agents will involve a training team which balances outside objectivity and expertness with inside diagnostic knowledge and affective commitment.

Motivational Support for Effort after Commitment

As we have reviewed earlier, in most fields of biological and physical technology it is possible to diffuse a new innovation by informational and demonstration programs of relatively short duration. But in the area of innovation in socialization practices, great emphasis must be placed on the amount and type of support which the socialization agent receives during the period of trying out a new practice and consolidating it as a part of his internal repertoire of values and skills. This means that socialization agencies should have an institutionalized, continuing function of in-service training for their staffs of socialization agents, and the community should sponsor such a program for the largest staff of socialization agents, the parents. It is a sad fact, for example, that few school systems have full-time training directors and training staffs; whereas no industrial concern would feel it could maintain its competitive position without a fully developed, continuing program of manpower training and retraining. When one member of a school board, who also happened to be president of a paper company, recently discovered this fact, he exclaimed, "You mean to tell me we use more intelligence in producing better paper than we do in raising better kids."

Differential Training Needs of Different Socialization Agents

The new impetus of socialization outreach programs deriving from the antipoverty efforts (supported by federal funds) for the intensified education of the socially and intellectually handicapped, the emphasis on resocialization of delinquents, and the retraining of the technologically displaced has created role demands for many new socialization agents. This has resulted in many challenging and difficult training situations where the socialization agents to be trained (for example, community volunteers, neighborhood aides, Head Start assistants, etc.) are from a social class or racial or ethnic background different from that of the trainers. Training a group of high school dropouts or a group of women from an underprivileged neighborhood to cope with the role requirements of a social service job is a training relationship and curriculum problem quite different from the training of middle-class volunteers to lead youth groups of middle-class young people in working in a nursery school. The facts of differences in social class, race, ethnic background, and orientation toward the disciplines of time, learning, and perspective, etc., cannot be ignored. Frank Reisman has pointed out that the action learning opportunities provided by role-playing technology are far more effective than verbal communication. One of the great needs in such a training situation is to provide opportunities for the trainees to achieve a sense of self-potency and interpersonal acceptance which will support the development of a motivation to learn and a readiness for a reciprocal influence relationship with their trainers. Perhaps the biggest lesson to be learned is the importance of designing training activities in such a way that there will be continuous feedback from the socialization agents to their trainers about their involvement in, and their evaluation of, the learning experience.

Training in Applied Behavioral Science

One of the crucial problems confronting any effort to improve socialization practice is the lack of training of socialization agents and also of socializees in the basic concepts and causal processes of human relations and in the valuing and understanding of the problem-solving process. As we have indicated previously, many socialization agents, both laymen and professionals, view scientists and science-based theory as impractical and too complex to understand. This posture serves as a difficult barrier to any rational improvement process which must, or should, be based on research knowledge and the best conceptualization we have available at any particular time in the development of the disciplines. It seems important to tackle this critical problem of "anti-intellectualism" and "anti-scientistism" head-on by providing opportunities for socialization agents and socializees to receive more effective basic education in the methods and substance of the relevant fields of scientific knowledge, and an understanding of scientists and how they work.

One illustration of potential developments in this field is the development of a series of "professional growth packages" which permits a teacher or a group of several teachers to work through a series of planned learning experiences in behavioral science in which the only equipment needed is a record player. The scientists speak directly to the teachers on banded records in which no conceptual presentation is more than six to ten minutes long. A listening guide is provided along with reading material, discussion material, additional reading references, and skill practice exercises to try out in the study group.

NEEDED DEVELOPMENT IN THE IMPROVEMENT OF SOCIALIZATION PRACTICES

It is time to step back now and look, with as comprehensive a perspective as possible, at the total socialization program of the society, and to ask: What are the priorities? Where is developmental work most needed? What types of innovation in socialization practice are most promising and need widespread promotion? Here is the beginning of such a priority list.

Dialogue about Socialization Objectives

Involvement of the expertness of our social and educational philosophers, religious leaders, and humanists is critically needed in order to focus on the concrete analysis of the basic goals and instrumental objectives of the socialization process. This should not be general philosophical analysis but should be disciplined dialogue with the scientists and with the practitioners to inquire into, and clarify, the varied goal orientations needed as basic guidelines for the performance of all socialization agents. This is not to say that a consensus should be achieved but rather that practice will be vastly improved if a motivated search for goals can be stimulated and a dialogue can be maintained which will blend the resources of the value experts, the scientists, and the practicing socialization agents.

Coordination of the Socialization Community

We have already noted the fact of the chaotic medley of socialization vested interests which impinge on the life space of the socializee. Certainly in our pluralistic society there is no place for a "socialization czar" to prevent client-raiding between the church, the school, the recreation association, and the family. But there is critical need for voluntary sharing of values and the development of programs of collaboration. We have demonstrated a genius for such voluntary coordination in other areas of community and national life. The socialization enterprise is perhaps our most crucial one from the point of view of the overall health and continuity of development of the nation. It is high time we gave priority to the coordination problems which are experienced every day by every child growing up among us.

In-service Education of Parents and Family Units

As we have noted, our largest and most influential population of socialization agents gets the least socialization into their role as socialization agents. On the one hand, parenthood has not been defined as a profession, and therefore no curriculum of professional training has been developed; on the other hand, parents have not been defined as volunteers, and thus do not receive the attention, commitment, and training opportunities offered to volunteers by the many child and youth-serving agencies. Perhaps as a defense against their sense of inadequacy, parents have not organized to demand more adequate training opportunities; and perhaps from a defensive sense of inadequacy and a misguided value orientation, the professional community has said the role of parent and the arena of family life are a private domain not to be entered unless there is a request for help. This is a great disservice to parents and family units and points to a basic weakening of the fabric of our society as it copes with the adjustment problems and development issues of rapid technological and social change. Not only must parents receive help in creating and filling their own socialization roles more effectively, but they must be helped to orient and support the child in his utilization of the other socialization situations such as the school, leisure-time activities, and employment opportunities.

Comprehensive Programs of School Improvement

The professional teams who make up the school system have been delegated a tremendously complex variety of socialization tasks. There is much confusion about the variety of these tasks and the hierarchy of priorities which should be maintained. Stimulating and guiding the unfolding of cognitive development and the acquisition of information about past, present, and future is a fantastically expanding task in itself. In addition there are the interdependent responsibilities for social-emotional growth and development, movement toward the selection and preparation for occupational and sex roles, the nurturance of physical health, development of leisure-time interests, and the development of motivation and skills in the area of citizenship. On the one hand, the school receives far too little in the way of collaboration from other segments of the community and far too much criticism for failure to achieve idealized standards; but on the other hand, it is typically very backward in utilizing the resources of social research and theory to improve its functioning as a subsystem of the community, as an organization, and as an association of small groups, called classrooms, engaged in a program of interaction between adults and children, committed to the achievement of certain educational objectives. As we have indicated earlier, school systems have lagged badly both in institutionalizing the in-service training function as a part of its manpower recruiting and development program, and in involving parents and socialization agents from other community segments in the program of the school and in involving older students in the education of younger students. Creative demonstrations in various of these areas do exist, but the total organization of the educational enterprise is inadequate in its support of the identification and diffusion of creative practices as they are innovated in a local school system.

Extension of Volunteerism and Sub-professionalism

Traditionally the American community has been relatively unique in the extent of its dependence on, and utilization of, volunteer efforts to man a variety of community functions, including the socialization of the young. But the increasing professionalism and specialization of the socialization function has tended to decrease the sense of significance of the volunteer worker and to decrease the importance of the volunteer role in the division of labor in the socialization community. This is partly true because the professional schools have neglected to build into their curriculum a value orientation toward, and training in the skills of, recruiting, training, and maintaining the motivation of volunteers. Also there has been no development of a clarified hierarchy of professional, sub-professional, and volunteer roles in a division of labor comparable to that which has developed in the field of nursing service or medical technology. With the increase in automation of housework, in early retirement, and in a shortened work week, there has been a tremendous increase in the amount of potential womanpower and manpower available for volunteer service. There have been very few innovations in the technique of identifying and recruiting such manpower, or in providing the type of continuing in-service training and involvement in goal-setting and program development which is needed to provide the volunteer with an adequate sense of personal fulfillment and social significance. We have already noted that a variety of sub-professional roles are beginning to emerge in the fields of education, social work, and leisure-time services. It will be interesting to see whether the professional establishments will be open enough to invite and provide the opportunity for upward mobility and continued training for the sub-professionals, or whether these roles will become predominantly routine and dead-end.

Utilization of Peer Culture Resources

Older siblings and older peers provide most children with the greatest single source of opportunity for value and behavior modeling. The peer who is three or four years older is more likely to be seen as a relevant "aspiration model" than those distant figures who fall into the category of grown-ups. But from the point of view of adult socialization agents, the cross-age relationships between peers tend to be dysfunctional and disruptive of adult socialization goals. Our experimentation with this problem has revealed that this is primarily true because adults have not sought the collaboration of older peers or, when they have, they have delegated routine social control responsibilities rather than provide training in the ideas and skills needed to do an effective job of working with the younger ones. Older peers have proved remarkably responsive to such opportunity for collaboration, have demonstrated a rapid "professionalization" of concepts and skills, and in addition have demonstrated a great increase in their own responsiveness, as socializees, to the influence attempts of the socialization agents. There are many areas of the socialization community where the manpower resources of older peers are needed and where youth can provide a necessary and sensitive linkage between the generations.

Involvement of the Socializees

Unfortunately we have not adequately recognized the vested interests which children and youth have in the direction and nature of their personal growth experience as learners and participants in the social process. There are exciting examples of the development of youth councils with significant community functions, invitations to young people to serve on policy boards of socialization agencies, and sharing with children the clarifications of the rationale and goals for their educational experience. These are very scattered, little-known demonstrations of what should become a policy of all segments of the socialization community: to involve the socializees to the greatest extent possible (conditioned by age level and maturity) in goal setting, in providing feedback about their response to their socialization experiences, and in taking initiative in innovating growth and development experiences for themselves. And perhaps most of all, the socializees need to receive direct training in solving the problems of coping with the multiple input of the socialization community and of developing personal potency to initiate directions for their own growth experiences.

Mobilization and Development of University Resources

As the other chapters of this volume have emphasized, there is a great demand for basic research to increase the range and validity of diagnostic insights needed by those who should give leadership to the engineering of improved socialization practices. In addition, there is a great need to develop high-level graduate training in applied behavioral science for "socialization engineers" who should be giving leadership to the research-and-development program needs of the socialization community and providing a systematic linkage between the resources of basic research and the operational needs of professional and volunteer agents. Also needed is a great expansion of university-linked demonstration centers where innovations in educational and social practice can be carefully developed and tested, under controlled field conditions, and then made available for widespread diffusion. And finally, programs of undergraduate education must encourage students to participate in the socialization programs of the community as a part of their undergraduate learning experiences. Many young people need to move from the limited perspective of baby-sitting to the wider horizons of internship and leadership in the community enterprise of rearing and educating the young.

REFERENCES

Benne, K. Education and the social sciences. In I. Morrissett (Ed.), *Social Sciences in the Schools: A Search for Rationale*. New York: Holt, Rinehart & Winston, 1968. Chap. 3.

Bennis, W., Benne, K., and Chin, R. (Eds.) *The Planning of Change: Readings in the Applied Behavioral Sciences*. New York: Holt, Rinehart & Winston, 1961.

Bradford, L., Gibb, J., and Benne, K. *T-Group Theory and Laboratory Method*. New York: John Wiley & Sons, 1964.

Brim, O. G., Jr. *Education for Child Rearing*. New York: Russell Sage Foundation, 1959.

Chesler, M., and Fox, R. *Role-Playing Methods in the Classroom*. Chicago: Science Research Associates, 1966.

Fox, R., Luszki, Margaret B., and Schmuck, R. *Diagnosing Classroom Learning Environment*. Chicago: Science Research Associates, 1966.

Harris, Marilyn. Bridging the generations. In R. Lippitt *et al.* (Eds.), *The World of Troubled Youth*. Reading, Mass.: Addison-Wesley Publishing Co., 1967. One in a series of six documentary, in-service, training packages.

Lippitt, R. The forgotten consumer: the child. In I. Morrissett (Ed.), *Social Sciences in the Schools: A Search for Rationale*. New York: Holt, Rinehart & Winston, 1968. Chap. 14.

Lippitt, R. The use of social research to improve social practice. *American Journal of Orthopsychiatry*, July 1965, 35, No. 4, pp. 663–69.

Lippitt, R. The youth culture, the school system and the socialization community. In A. J. Reiss (Ed.), *The School in a Changing Society*. Glencoe, Ill.: The Free Press of Glencoe, 1965.

Lippitt, R., Fox, R., and Schmuck, R. Innovating classroom practice to support achievement motivation and ego-development. In E. Bower and W. Hollister (Eds.), *Behavioral Science Frontiers in Education*. New York: John Wiley & Sons, 1967. Pp. 317–34.

Lippitt, R., Watson, Jeanne, and Westley, B. *Dynamics of Planned Change*. New York: Harcourt, Brace & Co., 1958.

Lippitt, R., *et al.* The teacher as innovator, seeker and sharer of new practices. In R. I. Miller (Ed.), *Perspectives on Educational Change*. Des Moines, Iowa: Meredith Press, 1966.

Lippitt, R., *et al.* *The World of Troubled Youth*. Reading, Mass.: Addison-Wesley Publishing Co., 1967. Six documentary, in-service, training packages, including recorded and written materials for the participants and special materials for the discussion leader.

NTL-IABS (National Training Laboratories–Institute for Applied Behavioral Science). Bibliographic listing of publications on training and change. National Training Laboratories, 1201 Sixteenth Street, N.W., Washington, D.C.

Schmuck, R., Chesler, M., and Lippitt, R. *Problem Solving to Improve Classroom Learning*. Chicago: Science Research Associates, 1966.

Watson, G. (Ed.) *Concepts for Social Change*. Washington, D.C.: National Training Laboratories, NEA, 1967.

Appendix A

I. Conferences and Conference Participants

Observational Methods in Research on Socialization Processes
Gould House, Tarrytown, New York
March 18–20, 1962

ORGANIZERS

Marian Radke Yarrow
National Institutes of Health

Harold L. Raush
National Institutes of Health

Stuart A. Altmann
University of Alberta

Roger G. Barker
University of Kansas

John D. Benjamin*
University of Colorado

Sidney W. Bijou
University of Washington

William Caudill
National Institutes of Health

John A. Clausen
University of California, Berkeley

Irven DeVore
University of California, Berkeley

D. Wells Goodrich
National Institutes of Health

John S. Harding
Cornell University

(Miss) Sadako Imamura
Harvard University

Richard A. Littman
University of Oregon

Eleanor E. Maccoby
Stanford University

Daniel R. Miller
University of Michigan

Francis H. Palmer
Social Science Research Council

Phil H Schoggen
University of Oregon

Fred L. Strodtbeck
University of Chicago

Beatrice B. Whiting
Harvard University

John W. M. Whiting
Harvard University

Herbert F. Wright
University of Kansas

* Deceased.

A brief description of the Conference is contained in *Items*, 1962, *16*, 17. Papers subsequently published include references 2, 7, 12, and 23 in Appendix B.

Socialization Theory: Relations between Social Structure and Psychological Structure
Tuscon, Arizona
December 7–9, 1962

ORGANIZER Daniel R. Miller
University of Michigan

Eric Bermann
Children's Psychiatric Hospital
Ann Arbor, Michigan

Orville G. Brim, Jr.
Russell Sage Foundation

John A. Clausen
University of California, Berkeley

John R. P. French, Jr.
University of Michigan

O. J. Harvey
University of Colorado

Alex Inkeles
Harvard University

Arnold Kaufman
Stanford University

Melvin L. Kohn
National Institute of Mental Health

Henry L. Lennard
Bureau of Applied Social Research

Robert A. LeVine
University of Chicago

Daniel J. Levinson
Harvard Medical School

Eleanor E. Maccoby
Stanford University

Francis H. Palmer
Social Science Research Council

Harold L. Raush
National Institute of Mental Health

Paul F. Secord
University of Nevada

M. Brewster Smith
University of California, Berkeley

Guy E. Swanson
University of Michigan

Ralph H. Turner
University of California, Los Angeles

Robert F. Winch
Northwestern University

Papers which were published, among those presented at the Conference, include references 14, 17, 20, 21, and 28 in Appendix B.

Socialization through the Life Cycle
New York City
May 17–19, 1963

ORGANIZER Orville G. Brim, Jr.
Russell Sage Foundation

Howard S. Becker
Stanford University

Charles E. Bidwell
University of Chicago

John A. Clausen
University of California, Berkeley

Leonard S. Cottrell, Jr.
Russell Sage Foundation

Neal Gross
Harvard University

Reuben L. Hill
University of Minnesota

Morris Janowitz
University of Chicago

Ronald Lippitt
University of Michigan

Henry S. Maas
University of California, Berkeley

Eleanor E. Maccoby
Stanford University

Daniel R. Miller
University of Michigan

Lloyd E. Ohlin
New York School of Social Work

Francis H. Palmer
Social Science Research Council

Albert J. Reiss, Jr.
University of Michigan

A. Kimball Romney
Stanford University

Irving Rosow
Western Reserve University

Alberta E. Siegel
Stanford University

Murray A. Straus
University of Minnesota

Yonina Talmon-Garber*
Harvard University

* Deceased

The Conference is described in reference 5, Appendix B. Other publications resulting from the Conference included references 3, 6, 24, and 27 of Appendix B.

Moral Development
Gould House, Tarrytown, New York
October 31–November 3, 1963

ORGANIZER Martin L. Hoffman
Merrill-Palmer Institute

Ethel Albert
University of California, Berkeley

Justin M. Aronfreed
University of Pennsylvania

Albert Bandura
Stanford University

Orville G. Brim, Jr.
Russell Sage Foundation

Urie Bronfenbrenner
Cornell University

Roger V. Burton
National Institute of Mental Health

John A. Clausen
University of California, Berkeley

Yehudi Cohen
Social Research, Inc.

Lawrence Freedman, M.D.
University of Chicago

Robert J. Havighurst
University of Chicago

Lawrence Kohlberg
University of Chicago

Ronald Lippitt
University of Michigan

Eleanor E. Maccoby
Stanford University

Albert J. Reiss, Jr.
University of Michigan

Richard A. Schmuck
University of Michigan

M. Brewster Smith
University of California, Berkeley

Melford E. Spiro
University of Washington

Beatrice B. Whiting
Harvard University

John W. M. Whiting
Harvard University

Ben Willerman*
Social Science Research Council

* Deceased

A brief description of the Conference is contained in *Items*, 1964, *18*, 9. Publications resulting from the Conference include references 1, 15, and 19 in Appendix B.

Socialization for Competence
San Juan, Puerto Rico
April 29–May 2, 1965

ORGANIZER M. Brewster Smith
University of California, Berkeley

Joseph M. Bobbitt
National Institute of Child Health and Human Development

Orville G. Brim, Jr.
Russell Sage Foundation

Nathan S. Caplan
University of Michigan

John A. Clausen
University of California, Berkeley

Elizabeth F. Colson
University of California, Berkeley

Elizabeth B. Davis
Harlem Hospital

Edward C. Devereux
Cornell University

Raphael S. Ezekiel
University of Michigan

J. McVicker Hunt
University of Illinois

Alex Inkeles
Harvard University

Ronald Lippitt
University of Michigan

Eleanor E. Maccoby
Stanford University

Patricia Minuchin
Bank Street College of Education

Bernard C. Rosen
University of Nebraska

Juan A. Rossello
University of Puerto Rico

Richard Snyder
Northwestern University

Burton L. White
Massachusetts Institute of Technology

Robert W. White
Harvard University

William F. Whyte
Cornell University

The Conference is described in reference 26, Appendix B. Conference papers subsequently published include references 4, 11, 16, and 29 in Appendix B.

II. Work Groups and Their Members

Linkages between Social Class and Socialization
University of Michigan

Martin G. Gold
Ronald Lippitt (Co-Chairman)
Daniel R. Miller
Oscar Oeser
Harold M. Proshansky
Stephen B. Withey (Co-Chairman)
Assistant:
Allen Guskin

Sex Differences
Stanford University

Roy G. D'Andrade
Irven DeVore
Sanford M. Dornbusch
David A. Hamburg
Lawrence Kohlberg
Eleanor E. Maccoby (Chairman)
Walter Mischel
A. Kimball Romney
Assistant:
Roberta M. Oetzel

Family Size and Birth Order as Influences upon Socialization and Personality
University of California, Berkeley

John A. Clausen (Chairman)
Paul H. Mussen
Edward E. Sampson
William T. Smelser
Louis H. Stewart
Ann M. Stout
Milton Yinger, visiting from Oberlin College
Assistants:
Francena T. Hancock
Judith R. Williams
Katherine Jako

Social Structure and Socialization in the Elementary School Classroom
Washington University

John C. Glidewell (Chairman)

Mildred B. Kantor

Louis M. Smith

Lorene A. Stringer

Assistant:

Beverly B. Carter

Peer Relations and Personality Development
University of Michigan

Gerald Gurin

Martin G. Gold

Richard A. Schmuck (Chairman)

Joseph Veroff

Assistant:

Anita Lohman

III. Commissioned Reviews

"American Longitudinal Research on Psychological Development," by Jerome Kagan. (See Appendix B, reference 18.)

"Socialization in Selected Situational Contexts: A Working Paper," by Judith R. Williams. (Dittoed working paper for Committee only.)

"Socialization Research in Germany," annotated bibliography and report by Gerhart Baumert and Heinz Karl, University of Marburg. (See Appendix B, Multilithed and Mimeographed Reports.)

"Problèmes de la Socialisation: Position des Auteurs de Langue Française. Analyses d'Ouvrages de Langue Française," prepared under the direction of P. H. Chombart de Lauwe, Groupe d'Ethnologie Sociale, Paris. (See Appendix B, Multilithed and Mimeographed Reports.)

"The School as an Agent of Socialization," by Hilde Himmelweit and Philip Sealy. (See Appendix B, Multilithed and Mimeographed Reports.)

Appendix B

I. Publications Deriving from or Relating to Activities Sponsored by the Committee

1. Aronfreed, J. *Conduct and Conscience: A Natural History of Internalization.* New York: Academic Press. (In press)
2. Barker, R. C. The stream of behavior as an empirical problem. In R. C. Barker (Ed.), *The Stream of Behavior.* New York: Appleton-Century-Crofts, 1963. Pp. 1–24.
3. Becker, H. S. Personal change in adult life. *Sociometry,* 1964, 27, 40–53.
4. Biber, Barbara, and Minuchin, Patricia. The role of the school in the socialization of competence. In B. Rosen *et al.* (Eds.), *Achievement in American Society.* Cambridge, Mass.: Schenkman Publishing Co. (In press)
5. Brim, O. G., Jr. Socialization through the life cycle. *Items,* 1964, *18,* 1–5.
6. Brim, O. G., Jr., and Wheeler, Stanton. *Socialization after Childhood: Two Essays.* New York: John Wiley & Sons, 1966.
7. Caudill, W., and Weinstein, Helen. Maternal care and infant behavior in Japanese and American urban middle-class families. In René Konig and R. Hill (Eds.), *Yearbook of the International Sociological Association.* Tokyo: ISFR, 1967.
8. Chombart de Lauwe, P. H. The interaction of person and society. *American Sociological Review,* 1966, 31, 237–48. Also published as L'interaction de la personne et de la société. *Bulletin de Psychologie,* 1966, 20, 1–13.
9. Clausen, J. A. Family structure, socialization, and personality. In Lois W. Hoffman and M. L. Hoffman (Eds.), *Review of Child Development Research.* Vol. 2. New York: Russell Sage Foundation, 1966. Pp. 1–53.
10. Clausen, J. A. Research on socialization and personality development in the United States and France: remarks on the paper by Professor Chombart de Lauwe. *American Sociological Review,* 1966, *31,* 248–57. Also published as Les recherches sur la socialisation et sur le développement de la personalité aux Etats Unis et en France. *Bulletin de Psychologie,* 1966, 20, 14–22.

11. Colson, Elizabeth. Competence and incompetence in the context of independence. *Current Anthropology*, 1967, *8*, 92–111.
12. DeVore, I. Mother-infant relations in baboons. In Harriet L. Rheingold (Ed.), *Maternal Care in Mammals*. New York: John Wiley & Sons, 1963. Pp. 305–35.
13. Glidewell, J. C., Kantor, Mildred B., Smith, L. M., and Stringer, Lorene A. Socialization and social structure in the classroom. In Lois W. Hoffman and M. L. Hoffman (Eds.), *Review of Child Development Research*. Vol. 2. New York: Russell Sage Foundation, 1966. Pp. 221–56.
14. Harvey, O. J., and Schroder, H. M. Cognitive aspects of self and motivation. In O. J. Harvey (Ed.), *Motivation and Social Interaction: Cognitive Determinants*. New York: The Ronald Press Co., 1963. Pp. 95–133.
15. Hoffman, M. L. Development of internal moral standards in children. In M. Strommen (Ed.), *Review of Research in Religious Development*. Des Moines, Iowa: Meredith Publishing Co. (In press)
16. Inkeles, A. A note on social structure and the socialization of competence. *Harvard Educational Review*, 1966, *36*, 265–83.
17. Inkeles, A., and Levinson, D. J. The person system and the sociocultural system in large-scale organizations. *Sociometry*, 1963, *26*, 217–29.
18. Kagan, J. American longitudinal research on psychological development. *Child Development*, 1964, *35*, 1–32.
19. Kohlberg, L. Piaget's approach to moral development: a reevaluation. *Merrill-Palmer Quarterly*. (In press)
20. Kohn, M. L. Social class and parent-child relationships: an interpretation. *American Journal of Sociology*, 1963, *68*, 471–80.
21. Levinson, D. J. Toward a new social psychology: problems in the convergence of sociology and psychology. *Merrill-Palmer Quarterly*, 1964, *10*, 77–88.
22. Maccoby, Eleanor E. (Ed.) *The Development of Sex Differences*. Stanford: Stanford University Press, 1966.
23. Raush, H. I. Interaction sequences. *Journal of Personality and Social Psychology*, 1965, *2*, 487–99.
24. Rostow, I. Forms and functions of adult socialization. *Social Forces*, 1965, *44*, 35–45.
25. Sampson, E. E. The study of ordinal position: antecedents and outcomes. In B. Maher (Ed.), *Progress in Experimental Personality Research*. Vol. 2. New York: Academic Press, 1965.
26. Smith, M. B. Socialization for competence. *Items*, 1965, *19*, 17–23.
27. Strauss, M. A. Power and support structure of the family in relation to socialization. *Journal of Marriage and the Family*, 1964, *26*, 318–26.
28. Swanson, G. E. On explanations of social interaction. *Sociometry*, 1965, *28*, 101–23.
29. White, B. L., and Held, R. Plasticity of sensorimotor development in the human infant. In Judy F. Rosenblith and W. Allinsmith (Eds.), *The Causes of Behavior: Readings in Child Development and Educational Psychology*. 2nd ed. Boston: Allyn & Bacon, 1966. Chap. 9.

II. Multilithed or Mimeographed Reports Prepared for the Committee

Baumert, G., and Karl, H. German research on socialization: a bibliography. Marburg, Germany, 1963. (Mimeo) Available in microfilm or microprint from A.D.I., Library of Congress. (See footnote 10, p. 58.)

Chombart de Lauwe, P. H. Problèmes de la socialisation: positions des auteurs de langue française; analyses d'ouvrages de langue française. Montrouge (Seine), France, 1964. (Mimeo)

*Clausen, J. A., with the assistance of Hancock, Francena, Williams, Judith, and Jako, Katherine. Family size and birth order as influences upon socialization and personality: bibliography and abstracts. Berkeley, California, 1965. (Multilith)

*Glidewell, J. C., Kantor, Mildred B., Smith, L. M., and Stringer, Lorene A. Social structure and socialization in the elementary school classroom. St. Louis County Health Department, Clayton, Missouri, 1965. (Multilith)

Himmelweit, Hilde T., and Sealy, A. P. The school as an agent of socialization. London, 1966. (Mimeo)

*Proshansky, H. (Ed.) Linking social class and socialization: toward a framework for analysis and research. Institute for Social Research, University of Michigan, Ann Arbor, Michigan, 1962. (Multilith)

Reiss, A. J., Jr. Social organization and socialization: variations on a theme about generations. Center for Research on Social Organization, University of Michigan, Ann Arbor, Michigan, 1965. (Multilith)

*Schmuck, R., and Lohman, Anita. Peer relations and personality development. Institute for Social Research, University of Michigan, Ann Arbor, Michigan, 1965. (Multilith)

*Yarrow, Marian R., and Raush, H. L. (Eds.) Observational methods in research on socialization processes: report of a conference. National Institute of Mental Health, 1962. (Multilith)

* A limited supply of this report is available from the issuing organization as of the date of publication of this volume.

Author Index

Subject Index